Furniture in the Ancient World
Origins & Evolution
3100–475 B.C.

Frontispiece.   Chest on legs. *Eighteenth Dynasty.*

FURNITURE IN THE ANCIENT WORLD

Origins & Evolution
3100–475 B.C.

Hollis S. Baker

with an Introduction by
Sir Gordon Russell CBE MC RDI

A Giniger Book
in association with
The Macmillan Company, New York

First published 1966

A Giniger Book in association with The Macmillan Company, New York

This book was designed and produced by George Rainbird Ltd, 2 Hyde Park Place, London W2, England

Printed and bound by Jarrold & Sons Ltd, Norwich, England

Library of Congress Catalog No. 66-23893

Printed in Great Britain

PREFACE

Nearly thirty years ago Hollis Baker, an American visitor in England, walked into my office at Broadway, Worcestershire, told me he was a furniture manufacturer on a busman's holiday and asked if he could see our works. He was so frank and enthusiastic that I liked him at once. He told me, among other things, that rather than completing his legal training he had entered a business started by his father, that their main demand at that time was for reproductions of English eighteenth-century furniture, that he was greatly interested in the history of the craft and had already collected a few pieces of antique furniture with a view to setting up a small furniture museum. This was in fact established in Grand Rapids in 1941, as the Baker Museum, and now contains about 1,400 items. All this added up to a personality which was certainly unusual, especially in the furniture industry, and over the years our frequent meetings and discussions both here and in the States cemented a friendship. We often disagreed about the value of making reproductions but neither of us had any doubts as to the importance of developing designs of our own age. We both felt that greater knowledge of any industry's background was a valuable way of stimulating interest in the things made and so maintaining quality for the future.

Quite a long time ago Hollis told me that he was impressed by the fact that although there were many books dealing with the history of furniture from medieval times until the early nineteenth century there were extremely few dealing with the earliest period, knowledge of which had been greatly extended by archaeological research. When did men start making furniture? What sort of furniture did they make? How long did it take to develop suitable ways of joining timber or, even further back, how long did it take to learn to saw trees into boards which could be joined? How was it that, although mortise-and-tenon and dovetail joints were well developed in Egypt 5,000 years ago, chests were still being made out of scooped-out tree trunks in England until the year 1500 at least and that boats are still being made in Africa in this way today? Hollis had acquired all the technical knowledge to enable him to assess the skills required, he was interested in design problems and fascinated by the extraordinary diversity of human ways of living, he had great patience and a lawyer's ability to marshal facts. And over the past few years he has been able – and wisely has been willing – to hand over most of his business problems to others. This has given him time to body forth his ideas in practical form. He has spent a great deal of time studying the subject in the countries concerned, and in the great museums of the world. He has even been so thorough as to buy a house on a Greek island in order to study the Mediterranean area at first hand! The result is a book which I feel will be of interest not only to historians and students, for whom it is likely to be of much value for a long time, but also to designers, interior decorators, and practical men of affairs in the furnishing industry by greatly increasing the width of vision of those who take the trouble – and so discover the pleasure – of reading it.

At first sight it may seem that a disproportionate amount of space has been given to Egypt. But the reason soon becomes clear. In this extraordinary country the conditions led to one of the earliest flowerings of civilized life, fed by the incredible bounty of the Nile. The belief in an afterlife in which tables, beds and chairs would still be necessary led to their being placed in the tombs

5

of the great. And again the climate is so extraordinarily favourable that wood – and even rush and woven linen – survived, in certain cases for 5,000 years. In other early civilizations knowledge of the furniture used comes largely from carvings in stone or paintings, which cannot give an adequate idea of the skill of design or workmanship. The economy of material, the excellence of the wood engineering and fitness for their purpose in such examples as the early stools and tables is quite remarkable. This gives them a quality akin to that of the best modern designs.

Anyone who studies this book with care will be unimaginative if he considers that, with all our boasted technological discoveries, progress as a whole has been adequate. Indeed, it would be true to say that we are in danger of claiming that constant restless change and progress are synonymous terms. Striving for perfection by slow – sometimes, in Egypt, too slow – evolution is something which might well be pondered by our generation, which is all too apt to sacrifice quality to speed.

GORDON RUSSELL

14.9.65

To my father, to whom I owe my introduction
to the fascinating world of furniture

CONTENTS

ACKNOWLEDGMENTS

Based almost entirely, as it is, on archaeological discoveries, this book would not have been possible without the assistance of a number of professional scholars in this field – to whom I am deeply indebted.

My original interest in ancient Egyptian household furniture stemmed from the collection in the British Museum in London; and, from the beginning, Dr I. E. S. Edwards, Keeper, and Mr T. G. H. James, Assistant Keeper of the Department of Egyptian Antiquities, have been generous in their encouragement and in making available the facilities of their department.

In the United States, John D. Cooney, Curator of Egyptian Art, Cleveland Museum of Art; Dr Henry C. Fischer, Curator of Egyptian Art, Metropolitan Museum of Art, New York; and Dr William S. Smith, Curator of the Department of Egyptian Art, Museum of Fine Arts, Boston, have each assisted me greatly since the beginning of this project in the search for material pertaining to ancient Egyptian furniture. I am particularly grateful to Mr Cooney for his critical comments and advice on the text of the Egyptian section and to Dr Smith for reading the first draft of the chapters which deal with the Archaic and Old Kingdom periods. Among other American Egyptologists who have given encouragement and help are Dr John A. Wilson and Dr Keith Seele of the Oriental Institute, Chicago.

Through the generosity of R. W. Hamilton, Keeper of the Ashmolean Museum, Oxford, it was made possible to refer directly to Howard Carter's original notes relating to the Tutankhamun discoveries and to present for the first time a comprehensive survey of the magnificent furniture from this tomb. This was further facilitated by the friendly cooperation of Dr Victor A. Girgis, Chief Keeper of the Cairo Museum, and by Dr Fischer of the Metropolitan Museum.

Likewise, as regards the remarkable collection of household furniture from the tomb of the Architect Kha, I am indebted to Dr Silvio C. Curto, Director of the Egyptian Museum of Turin, Italy, and Dr Ernesto Scamuzzi, formerly Soprintendente all'Egittologia, for the opportunity of publishing this in its entirety. I would also like to express my appreciation to Mme Christiane Desroches-Noblecourt, Conservateur-en-Chef, Department of Egyptian Antiquities, Louvre Museum; Prof. W. B. Emery, Professor of Egyptology, University College, London; Dr Zaki Saad, formerly Chief Inspector, Department of Antiquities, Cairo; Prof. Giacomo Caputò, Soprintendenza alle antichità, Etruria and Director, Archaeological Museum, Florence, Italy; T. Burton Brown, Keeper of Egyptology, University of Manchester Museum, Manchester, England; and Miss Louise A. Shier, Curator, Kelsey Museum of Archaeology, University of Michigan.

In the research for material relating to ancient Near Eastern furniture, Charles Wilkinson, formerly Curator, Department of Near Eastern Art, Metropolitan Museum of Art; Erle Leichty, then staff member, Oriental Institute, Chicago, and now Professor of Near Eastern Art at the University of Minnesota; and Dr George F. Dales, Assistant Curator in charge of South Asia Section, University Museum, Philadelphia, were of particular assistance. In addition, Dr Dales reviewed the first drafts of the Near Eastern chapters and helped to bring order to the confused lot of material which had been assembled.

For other material I am greatly indebted to Dr Faisal el Wailly, Director of Antiquities, Iraq Museum, Baghdad, for making available views of the Khorsabad reliefs not hitherto published; to Dr Rodney S. Young, Curator, Mediterranean Section, University Museum, Philadelphia, and director of the excavations at Gordion, for making available the files and photographs of the expedition; and to Winifred Needler of the Royal Ontario Museum and Kathleen M. Kenyon, Principal of St Hugh's College, Oxford, Director, British School of Archaeology in Jerusalem, for the opportunity of presenting in detail the results of the Jericho expedition pertaining to furniture.

In the course of organizing the Near Eastern section I have had the benefit also of the advice of Dr Edmond Sollberger, Assistant Keeper of Western Asiatic Antiquities, British Museum, who read the original rough draft; Dr Samuel N. Kramer, Curator of Tablet Collections, Near Eastern Section, University Museum, Philadelphia, who read the section dealing with Sumer; and Mr D. J. Wiseman, Professor of Ancient Semitic Languages and Civilizations, University of London, who read the chapter on Palestine.

On the subject of ancient furniture in the Aegean, I conferred at the beginning of this project with Miss Gisela M. A. Richter, formerly Curator of Classical Art, Metropolitan Museum, New York, whose history of Greek, Etruscan and Roman furniture was then out of print; and also with Dr Dietrich Von Bothmer, Curator of Classical Art of the Metropolitan Museum. For the assembling of material for the Aegean section of the book I am especially grateful to R. W. Hamilton, Keeper of the Ashmolean Museum, and H. W. Catling, Senior Assistant Keeper; Dr Henry Robinson, Director, American School of Classical Studies, Athens; Mrs Eleftherios Saridis, Athens; and the staff of the National Museum in Athens. Most of all I am deeply grateful to Dr Reynold Higgins, Deputy Keeper of Greek and Roman Antiquities in the British Museum, for making available the facilities of this department and for his personal interest.

Principal credit for the final completion of the Egyptian Section of this work should go to T. G. H. James of the British Museum, who, in addition to his critical editing of the text, has greatly assisted me by rewriting the Egyptian reference notes. Likewise I am indebted to Dr Edmond Sollberger of the British Museum for his critical comments on the final draft of the Near Eastern section, and Mr T. C. Mitchell, Research Assistant of the Western Asiatic Department, for the revision of the notes relative thereto. To Dr Reynold Higgins, also of the British Museum, I am greatly indebted for correcting and revising the reference notes of the Aegean section, as well as for his checking of the final text of this part of the book. I wish to make special acknowledgment also to the Trustees of the British Museum for the privilege of using the library and other facilities of this great institution.

But although the scholars whose names I have mentioned have given generously of their time and personal interest, it must be emphasized that any dubious assumptions or errors of fact are purely my own responsibility.

I regret that it is not possible to give proper acknowledgments to all those others who have contributed to the completion of this project, but special mention should be made of Miss Barbara Sewell, formerly Secretary of the Griffith Institute, now Secretary of the Oriental Institute, Oxford, for her painstaking work in transcribing the Carter records pertaining to the Tutankhamun furniture and for her comments on the text of this chapter of the book; and also Mrs John Switalski, Reference Secretary of the Oriental Institute, Chicago, for her assistance in assembling the material relating to the Khorsabad and Mereruka furniture. Special mention should also be made of the drawings by Mr H. M. Stewart, of the Institute of Technology, London, which appear in the Egyptian section, and the measured drawings by Margaret MacDonald-Taylor, formerly of the Royal College of Art, at the end of the book.

I wish to thank Dr Richard Tiemersma, Professor of English at Calvin College, Grand Rapids, Michigan, for his valuable suggestions regarding the form of the text, and for the reading of the galley proofs. To my secretary, Miss Victoria Birch, I wish to express appreciation for her patience and efficiency in typing the various drafts which preceded the final version.

These are those who have contributed encouragement, professional advice and other assistance in bringing this work to the point of publication. But at this point it would still have been stillborn except for the tireless efforts and technical assistance of Mrs Joy Law of the Royal College of Art (formerly Executive Editor of George Rainbird Ltd) and the personal sympathy of George Rainbird himself, together with the facilities of his organization. To my friend of long standing, Sir Gordon Russell, founder and, for twelve years, Director of the Council of Industrial Design, London, noted for his contribution to contemporary design, I wish to express my deep appreciation for his kindness in writing the foreword. And to my wife I owe my gratitude for her understanding and consideration, over and beyond the call of duty, during the long period of gestation of this book.

H.S.B.

INTRODUCTION

Is there anything whereof
it can be said, See, this is new?
It hath been already of old
time, which was before us.
Ecclesiastes, 1:10

Compared with the important place which furniture had in the life of the ancient world, relatively little attention has been given to the subject of ancient furniture. In ancient Egypt it was traditional that the furniture of the pharaohs be taken with them to the tomb in the belief that they could continue to enjoy it in the afterlife. In ancient Nineveh and Khorsabad the rulers of Assyria prized so highly the furniture received as tribute that they caused it to be sculptured on the bas-reliefs which decorated their great temples and palaces. And in ancient Greece furniture was a favourite subject of artists, who depicted it in meticulous detail in the scenes they painted on Greek vases. But although furniture is mentioned in the written records from the beginning of history and is represented innumerable times in the sculptures and paintings of ancient civilizations, no comprehensive work exists on the subject of ancient furniture as a whole.

That this should be so seems curious when we consider that most of the traditional techniques of cabinet-making were perfected long before the beginning of the Christian era, and that several hundred pieces of Egyptian furniture more than three thousand years old still exist in an excellent state of preservation. To be sure, the individual discoveries made by archaeologists have been studied carefully and described in detail. Their scholarly publications, however, ordinarily reach only a specialized audience and are not known to the general public, while the attention given to the subject of ancient furniture by furniture historians is usually limited to a brief summary prior to a discussion of 'period' or 'modern' furniture. And writers on the subject of ancient art and artifacts rarely mention furniture at all in the many elaborate publications which have appeared recently. As a result it is not generally known, even by students of design, what a large quantity of furniture and wide variety of types actually existed in antiquity.

Because of this paucity of books on the subject no separate bibliographical list will be given; where reference is made to other works the source will be given in the notes. Special mention must be made, however, of the scholarly work by G. M. A. Richter, first published in 1926, on the subject of Greek, Etruscan and Roman furniture. Of the fourteen hundred works on furniture listed in the files of the New York Public Library Miss Richter's is the only book listed under the heading of Ancient Furniture. But although this is a most important study, it deals with only a limited segment of the subject.[1] It is our intent, on the other hand, to consider ancient furniture as a whole and to compare the types that evolved in the different civilizations of the ancient world.[2]

In a work covering so broad a subject it is necessary, of course, to set some limitations as to space and time. The geographical areas are limited to Egypt, the Near East and the Aegean. The furniture of China and other Far East countries is not included, since up until this time little or nothing has been discovered from the ancient periods with which we are dealing.[3] In point of time, our study begins with the fourth millennium B.C. and covers a period of approximately twenty-five centuries ending with the Classical era in Greece. The Early Greek section of our discussion is condensed because of the comprehensive study given the furniture of this period by Miss Richter; and the furniture of classical times is mentioned only briefly because it falls outside the somewhat arbitrary limits which have been set.

Special emphasis is given to three periods of Egyptian history – the Early Dynastic, the Old Kingdom and the New Kingdom. Likewise in our discussion of Near Eastern furniture and in that of the Aegean area, some periods will be discussed in detail, and others, where the record is lacking or is not significant, will be mentioned only briefly. It has been impossible also to avoid certain other omissions in making our selections from the vast quantity of material that exists. The objective, however, has been to consider the principal design types of antiquity, their origins, their developments and their continuing influence. In most instances the description of individual pieces has been made brief to avoid constant repetition. Many of the details are best understood from the illustrations, and a wordy description is superfluous. In any case, the main value from the point of the student of design will be that of the illustrations themselves. Consequently our emphasis is placed on the visual records rather than on the written records.

It will obviously be difficult to avoid an overemphasis on Egyptian furniture, since this is the only ancient furniture of which we have both the representations in art and the actual furniture itself. At one time I considered limiting this work to only those pieces which had actually been discovered in the excavations of archaeologists. To have done so, however, would have meant producing a book devoted exclusively to Egyptian furniture and confined to those examples which had escaped the vicissitudes of time. Furthermore this would have meant excluding the wide variety of designs that are represented in the art of the Near East and the Aegean. Obviously, therefore, in order to consider ancient furniture as a whole, it is necessary to include the representations in sculpture and painting. This procedure has the added value of giving us some intriguing pictures of furniture in actual use.

Since my own first interest is in design, and since this book deals primarily with the appearance of furniture rather than its function, it seems fitting to point out that from the very beginning artists and craftsmen have striven to create what to them was beautiful as well as useful. It should be noted also that in ancient times the terms 'artist' and 'craftsman' were synonymous. The ideal of beauty, however, is not a constant thing, and at different times and in different countries it varies widely – not only in ancient times but also in our more recent history. Within a relatively short time, in terms of the overall history of furniture, the range of styles has included Gothic, Renaissance, Elizabethan, Jacobean, Queen Anne, Louis XIV, Louis XV, Louis XVI, Chippendale, Hepplewhite, Sheraton, Empire, Directoire, Beidemeier, William Morris, Art Nouveau and Mission

– to name only some of the more prominent styles that have been fashionable. And today, along with the styles inherited from the past, we have a style called 'modern'.

It is tempting to elaborate on the historical background and romantic associations of the furniture which is pictured from the ancient past. But many books have been written about the life and arts of these ancient peoples – even if not about their furniture – and I have endeavoured instead to limit myself to a factual survey of furniture as it existed within the period under discussion. Even without other embellishment, however, this long pageant of furniture is also history in a broader sense, in which we see reflected the lives of the people who made and who used this ancient furniture.

From the practical viewpoint, a knowledge of the art forms and techniques of the past is essential to an understanding of the present. It is not intended, however, that this review of the furniture of antiquity should encourage a revival of Egyptian, Assyrian or Greek styles in furniture. I only hope that it will prove interesting to the curious and be helpful in carrying on the continuing tradition of furniture design which has its roots so deeply embedded in the past.

H.S.B.
Grand Rapids, Michigan, 1965

Colour plate II. Stela of Wepemnefert. *Fourth Dynasty.*

PART I: EGYPT

EGYPTIAN CHRONOLOGY
c. 3100–1085 B.C.

(Down to the Middle Kingdom, dates for individual reigns are uncertain)

Early Dynastic Period

First Dynasty: c. 3100–2890 B.C.
Narmer (Menes)
Aha
Djer
Djet
Den
Anedjib
Semerkhet
Qaa

Second Dynasty: c. 2890–2686 B.C.
Hotepsekhemwy
Raneb
Nynetjer
Peribsen
Khasekhem
Khasekhemwy

The Old Kingdom

Third Dynasty: c. 2686–2613 B.C.
Sanakhte
Zoser
Sekhemkhet
Khaba
Huni

Fourth Dynasty: c. 2613–2494 B.C.
Sneferu
Cheops
Radedef
Chephren
Baufre
Mycerinus
Shepseskaf
Dedefptah

Fifth Dynasty: c. 2494–2345 B.C.
Userkaf
Sahure
Neferirkare
Shepseskare
Neferefre
Nyuserre
Menkauhor
Djedkare
Unas

Sixth Dynasty: c. 2345–2181 B.C.
Teti
Userkare
Pepi I
Merenre I
Pepi II
Merenre II

First Intermediate Period

Between the Old and Middle King-doms came a period of disorganization (c. 2181–2133 B.C.) which included the Seventh to Tenth Dynasties.

Middle Kingdom

Eleventh Dynasty: c. 2133–1991 B.C. (Principal Kings)
Mentuhotpe I
Inyotef I–III
Mentuhotpe II–IV

Twelfth Dynasty: c. 1991–1786 B.C. (Principal Kings)
Ammenemes I: 1991–1962 B.C.
Sesostris I: 1971–1928 B.C.
Sesostris III: 1878–1843 B.C.
Ammenemes III: 1842–1797 B.C.

Thirteenth Dynasty: c. 1786–1633 B.C. (Principal Kings)
Sebekhotpe III
Neferhotep

Second Intermediate Period

Between the Middle and New King-doms Egypt again entered into a state of political confusion due largely to the rise of power of Asiatic rulers called Hyksos. The Fourteenth and Sixteenth Dynasties are very obscure.

Fifteenth Dynasty: c. 1674–1567 B.C. (Hyksos. Principal Kings)
Sheshi
Khyan
Apophis I
Apophis II

Seventeenth Dynasty: c. 1650–1567 B.C. (Theban. Principal Kings)
Seqenenre
Kamose

New Kingdom

Eighteenth Dynasty: c. 1567–1320 B.C.
Amosis: 1570–1546 B.C.
Amenophis I: 1546–1526 B.C.
Tuthmosis I: 1525–1512 B.C.
Tuthmosis II: 1512–1504 B.C.
Hatshepsut: 1503–1482 B.C.
Tuthmosis III: 1504–1450 B.C.
Amenophis II: 1450–1425 B.C.
Tuthmosis IV: 1425–1417 B.C.
Amenophis III: 1417–1379 B.C.
Akhenaten: 1379–1362 B.C.
Smenkhkare: 1364–1361 B.C.
Tutankhamun: 1361–1352 B.C.
Ay: 1352–1348 B.C.
Horemheb: 1348–1320 B.C.

Nineteenth Dynasty: c. 1320–1200 B.C. (Principal Kings)
Ramesses I: 1320–1318 B.C.
Sethos I: 1318–1304 B.C.
Ramesses II: 1304–1237 B.C.
Merneptah: 1236–1223 B.C.
Amenmesses: 1222–1217 B.C.
Sethos II: 1216–1210 B.C.

Twentieth Dynasty: c. 1200–1085 B.C.
Sethnakhte: 1200–1198 B.C.
Ramesses III: 1198–1166 B.C.
Ramesses IV–XI: 1166–1085 B.C.

Following the New Kingdom there came a long period of political and cultural decline only occasionally interrupted by moments of revival. The Twenty-seventh Dynasty (525–404 B.C.) consisted of Assyrian kings who ruled Egypt as part of the Assyrian Empire. Although they were followed by native rulers for a short period, in 332 B.C. Egypt was conquered by Alexander the Great.

THE EARLY BEGINNINGS: DYNASTIES I, II AND III
(c. 3100–2613 B.C.)

By the latter part of the fourth millennium B.C. (some five hundred years before the building of the pyramids), furniture in which the rudiments of traditional Egyptian design are clearly evident was being made in the Nile Valley. Shortly before this time, tools of copper had become available; and even though copper is a soft metal, the new tools[1] were a great advance over the neolithic implements of flint and made possible the cabinet-work that would have been difficult, if not impossible, hitherto. By the beginning of the First Dynasty, the basic principles of woodworking were already well established, and the mortise and tenon joint – one of the most practical inventions of the ancient woodworkers – was in common use.

But until quite recently this remote period was shrouded in deep mystery and virtually nothing was known of its craftsmen and their accomplishments. Excavations early in the nineteenth century had yielded furniture from the Eighteenth Dynasty (c. 1567–1320 B.C.), and it was known from ancient sculptures that furniture was already in use in Egypt long before this time. However, until the first years of the present century, knowledge of ancient Egypt began at about the time of Cheops, builder of the Great Pyramid at Giza (c. 2600 B.C.). There were ancient 'king lists' giving the names of the first rulers, but it was thought by many authorities that these were legendary rather than real people. The first actual evidence of the beginning years of Egyptian civilization came with the discoveries of First Dynasty tombs at Hierakonpolis, Naqada and Abydos between 1894 and 1897. Soon after, at the turn of the century, Sir William Flinders Petrie began his epochal work at Abydos, and by his painstaking methods and scholarly research established that these early rulers had actually existed and moreover that their culture was far more advanced than had previously been supposed.[2]

In these tombs, and in others excavated later, notably by Petrie at Tarkhan[3] and by Professor W. B. Emery at Saqqara,[4] were found the remains of the oldest known wooden furniture, dating from about 3100 B.C. – five thousand years ago. Although for the most part the remains are fragmentary, it is evident that this furniture represents more than just the first naïve efforts of a primitive people, and that the early beginnings of furniture in Egypt are much more ancient than was previously suspected.

The survival of this early furniture is mainly due to the Egyptian's firm belief in life after death, which resulted in the taking of worldly goods, suitable to his status in life, into his tomb for use in the afterlife. The tombs of the kings and great nobles of the early dynasties consisted of substructures dug into the rock, containing the burial chamber and storerooms, and massive brick superstructures called *mastabas*, containing further storerooms. The exterior walls of these *mastabas* were ornamented with sunken vertical panelling to give the appearance of palace walls. Within the storerooms were placed food and clothing, jewellery, household furniture and other useful goods and chattels.

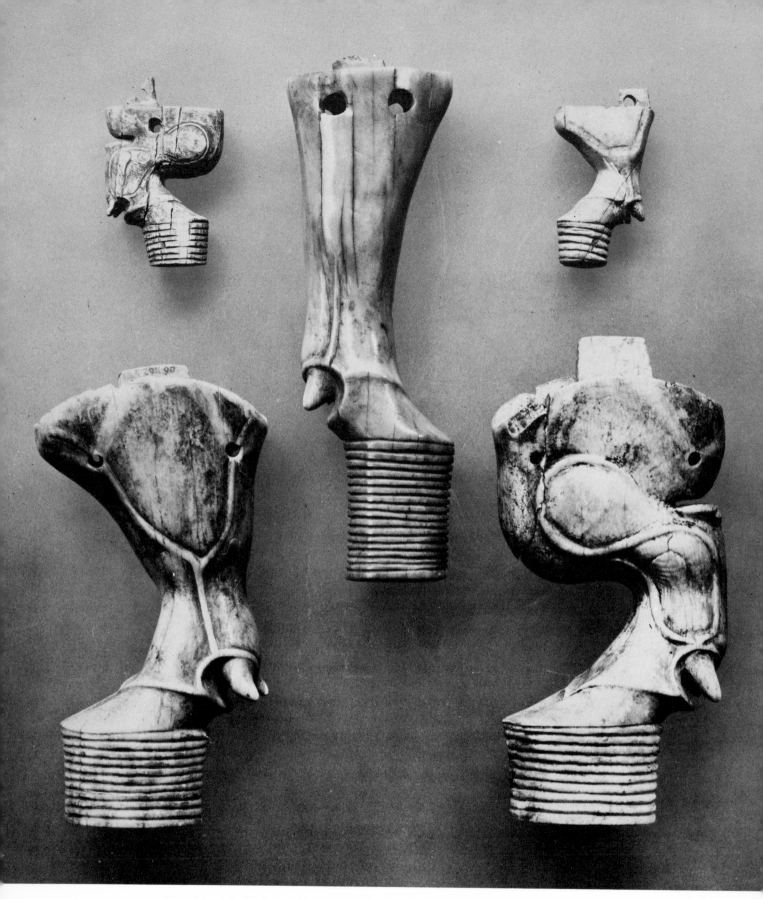

1 Carved ivory bull's legs used as supports for stools, couches and small chests. *First Dynasty*.

The size of the tombs and the exceptionally dry climate helped to preserve these objects, even though in many cases they were made of perishable materials. Despite repeated tomb robberies for the precious metals and other valuables, there are enough fragments of furniture left to give us a fairly good idea of what existed in the Early Dynastic period. They show both an advanced knowledge of the principles of joinery and also considerable skill in the associated arts of carving and inlaying.

Actual furniture or fragments found

Among the earliest examples of the carver's art are five ivory legs found at Abydos and now in the Metropolitan Museum of Art, New York, which date from about 3100 B.C. and originally served as supports for furniture (fig. 1). Tangible evidence of the skill of the early craftsmen, they exhibit crisp carving and a design combining realism with a highly stylized sense of form which served as a model for the furniture-makers of Egypt for the next three thousand years.

The bull's leg, usually of wood but sometimes of ivory, was used as a furniture support from the earliest period, and it has been suggested that the form was adopted for religious reasons. At Saqqara in one of the great First Dynasty tombs found by Emery there was a series of bull-heads fashioned over actual bull-skulls on the 'bench' surrounding the superstructure.[5] These doubtless had a religious significance; and there was also the famous mausoleum of sacred bulls – the Serapeum – in later times at Saqqara. There is, however, no evidence that the use of the bull's leg on furniture had any religious connotation. It is true that any animal leg may seem an elaborate and unlikely support for primitive furniture, but the early craftsman in Egypt naturally found his inspiration in the objects of the world around him. Not only were bull's legs and lion's legs used as furniture supports, but floral motifs such as the lotus and papyrus were employed quite early for furniture decoration and also for architectural elements.

It will be noted from their dimensions that these legs from the Metropolitan Museum are smaller than would normally be expected of furniture supports, the tallest being only about seven inches high. Ancient Egyptian beds were, however, low in height, rarely exceeding twelve inches, and the early stools were extremely low compared with modern standards. The primary function of beds was, of course, to raise the body off the ground, and so legs of only a few inches were necessary. As to the lowness of the seating pieces, the short stature of the early Egyptian people may have had some influence, their average height being only a few inches over five feet.[6] They were accustomed, also, to squatting on the ground.

At the bottom of each of the legs illustrated is a short beaded cylinder, a typical detail of the Early Dynastic period. Originally probably intended to protect the delicate hoof, it became a device used throughout Egyptian history, sometimes being sheathed with metal. The smaller legs have flat tops and were probably supports for a toilet box; the larger ones have a cove section and tenon at the top to carry the rounded rails of a bed or stool (fig. 2). These taller legs also have holes to permit lashing them to the frame; it is doubtful whether glue was used at this early period, but a well-fitted joint could be

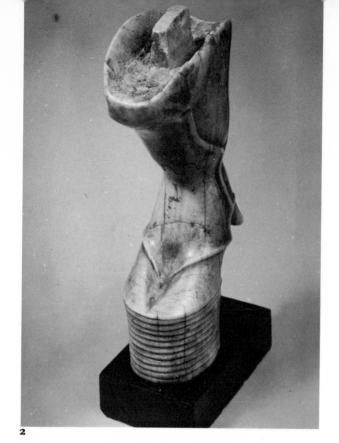

2   3

firmly secured by the use of leather thongs.[7] The Egyptians understood the tanning of leather and undoubtedly knew that thongs soaked in water would shrink and then tighten in drying. In the individual example illustrated from the Metropolitan Museum, the ivory block from which the leg is carved consists of two pieces joined, as can be seen from the serrated pattern in the middle of the leg where the joint occurs.

Among the furniture fragments found by Emery at Saqqara there were three miniature ivory legs resembling those illustrated but measuring less than one and a half inches in height, which were most certainly supports for a game box, since ivory markers or counters were found near by.[8] Ivory carved legs of larger sizes were also found at Saqqara and elsewhere, and fine specimens are to be seen in the Louvre and the Berlin Museum.

But although quite a number of ivory examples have been found, no doubt legs made of wood were more common. Usually these are plainer and lack the fine carving of the ivory specimens. On one example from Tarkhan, however, now in the Petrie Collection in University College, London, the veins on the side are clearly delineated (fig. 3). The leg, however, is rather badly defaced as it was broken in two parts when found in the tomb and the lower section had become stained almost black. In this instance the leg is carved on one side only, the opposite being left plain, as is also true of the smallest legs in figure 1. The larger two of the Metropolitan Museum ivory legs are carved on both sides.

In First Dynasty tombs excavated by Petrie at Tarkhan, some of which could be dated as early as King Narmer, a number of beds in a fairly good state of preservation were found. These represent four distinct types of construction, as can be seen in the photographs taken shortly after the discovery (fig. 4).[9] Fragments of their woven coverings were also found which give a good idea of the weaving patterns that were employed (fig. 5). The most primitive of the beds is constructed of four angular knee-pieces of a

22   2 Ivory leg showing the cove and tenon at the top. *First Dynasty.*

                              3 Carved wooden bull's leg. *First Dynasty.*

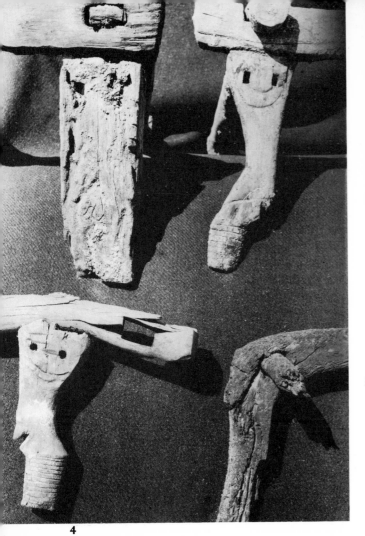

4 Details of methods of corner construction used in beds. *Early Dynastic*.

5 Parts of bed-coverings made of woven rushes. *Early Dynastic*.

tree, the short parts forming the legs and the longer sections the rails, like the crude First Dynasty bed in Berlin (fig. 6). At the bend of each piece a hole is cut to receive the end of the next, which meets it at right angles. In this type of bed the webbing is woven around the frame. A variation occurs where each of the end poles is bent in a U-shape into which the straight side-rails are tenoned. In another of the more primitive types the cross-rails are notched into the long poles from above, as in the bed or bier from Tarkhan now in the Metropolitan Museum (fig. 7).

Of the various types, however, the most common found here, as well as in other tombs of the period, has carved bull's legs of wood, which are mortised into the side-rails from below. Usually these long rails are round, but occasionally they are square with bevelled edges; the end-rails are fastened into the side-rails with mortise and tenon joints, sometimes secured with a dowel from above. The largest and best preserved of the beds (figs. 8, 9), found by Petrie at Tarkhan, is now in the Manchester Museum. It has bull's legs of wood which are well carved, and, instead of the cover of woven rush found on most of the beds, there was webbing made of leather straps woven through slots in the sides and bottoms of the rails. This bed, the longest of those found at Tarkhan, is sixty-nine inches long – but is still considerably shorter than modern beds which are usually seventy-eight inches in length.[10] Other examples resembling the Manchester bed are in Berlin, Cairo and the Oriental Institute in Chicago.

23

6

7

6 Primitive wooden bed frame. *Early Dynastic.*

7 Wooden bed frame with bull's legs and cross-rails notched into side-rails. *Early Dynastic.*

8 Bed with carved bull's legs attached with mortise and tenon joints. *Early Dynastic.*

Although all these different types of beds were apparently in use during the same period, the differences that exist in their construction suggest stages of development which in all likelihood preceded the Manchester bed. Certainly the construction in which the leg is lashed to the side-rail without a tenon, and the end-rail is notched in from above, represents a less advanced form; the crude Berlin bed (fig. 6) is even more primitive. It is characteristic, however, of Egyptian furniture, as indeed of other Egyptian works, that the early forms continued with little change over long periods of time; developments in design can be traced only intermittently as new styles appeared or variations were made in the old.

Evidence of the variety and quantity of copper tools in use by woodworkers in the early part of the First Dynasty is given by the hoard found by Emery in Tomb 3471 at Saqqara, which can be dated, on the basis of the inscriptions on jar-sealings discovered in the tomb, to the reign of Djer, the third king of the dynasty.[11] There were ninety-eight

24

adzes, the chief woodworking tool of ancient Egypt, which was used also in the place of the plane; they varied in size and shape, no doubt according to the uses for which they were intended. In addition there were fifty-one chisels, seven saws, some with their handles intact, and several hundred copper knives, engraving tools and awls. It is difficult to account for the vast quantity of woodworking tools in this one tomb, but it is possible that the owner was a high official whose duties involved the manufacturing of copper articles or the overseeing of woodwork, and so a good stock had been supplied in his burial equipment for his afterlife. The tomb also contained a large number of furniture fragments which give valuable evidence of what were undoubtedly the ordinary furniture types of the First Dynasty.

One significant find was a bed with bull's legs, well enough preserved to permit an accurate reconstruction, which Emery illustrates in a drawing showing the mortise and tenon joints with which it was fastened together, and the method of lashing the legs with leather thongs (fig. 10).[12] The rails are slotted at the side and bottom to receive the leather straps with which the covering was attached to the frame. Both the beaded drums at the bottom of the legs and the knob ornaments of the side-rails were covered with sheet copper. Only fragments remained of the other furniture. Since it presents a first-hand picture of the wooden contents of an Early Dynastic tomb, as well as of the problems facing the archaeologist in piecing these fragmentary remains together, the list given by Emery in his account of the excavations is quoted here, with the corresponding catalogue numbers.[13]

No. 538. Fragments of a large wooden bed. All four bull legs have been preserved as has one of the end rods together with the copper encased butts of the long side rods. Sufficient evidence remains for an accurate reconstruction. Max. length of bed not ascertainable. Max. width 66·0 cms. Height 24·0 cms. Max. diam. of rods 5·5 cms. Max. diam. of copper encased knobs 9·0 cms.

No. 539. Fragments of a large wooden bed of almost identical design to No. 538. Length and width not ascertainable. Height 36·0 cms. Max. diam. of rods 6·0 cms. Max. diam. of copper encased knobs 11·3 cms.

No. 540. Fragments of a wooden chair or small bed. The copper encased knobs of the side

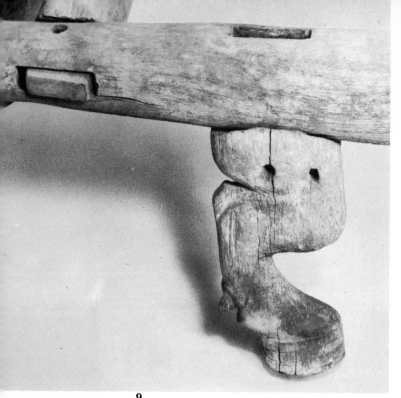

9

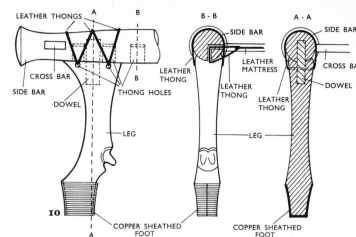

10 Construction details of a bed. *First Dynasty*.

9 Detail of bed in figure 8 showing leg and method of joining. *Early Dynastic*.

rods are preserved but no trace remained of the legs. The seat was held with leather thongs. Width and height not ascertainable. Max. diam. of rods 4·5 cms. Max. diam. of copper encased knobs 6·5 cms.

No. 541. Part of what was perhaps a double bracket of wood to strengthen the underside of a chair. It has been secured by four wooden pegs. Length 42 cms.

No. 542. Fragments of a small chair of hardwood. . . . The chair rested on finely carved bull legs measuring 15·5 cms. in height. The seat was apparently not formed by the usual leather straps, but by flat pieces of wood 1·5 cms. thick.

No. 543. Fragments of a hardwood stool eaten by white ants. It originally had a seat of leather straps and was embellished with the usual copper encased knobs. No trace of the legs remains.

No. 544. Finely carved bull leg of hardwood. The joint shows it supported a flat surface, possibly a gaming board or box. Height 8·5 cms.

No. 545. Finely carved bull leg of hardwood. Like No. 544 it supported a flat surface. Height 12·4 cms.

No. 546. Fragments of a wooden canopy with posts similar to those featured on the walls of the tomb of Hesy (Quibell, *Tomb of Hesy*, Pl. XVIII). . . . There is evidence to show that the capitals of the upright posts were encased with sheet copper. Max. diam. of posts 3·4 cms. Max. width of cross pieces 3·0 cms.

Except for beds, no wooden furniture of consequence has survived complete from the Early Dynastic period. There are only crude pieces such as a rough table and small box with a lid now in the Berlin Museum (figs. 11, 12),[14] and the small partitioned box found in Tomb 3504 at Saqqara which was probably designed to hold gaming pieces (fig. 13).[15] Although insignificant in appearance this small box is important because it shows some of the joinery details in use at this early period. The sides are notched to receive the ends, and the ends of the partitions fit into grooves in the same manner as they would today. The many coffins which survive are a better source of information; they are of various

11

12

11 Rough table with legs, cut from a single piece of wood. *Early Dynastic.*

12 Box with a sliding lid. *Early Dynastic.*

13 Box with partitions, possibly used for gaming pieces. *First Dynasty.*

13

shapes and sizes and display details of construction no doubt similar to those used in domestic chests designed for the storage of clothing, linen and other equipment (see colour plate XA).

Fragments belonging to household storage chests have also been found at Saqqara and elsewhere, but no such chests have survived intact from the Early Dynastic period. A burial chest in the Metropolitan Museum, although not a piece of furniture in the accepted meaning of the term, is shown, however, partly as an example of early cabinet construction, and partly because it represents what might equally well have served as a storage chest in an Egyptian household (fig. 14). It has panelled sides and a vaulted lid, a form which is thought to simulate the exterior appearance of palaces and other buildings of the period.

Although our primary interest is in wooden furniture, a stone table found by Petrie at Saqqara is worthy of note. Stone tables were apparently in general use in the Early Dynastic period; not only the pedestal offering tables which appear in stelae, but also tables which were low in height with a top rounded at one end supported by three round legs (fig. 15). It appears likely that similar tables were also made in wood, as well as other types represented in the sculptural representations, although none has survived.

Little evidence of the advanced culture attained during this period appears in the fragmentary furniture which has survived, except for the beautifully carved legs of ivory

27

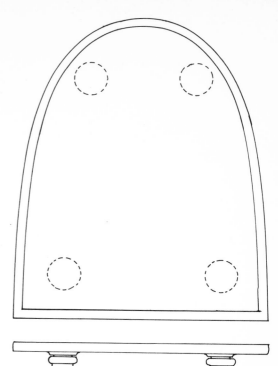

14

14 Wooden coffin with panelled façade sides and a vaulted roof. *Second–Third Dynasty.*

15 Drawing of the top and sides of a stone table with detachable legs. *First Dynasty.*

15

illustrated at the beginning of this chapter. But even if no example of more refined furniture has been preserved, some indication of the sophisticated sense of design and luxurious way of life already developing at this early time can be obtained from small fragments of carved wood, inlays of glazed composition and ivory, shreds of gold ornamentation with embossed and chased designs, and remnants of elaborate jewellery of gold and semi-precious stones salvaged from the ruins of the great tombs.[16] An indication of the variety of pattern and design is seen in a number of pieces now in the Berlin Museum (fig. 16). Of larger pieces which have survived, one of the most interesting is a portion of the lid of a small box, consisting of two fragments found separately by Amélineau and Petrie at Abydos and now united in the Ashmolean Museum, Oxford (fig. 17). This lid is of especial significance, since it came from the tomb of King Semerkhet of the First Dynasty and is among the earliest examples of delicate wood-carving and inlay. The outer face of the lid has a pattern based on the motif of the bound reeds used in matting, one of the first decorative designs; in the centre of the border is the *serekh*, a rectangular frame surmounted by a falcon representing the god Horus, within which the royal name is inscribed above a pattern representing a palace façade. The inner face is inlaid in a geometrical pattern with thin triangles of glazed composition (Egyptian faience, a material made of powdered quartz, moulded and fused, which had been discovered in late Pre-dynastic times).

All these examples of actual furniture surviving from the Early Dynastic period have come by chance from tombs of the First Dynasty. Little of importance in the way of

28

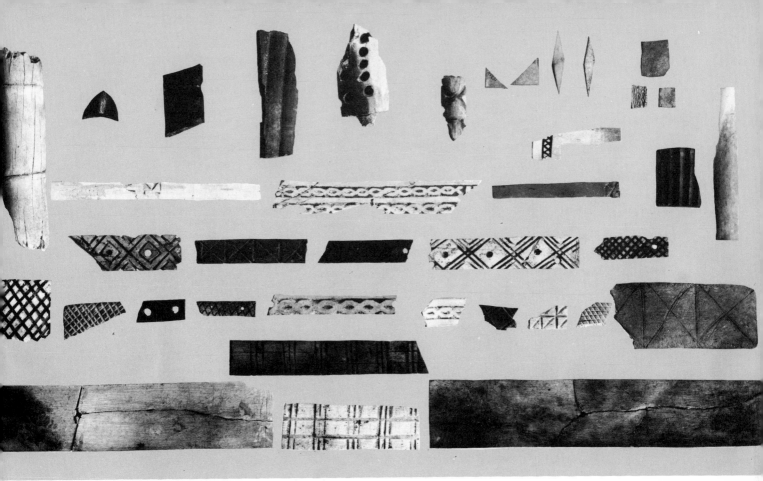

16

furniture remains has been found in the Second Dynasty tombs that have been excavated, but they do, however, contain important sculptural representations of furniture, and one tomb of the early Third Dynasty (that of Hesy-Re) contained remarkable painted representations of furniture. This representational material helps not only in the interpretation of the fragmentary finds from the earlier period, but also illustrates the continuity of design that existed in the Second and Third Dynasties (see pages 33–37).

Furniture in sculpture

Our most valuable evidence of the actual appearance of the stools in use during the Early Dynastic period is to be seen on the carved stelae found in private tombs dating from the late First and the Second Dynasty. The customary scene found on these stelae shows the owner of the tomb seated on a stool in front of a round pedestal table on which offerings are represented. The purpose of these stelae was not that of the modern gravestone – to commemorate the deceased person – but to serve as a magical means by which the deceased could continue to enjoy the good things of life. But although many fragments of actual stools have been found in excavations, unfortunately none has been found complete, or that could be reconstructed. This is true likewise of the pedestal tables, but it seems that in most cases these were made of stone or pottery.

One of the most fruitful sources of these stelae is the Early Dynastic cemetery at Helwan on the east bank of the Nile opposite Saqqara. Here the Egyptian Egyptologist

16 Fragments of wood and ivory with carved ornaments, from furniture. *Early Dynastic.*

17

17 Parts of a box lid carved with a bound-reed pattern and inlaid with thin plaques of faience. *First Dynasty*.

18 Typical Early Dynastic stool on the stela of Menkhefnefer. *Second Dynasty*.

19 Stool with a woven rush seat, on the stela of the lady Heken. *Second Dynasty*.

Zaki Saad, between 1942 and 1955, made important discoveries of Second Dynasty tombs in many of which he found stelae set in chimney-like holes in the roofs of burial chambers. He has published twenty-five of these so-called 'ceiling' stelae,[17] on all but four of which are shown stools with legs of the bull's leg design resembling the carved legs found in the First Dynasty tombs. Seats of woven rush are indicated in some cases, with projecting side-rails which terminate in knob-like ornaments simulating papyrus flowers, like those discovered by Emery at Saqqara. These stools no doubt carry on the traditions of the First Dynasty, but the only earlier example so far known is that on a stela found at Saqqara in a tomb dated to the reign of Qaa, the last king of the First Dynasty (*c.*2900 B.C.).[18] The stool represented in this stela, which belonged to a nobleman named Merka, closely resembles those in the Helwan stelae, but its outlines are rather vague, and consequently only the latter are illustrated here.

A typical example of the Helwan stool is found on the stela of an official whose name is given as Menkhefnefer (fig. 18). The legs are squat and heavy, which is characteristic of the stools on these stelae, but the seat is furnished with the added luxury of a cushion. On another stela, made for the lady Heken (fig. 19), the top of the stool with its woven seat is represented. Because of his lack of knowledge of perspective the artist has shown the top from above, in plan, as it were, but the base in profile. The omission of the front leg of the stool, as in this example, is not uncommon on early stelae; the artist possibly considered that the front leg would be concealed behind the human legs, both of which are often represented, but more probably this is just another of the conventions found in early Egyptian art.

18   19

Other representations of the animal-leg stool occur on stelae found set in niches in
Second Dynasty tombs at Saqqara. In general design the stools represented in these
'niche' stelae are similar to those of the Helwan 'ceiling' stelae, but they are usually better
executed and in a more refined style. In the example illustrated (fig. 20), the lashings
around the seat-rail are indicated and also what appears to be a flat cushion. The papyrus
flower terminals of the side-rail are also shown in detail, the front terminal being sharply
outlined against the leg of the seated person.[19] Occasionally, as in this example, the seats
had flower terminals at both the front and back of the side-rails; but in the majority of
instances this ornamentation appears only at the back.

On one of the Helwan stelae there is a seat which most probably represents an early
primitive type. It occurs on the stela of the priestly official Menka-Heqet (fig. 21), and it
is represented as a solid block scored with a number of vertical lines – a form found also
in Sumerian sculpture and cylinder seals (see fig. 272). These lines undoubtedly indicate
a feature of the construction and may here be interpreted either as slats or as a woven
construction, more probably the latter. At the back the seat has the raised flange of a
rudimentary back-rest. The stools with bull's legs, which were prevalent in the Early
Dynastic period, were undoubtedly antedated by a seat with a simple box frame. This type
is thought to have served as the model for the hieroglyphic sign ⊞, the yellow colour
and detail found on early examples of this sign suggesting that such stools were originally
made of reed-work. By the time of the Second Dynasty this primitive form had been
developed into a seat made with a wooden framework, represented in sculptures as the
formal seat of royalty and other important persons.

20

20 Stool with papyrus terminals and well-carved bull's
legs lashed to side-rail on a 'niche' stela. *Second Dynasty*.

2

21 Stool exhibiting slat or wicker-work construction on
the stela of Menka-Heqet. *Second Dynasty*.

This formal seat occurs in a number of statues which vary in quality of workmanship
from clumsy early examples, such as the one illustrated from Berlin (fig. 22), to the well-
carved diorite statue of a princess in the Turin Museum, which dates from the Third
Dynasty (fig. 23). In these seats the lower piece which formed the bottom part of the
square of the frame has been eliminated, and there are four straight legs strengthened by
bent wooden braces placed between them and the top – a characteristic detail of ancient
Egyptian cabinet-work. In some cases, as in that of the Turin statue, a low back-rest is
added.

Although the stool came first, the chair with a high back appeared as early as the
Second Dynasty. Used at first only by nobles and high officials, it was a symbol of high
rank and did not come into general use until much later. Among the earliest examples is
the one shown on the 'niche' stela of the princess Sehefner from Saqqara (fig. 24).[20] This
chair, derived from the low square stool with straight legs, displays a sophisticated and
modern-looking design in its slender members and the cross-stretchers below with which
it is strengthened. A seat cushion which continued up over the back gave additional
comfort. Another example, almost exactly the same in design, occurs on the Helwan
'ceiling' stela of the prince Nisu-Heqet (fig. 25). It should be noted that both of these
early high-backed chairs have straight legs. Although the bull's leg was in use from the

Colour plate III. Mereruka and his wife seated on a bed. *Sixth Dynasty*.

22   23

beginning of the First Dynasty, the high-backed chair with animal legs does not appear
in sculpture until the time of the Old Kingdom.

The furniture of Hesy-Re

By the end of the Early Dynastic period the upper-class Egyptian home contained a
considerable variety of furniture. The best evidence of this variety, however, comes not
from the fragments of furniture which have been found, nor from sculptures, but from
the paintings on the walls of the tomb of Hesy-Re, a high scribal official of the Third
Dynasty who lived in the reign of Zoser, about 2650 B.C. This tomb belongs, strictly
speaking, to the Old Kingdom, but it comes very early in this period, and the furniture
represented is doubtless very close in design to that which existed at the end of the Early
Dynastic period.

Like so many others, this tomb, discovered first by A. F. F. Mariette in the mid-
nineteenth century, had been plundered in ancient times. One side of the long corridor
chapel in the tomb contained a series of eleven niches in which were set wooden panels
bearing beautifully carved representations of Hesy-Re. Of the eleven panels, five have
survived in a relatively good state and are now in the Cairo Museum. On four of these,

22 Statuette of a man seated on a primitive stool with straight legs and curved braces. *Second Dynasty.*   33

23 Statue of a princess seated on a rectangular stool with a low back. *Third Dynasty.*

24 Straight-backed chair with cushion, on the stela of Sehefner. *Second Dynasty.*

25 Straight-backed chair without cushion, on the stela of Nisu-Heqet. *Second Dynasty.*

Hesy-Re appears standing; on the fifth, one of the finest examples of ancient wood-carving, he is portrayed seated (fig. 26). As Overseer of the Scribes of the King, he is depicted with his scribal equipment, seated on the traditional stool with animal legs, facing an offering table loaded with half-loaves of bread, represented in the formal stylized Egyptian manner. The inscriptions above his head and above the table record his name and titles and specify the offerings he is to receive. But although the stool is traditional in form, its slender rounded side-rails and slim gazelle-like leg are a later refinement.

The tomb became sanded up after this first modern excavation and was re-excavated in 1911 by J. E. Quibell.[21] Of the furniture originally placed in the tomb only a few traces remained – some pieces of inlay, a strip of gold foil, a plaque of green glazed composition, and the broken parts of thirteen small tables made of alabaster and porphyry.[22] More important, however, Quibell discovered on the wall of the corridor chapel opposite the wall of the niches an extraordinary series of paintings of contemporary furniture, either not recorded by Mariette or never published. The colours were dulled, and in some places the plaster background had fallen away, but the outlines of the furniture were clearly discernible and were carefully copied by Quibell. The manner in which the furniture was represented was quite different from the type of decoration usually found in Egyptian tombs. There was a series of long rectangular panels in which were portrayed individual pieces of furniture and a large number of other household articles, forming, as it were, a pictorial inventory. Representing as they do the furnishings used in a fine Egyptian home forty-five hundred years ago, these paintings are of the greatest importance.

34   26 Wooden panel of Hesy-Re who is shown seated on a stool with a slender gazelle-like leg. *Third Dynasty.*

27a

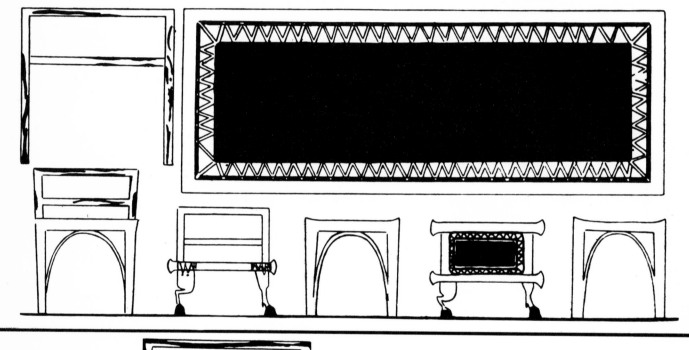

b

c

36

Most surprising of the pieces depicted are four cabinets on legs (two of which are shown) (fig. 27a), which closely resemble actual cabinets found in the tomb of King Tutankhamun, dating thirteen hundred years later. On parts of the cabinets graining is indicated to represent wood surfaces; solid or clear areas probably indicate the gilded or painted parts. Judging from the finds made in the tomb of Queen Hetepheres, dated only a little later, we may reasonably assume that the carved hieroglyphs were covered with gold and that other parts were decorated with inlays of Egyptian faience. It is also likely that the cabinets opened from the top and were divided internally by compartments to hold jewellery, cosmetics and other small personal belongings, in the same manner as the Tutankhamun cabinets. Above the panels in which the cabinets are portrayed are four shafts with finials, presumed to represent the supports of a bed canopy. Such a canopy intended to be hung with netting or curtains was actually found in the tomb of Queen Hetepheres.

Other objects of great interest are the small pieces illustrated in figure 27b. In the upper left corner is the 'basic' table with plain straight legs and stretchers, not only the first type of wooden table to appear in ancient Egypt, but also the prototype of the 'modern' table in use today in various sizes and proportions. Three stools are represented, of which two have the typical curved braces used by Egyptian cabinet-makers to strengthen the joints. The third stool has the traditional animal legs with rounded side-rails and a leather seat attached by lashings. It is interesting to note that these lashings do not appear at the top of the frame. It was customary to cut the slots on the side and bottom parts of the rails, and consequently the slots with the lashings passing through them do not appear on the frame itself when the seat is viewed from above. Special note should be made of the drawing of the stool in which the papyrus ornaments appear at both ends of the side-rails as on the 'niche' stela in figure 20.

At the lower left in figure 27b are two chairs similar to the stools except for the addition of the backs. The design of the back is basic and represents a practical construction, but we do not know if this was a common type because chairs are usually rendered in profile and a direct view of the back is not shown. The long frame with a panel attached by lashings which appears in this same painting presumably represents a bed with a leather covering as seen from above. A number of beds are portrayed, mostly with typical animal legs; but there is also a curious new type of support shown, which appears like a bent piece of wood (fig. 27c). At one end of each bed a rectangular frame is added which seems to be a separate construction with straight legs – evidently the forerunner of the foot-board commonly used on Egyptian beds from this time on.

Besides the furniture represented in these extraordinary paintings there were also brilliant wall hangings, head-rests stored in boxes, games with markers and game boxes, and vessels of various sorts. But despite the lack of any comparable record, there is no reason to believe this to be an isolated instance of luxury. Though Hesy-Re was an important individual it is probable that the furnishings of the royal palaces were even more luxurious. The panelled palace façades represented on First Dynasty royal stelae indicate that the king's residence was an imposing structure even at that early age, and it no doubt contained more and finer furniture than the home of a private person, however

27a Tomb painting with cabinets on legs incorporating hieroglyphic signs as ornaments. *Third Dynasty.*   37

 b Tomb painting with household furniture – tables, chairs, stools and a bed in plan. *Third Dynasty.*

 c Tomb painting showing beds. *Third Dynasty.*

well-to-do. And in the architectural ruins that surround the Step Pyramid of Zoser at Saqqara there is incontrovertible evidence in stone of the elegance of the royal buildings of the Third Dynasty.[23]

Shortly after Petrie's historic discoveries in the First Dynasty tombs at Abydos, the distinguished archaeologist J. H. Breasted, in his classic history of Egypt, published in 1905, wrote of the furnishings of an Early Dynastic palace saying, in part, as follows:

> The furniture of such a palace, even in this remote age was magnificent and of fine artistic quality. . . . The less substantial furniture has for the most part perished, but chests of ebony inlaid with ivory and stools with legs of ivory magnificently carved to represent bull's legs,

28 The reconstructed chair of Queen Hetepheres with the original gold covering. *Fourth Dynasty.*

have survived in fragments. Glaze was now more thoroughly mastered than before, and incrustation with glazed plaques and ivory was practised.[24]

Although this account was based on the somewhat limited knowledge of the time it was written, the later discoveries have proved conclusively that the basic traditional forms of Egyptian furniture, reproduced from the Old Kingdom to the Ptolemaic period, were already established by the end of the Third Dynasty. In the techniques of wood-working also, the principles already evolved set the pattern for the future, and they have continued with little change until the present time. New tools have been invented and machines now turn out much of the work formerly done by hand, but the basic joinery is much the same today as it was forty-six centuries ago.

2

THE OLD KINGDOM
(2686–2181 B.C.)

Although the term 'Old Kingdom' is now used by archaeologists to cover the period of the Third to the Sixth Dynasties, the little surviving material pertaining to furniture of the Third Dynasty (the Hesy-Re panels and paintings) has already been discussed.

But even though adhering to the traditions of design and form established during the Early Dynastic period, the arts and architecture of ancient Egypt reached the peak of their development during the five hundred years which begin with the Fourth Dynasty. The vitality and creative urge of the era were combined with a restrained elegance of design and technical skill to a degree never surpassed and rarely equalled in the history of Egyptian art, as is evident in the masterpieces of ancient royal furniture found in the tomb of Queen Hetepheres. Her golden arm-chair (fig. 28 and colour plate IVA) and the other pieces discovered in the tomb give striking evidence of the elegance of palace furniture of this early period.

The furniture of Hetepheres

Queen Hetepheres was the wife of Sneferu, the first king of the Fourth Dynasty, who built a pyramid-tomb for himself at Dahshur, and the mother of Cheops, who built the Great Pyramid at Giza about 2580 B.C. Nothing remains of the rich treasures and furniture which were undoubtedly buried with these great kings: their tombs, like those of the other rulers of the Old Kingdom, were robbed thousands of years ago; but strangely enough the furniture of Cheops' mother has been preserved and can still be seen in the Cairo Museum restored to a condition very close to that in which it existed forty-six centuries ago.

It was discovered in 1925 by an expedition from Harvard University and the Boston Museum of Fine Arts under Dr G. A. Reisner. At the bottom of a deep shaft near the Great Pyramid at Giza the excavators found a small chamber containing the queen's burial

39

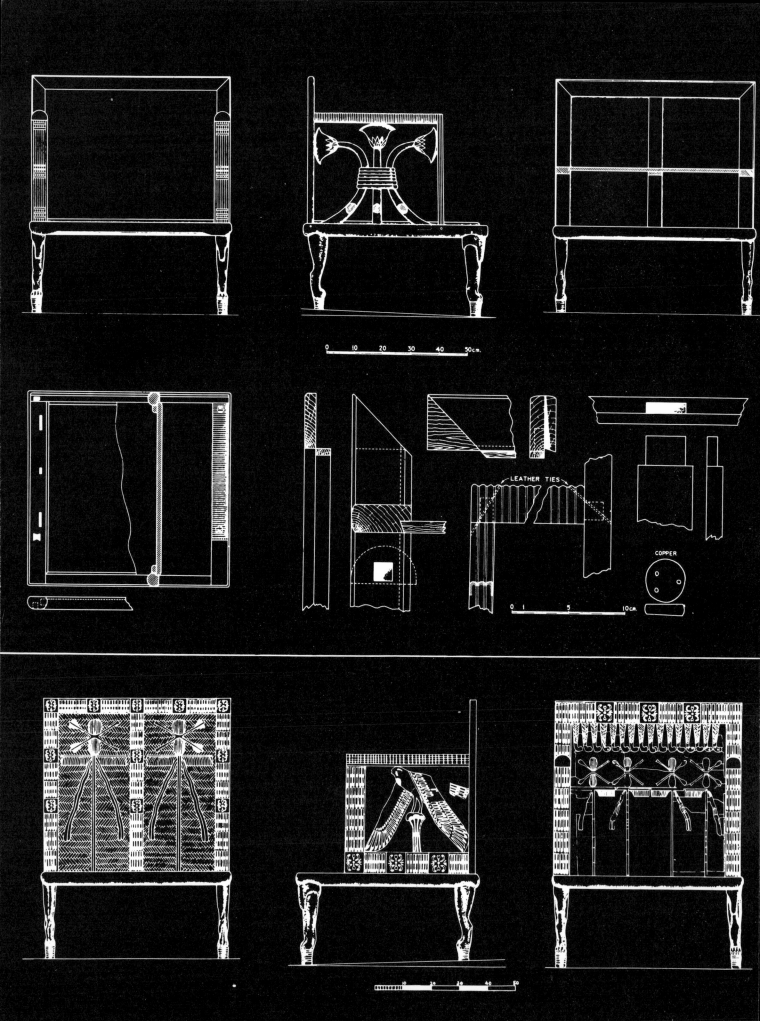

0   10   20   30   40   50 cm.

LEATHER TIES

COPPER

0   1   5   10 cm.

10   20   40   50

equipment, no doubt transferred there after her proper tomb had been violated. The original tomb was probably at Dahshur, near one of the pyramids built by her husband Sneferu. The most plausible explanation of what occurred seems to be that of Dr Reisner: that this tomb had been broken into during the reign of Cheops, that the robbery was discovered and that the remaining contents of the tomb were taken to the chamber at Giza. Although the mummy of the queen had been stolen from its alabaster coffin, the sarcophagus and the funeral equipment were stored as in a proper burial, and this time the grave was successfully concealed. The upper part of the shaft was filled with stones similar to those lying around, and the ground above was effectively camouflaged with a layer of debris. Consequently, when the chamber was re-opened in modern times, its contents were found unmolested. The record of the discovery and of the recovery and reconstruction of the furniture is one of the most fascinating stories in the history of archaeology.[1]

The arm-chair of Queen Hetepheres is unique in being the most ancient chair extant and the only one to survive from the Old Kingdom. Entirely covered with gold except for the back panel and the seat, it is also one of the most beautiful examples of ancient design and workmanship. Although much of the original wood of the chair had been reduced to a fine powder, the gold sheathings and the inlays of various other materials retained their original shapes and relative positions, and therefore an accurate reconstruction was possible. These parts have been re-joined and appear today much as they would have done originally, except for the patina they have acquired. The back and seat have been restored with plain wooden panels on the supposition that a cushion was thrown over them, as is seen in so many Old Kingdom sculptural representations. Nothing remained that could definitely be identified as part of an ornamented seat and back, but in the space beneath the chair were found torn fragments of gold-foil which could be reassembled to form part of the figure of a seated woman smelling a lotus flower. This figure had been raised in the surface of the gold by applying the foil over a carved wooden surface, and although the proportions of the figure do not fit well with those of the back of the chair, it is possible that it did form part of the decoration of a back panel similar to that on the chair of Sitamun of the Eighteenth Dynasty (fig. 74). However, it is more likely that the fragments formed part of the lid of a small box, the wood of which has vanished.[2]

The chair is low, with a wide and deep seat sloping slightly from front to back. Its supports, in the form of the fore and hind legs of a lion, rest on the traditional beaded drums. At this time the feline type of leg began to replace the hoof type used in the Early Dynastic period, and from now on the lion's leg is the form most generally used. Like the rest of the chair, the legs are covered with thin gold sheet except for their bases, which are shod with disks of copper. The outstanding feature of the design, however, is the motif employed in the side panels: a group of three boldly carved papyrus flowers bound together (fig. 28). The face of the arm-supports has a finely drawn mat pattern, while the upper surface of the arms has a semi-circular shape with a crosswise beading. As a whole the chair has a vigour and a restrained elegance which render it uniquely important in the history of furniture design.

29 Scale drawings of the reconstructed chair of Queen Hetepheres. *Fourth Dynasty.*

30 Scale drawings of the second chair of Queen Hetepheres. *Fourth Dynasty.*

Sufficient traces of the details of its construction remained to ascertain the joining of the wooden parts (fig. 29). The legs, frames and arm-supports are fastened together with mortise and tenon joints secured with wooden pins. The joints of the arm-rests, both at front and back, are further strengthened by leather thongs passed diagonally through the tenons, the leather ties being concealed with small gold patches where they appear on the surface. Dowels are used to fasten the stems of the papyrus flowers of the side panels to the central tie uniting them, and these floral groups are dowelled into the back, the arm-rests and the arm-supports.

A second arm-chair, of which fragments were also found in the chamber, had deteriorated beyond the possibility of reconstruction. Nevertheless, its general outline could be determined from the pieces of inlay and the metal parts which remained (fig. 30). Its basic form is similar to that of the other chair, with gold-covered legs of animal design. The ornamentation of the back and sides is, however, totally different. Both surfaces of the back are elaborately decorated with designs incorporating religious symbols. On the inner surface the principal symbols are executed in inlay of coloured composition,[3] set in a background of gold sheeting; on the outer surface the symbols are modelled in plaster and overlaid with gold, being set in a background of blue composition inlays arranged in a criss-cross pattern imitating a woven design. The motif used in the open-work sides

31

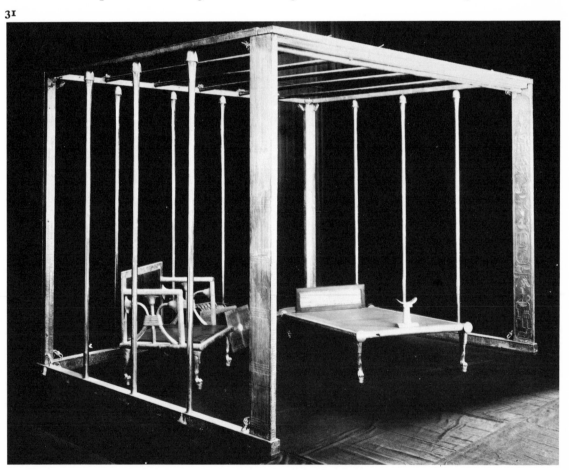

31 The reconstructed bed canopy of Queen Hetepheres, with bed and chair. *Fourth Dynasty*.

32 Part of a scene from the tomb of Queen Meresankh III, showing bed-making under a canopy. *Fourth Dynasty.*

was that of the falcon of Horus shown perched on a palm-column, its wings opened downwards in the conventional attitude of protection. The frames of the sides and the back were also inlaid with coloured composition in a formal design of a feather pattern with occasional rosettes.

The queen's furniture included an ingeniously constructed gold-covered canopy which formed an enclosed place for the bed, probably partly for protection from insects and partly for privacy (fig. 31). Fragments have survived of contemporary linen fine enough to serve as mosquito-netting; pieces of heavier woven materials, which could have served for bed curtains, have also been preserved. Copper hooks were placed around the inner edge of the top frame for attaching the curtains and also, apparently, a roofing cloth. A relief in the tomb-chapel of Queen Meresankh at Giza shows a similar canopy under which servants are portrayed making up a bed (fig. 32).[4]

The woodwork of the canopy was carved with a mat pattern, except for the inner faces of the uprights forming the jambs of the entrance. These faces carried inscriptions giving the titles of King Sneferu. Gold sheeting was beaten over the wood to take the impression of the carving, which then appeared as gilded relief-work. The individual signs of the inscriptions are carved with great beauty and skill and the small details on the insect and bird forms were clearly tooled with a sharp instrument. The over-all result is one of great charm – an effective combination of raised forms and incised patterns (fig. 33).[5] All the elements were fastened together in such a way that the structure could be dismantled and re-assembled with ease. The intricate series of joints reflect cabinet-making ability of the first order, the joining members being sheathed in copper. (For the various joints used in the construction, see the series of photographs made from the reconstruction in Cairo and reproduced in fig. 34.)[6]

The curtain box, in which the canopy hangings were placed when not in use, was also covered with gold and elaborately ornamented with composition inlays of blue-green and black (fig. 35). But here the designs and inscriptions were first carved as depressions in the wood rather than in relief as on the canopy. Very thin sheets of gold were laid over the surfaces to form the background; the gold covering the incised designs was cut out and the edges of the metal pressed into the depressions; the inlays were then inserted into the depressions. The end of the box opposite to that illustrated carries a small inlaid figure of Sneferu. The sides were fitted together with wooden pegs, and the underside of the lid had two battens to give it strength and to hold it in place. In the centre of the lid was a knob.

The queen's bed obviously derives from the Early Dynastic types which we have seen previously, in which the legs, of animal design, were likewise lashed to the rails with thongs (fig. 37). This bed, however, has a much more pronounced slope toward the

33 Details of the raised inscriptions on the sheet gold covering one of the uprights of the canopy of Queen Hetepheres. *Fourth Dynasty.*

34 Constructional details of the canopy of Queen Hetepheres. *Fourth Dynasty.*

33

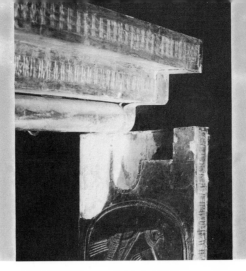

34

foot-board, and the legs are made in the shape of stylized lion's legs with claws, instead of the bull's legs of the primitive beds. The foot-board is inlaid on the face with composition in feather and flower rosette patterns. In place of the usual covering of matting or leather thongs, there was a solid board fitted into grooves cut in the inner sides of the frame-rails, forming a base on which the mattress was placed. The legs were covered with a heavy sheathing of gold, as were the rounded side-rails, which terminated in simplified papyrus flower ornaments.

A head-rest was found inside a gold-covered box. Originally of wood and overlaid with thin sheets of gold and silver, it survived only as a metal shell (fig. 36). It may be well to mention here that the Egyptians slept with their feet towards the bed panel, their heads resting on rigid head-rests set at the other end. It is easy to understand why women in countries like Japan might wish to protect their elaborate head-dresses by using head-rests, but it is difficult to understand why the Egyptians, who shaved their heads, should adopt such an apparently uncomfortable habit. Yet a head-rest, carefully cut to fit a particular head, might, in spite of the intractability of the material, offer more comfort on a hot, sticky night than a pillow of soft, clinging down. A head-rest might, furthermore, be cushioned in some way, like one in the Metropolitan Museum where the hard upper surface has been softened with linen bandages. The usual design of head-rests consisted of a curved upper section supported by a column, ordinarily plain, but occasionally fluted, and sometimes very elaborate, resting on a base. Although those in daily use were ordinarily made of wood, more formal ones were made of alabaster or other stone, and those made for royalty were even covered with precious metals, as was that found in the tomb of Queen Hetepheres.[7]

The carrying chair (fig. 38) was apparently made at a later date than the canopy and the curtain box. In the inscriptions which it bears, Hetepheres is called 'Mother of the King of Upper and Lower Egypt', that is, mother of Cheops. This implies that she received the carrying chair as a gift from Cheops after he had become king, whereas the canopy and the box are inscribed with the name of Sneferu. On the carrying chair are four lines of inscription composed of small individual hieroglyphs made of solid gold. Originally they were set in narrow wooden bands (probably ebony), one band running horizontally across the middle of the face of the back panel, and three running vertically down the reverse side of the same panel. The gold casing of the frame is somewhat heavier than that on the other furniture, and it bears a matting design of fine cross-lines

45

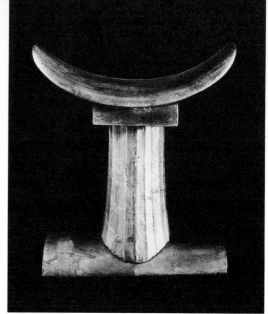

that appears to have been stamped in the metal with a die. The original wood was in a better state of preservation than that of any of the other pieces, but when the reconstruction was made it was found necessary in this piece also to use new wood for the panels and carrying poles.

The ends of the carrying poles of this chair terminate in heavy gold ornaments in the form of palm leaf capitals similar to those which appear on granite columns during the Fifth Dynasty. This use of the palm as a furniture ornament, however, seems to be an isolated instance. As a general rule the terminals which appear on chairs, stools and beds derive from the open papyrus flower or, in rare instances, from the lotus flower.[8] For the purpose of comparison, drawings of the three types are illustrated.

(a) PALM   (b) PAPYRUS   (c) LOTUS

Another inlaid box, which has not yet been reconstructed, was the most richly decorated object in the tomb. It carried inlays of feather patterns and flower rosettes similar to those on the back of the second arm-chair, but the background metal in this case was silver, and has almost entirely disintegrated. In this chest were personal belongings of the queen including gold and copper razors and other toilet articles, and a small gold-covered box containing silver bracelets which were left behind by the robbers who stripped Hetepheres' more valuable jewellery from her first tomb (fig. 39).

This unique collection of furniture would have been lost for ever had it not been for the painstaking care and scientific methods employed by Dr Reisner and his staff. Most of the wood had decayed to the consistency of cigar ash, leaving the gold sheathing and inlays without any substance to support them. Every scrap of gold, inlay and other material was recorded by photography and drawings exactly as it was found at the time of excavation. Each piece was then removed with a care that would have been unthinkable in the early days of excavation in Egypt and that has rarely been equalled since. Then followed years of meticulous study and careful reconstruction until the golden arm-chair, the

46

38 The reconstructed carrying chair of Queen Hetepheres, framed and ornamented with gold. *Fourth Dynasty.*

35 The reconstructed curtain box of Queen Hetepheres. It is covered with gold and inlaid with faience. *Fourth Dynasty.*

36 Queen Hetepheres' head-rest of wood overlaid with gold and silver. *Fourth Dynasty.*

37 The reconstructed bed of Queen Hetepheres. The legs and rails are overlaid with gold, and the foot-board is inlaid with faience. *Fourth Dynasty.*

37

carrying chair and the bed were completed in 1929, the canopy in 1932, and the long box in 1939, fourteen years after the first discovery.

What might have been only an incomprehensible heap of fragments had been transformed into a priceless group of ancient furniture.[9] These pieces, now kept in the Cairo Museum, have a restraint and dignified elegance that contrast markedly with the brilliant exuberance of the furniture of King Tutankhamun, exhibited near by. Replicas may also be seen in the Boston Museum of Fine Arts, made in meticulous detail in accordance with the originals.

The objects from the tomb of Hetepheres are remarkable not only as rare pieces of furniture from the Old Kingdom, but also for the lavish use of gold. They reveal that this metal was used in quantity already at this early period, although few traces of it have been found on objects of the same date discovered elsewhere. An account has, however, been published of some rather similar material found at Dorak on the Sea of Marmora in Turkey.[10] It comprises fragments of furniture apparently made in Egypt during the reign of King Sahure of the Fifth Dynasty (about 2485 B.C.), and presumably was a gift to some Oriental ruler. The report of this find states that it includes parts of a wooden chair or throne plated with gold, a furniture ornament consisting of a strip of gold inscribed with the name of Sahure, and gold-covered animal feet. No further information is available on this interesting discovery, the objects from which are in private hands. From them and

38

39

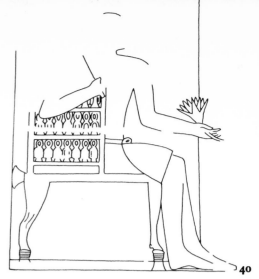

40

41

39 Reconstructed gold-covered box of Queen Hetepheres, used to hold her bracelets. *Fourth Dynasty.*

40 Seshem-nefer seated in an arm-chair with side panels decorated with cut-out hieroglyphic signs. *Fifth Dynasty.*

41 A man and his wife seated side by side on a double arm-chair. *Fifth Dynasty.*

42 Rashepses seated in an arm-chair with a high back, decorated with a mat pattern, possibly representing inlay. *Fifth Dynasty.*

42

from the Hetepheres pieces, it is clear that gold was more plentiful than the few scanty remains would otherwise indicate, and this view is borne out by the references in ancient texts to the use of gold for the ornamentation of furniture.[11] Gold was of course the first objective of the ancient tomb robbers, who were thorough in removing every particle they could find.

Furniture in sculpture

A number of high-backed arm-chairs, similar to those of Queen Hetepheres, except for their ornamentation, appear in the reliefs of Old Kingdom tombs. In some cases the legs have the lion design with claws, and in others they take the form of bull's leg with hoof, so common in the Early Dynastic period; both types are used at the same time in the Old Kingdom. The latter, at this period, was more slender and attenuated than its Second Dynasty counterpart and sometimes resembled the leg of an antelope, like those on the carved wood panel of Hesy-Re (fig. 26).

For the most part these arm-chairs have plain side panels, but an interesting variation is found in the preliminary drawing for an unfinished relief in the tomb of a man named Seshem-nefer (fig. 40).[12] Although the upper parts of the seated figure and of the chair-back are defaced, the design of the side panel is clearly visible. Within the frame formed by the arm-rest there are three rows made up of the hieroglyphic sign sometimes called the 'girdle of Isis' (⧖), similar to those on the cabinets in the Hesy-Re wall-paintings. These signs were probably made in open-work and, to judge from the Hetepheres furniture, were most likely embellished with gold and inlays. A similar design is found in the arm panel of another chair which forms part of the decorations in the tomb of a man named Shepseskaf-ankh.[13] The representation of this chair is badly defaced, but the design of the panel is clearly indicated: there were four rows of the same hieroglyphic sign,

49

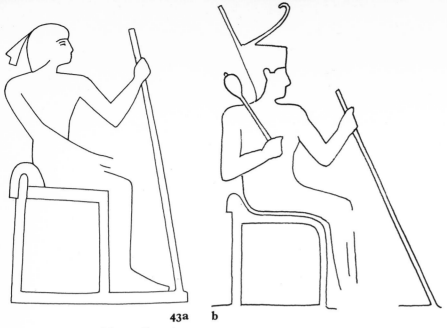

43a   b

although only two rows are now to be seen. Both these chairs have the typical papyrus flower terminal ornaments which are lacking on the Hetepheres chair.

In one representation of a chair, in a *mastaba* at Saqqara, the back panel carries a mat pattern resembling that on the inlaid Hetepheres chair (fig. 42). Depicting the chair back in full, the Egyptian artist has in this case departed from his normal custom of showing objects in profile, his intention no doubt being to emphasize the decorative detail on the panel. It is possible that the original of the chair had its decoration executed in composition inlays as in the Hetepheres chair; but the framing of the back suggests that the pattern was more probably carved in the wood – a technique of design dating from the Early Dynastic period – and perhaps covered with gold.

A similar type of chair with a plain side panel is depicted on a curious relief in the Louvre (fig. 41).[14] On this chair the husband and wife are seated, apparently in tandem, the one behind the other, another representational convention of the Egyptian artist who could not cope realistically with perspective; probably the couple sat side by side on a wide seat. Such representations are not uncommon, and later, in the New Kingdom, the wide double chair with two persons seated side by side appears in sculpture in the round (fig. 180).

The types of seats found in the Early Dynastic period, and discussed in the last chapter, persisted into the Old Kingdom. The rectangular armless chair with a low back, over which a cushion was draped, continued to be used in the portrayal of seated kings. On one end of the curtain box of Hetepheres, King Sneferu is shown seated on such a chair[15] (fig. 43a). Cheops is portrayed on an almost identical seat in an inscription in high relief in the alabaster quarries at Hatnub in Middle Egypt (fig. 43b). In a less formal scene in which Queen Meresankh, the grand-daughter of Cheops, is depicted in a boat being rowed in the marshes, she sits on a similar chair with an inner rectangular frame (fig. 44). This detail, no doubt added to give rigidity to the seat, is represented hundreds of times in the paintings and sculptures of this and later periods.

Shortly after the time of Cheops more elaborate motifs appear on royal thrones; the throne occupied by Chephren in the famous diorite statue in Cairo exhibits several new features. The legs, which are of the lion type, are shown as being in each case doubled,

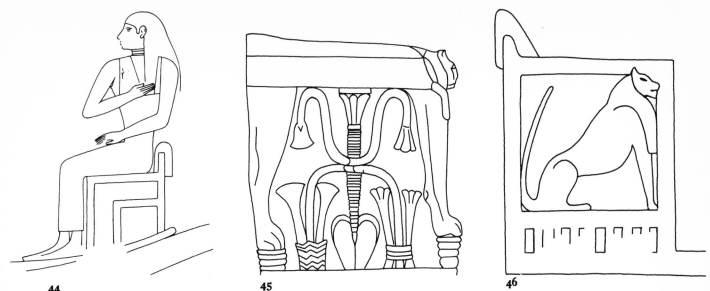

44   45   46

and the front pairs on each side of the chair are surmounted by lion heads; from the front, therefore, Chephren's legs appear to be flanked by lion figures with long attenuated legs.[16] The spaces between the front and back legs on each side are filled with a plant design (fig. 45). Like so much of the ornamentation in Egyptian art, this plant design has a special significance as well as being attractive in itself. It consists of two plants symbolic of Upper and Lower Egypt bound with a hieroglyph meaning 'joined together'. The whole design celebrated pictorially the union of the two kingdoms of Upper and Lower Egypt. It was first used (although not as an element in furniture design) in the Early Dynastic period, and continued as a favourite motif associated with the king for thousands of years.[17]

Lion motifs are usually associated with royal thrones, except for the lion's leg which had begun to supersede the bull's leg in the Third Dynasty, and which was used for the chairs of private individuals as well as for those of royalty. Two other statues of Chephren show the heads and foreparts of lions,[18] and a little later, on the throne of Queen Meresankh III, the complete animal figure is placed within the frame of the rectangular seat (fig. 46). The complete figure also appears set between the arm and the seat in a relief showing a chair with lion's legs (fig. 47). Again, to judge from the ornamentation of the Hetepheres furniture, it may reasonably be assumed that these figures were gilded or inlaid with coloured composition. Some evidence in support of this assumption is given by the colours preserved on the figures of lions in furniture in other reliefs. In one instance the lion is painted in brilliant yellow with a green-striped mane, and in another he is yellow with stripes of red on his mane; the yellow almost certainly represented a covering of gold.[19]

The straight-legged chair seen on Second Dynasty Helwan and Saqqara stelae is not often found in reliefs and paintings of the Old Kingdom, but its survival and further development can be seen in the relief carved on the outside of the limestone sarcophagus of the princess Kauit of the Eleventh Dynasty (about 2050 B.C.), now in the Cairo Museum. This finely carved scene shows the charming figure of the princess at her toilet, holding a mirror, while a maid adjusts her hair ornaments and a male servant pours a drink. She is seated on a simple arm-chair which might have been made yesterday. The

47

47 Arm-chair with lion figure incorporated in the side panel. *Fourth Dynasty.*

48 High-backed arm-chair in a toilet scene on the sarcophagus of the princess Kauit. *Eleventh Dynasty.*

stretcher is lower than that found in the Early Dynastic high-backed chair, and a low rectangular open arm-rest has been added; a cushion is thrown over the back (fig. 48). The wood sections, the scale and the restrained design resemble the furniture of the twentieth century more than they do the usual concept of four-thousand-year-old Egyptian furniture. In another scene on the same sarcophagus Kauit is shown again, seated on a high-backed chair but without arm-rest or cushion.[20]

The chair shown in figure 49 exhibits a marked deviation from the usual forms. It occurs in a scene from the *mastaba* of Ipy at Saqqara, now in the Cairo Museum,[21] in which the deceased owner is shown being carried in a palanquin. He sits on a high-backed chair which has four plain vertical supports below the seat. It is not quite clear from the relief whether these supports are in fact legs, or whether the side of the seat is panelled, in which case the two outer supports would be part of the frame and the two inner supports would be battens. Solid chair-sides, decorated in different ways, are frequently represented in later Egyptian periods, whereas an open construction of the form shown is most unusual. It is interesting to note, however, that stools with a series of vertical supports, either with or without a frame, are often depicted in the Near Eastern seals of approximately this time. Another interesting feature of the Ipy chair is that it has a foot-stool extending forward which also exhibits small vertical supports or battens.

Of the various types of seat which continued from the Early Dynastic period into the Old Kingdom, the most common is the stool with animal legs and papyrus flower terminals. Since the Old Kingdom stools differ so little from their early prototypes, only two of many are illustrated here. The first occurs on the slab-stela of Wepemnefert of the Fourth Dynasty from Giza, and now in the Museum of Anthropology, University of California. It is one of the best preserved examples of an early Old Kingdom painted relief (colour plate II). The basic form of the stool has not changed, but the legs and other details have a refinement, compared with those found on Second Dynasty stelae, that is already apparent in the stool of Hesy-Re (fig. 26). In the painting, the wooden parts of the stool, distinctively coloured and grained, are clearly differentiated from the parts covered with metal – the papyrus flower terminal and the beaded cylinders which support the legs. The cushion on the seat and the gown worn by Wepemnefert are both coloured white, indicating no doubt that both were made of linen.

52

48

A similar design of stool is shown on the stela of Rahotep from his tomb in Maidum and now in the British Museum (fig. 50). Rahotep, a son of Sneferu who flourished during the reign of Cheops, is best known for the famous statues of himself and his wife Nefert, among the greatest treasures of the Cairo Museum.[22] The stool on his stela, like that on one of the Helwan stelae, is represented with a view of the seat rendered in plan. Here, as in the stela of Wepemnefert, there is a marked advance in the technical quality of the relief as well as in the design of the stool, in comparison with the somewhat crude examples of Early Dynastic date. On both these Fourth Dynasty stelae the seated person faced the traditional offering-table, which was made of stone, or possibly of pottery, on which are placed loaves of bread represented in a conventional manner.

As in the case of the high-backed arm-chair (fig. 41), the animal-leg stool is sometimes shown in a double version (fig. 51). In this instance, where the legs of the wife are outlined against the side of the seat, it may seem far-fetched to surmise that the two persons were seated side by side. Perhaps what is represented here is an unusual, elongated bench rather than the usual double seat. On the other hand, the Egyptian artist, faced with depicting something a little out of the ordinary, frequently used solutions which, to us, produce a bizarre or distorted result.

53

49 50

49 Relief of Ipy seated on a high-backed chair with possibly a panelled base. *Sixth Dynasty.*

50 Stela of Rahotep showing a stool with slender bull's legs, the seat represented in plan, and with a cushion. *Fourth Dynasty.*

51

The furniture of Mereruka

Apart from the actual furniture of Queen Hetepheres, our best idea of the furniture of the Old Kingdom comes from the scenes in the tombs of the high officials of the period. The most complete picture of the wide range of pieces found in the palaces and houses of the time can be obtained from the multi-roomed *mastaba*-tombs of the Fifth and Sixth Dynasties at Saqqara. The biggest is that made for Mereruka, a vizier under Teti, the first king of the Sixth Dynasty (about 2345–2333 B.C.).[23] The great bulk and solidity of these structures account for the preservation of the painted reliefs. Many scenes show pieces of furniture of types commonly in use during the late Old Kingdom. In one scene Mereruka is portrayed sitting on a finely carved stool of which the lion's paws are clearly delineated; in front of him is a round offering-table; at the right of the scene is the end section of a straight-legged small square or rectangular table (fig. 52).

One of the most intriguing of the painted reliefs in this tomb is that in which Mereruka and his wife sit facing one another on a heavily cushioned bed with a high board at one end and a foot-board with a cushion at the other (colour plate III and fig. 53). He holds a fly-whisk, while she entertains him by playing on a stringed musical instrument. The bed has heavy legs with lion's claws, resting on a base. The legs and frame of the bed are painted and grained so that they represent wood. The cones on which the legs rest are plain and painted a different colour – probably to indicate a metal covering. Of particular interest are the six tables which appear beneath the bed. Two are nearly identical; the others differ from each other slightly in size and in the arrangement of their parts, although their details are similar. They deserve careful study and are clearly enough drawn to be successfully reproduced by a modern cabinet-maker. The proportions are excellent, and the cove edge of the top and the flowing lines of the base between legs and stretcher are attractive details of design (fig. 55).

A characteristic feature of the decoration found in tombs of this kind is the series of scenes depicting activities common in the daily life of the deceased, including representations of various craftsmen at work. In one of these scenes there are heavy tables, evidently intended to carry the materials on which the artisans are working (fig. 54). In another scene there is a series of tables of lighter scale which, representing as they do the basic table used from the earliest times until today, have a special place in the history of furniture (fig. 56). Plain in design, with flush stretchers to strengthen them, they appear in a variety of sizes and shapes. Occasionally the top is left open to make room for a rack to hold vases or other vessels. Although no actual tables of this type have survived from the Old Kingdom, copper models have been found in Old Kingdom tombs.[24] Figure 59 illustrates such a model, now in the British Museum, made for the lector-priest Idy who lived during the Sixth Dynasty and was buried at Abydos. Its top is in the form of the conventional offering-table with a projection on one side which, on an actual offering-table, may have carried a channel to drain liquids poured on the table. The top also has small circular holes cut in it to hold vessels with pointed or rounded bases.

One of the ritual scenes in the tomb of Mereruka shows a procession of men carrying gabled chests on poles (fig. 57). As with the tables, no household chests survive from this

51 Stela of Intef on which the owner and his wife are shown sitting on a double stool or bench with lion's legs. *Eleventh Dynasty.*

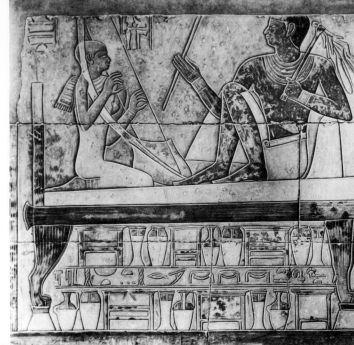

52 Mereruka seated on a lion-legged chair with a low back. *Sixth Dynasty.*

53 Mereruka and his wife seated on a bed with a thick mattress. Beneath the bed are pots and six tables (see fig. 54). *Sixth Dynasty.* (See colour plate III.)

period, but examples with peaked tops, almost identical to those shown here, have been found in New Kingdom tombs. Such chests, used for the storage of linen, clothing and other personal belongings, formed an important part of the furniture in early Egyptian households, since there were no cupboards or bureaux. Their appearance in these reliefs provides indisputable evidence that they were in use in the Old Kingdom, and it may be inferred that chests of the same kind were also used in earlier periods.

The scenes in Old Kingdom tombs amply illustrate the importance of furniture in the simple everyday life of the times. As we have seen, stools were used not only in the home but also in the workshop. In a relief from a tomb at Giza we see a sculptor at work on a statue with his arms upraised, seated on a splay-leg stool (fig. 60). Similarly, Mereruka, going about his business on the Nile, is represented sitting on a stool with carved legs in the stern of his boat (fig. 62). In yet another scene set on the Nile, the stool in the stern of the boat is replaced by a bed, which is enclosed within a light structure to protect the vizier from the hot sun (fig. 63).

The Fifth Dynasty tomb of Nykauhor and Sekhem-hathor, also in the necropolis of Saqqara, contains one scene of special interest: two men are shown playing a board game, something like draughts, at a table which in its proportions and design could well serve as the model for the present-day 'cocktail table' (fig. 61). The individual details of design, as well as the over-all appearance of this table, exemplify the resemblances which frequently occur between the furniture of ancient Egypt and that of our own times. In a similar scene,

56

Colour plate IV*a*. Chair of Hetepheres. *Fourth Dynasty.*

b. Chair of Sitamun. *Eighteenth Dynasty.*

Mereruka and his son are shown playing a game on a table of like proportions, although simpler in design (fig. 58).

Minor variations within the established forms occur throughout the Old Kingdom; but, unfortunately, the gaps which exist in the records make it impossible to discuss the development of ancient Egyptian furniture in a neat chronological sequence. What seems to be new often represents something inherited from an earlier period, and the continued repetition of Old Kingdom forms is conspicuous on the stelae of the Transitional and Middle Kingdom periods. Only rarely is there a marked variation from the traditional types, but one significant new development occurs at about the time of the Twelfth Dynasty, when an inclined back-rest is added to the usual vertical back of the chair. I do not know of any precedent for this in Old Kingdom representations, and if none exists this is the first appearance of what was to become the most popular chair during the Eighteenth Dynasty.

When we consider how few actual examples of furniture have survived from the Old Kingdom, it is indeed curious that fate has preserved for us the elaborate pieces belonging to Queen Hetepheres. Such furniture was, of course, far removed in elegance and ornamentation from what was used by ordinary Egyptians during this period. It is unique of its kind; for we know no precedents for it, nor has any furniture of comparable elegance survived except for the royal furniture of the Eighteenth Dynasty described in the next chapter.

55

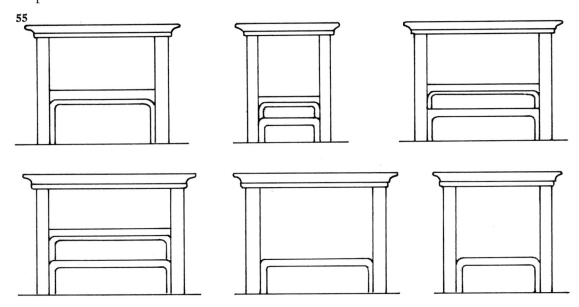

54 Scene of craftsmen at work, using substantially built tables to support heavy work. *Sixth Dynasty.*

55 Low tables with cove-edged tops (see fig. 54). *Sixth Dynasty.*

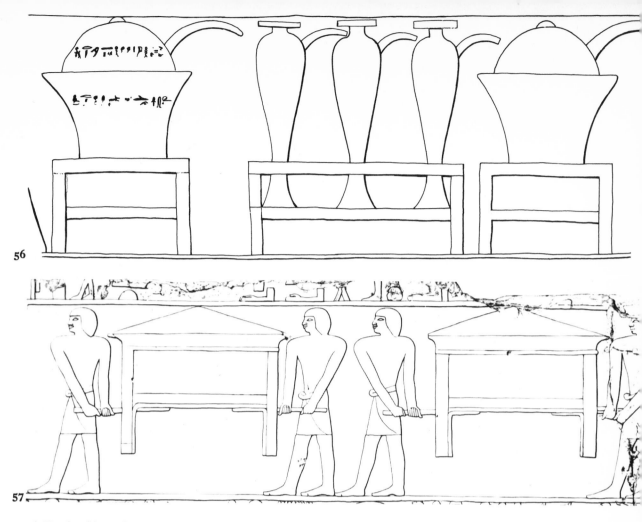

56

57

56 Simple tables and a stand for vessels, from the tomb of Mereruka. *Sixth Dynasty*.

57 Servants carrying gable-topped storage chests. *Sixth Dynasty*.

58 Mereruka and his son play 'draughts' on a low table of simple design. *Sixth Dynasty*.

58

59 Copper offering-stand with model vessels. *Sixth Dynasty*.

60 Sculptor at work seated on a splay-leg stool. *Fifth Dynasty*.

61 Two men play 'draughts' on a low table. *Fifth Dynasty*.

62 Mereruka sits on a stool as he sails on the Nile. *Sixth Dynasty*.

63 Bed-making scene on board ship. The bed is set beneath an awning. *Sixth Dynasty*.

PALACE FURNITURE OF THE EIGHTEENTH DYNASTY
(1567–1320 B.C.)

More than a thousand years elapsed between the time of Queen Hetepheres and the Eighteenth Dynasty to which our next examples of palace furniture belong. But although no furniture has survived from this intervening period, the pieces represented in sculptured reliefs indicate that the traditions of the Old Kingdom persisted with little change.[1] Shortly after the beginning of the Eighteenth Dynasty, however, new trends are apparent.

At this time Egypt had reached the height of her power and prosperity. The Egyptian kings controlled the area from the Euphrates River in the east to Nubia in the south; and increased contacts with Crete and the other Aegean islands, as well as trade with distant lands, spread the Egyptian influence throughout the ancient world. In one respect Egypt at this time resembled England and France in the eighteenth century: in both instances a wealth of ornamental detail was lavished on the furniture made by the artists and artisans of the times for their royal patrons. As might be expected, in Egypt the finest furniture was reserved for the pharaoh himself, who was not only the king, but also was worshipped as a god, and whose choicest pieces of furniture accompanied him to the tomb.

Not all the fine furniture produced in the royal workshops was, however, kept for use in the royal palaces. Some was sent abroad by kings of the Eighteenth Dynasty as presents to rulers of neighbouring states, and some to subject princes – a clear sign of the high regard in which such furniture was held. One of the cuneiform tablets found at El-Amarna, included in the diplomatic archives of about 1390 B.C., contains the account of the furniture sent by Amenophis III to the king of Babylon, Kadashman-Kharbe I:

> Behold, I have sent thee as a present
> for the new house, by the hand of Sutti
> one bed of ebony, overlaid with ivory and gold;
> three beds of ebony, overlaid with gold;
> one head-rest of ebony, overlaid with gold;
> one large chair of ebony, overlaid with gold;
> five chairs of ebony, overlaid with gold;
> —footstools of ebony, overlaid with gold.[2]

Another tablet states that Amenophis IV (Akhenaten) sent Burna-Buriash, who was then the king of Babylon, similar gifts:

> One bedstead, overlaid with gold, whose feet are protective deities.
> One bedstead, overlaid with gold; one part for the head, overlaid with gold.
> Five wooden arks, overlaid with gold.

Two chairs, which are overlaid with gold.
[There follow seven lines, not translated, which apparently refer to other chairs, after which many other articles are listed.]
Three bedsteads, of pure silver; one for the head of pure silver.
One ark overlaid with silver.[3]

Although in all periods there is a marked difference between the furniture made in the royal workshops for the use of royalty and that produced for common use, there remains a close relationship between them in basic forms. The differences lie chiefly in the quality of workmanship and the elaboration of ornament. Even in the palaces, however, a distinction must be made between the elegant furniture made for the personal use of royalty and the simple pieces required for storage and for everyday household requirements. Hence the terms 'royal' furniture and 'palace' furniture are not necessarily synonymous and, in preparation for the afterlife, what was placed in the royal tomb varied from the most elegant to the purely practical.

That so much of the more elaborate furniture was covered or ornamented with gold is one reason, perhaps the greatest single reason, why so little royal furniture has survived. The great wealth known to have been buried in the royal tombs proved an irresistible temptation to plunderers, who not only looted jewellery and valuable ornaments, but, when they had the opportunity, stripped the furniture as well, breaking it up or burning the wooden parts in order to obtain the precious metal with which it was decorated. For the most part the gilding on ancient Egyptian furniture did not consist of extremely thin gold-leaf (although the Egyptians did in fact prepare gold-leaf which closely approached the modern product in fineness), but of relatively heavy gold-foil or sheathing. Hence it was, along with the other valuables in the royal tombs, well worthy of the robbers' attention.[4]

Before examples of royal furniture were found in this century, there were indications that elegant and elaborate furniture did exist in ancient Egypt. The scholars and artists who accompanied Napoleon's expedition to Egypt and who made the first systematic survey of the paintings in temples and tombs found many scenes in which elaborate chairs and beds were represented; and in the years which followed, countless other similar representations were discovered by archaeologists. Additional evidence came from ancient writings containing descriptions of the rare woods used and of the ornamentation of gold, silver, ivory and costly inlays. But the excavations of the nineteenth century yielded only a few fragments of actual royal furniture, such as the parts of a bed in the British Museum made of fine hardwood ornamented on the legs with gold cobras' heads (fig. 64) and on the foot-board (fig. 65) with ebony cobras decorated with tiny silver rings. Otherwise, only the simpler pieces of ordinary household furniture were discovered.

In the great temple of Queen Hatshepsut at Deir el-Bahari there is a relief showing an arm-chair which is clearly the forerunner, if not the prototype, for the chair of the princess Sitamun of slightly later date. Although the relief is cracked and the design of the side panel is defaced, the form is clearly outlined (fig. 66). The head of the lion above the foreleg continues the traditional design of the Old Kingdom, but the slanting back-rest,

61

64

65

64 Leg from a royal bed decorated with cobras of gold sheet, and with silver on the hoof. *Eighteenth Dynasty.*

which forms an open triangle with the straight back and the seat, represents a form which was newly developed in the Middle Kingdom. In a later relief of Amenophis III dating from about 1400 B.C. another chair of the same general form is depicted (fig. 67). In this example, however, there is a new refinement in the design, and the motif of the bound plants of Upper and Lower Egypt is added beneath the seat. Between the arm and the seat is an elaborately carved and inlaid pattern such as may have filled the blank panel of the chair in the Hatshepsut relief. That the detail of this ornamentation is based on what actually existed, and is not just the result of the artist's imagination, is indicated by fragments from the tomb of Tuthmosis IV (about 1417 B.C.) in the Boston Museum, which have been assembled to form parts of an almost identical panel.[5]

The furniture of Yuia and Thuiu

At the beginning of the present century the sketchy record of the palace furniture of ancient Egypt was augmented by the sensational finds in the tomb of Yuia and Thuiu, parents of the wife of Amenophis III. This tomb was the first ever found in the royal necropolis of the Valley of the Kings which had not been completely looted, and in it were pieces of carved and gilded furniture inscribed with the names of Amenophis III, his wife, Queen Tiye and their daughter, the princess Sitamun. Then in 1922 the tomb of King Tutankhamun was discovered, followed in 1925 by the finding of the Old Kingdom tomb of Queen Hetepheres at Giza.

The tomb of Yuia and Thuiu was discovered in 1905 by Theodore M. Davis, an American archaeologist, in what would seem to be a most unpromising site.[6] It was located in a side valley off the main Valley of the Kings between two unfinished tombs, one begun for Ramesses III (but never completed) and one inscribed with the name of

65 Foot-board end of a royal bed. The struts supporting the foot-board carry figures of cobras embellished with small silver rings. *Eighteenth Dynasty.*

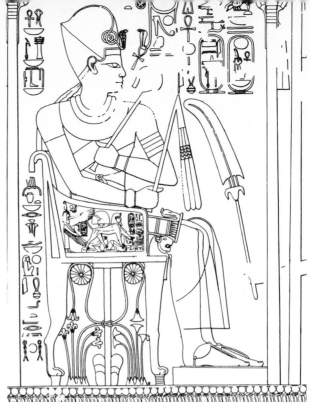

66 Drawing showing Queen Hatshepsut's chair with lion-head rising above the foreleg. *Eighteenth Dynasty*.

Ramesses XI. Both had been excavated long before, and the debris from the excavations covered the entrance to the tomb in the middle. As usual, the robbers had been there first, but, whereas the adjoining tombs had been completely looted, only small articles of jewellery which could easily be concealed had been taken from the tomb of Yuia and Thuiu. Apart from this robbery, which probably took place soon after the burial, the tomb had remained undisturbed for about thirty-three hundred years.

As befitted the parents of Queen Tiye, Yuia and Thuiu were buried like royalty in the Valley of the Kings. Although not of royal birth themselves, they were part of the royal household, and important personages in their own right. Much of the elegant furniture found in the tomb was doubtless a gift from the king, their son-in-law, who had sent similar furniture as gifts to the king of Babylon, Kadashman-Kharbe I.

The tomb contained three carved and gilded chairs, two decorated cabinets for jewellery, three beds and a number of storage chests, some decorated and some plain. The most important of the chairs was an arm-chair inscribed with the name of princess Sitamun, who is described as "the beloved eldest daughter of the King" and who was quite likely also the favourite of her grandparents (fig. 68). Since this was the first truly royal chair to be discovered, and because it represents the prevailing type of the Eighteenth Dynasty, it is described here in more detail than will be possible, or desirable, in most other instances. Its form is similar to the earlier throne of Queen Hatshepsut (fig. 66) and in each there is the strongly marked triangular opening between the vertical back and the slanting back-rest, which is characteristic of the profile view of chairs in contemporary paintings and sculptures.

The carved legs, representing the fore and hind legs of a lion, and the silver-covered beaded drums on which they rest are typical Old Kingdom details, but the concave curved back-rest, the shape of the arm, the rounded stretchers and the motifs of the

67 King Amenophis III seated in state on a chair with elaborately carved side panels, and with the motif of 'union of the two lands' between the legs. *Eighteenth Dynasty*.

63

68 Front view of the chair of princess Sitamun. *Eighteenth Dynasty.*

69 Drawing of the scene on the back of the chair of Sitamun. The carving is covered with gold-foil. *Eighteenth Dynasty.*

68

carvings are distinctive features of the New Kingdom period. The wood of which the chair is made is reddish in colour with elaborate decorations in gold-leaf. A conspicuous feature of the carved ornamentation is the pair of women's heads above the front legs which take the place of the lion-heads seen on the throne of Queen Hatshepsut. The crowns, elaborate collars and faces of these heads are gilded; the wigs are left in a plain dark wood. Otherwise all the carved decoration, except for the feather-design panels in the outer side of the back, is gold-covered (fig. 70).

Legs, seat-frame, arms and back are fastened together with mortise and tenon joints, reinforced in some places with bronze nails. At the back, a vertical framework braces the back-rest, forming in side view the characteristic triangular opening which has been mentioned above. But although this detail appears in some Middle Kingdom representations of chairs in reliefs, they give no indication as to when the curve was introduced in the back-rest, a luxury in common use by the time of the Eighteenth Dynasty. Both the back and the frame of the seat are veneered with some species of tropical wood, which is glued and pinned down with small wooden pins. The seat, which is well preserved, is made of strands consisting of four strings each, the strands being woven over and under one another and fastened through holes in the frame of the seat. Soon after the discovery a facsimile of this chair was made in Cairo (illustrated in colour plate IVB).

On the inside of the back is a delicately carved and gilded double scene in low relief in which the princess Sitamun is shown seated, receiving an elaborate collar from an

64

70 Back view of the chair of Sitamun, showing the carved side panel and the supporting struts of the back. *Eighteenth Dynasty*.

attendant (fig. 69). The hieroglyphs describe the scene as "presentation of gold of the Southern Countries". Sitamun is seated on an arm-chair of interesting design, and the action is shown taking place within a kiosk, or bower, the top frame of which has pendant lotus flowers and buds. Above is the winged sun-disk with pendant cobras (*uraei*), a commonly used motif which dates back to the Old Kingdom. On the insides of the arm panels are other scenes, carved in the same way as the back panel, which represent maidens bearing dishes piled with gold rings. The mouldings of the arm-rests are also covered with gold, somewhat heavier than the leaf used on the carved relief, and burnished so that it resembles solid metal.

Very different from the stylized detail of the figures on the insides of the arm panels are the spirited carvings on the outsides (fig. 71). The strange-looking beasts which appear here were popular Egyptian household gods. On the left side there are three dancing figures representing the god Bes, a genial bearded creature who frequently appears as an ornament on Egyptian furniture. Partly human in form, he has the tail, mane and ears of a lion, and he was regarded as a potent protector against the tangible terrors of life, such as snakes, and also the intangible. Sometimes he is shown wearing a panther skin, sometimes a kilt, and he is often portrayed dancing and beating a tambourine or wielding knives, as he is on this panel. On the outside of the other arm panel (fig. 72) the goddess Thoeris appears between two figures of Bes. She is the hippopotamus goddess, almost always shown standing and pregnant – the patroness of women in childbirth. In spite of

65

71 Left side panel of the chair of Sitamun. Figures of Bes beat tambourines and flourish knives to keep away evil. *Eighteenth Dynasty.*

their formidable appearances these were friendly gods who guarded the household and especially watched over sleeping people.

A second chair, smaller in scale, described by Davis as a child's chair, bears the names of Tiye and Sitamun on the inside of the back panel (fig. 73). It is quite likely that this small chair was used by the princess in her childhood and was later replaced by her large arm-chair. Except for the bases of the legs and the braces under the seat, which were silvered, the entire chair was covered with gold-leaf over gesso, and it must have presented a brilliant appearance when it was new. The inside of the back panel is finely carved in the same technique used on the back of the larger chair (fig. 74). The scene shows Queen Tiye seated on an elegant arm-chair in a papyrus boat, accompanied by two princesses and a cat; the princess in front is named as Sitamun, the other is unnamed. The queen is described as "the great royal wife, Tiye".

On the outside of the back the dancing figure of the god Bes is carved in low relief, partially hidden by the central back strut. Here the god has outspread wings and knives fastened to his feet. He carries baskets filled with protective amulets. As in the larger chair, the back-rest is rounded, slants backwards, and is supported from behind by three struts. The open panels of the arm-frames are filled by figures of Bes and Thoeris which were carved separately and tenoned in; these are flat pieces, about half an inch thick,

66

72

72 Right side panel of the chair of Sitamun. The hippopotamus goddess Thoeris in company with two Bes figures. *Eighteenth Dynasty.*

carefully worked as bas-reliefs on both sides. Apparently the chair had been used a great deal. Before it was placed in the tomb the woven seat had been replaced with a plain board painted yellow above and silvered below; in places the gilding of the ornamentation had been worn through and patched. On each side one of the cut-out gilded figures of Bes is broken out, but possibly this occurred some time after the burial.

The most striking feature of the third chair is the group of carvings found in the side panels: on the right an ibex is about to kneel down with a cluster of papyrus flowers over its back, and on the left is a hieroglyphic combination of two signs of 'life', with the sign for 'protection' between, below which is the sign for 'gold' – motifs of very differing character brought together in a charming manner (fig. 75). In the back, however, the design is more conventional, with figures of the household gods Bes and Thoeris again appearing in the cut-out and gilded carvings (fig. 76). Bes is shown in silhouette with arms akimbo, flanked by two figures of the hippopotamus goddess facing inwards; in both cases he carries knives and the sign of 'protection', and the three deities stand on signs for 'gold'. The highlights indicate the parts which are covered with gold; the wood, which is naturally of a reddish colour, was coloured with dark paint. Unlike the other two chairs, which have curved and slanted back-rests, this one has a straight back with a simple framed construction resting on the seat-frame. In the attractive watercolour

67

73

74

73 The small chair of princess Sitamun, made of carved wood overlaid with gilded gesso. *Eighteenth Dynasty.*

painted by Howard Carter, who was a member of Davis's staff at the time of the excavation of this tomb, the pleasant contrast between the dark wood and the gold ornamentation is brought out; in this painting (colour plate V) can also be seen the small cushion of figured linen stuffed with pigeon feathers which was found in the tomb and which was thought to belong with this chair. The original woven seat of the chair was replaced with a white painted board before it was put in the tomb.

Besides these chairs, two of the most striking pieces found in the tomb are the small decorated cabinets on legs, intended to hold jewellery, cosmetics and other personal belongings. The one with the rounded top has its legs and frame inlaid in a pattern of rectangles made of pieces of ebony, ivory stained red and blue-glazed faience (fig. 77). The upper panels of the ends and the sides, and two panels on the top are inlaid with large plaques of blue-glazed composition with inscriptions in raised relief, the individual signs of which are gilded. The side panels and one end panel bear the names and titles of King Amenophis III; the other end panel carries the name of Queen Tiye. On the lid the decoration, repeated on each panel, consists of two cartouches containing the names of Amenophis III surmounted by double feathers and the sun-disk with royal *uraei*, above a figure of the god of eternity (Heh), who holds two notched palm branches, the notches (which were presumed to be infinite) representing the years of the king's reign. The lower panels of the sides and ends consist of open-work groups of hieroglyphs behind which is a background of red-stained linen of fine texture. The interior, which is divided into small compartments, was also originally lined with red linen.

68

74 Scene on the back panel of the small chair of Sitamun. Queen Tiye receives flowers from Sitamun. *Eighteenth Dynasty*.

75 Side panel of the chair with bold cut-out designs, here consisting of an ibex, flowers and a group of amuletic signs; partly gilded. *Eighteenth Dynasty*.

75

A second small cabinet with splayed legs and a heavy cove moulding under the top bears the names of Amenophis III on the wooden knobs with which the lid was secured (fig. 78). Three carved and gilded hieroglyphs representing 'life' ♀, 'stability' ∏, and 'dominion' ⌐, repeated continuously, form the attractive decorative motifs for the sides and ends and are set against a background of blue-glazed composition. The base of the chest exhibits a characteristic detail of the Eighteenth Dynasty (and reminiscent of the work of Chippendale in the eighteenth century) in the lattice-like design of cross-struts between the legs, which is both functional and ornamental. The lid consists of two leaves, hinged at the sides and overlapping in the middle. It was secured partly by a cord wound round the two knobs and partly by two wooden bolts which slide in bronze hoops. The lid is decorated, like that of the round-topped cabinet, with cartouches of Amenophis III and figures of the god Heh.

The reed and papyrus chest shown in figure 79, which is obviously an ancestor of the summer 'reed furniture' of today, served a very special purpose. It contained the wigs of the lady Thuiu, who, following the custom of the day, had her head shaved for hygienic reasons; she consequently needed a suitable place to keep these important adjuncts to her wardrobe. The general construction of the chest and the wrapping of the joints between the stretchers and the legs of the chest anticipate the methods used in the making of reed and cane furniture at the present time. The little openings in the sides resemble the barred windows of a house and give the chest an architectural look – a popular device of Egyptian cabinet-makers, who often designed chests with sides resembling the façades of houses.

69

In addition to the wig chest made of reed and papyrus, the tomb equipment included three other chests made of wood, two of which form a pair nearly identical in size and shape, although differing slightly in their decoration (fig. 80). The lids are heavy and rounded at the front, slanting downwards towards the back in the manner traditionally used for the tops of shrines as well as other structures and for chests in ancient Egypt. On the top at the thick end is a large knob, painted with a rosette design, by which the lid was secured with a cord lashed to a similar knob on the front of the chest below. Unlike the more elaborate furniture, which is ornamented with gold and inlays, both chests are painted on a gesso base in imitation of precious woods, ivory inlay and gold, with the background largely in black or dark red. The cavetto cornices, architectural in character, are painted black and white; the torus mouldings beneath are painted yellow; the panels are framed with black and white lines simulating ebony and ivory. A line of hieroglyphs in black on a yellow ground runs down the middle of one lid, invoking posthumous benefits for Yuia; on the other is a similar band except that the hieroglyphs are yellow and the ground black. The chest with the inscription also has, on the sides and lid, additional

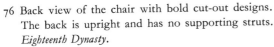

76 Back view of the chair with bold cut-out designs.
The back is upright and has no supporting struts.
Eighteenth Dynasty.

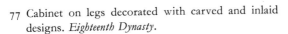

77 Cabinet on legs decorated with carved and inlaid
designs. *Eighteenth Dynasty.*

78 Cabinet with splayed legs and lattice-work cross-
struts. *Eighteenth Dynasty.*

ornamentation consisting of a chequered pattern of black and white squares contained within frames of black, white and blue rectangles.

The third wooden chest, smaller than the others and rectangular, is also painted; but the signs of 'life' and 'dominion' used as decorative motifs on the sides, as well as on the edges of the sides and lid, were originally covered with a thin gold-foil, now tarnished to a dull brownish colour (fig. 81). The field of the side panels is painted a dark blue to simulate glazed composition, and the ornamentation of the top and the whole of the interior is painted yellow. As on the other chests, knobs are provided for fastening. These three chests are of the type used for household purposes. The tomb contained two others, also of shrine shape, larger and more elaborately decorated, which rest on runners. In addition to hieroglyphic inscriptions, their sides bear full-length figures of Isis, Nephthys and other Egyptian deities. These two chests are not illustrated because they cannot properly be called household furniture, having been made specifically to hold the canopic jars in which were placed the embalmed entrails of the deceased persons.[7]

All three of the beds found in the tomb are of the traditional type, with wooden

79

80

81

79 Wig box made of papyrus and reed. Note the wrapping of the joints between the stretchers, the legs and the struts. *Eighteenth Dynasty.*

80 Shrine-shaped storage chests with painting simulating inlay. *Eighteenth Dynasty.*

81 Small storage chest, partly painted and partly gilded. *Eighteenth Dynasty.*

82a Inside of the foot-board of Yuia's bed. The figures of Bes and Thoeris are of gilded plaster. *Eighteenth Dynasty.*

 b Back of the foot-board of Yuia's bed. *Eighteenth Dynasty.*

carved legs representing the fore and hind legs of a lion, which face towards the head of the bed, and with a panel above the opposite end serving as a foot-board. In their joinery and woven coverings the beds resemble those found from the Early Dynastic period and the Old Kingdom, but they exhibit a considerable refinement of design, as can be seen in the largest of the beds, probably Yuia's own (fig. 83). This is the finest of the three beds with the carvings and some of the other parts covered in gold. The side-rails are made with a rectangular section, smoothly finished, and they dip from head to foot in a long curve. In this the bed differs markedly from that of Queen Hetepheres, where the side-rails are long, straight, rounded poles. It is also different in that, having fore and hind legs of approximately the same height, it lacks the pronounced slope of the earlier example. The moulding at the top of the foot-board, and the long curved braces which secure it to the frame are covered with gold sheet, as are the carved feet and the ends of the cross-stretchers between the legs. The bases of the feet are shod with silver. The wood used in the construction of the bed is of an ordinary kind veneered with a superior cabinet-wood, probably imported. This veneer is about $\frac{1}{4}$ in. thick and fastened to the frame with pegs.

   The panels of the foot-board are the most striking feature of the bed (figs. 82a,b). They show again figures of the god Bes with his tambourine, and the hippopotamus goddess Thoeris, carved in gilded plaster, although the style is somewhat different from that found on the chairs. These figures appear on both sides of the foot-board, and in the centre panel on the back Bes is shown holding hieroglyphic signs which were believed to give protection to whoever might be the occupant of the bed. The three panels are

separated by gold-covered rods which curve over the top of the foot-board; these rods show knob-like swellings in their centres which in fact represent pairs of papyrus flowers set mouth to mouth, a typical ornamental detail found on Eighteenth Dynasty beds.

The bed shown in figure 84 is slightly shorter and may have belonged to Yuia's wife, Thuiu. It is similar in form, and is also made in ordinary wood veneered with hardwood. On the inside of its foot-board there are three panels carrying representations of the god Bes, carved in gesso and silvered. A third bed of similar shape is constructed of coarse plain wood, painted black, with the foot-board painted with white lines to simulate ivory inlay (fig. 85).[8]

In addition to the wooden furniture, the tomb contained a very fine chariot, the rims of the wheels of which were made of sections of wood which had been bent and cleverly spliced together with a binding of metal bands. One of Yuia's titles was 'Overseer of Horses', and he would, no doubt, consider a chariot as an important part of his equipment in the afterlife.[9] For nearly twenty years this remarkable collection of furniture

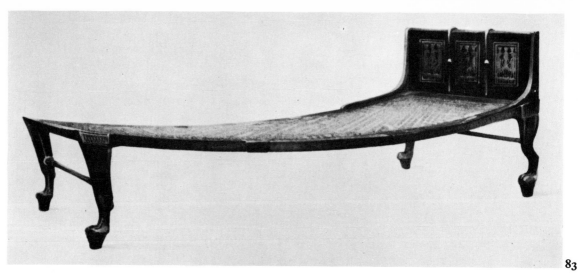

83

83 Bed, probably Yuia's own, with side-rails dipping from front to rear. *Eighteenth Dynasty.*

84

84 Bed, probably Thuiu's own. The panels on the foot-board are of carved plaster overlaid with silver-foil. *Eighteenth Dynasty.*

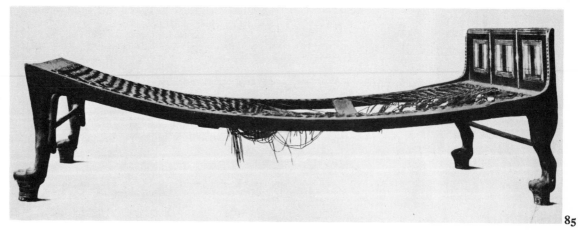

85

85 Bed of black-painted wood with white-painted decoration on the foot-board to represent ivory inlay. *Eighteenth Dynasty.*

remained unique. Now the brilliance of the gold has tarnished, the colours have dulled, and visitors to the Cairo Museum pass by with hardly a glance at the furniture of Yuia and Thuiu, which is overshadowed by the gorgeous treasures of King Tutankhamun, exhibited near by in the museum.

4   THE FURNITURE OF KING TUTANKHAMUN
(c. 1352 B.C.)

Although the finding of the elegant furniture of Yuia and Thuiu had given glimpses of the luxurious palace furniture of the Eighteenth Dynasty, it was not until the discovery of the tomb of King Tutankhamun in 1922 that the full range of royal furnishings became apparent. This fabulous collection of furniture and other treasures, instead of coming from one of the great tombs, as might have been expected, was found in the smallest of the royal tombs in the Valley of the Kings. The young king, who died before he was twenty years old, did not have time to build a suitable tomb, and the one in which he was buried was probably intended for his mentor and successor Ay. But as a result of this spectacular discovery the name Tutankhamun has become a household word, typifying the splendour of ancient Egypt.

Like the tomb of Yuia and Thuiu, that of King Tutankhamun was found in an unlikely spot, hidden under boulders, limestone chippings and ancient workmen's huts below the tomb of Ramesses VI. There was little hope of finding another tomb in the Valley of the Kings, and the chance of one surviving unscathed was remote, since those already excavated had been looted; so this discovery, by Howard Carter, leader of the Carnarvon expedition, was particularly exciting. As usual, the tomb robbers had been there first; but, for whatever reasons, only a relatively small amount of damage was done, and they departed leaving most of the treasures behind. When we consider the wealth of gold which remained, it is a wonder that Tutankhamun's tomb should have escaped the usual fate. The large quantity of precious metal used in the ornamentation of the furniture, and for statues, jewellery and other objects, is indicated by the weight of the solid gold inner coffin, bearing the likeness of the king, which amounts to two thousand four hundred and forty-eight pounds.

The reports of the discovery of the tomb in 1922 aroused world-wide curiosity, and the romantic episode of its opening has been recounted many times. But although there have been various publications which describe the discovery and the contents of the tomb in general, there has been no comprehensive account of the furniture as a whole. In his three-volume popular work, *The Tomb of Tut·Ankh·Amen*, published soon after the discovery, Carter included photographs of about twenty pieces of furniture, and individual pieces have been illustrated and described in other publications.[1] In most instances, however, the furniture is given secondary importance compared with the other richer treasures found, and the less sensational pieces of furniture have necessarily been omitted from these general publications.

The persistent traditions of design and ornament established in the early periods of ancient Egypt are still conspicuous in the Tutankhamun furniture, but new influences appear in the freedom of design and in the exuberance of the applied decoration. These innovations, however, were not due to the young king, although apparently they also reflected his own taste, but were the result of the influence of his father-in-law, King Akhenaten. Since the history of this remarkable man had so direct an effect on the furniture illustrated in this chapter, it seems appropriate to review briefly the events which preceded the accession of Tutankhamun to the throne.

Akhenaten was the son of Amenophis III and Tiye, and thus the son-in-law of Yuia and Thuiu. Unlike his more practical father, who ruled for nearly forty years, the son was a visionary and a reformer whose chief interests were religion and the arts. He was a fanatical believer in one god, the Aten (represented by the sun-disk), and he changed his name from Amenophis ('Amun is content') to Akhenaten ('He who is useful for the Aten'). He abandoned the old religion of Amun, and left his capital at Thebes to build a new city where he would not be directly exposed to the powerful priests of Amun. The new city was called Akhetaten ('Horizon of the Aten') and was located to the north of Thebes on a site now called El-Amarna. In addition to a temple for the worship of Aten, palaces for the king, houses for city dwellers, villas with walled gardens for the well-to-do and special quarters for the artisans were also built. Here Akhenaten fostered a revolution in the arts as well as in religion, and a remarkable degree of proficiency was developed in the crafts and decorative arts.

A striking example of the new informality expressed in the sculpture of the period is seen in a relief depicting the royal family (fig. 86). In this intimate scene the king and his wife are shown sitting on typical stools of the period, and playing with their three doll-like daughters while the sun-god shines on them from above. Instead of appearing in the rigid pose characteristic of traditional Egyptian art, Akhenaten is portrayed relaxed on his seat in a highly informal manner.[2]

One of the three little princesses later became the wife of Tutankhamun, who, following the brief interim rule of Smenkhkare, was made king when he was still a very young boy, perhaps twelve or thirteen years old. Not long before he came to the throne, steps were taken to re-establish the old religion; Thebes became again the royal residence and the new city of Akhetaten was abandoned. The influence of Akhenaten's revolution continued to some extent, however, and the freedom and naturalism of the arts of this brief epoch are clearly reflected in the Tutankhamun furniture. Some pieces were undoubtedly made before the rehabilitation of Amun was completed, because they bear the name Tutankhaten – the form used by the king in his early life – and other pieces carry both forms – Tutankhaten and Tutankhamun.

Altogether about fifty pieces of furniture, ranging from elaborately decorated throne-chairs to the more ordinary stools and chests, were found all jumbled together in the tomb (figs. 87, 88). In the descriptions which follow, I have relied for my final authority on Carter's original card file, now in the possession of the Griffith Institute in the

86 The royal family of Amarna seated on typical stools of the period, and using upholstered foot-stools. *Eighteenth Dynasty.*

Ashmolean Museum in Oxford. Although I have viewed the individual objects personally a number of times in the Cairo Museum, many details are unavoidably missed in a brief inspection and only examination in a laboratory can determine the fine points involved. Carter's notes were made with his usual meticulous thoroughness and are the result of first-hand observation, supplemented by years of continuing research intended to lead to a definitive publication on the tomb and its contents, but which so far has unfortunately not been realized. Throughout the remainder of this chapter those parts of the descriptions given as quotations (unless otherwise indicated) are taken verbatim from Carter's notes.[3]

Thrones and chairs

The piece which best typifies the sumptuous furniture of King Tutankhamun is his gold-covered arm-chair, or 'the golden throne', as it is often called (colour plate VI), with its magnificent gold and inlaid back panel. The legs, in the stylized form of the fore and hind legs of a lion, are traditional, as are the carved lion's heads which top them. Side panels take the form of cobras wearing the double crown of the king of Upper and Lower Egypt, with falcon wings overlaid with silver and gold, the eyes and other parts inlaid with glass (fig. 89). On the outside back, papyrus plants are carved in the gold panels, the upright stiles being inscribed with hieroglyphs giving the names and titles of the king in both the Amun and Aten forms; between the stiles there are four free-standing *uraei*, symbols of royalty (fig. 90). Originally the space between seat and stretchers was filled with the traditional carved wood grille-work of interlacing plants of Upper and Lower Egypt; but this, unfortunately, had been torn out by the robbers for the sake of its gold covering. Beneath all the elaborate ornamentation the method of construction is similar to that of the chair of the princess Sitamun (fig. 68), the legs, seat and back being secured by a series of interlocking mortise and tenon joints.

As an individual work of art, the inside back panel (colour plate VII) is the outstanding feature of the chair. The sun-disk, the Aten, shines from above, and the continuing influence of the Akhenaten revolution in art is apparent in the sensitive and intimate scene of the king being anointed by his slender young wife. Faience and coloured glass with lapis lazuli and translucent calcite are inlaid against a background of sheet gold mounted on a wood base. In spite of the limitations of the materials, the artist has managed to

87 View of the inside of the tomb of Tutankhamun at the time of discovery, showing the jumble of furniture, including the Hathor couch. *Eighteenth Dynasty.*

achieve a charming and rather realistic effect. Robes are of silver, the bodies of a dark red opaque glass, and the wigs and the wooden parts of the chair of brilliant blue lapis lazuli. At the top is a frieze of cobras with disks on their heads set above an elaborate geometric design; and below is a dado with a pattern of simplified 'false doorways', all executed in faience, glass and calcite. The seat is similarly inlaid. The technique of inlaying, which had been known from the First Dynasty, reaches its highest development here and is used to tell a story rather than to produce geometric patterns only.

The chair without arms represented in the inlays of the back panel is of considerable interest, differing in several respects from the golden throne itself. The legs and inter-lacing grille-work are similar but there are no arms, and the thick cushion which rolls over the curve at the top gives the upper part an appearance not unlike that of a French Empire design of the early nineteenth century. Inscribed above are hieroglyphs giving the titles of the king and queen, which are translated by Carter in part as follows: "King of Upper and Lower Egypt, Nebkheperuré, son of Ré, Tutankhamun, ruler of the Southern On, given life like Ré, and the hereditary princess, great of favour, the beloved sweet of life, mistress of Upper and Lower Egypt, lady of the two lands, Ankhesenamun, living for ever and ever."

88 View of the inside of the tomb of Tutankhamun at the time of discovery, showing the Thoeris couch, the chariot and other furniture piled haphazardly. *Eighteenth Dynasty.*

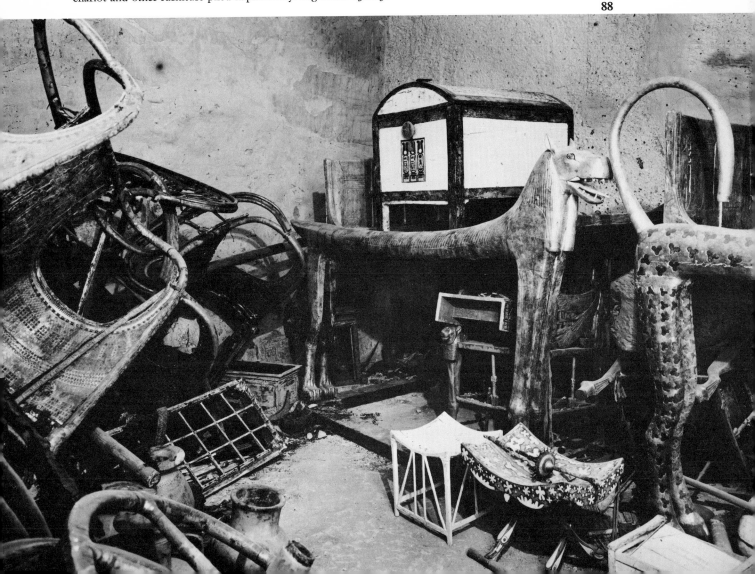

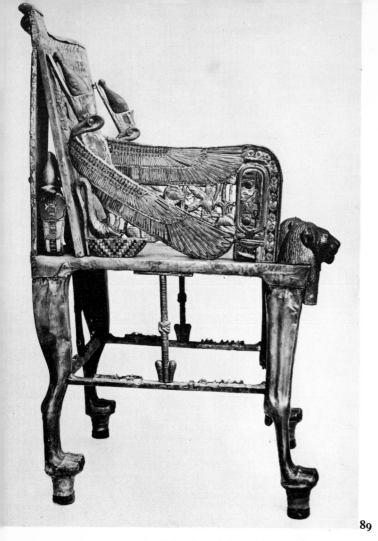

89

89 Side view of the golden throne. The panel is in the form of a winged cobra. *Eighteenth Dynasty.*

90 Back view of the golden throne. The spaces between the supporting upright stiles are occupied by pairs of cobras. *Eighteenth Dynasty.*

What is known as the 'ceremonial chair' (fig. 91) differs greatly in design. In his original notes Howard Carter describes this as:

fashioned of ebony and ivory, partially plated with thin sheet gold inlaid with natural stones, glaze and polychrome glass . . . the seat made of ebony and inlaid with irregular shaped pieces of ivory to imitate the blotchy markings of a hide like that of the Nubian goat. Central part of seat is ornamented with a series of small panels of ivory, stained to imitate various piebald hides. The back panel comprises small panels obviously inspired by panelling common to outer walls of earlier and contemporary buildings.

Originally there had been a gold-covered grille-work of intertwined plants beneath the seat; but, as in the case of the golden throne, this had in part been torn off by the tomb robbers. The base resembles that of a folding stool with supports terminating in the carved heads of ducks inlaid with ivory, a typical detail of the period, the cross-bars being held between their beaks. The seat is deeply curved and relates well to the vertical

80   Colour plate V. Chair with side-panel of cut-out designs. *Eighteenth Dynasty.*

91 The ceremonial chair and ceremonial foot-stool. *Eighteenth Dynasty*.

92 Back view of the ceremonial chair. The gold-covered panel has a large figure of the vulture goddess Nekhbet. Note the Cretan spirals. *Eighteenth Dynasty.*

93 Foot-stool with painted plaster decoration. *Eighteenth Dynasty.*

94 Top of the ceremonial foot-stool. The figures of the nine traditional enemies are of gold and hardwood. *Eighteenth Dynasty.*

rectangle of the back, which is slightly curved and is strengthened with bent wooden brackets where it joins the seat. The cross-rail at the top is ornamented with a golden disk, below which is the vulture goddess Nekhbet, the vertical panels being inlaid with strips of ebony and ivory on which are inscriptions giving the king's name in its earlier form, Tutankhaten. The outer side of the back of the chair carries a large representation in gold of Nekhbet, and supporting decoration which includes spirals of a contemporary Cretan type. The upright supporting stiles of the back are also inlaid with the king's titles and earlier name (fig. 92). There are gold-covered fittings at the joints, and the underside of the curved seat is backed with leather. Although the chair as a whole is a curious assembly of unrelated motifs, the diverse parts are combined to form a dignified and impressive oriental chair of state.

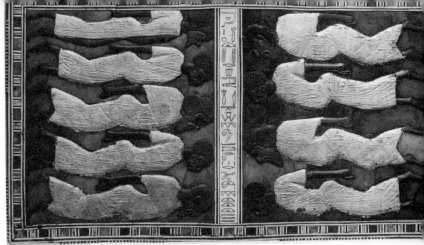

93   94

With the ceremonial chair was a foot-stool (fig. 94) inlaid with nine bound figures, four reddish and five black, representing the nine traditional enemies of Egypt. The solid wood of the stool is "veneered with ebony, ivory, faience, glass and natural stone ornament . . . the heads, limbs and exposed parts of bodies of Asiatics of dark brown wood, head-dresses of ebony". The variation in colour between the flesh tones of the two groups of captives indicates the difference in their racial origins, red for Asiatics and black for Negroes, and the fine drawing of the faces expresses their different national physiognomies. The pharaohs by this means symbolized their conquests, placing their enemies permanently under their feet. On the foot-stool of the golden throne, six figures were represented, and on another foot-stool there were two (fig. 93).[4]

The third chair is made of a finely grained reddish wood resembling cedar and has a superbly carved open-work back panel (figs. 95, 96). Above this, on the top-rail, is a winged solar disk made of embossed sheet gold. The curved braces between seat and back are also covered with sheet gold as was the grille-work below of the intertwined plant design; this, however, as in the golden throne, had been torn out by the tomb robbers. The claws of the lion's feet are realistically carved in ivory and rest on supports sheathed in gold and shod in bronze. The seat, made of wood, is deeply curved with a double cove, unlike the flat seat of the golden throne and that of the ceremonial chair, which has a one-way curve.

It is amazing that the delicately carved wood parts of the back panel in this chair should have survived intact while the gold-covered grilles below were being wrenched away. These remarkable carvings have, as usual, a symbolic meaning and were intended to assure the king of eternal life. The god in the centre (Heh) has a large symbol of life over one of his outstretched arms and with his hands he grasps notched palm branches, the whole representation forming the hieroglyphic symbol for millions of years. On each side of the figure are two panels; the smaller ones contain the principal titles and names of the king; the larger ones, taking the form of the traditional *serekh*, are surmounted by figures of crowned Horus falcons, *uraei* and sun-disks, and they carry the so-called Horus-name of the king.

A chair of similar form but less delicately carved is painted white over a gesso base (figs. 97, 98). The legs are of the typical animal design, with feet capped with copper and bronze, and the seat also has the double cove shape of the chair. In this instance, however, the intertwined plant design beneath the seat is intact, no doubt because there was no gold covering to attract the robbers. Parts such as these were especially tempting

95

95 Wooden chair with gold-covered decoration. Note the double-curved seat. *Eighteenth Dynasty.*

96 Back of the wooden chair containing an open-work panel with a figure of the god Heh, partly gilded. *Eighteenth Dynasty.*

when covered with gold, as they were easy to break into bits and conceal, and the metal could readily be recovered, probably by burning the wood. Since this is the first uninjured example pictured of this traditional detail in an actual piece, it may be well to consider its significance further at this point. It consists of the hieroglyphic sign ♀ (meaning 'to unite') joining intertwined plants symbolizing Upper and Lower Egypt. Besides making a very decorative design, it represents graphically the unification of the two parts of the country under one king; it appears carved on the sides of thrones in statuary as early as the Old Kingdom (fig. 45).

Framed in the back above is the carved design of an 'open-winged hawk', with the 'prenomen and nomen of the king' in the rail above. The tail of the hawk rests on the symbol for gold and below its wings are the symbols of life and well-being. As in the chair with the elegantly carved back panel, it is surprising that such fragile pieces of brittle wood should have survived without damage.

There was also a little arm-chair (fig. 99) which was perhaps the king's when he was a child. Carter describes it as "solid ebony . . . overlaid and inlaid with ivory with studded rivets and panels in gold". The outer sides of the panels are decorated with "a wounded oryx and desert plant surrounded by a scroll pattern"; inside is a "simple desert plant device surrounded by the common rectangular pattern". The back is boldly inlaid with strips of ivory and small repeated patterns. Gold is used to ornament the ends of the

84

97   98

rounded stretchers, and again we see the lifelike lion's claws made of ivory. Beneath the seat is a trellis-like bracing which is one of the popular details of the period.

Stools

This same trellis- or lattice-work forms the design motif for a simple but elegant stool, originally painted white, which is one of the most attractive and functional designs of Eighteenth Dynasty furniture (fig. 100). Here the delicate members form a pattern which has both structural strength and rhythmic movement. The double cove seat of wood slats has an interesting shape, meeting the legs with a reverse curve, which contrasts pleasantly with the geometric form below. The thin edge of the seat relates nicely to the delicate struts beneath.

A second small stool (fig. 101) of similar design is beautifully constructed of a fine cabinet-wood, resembling cedar, finished in a natural colour. The skill and care lavished on this little stool demonstrate, as much as do the more elaborate pieces, the fine work of the ancient Egyptian cabinet-makers. It is one of the most attractive examples of ancient furniture design, and reproductions of it are made today by Hatoun, a cabinet-maker in Cairo. The seat has five slats, two veneered with ivory and three with ebony, with strips of ivory and of ebony as a border on each side, and there were also small ivory bosses attached with ebony pins. Stools with a lattice-base such as these two are frequently seen

97 White-painted chair. The plant motif between the legs is here intact. *Eighteenth Dynasty.*

98 Side view of the white-painted chair showing the stiles supporting the back and the deep curves of the seat. *Eighteenth Dynasty.*

99 Child's arm-chair of heavy design, with lattice-work bracing beneath the seat. *Eighteenth Dynasty.*

99

in reliefs of the New Kingdom, as in the scene of Akhenaten and his family (fig. 86). It should be noted, however, that whereas in this relief the king is shown seated on a lattice-base stool, the queen's stool has the intertwined plant design beneath the seat. It seems also that the relief represents stools made of reed or cane instead of wood. Such materials, including the hard centre spine of the palm leaf, were often used in the construction of ancient Egyptian furniture.

A lattice-type stool of reed-construction similar to the one in the relief, and also a chair of combined wood and reed were included among the furnishings. These can be discerned in the photographs taken in the tomb before the furniture was removed, but separate photographs are not available at this time.

Although the reliefs indicate that the stool with the intertwined grille-work was not unusual, there was only one found in the tomb (colour plate VIII). This has an attractive design, with a deeply curving double cove seat and carved animal legs. Except for the feet and the grilles, the stool is painted white; the grilles, however, are covered with a thin sheet of gold and are the only gold-covered ones that have escaped intact. The feet and bases of the legs are capped with copper and bronze.

A third form of stool, very popular in this period, has crossed supports terminating in carved and ivory-inlaid duck-heads, their bills grasping cross-bars which rest on the floor (fig. 102). Although such stools were often made so that they could be folded, this one has a rigid wooden top with pieces of ivory inlaid to simulate the irregular markings

100

101

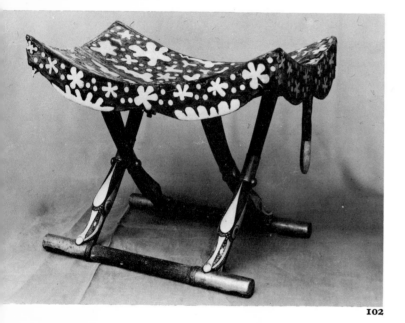

102

100 White-painted stool with double cove seat and lattice-work bracing. *Eighteenth Dynasty.*

101 Red wood stool with a seat made of slats veneered with ivory and ebony. *Eighteenth Dynasty.*

102 Stool in the form of a folding seat with the seat simulating an animal skin. *Eighteenth Dynasty.*

103 Duck-legged folding stools, originally with leather seats. *Eighteenth Dynasty.*

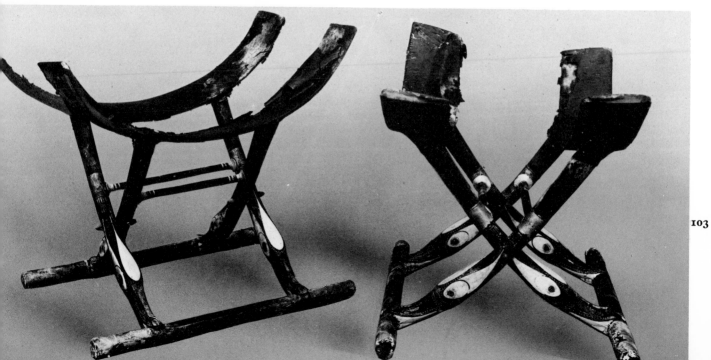

103

of an animal skin. Down the centre of the seat is a strip of reddish wood inlay designed to imitate the backbone of an animal. At one end is a pendant piece intended to represent the tail, a not uncommon detail of the stools pictured in Theban tomb reliefs and paintings.[5]

Two stools of similar design to the one above, but constructed so that they could be folded, were also included in the tomb furnishings (fig. 103). The seats were made of leather to provide flexibility for folding; red leather in one stool and black in the other, as we can tell from some fragments still adhering to the curved seat-rails. Otherwise there was very little difference either in design or size between the two stools. Their legs pivoted on bronze pins; the duck heads were inlaid with ivory, and there were ivory ferrules and bands of gold where stretchers and legs were joined. Since the photographs convey only an inadequate impression of the intricate detail involved in these apparently simple pieces, Carter's meticulously detailed description of one of the stools is quoted in full as it appears in the original longhand notes.

Object 139: Stool of ebony, ivory, gold and leather. Seat consisted of two curved slats of wood 42·5 × 7·5 × ·7 cms from horizontal. Outer edges rounded. Curved in centre 8·5 cms from horizontal. Slats set to incline slightly inwards. These slats covered with red leather, which continued between them to form seat. Seat part of this leather had almost entirely disappeared, having melted to a glue-like substance. Scraps remaining showed that there had been a stamped pattern on the leather. Underneath, running diagonally from cover to cover extra slips 1·1 cms wide. Legs: to the seat were attached diagonally four round legs, two to each slat, which crossed in their centres, and were fastened together by bronze pins which transfixed the crossed legs, the pins being held at either end by conical caps of wood. The inner cap in each case was pierced by the pin and acted as a kind of washer; the outer cap covered the point of the pin. Caps about 1 cm in diam., projected ·8 cm. Upper part of legs oval in sections 3 × 2 cms at top, thinning down to 2·2 × 1·7 cms at crossing. Below crossing the legs thickened and were carved to represent ducks' heads. At 9 cms from top of legs a band of gold leaf 3 cms wide with reinforced edges ·2 cm wide. Below this, on inner half only, band of decoration 3 cms wide, in yellow bark. Details of ducks' heads of ivory inlay. Open mouth ivory inlay, with a central slip of reddened ivory to represent tongue. Eye frame in gold or silver, with pupil of paste(?) of doubtful colour (in other stool red). Ducks' head at widest point 3 × 2·8 cms. In ducks' open mouths cross bars of ebony 38·5 cms long × 2·3 cms in diam. Between ducks' heads and ends of these bars covered with gesso overlaid with gold. Under sides of these bars in centre, where they rested on ground, covered with yellow bark. Bronze pins with ivory washers ·7 cm in diam. fastened ducks' heads to these bars. On upper part of legs, in centre of the gold bands round cross bars of ebony 1 cm in diam. Where they joined legs there were flaring caps of ivory 1·3 cms long, 2·5 × 2 cms at legs. Ends of these were concave to fit legs. Inside these bands ·7 cm wide, consisting of three narrow rings of ivory with ·1 cm of ebony between each. Leather from seat. Undoubtedly goat skin. (There is no evidence to show whether the leather was tanned or how it was tanned.)

A different version of the cross-legged stool is represented in another intimate scene of King Tutankhamun and his wife on one panel of a gold-covered shrine-shaped coffer (fig. 104), but no actual example of such a type was found in the tomb. The king sits on the stool while the queen is seated on a cushion at her husband's feet with her elbow resting informally on his knee. The stool, which has a thick cushion, has crossed legs

104

terminating in claws which clasp what seems to be a ball, much as in our own traditional 'ball and claw' design; more likely, however, what appears as a rounded ball is really the end of a transverse rod like those in the other stools illustrated.

The most elegant of the smaller pieces is the three-legged stool or table with a beautifully pierced and carved top in the shape of an elongated half circle (fig. 105a,b,c). Around the top, ornamented with fine carving in relief representing lions bound head to tail, runs a finely carved spiral pattern which is repeated on the edge. This design, Aegean in character,

90

105a

b

c

104 Scene showing Tutankhamun seated on a folding
stool with a cushion. *Eighteenth Dynasty.*

105a Three-legged stool or table with Cretan spiral
decoration around the rim. *Eighteenth Dynasty.*
  b Top side of stool or table. Two lions bound head
  to tail form the seat.
  c Underside of stool or table. Note the bracing.

is attributed to the influence of artists from Crete, which had reached the peak of its power
shortly before this time. The legs of the table (as I prefer to call it, since it does not seem
intended to be sat upon) are joined together by curved stretchers with the claws and
tendons of the feet meticulously carved on the inside as well as outside. Painted white
over gesso, it is a beautiful example of design and craftsmanship.

Cabinets and chests

Two small cabinets on legs resemble those painted on the walls of the tomb of Hesy-Re
thirteen hundred years earlier (fig. 27a). In the Tutankhamun examples there are similar
carved bands of hieroglyphs, the alternate ones being gilded. Each of the cabinets had
gold-covered knobs on top and face so that the lids could be fastened in the usual manner
with cords, and their interiors were divided into small compartments. They have frame-
works of ebony with panels of red-brown wood, probably cedar. In the handsome example
illustrated in the frontispiece, the frame is inscribed with hieroglyphic texts filled in with
a yellowish pigment (fig. 106). Although these consist of phrases in glorification of

106   **107**

the king, the resulting effect for our Western eyes is that of attractive patterns, rather like the effect produced by Japanese calligraphy. The legs and framing of the second chest are plain (fig. 107). Intended for jewellery or toilet articles, these two cabinets, together with the two from the tomb of Yuia and Thuiu, are the only surviving examples of what must have been a popular piece of furniture for the boudoir of an elegant Egyptian lady.

A more simple but well-proportioned small cabinet on legs (fig. 108) might pass as a 'Chinese Chippendale' commode of the eighteenth century, although it is three thousand years earlier in date. Here we see again the lattice design with angle struts, which is both attractive and practical from the standpoint of good construction. Large ivory knobs on top and front were used, as was customary, to secure the lid. A stripping of ivory which surrounds the top panels is the only other ornamentation except for the bronze caps of the legs. The wood is described by Carter as a combination of ebony and redwood, the latter probably being some form of cedar.

In total there were more than thirty chests in the tomb, varying from small jewellery coffers to large chests for bedding and household linen. Since there were no storage bureaux or cabinets as are used today, the chest in its various forms provided the necessary storage facilities for all kinds of household goods in the Eighteenth Dynasty as in the earlier periods. In style and construction they ranged from simple boxes for use in storage rooms to elegant pieces, carved and decorated, which would be part of the furnishings of the royal apartments in the king's palace. Since the chests served as containers for all

92

106 Chest on legs, with bands of cut-out hieroglyphs and inscribed texts on legs. (See frontispiece.)

107 Chest on legs, partly gilded, and with hieroglyphic decoration. *Eighteenth Dynasty*.

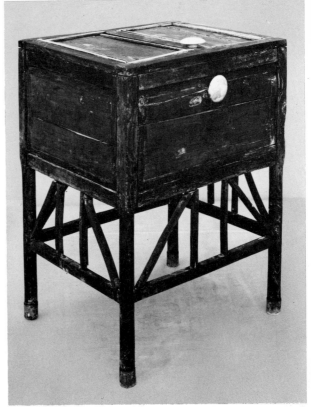

108 Chest on legs with lattice-type base and angle struts. *Eighteenth Dynasty*.

108

kinds of small articles, their interiors were frequently divided, sometimes into small boxes. When found they contained a great variety of articles, not only linen and clothing but also ceramics, jewellery, wigs, cosmetics, small statues and personal souvenirs – whatever might be wanted in the afterlife.

One of the more elaborate of the chests is a low rectangular casket ornamented on all four sides with double bands of carved and gilded hieroglyphs (fig. 109). The legs terminate in square feet shod with silver caps. The interior is divided into sixteen small compartments, the divisions being edged with ivory. The top is a fine example of the use of hieroglyphs and inscriptions as furniture ornaments (fig. 111). To help in the identification of the hieroglyphs most frequently referred to, a small chart is given for convenient reference (fig. 110). The repetitive pattern, however, of symbols such as *ankh, was, djed* and *neb*, unlike the acanthus leaf or honeysuckle flower in Greece, which were purely ornamental, had great magical significance for the Egyptians, and the chief purpose of these hieroglyphs was to ensure the well-being of the departed in his afterlife.

Among the art treasures of the tomb is the magnificent 'painted chest' bearing scenes on its sides which portray the king hunting wild beasts and battling with his enemies (fig. 112). Although obviously the young pharaoh did not single-handed slaughter these animals or his opponents in such large numbers as depicted, the exaggerated portrayal of events was the prerogative of the Egyptian kings. Unfortunately the photograph does not convey an adequate impression of either the colour tones or the quality of the painting,

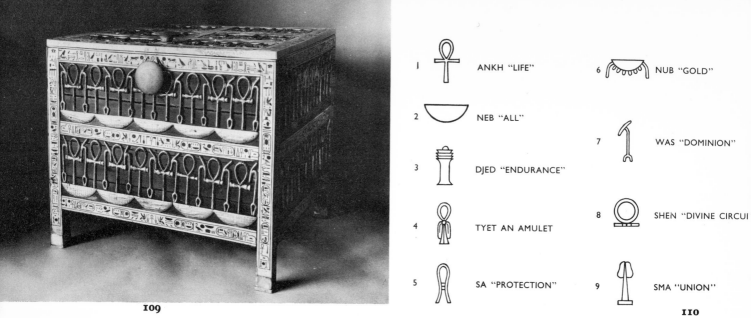

1	ANKH "LIFE"		6	NUB "GOLD"
2	NEB "ALL"			
3	DJED "ENDURANCE"		7	WAS "DOMINION"
4	TYET AN AMULET		8	SHEN "DIVINE CIRCUI
5	SA "PROTECTION"		9	SMA "UNION"

which is done over a gesso base. Even in the original, a magnifying glass is needed to see the minute detail of the fine decorations of the horse's trappings or the gay little tufts of flowers in the desert scenes (fig. 113).[6]

The long plain rectangular box (fig. 114) with a lattice design beneath resembles a modern blanket chest and was probably used for the storage of linen, of which a great deal was used in an ancient Egyptian household. The stretchers, with the angle struts and vertical members above, form girder-like supports that would doubtless help to keep the bottom straight, but more likely were intended to add a touch of design to an otherwise plain piece. Even in the very simple pieces the Egyptian artisan often tried to produce what he considered beautiful as well as useful. Panels covered with white gesso are enclosed by a black painted frame. The lattice and bottom strips are coloured red, and the top is divided into three sections by painted bands which terminate in large round knobs. Straightforward design and the effective use of black frames and red bands against the white ground give this piece a somewhat modern look.

The large chest with gabled top (fig. 115) is very much like the chests previously illustrated from the tomb of Mereruka (fig. 57), which are one thousand years earlier in date. Like those, this chest is equipped with removable poles with which it could be carried. The frame of the chest is ebony, inlaid with ivory hieroglyphs; the cedar panels are outlined with bands of ivory. On the end and lid are large gold-covered knobs.

An example of the great amount of detail sometimes expended on household chests is seen in an elaborate rectangular box veneered over softwood with ivory and ebony, which stands on four square feet (fig. 116). The front is inlaid with ivory and ebony marquetry in a complicated herring-bone design with an ivory centre panel, on which the Horus-name of the king is engraved and filled in with black pigment, and the ends and back are ornamented with similar herring-bone patterns. The legs and cross-rails of ivory veneer are studded with small gold buttons. Carter states that each of the face and back panels contains some six thousand five hundred separate pieces of marquetry and that each of the ends contains approximately five thousand five hundred pieces. On the lid are an additional nine thousand pieces, making the amazing total of thirty-three thousand pieces individually glued in place.

94

109 Casket with rails and stiles veneered with ivory. The applied hieroglyphs are gilded. *Eighteenth Dynasty.*

110 Hieroglyphs commonly used as decorative elements on furniture.

111 Lid of a casket with hieroglyphs used in a decorative manner. *Eighteenth Dynasty.*

III

Other chests have sloping shrine-shaped lids similar to those on chests found in the tomb of Yuia and Thuiu (figs. 80, 81). In these chests the heavy part of the cover appears at the point of closure, helping the top to fit firmly, but this construction seems to be solely a feature of design without any practical intent. The shape, however, may have had some special significance, as shrines, both large and small, were customarily made in the same form. A small matching pair of shrine-shaped chests are constructed of a dark reddish-brown wood inlaid with strips of ivory and ebony (fig. 118). The feet are capped with bronze, and the interiors of each are divided into two sections.

A larger shrine-shaped chest, one of the most elaborately decorated of all the storage pieces, is a striking example of the almost limitless effort and detail expended on the furniture of King Tutankhamun (fig. 117). On the panel on the top is depicted a charming scene of the king and queen, in which she presents her young husband with a bouquet of flowers (fig. 119). Rather than our usual brief summary, the full description in Carter's notes is quoted to emphasize the intricate ornamentation of this elaborate piece.

Object 540. This casket is an admirable example of the highly decorative type produced by the artisans of the reign. Its structure is architectural in spirit, it being designed after the form of a shrine. The box proper has an entablature comprising an ebony edged cornice of gesso-gilt, a green wood torus-moulding, and a narrow plain ebony frieze. On each of its four sides are broad rails and stiles of veneered ivory which form oblong rectangular centre panels. These panels – bordered with rectangular and garland patterns of inlaid ivory, ebony, faience, glass and calcite – are veneered with ivory luxuriantly carved and stained with floral, animal and hunting motifs. The box stands upon four square legs, which are ferruled with bronze caps, and its four corners are embellished with minute cubes and strips of ebony and ivory.

The carved and stained ivory scene upon the front panel depicts the King seated upon a cushioned chair (decorated with garlands), shooting wild-fowl and fish with bow and arrow. His feet rest upon a cushioned footstool, and squatting beside them is the Queen, holding in her right hand a lotus flower, and in her left an arrow, while she looks up appealingly to the King. In front of the royal couple is a small rectangular pond full of water-lilies and fish, and above are arrow-pierced fleeing wild-fowl. Below the pond is an attendant bringing the King's quarry – a large fish and a wild duck – each impaled upon an arrow. The field of the

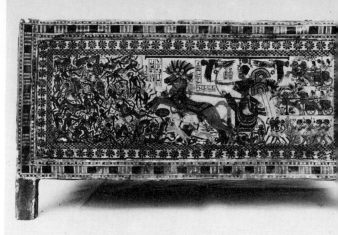

113

112

114

115

112 Elaborately painted box, decorated on all sides with scenes painted on gesso. *Eighteenth Dynasty.*

113 One side of the painted box showing Tutankhamun in battle against the Nubians. *Eighteenth Dynasty.*

114 White painted wooden chest, probably for storing linen. *Eighteenth Dynasty.*

115 Chest with gabled top and removable poles for carrying. *Eighteenth Dynasty.*

116 Chest with ivory veneered frame inlaid with ivory and ebony in a herring-bone pattern. *Eighteenth Dynasty.*

116

Colour plate VI.
    Golden throne of Tutankhamun. *Eighteenth Dynasty.*

background is filled in with conventional garlands, bouquets and plants, among which the mandragora is prominently figured.

The scenes upon the side and back panels represent scampering animals – bulls, bull-calves and ibexes – which, in some instances, are being attacked by a lion, a cheetah, a leopard and hounds. The background to these animal motifs is filled in with similar conventional flora like the fowling scene upon the front panel, described above.

But the chief glory of this casket is the ivory panel upon the lid carved in delicate low relief like a Greek coin. Here the royal couple are represented in a pavilion bedecked with festoons of flowers, and the vine. The King, leaning slightly on his walking-staff, accepts bouquets from his charming consort who is attired in an open flowing robe; while in a frieze below, two court maidens gather flowers and the fruit of the mandrake for their charges. Surrounding this scene is a conventional floral border, also of carved and stained ivory, and the usual rectangular pattern of inlaid ivory, ebony, faience and calcite. Above, on the curvature of the lid, is a long, narrow inlaid panel of floral design in carved and stained ivory. The knobs on this box are of wood gesso-gilt.

Lid of Casket: basic-wood of soft reddish brown (?) wood. Overlaid with slabs of ivory – the panels carved in bas-relief and stained, these have been nailed (copper) to the wood causing the ivory to crack badly; the long strips of ivory are quite plain and bent to fit the round part of the lid. Glue has been used as an adhesive in every case.

Borders: around panels; dark blue faience, calcite, ivory and ebony – the faience and calcite have a stucco or plaster backing. Edges of lid – long strips of ivory and ebony, with small cubes of ivory and ebony forming a chequer border. The long strips of ivory measure 66·0 cms in length and 4·0 cms broad, and about 3 mms in thickness.

Another elegant chest with a sloping top has an interesting design in the side panels in which pairs of *uraei* alternate with cartouches enclosing the titles of the king (fig. 120). The shape resembles that of the three preceding chests, but the heavy beaded cove of the cornice finishes flush with the face of the chest without the usual torus moulding. The wood surface was covered with gold-leaf over a gesso base.

A rectangular ivory veneered chest with heavy square legs and a domed top (fig. 121)

117

118

117 Shrine-shaped chest with ivory veneered frame, and faience, calcite and ivory inlays. *Eighteenth Dynasty.*

118 A pair of shrine-shaped storage chests with bronze staples for suspension, perhaps during travel. *Eighteenth Dynasty.*

has an even larger number of pieces of inlay than the chest in figure 116. Carter states that the total number of small pieces on the four sides and vaulted top amounts to forty-seven thousand. As in the previous instance, the frame is outlined with narrow strips of ebony veneer; the interior is painted a 'pinkish red'. The chest had been ransacked by tomb robbers but still contained some of the king's jewellery which had been tied up in linen and sealed.

Very different in shape is a chest (fig. 122) which, when viewed from above, appears in the shape of a cartouche enclosing the name of the king (fig. 123). The traditional cartouche, as seen in inscriptions, represented an oval made of rope within which was placed the royal name; at one end of the oval is a transverse line which stands for the tie of the rope. This tie is represented in the chest by an attached rectangular slab at one end which serves no practical purpose but is added to complete the cartouche form. The body of the chest is of natural wood on which are carved three bands of hieroglyphic inscriptions. When found in the tomb the chest contained five pairs of earrings, a scarab of hard green stone, a mirror case in form of an *ankh*, a fine cambric-like linen shawl, a sceptre, two flagellums (a symbol of royalty), pectorals, bracelets, pendants and a beadwork ornament resembling a stole. On the surface of the lid, which is covered with a sheet of gold, are boldly carved hieroglyphs of ebony and ivory, stained red, which form the king's personal name, Tutankhamun.

A simpler chest (fig. 124), ornamented with an inlaid band of hieroglyphs similar to those in the cartouche chest, has an interesting variation from the usual construction in

119

120

121

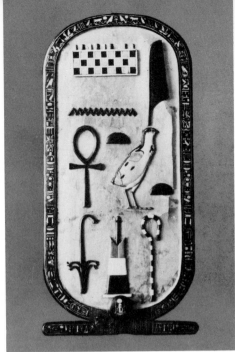

122 Deep chest in the form (in plan) of a cartouche. The lines of text are carved and filled with blue paint. *Eighteenth Dynasty*.

123 Lid of the cartouche-shaped chest. The background is gilded and the signs are carved ebony and stained ivory; the surround is of ebony inlaid with ivory. *Eighteenth Dynasty*.

the raised band of wood that runs around the bottom above the short legs. Among the undecorated chests is one with a gabled top (fig. 125) similar to figure 115, with a bold cove cornice. This is constructed with heavy corner posts and is made of a plain, ordinary wood painted white. There were a number of other plain rectangular chests with flat tops, mostly painted white, such as were used for storage in ordinary households (discussed in Chapters 5 and 6).

In addition to the utilitarian furniture, there were boxes to hold the games of which the ancient Egyptians were fond. The pieces of one of these games were housed in a small wooden chest which has carved lion's legs similar to those used on furniture (fig. 126). Like the more important objects, this is embellished with gold and ivory, and the claws of the feet are carved out of ivory. Within the drawer with which it is fitted were found two ivory knucklebones and four playing sticks, one pair ending in the form of a human finger, the other pair terminating in fox's heads made of ebony and ivory. A second gaming box had its top marked out with gilded divisions and contained a drawer at each end in which there were twenty playing pieces, large and small.

There were also a number of boxes and chests constructed of materials other than wood and used to hold jewellery and other valuables. Since such caskets formed an important part of the palace furnishings, three are illustrated even though they do not enter the category of wood furniture. The first, made of papyrus pith and lined with linen, was used for storing writing materials (fig. 127). The second, constructed of solid ivory and ornamented with gold, was probably used as a jewel box (fig. 128). The third, which served a similar purpose, is constructed entirely of alabaster, with incised decoration filled with black and red paint (fig. 129).

Altogether, twenty chests have been illustrated, seemingly a disproportionate number in comparison with the other types of furniture shown. The concentration of effort by the ancient cabinet-makers on furniture of this sort, however, can be explained by the importance of these pieces in the Egyptian household. They represent also some of the finest examples of ancient craftsmanship.

119 Scene on the lid of the ivory casket. Tutankhamun and his wife in a garden. *Eighteenth Dynasty*.

120 Chest with a sloping top. *Eighteenth Dynasty*.

121 Casket with domed lid and marquetry panels. *Eighteenth Dynasty*.

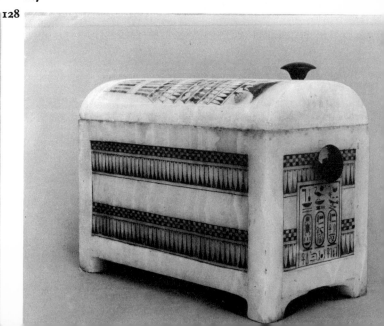

124   125

126   127

128

124 Chest of solid construction with a raised band of wood around the base. *Eighteenth Dynasty.*

125 Plain storage chest with gabled top. *Eighteenth Dynasty.*

126 Wooden game box, set on a stool with lion's legs, supported on a sledge. *Eighteenth Dynasty.*

127 Box of papyrus pith lined with linen and painted with ritual scenes. *Eighteenth Dynasty.*

128 Solid ivory jewel casket with gold mountings and fittings. Each side-panel is made of a single piece of ivory. *Eighteenth Dynasty.*

129 Solid alabaster box with obsidian knobs. *Eighteenth Dynasty.*

130 Canopic shrine, consisting of a canopy on a sledge, enclosing a shrine-shaped chest, protected by four goddesses (Isis and Selkis visible here). *Eighteenth Dynasty.*

130

The four great carved and gilded shrines found in the tomb are worthy of note as impressive examples of woodworking, the largest being nearly eight feet high. They were graduated in size to fit inside each other, the smallest one containing the sarcophagus of King Tutankhamun. Constructed of wood planking, probably cedar of Lebanon, these large structures, after thirty-three hundred years, are still remarkably free from warping and splitting. The construction details exhibit great skill, the shrines being built in sections so they could be taken through the narrow entrance of the tomb in parts and assembled in place. The ingenious series of cabinet joints which fastened the sides were constructed to lock permanently when brought together, and each section of the shrine was carefully numbered and marked to show how the pieces fitted to each other. Although this is cabinet-making on a grand scale, the shrines, of course, do not come in the category of furniture.

A somewhat smaller shrine, however, which contained the calcite canopic chest, is illustrated as furniture since it repeats in larger scale the ornamental details used in some of the palace furniture (fig. 130). The same traditional patterns occur in the chased gold covering of the panels; the cornice is similar, although its members are larger; and free-standing gold *uraei* ornament the sides and crown the top. Of great interest also are the carved and gilded wooden figures which stand at the four sides of the shrine.

131 Gilded wooden figures of three of the protective goddesses: Neith, Isis and Selkis (the fourth is Nephthys). *Eighteenth Dynasty*.

132 Bed completely overlaid with gold bearing incised decoration. The sagging stretchers allow for the sinking of the mattress. *Eighteenth Dynasty*.

133 Foot-board of the gold-covered bed. The decoration is wholly floral, the motif on the central panel symbolizing the union of Upper and Lower Egypt. *Eighteenth Dynasty*.

131

Wood-carving is a conspicuous feature of the more elaborate furniture of ancient Egypt, and the carvers were master craftsmen. Usually the carving appears in low relief, but outstanding examples of carving in the round are seen in the four figures which guarded the canopic chest containing the viscera. As is usually the case in Egyptian art, the figures have a symbolic significance, representing the goddesses Isis, Nephthys, Neith and Selkis. In their original positions they were the guardians of the chest, standing one on each side, with outstretched arms and facing inward. But away from their formal setting the three beautifully carved small goddesses (fig. 131) appear as charming maidens in the prelude to a dance, and the Amarna influence is apparent in their realistic, fully revealed contours and softly flowing pleated garments.

Beds and head-rests

In the beds found in the tomb, as well as in the other categories of furniture, there is a great deal of carving. Altogether there are five beds, three of which have elaborately carved foot-boards in addition to the usual carved legs. The most elegant of these (figs. 132, 133) is completely covered with heavy gold sheet which still retains a considerable sheen. As in the other Tutankhamun beds, the frame is slightly curved, dipping in the

102

132

133

centre, with a covering of woven mesh. The legs, in the form of the fore and hind legs of a lion, are also similar to those of the other beds, but the outstanding feature is the beautifully carved foot-board with papyrus and lotus patterns in the panels, which are divided by the customary 'panel binding' – slender rods which curve over the top and represent papyrus stems with joined flowers in the centre. The designs were first carved in the wood, then covered with gold sheet which was pressed into shape and chased with small tools. Across the top and bottom of the foot-board are bands with an incised pattern; the narrow panels at the ends are filled with other decorative patterns. The foot-board is secured to the frame by curved braces covered with heavy gold sheet on which are gold studs which cover the dowel ends. Beneath the frame are curved supports of leather apparently intended to support the matting if it should sag.

The second bed (figs. 134, 135) has the same general form but has a very different treatment in the design of its foot-board. The three panels, which are divided by the usual papyrus rods, each contain three carved and cut-out figures decorated with gold-leaf. The god Bes, who is frequently represented in the Yuia and Thuiu furniture, crouches in the centre and is faced on each side by a standing lion with his forepaws resting on the hieroglyph signifying protection. On the ebony bands framing the foot-board at top and ends are inscriptions, filled with yellow paint, which repeat magic formulae on behalf of

134

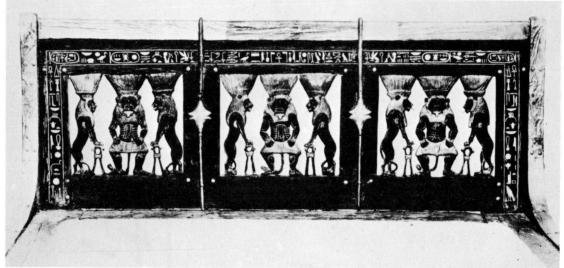

135

the king. The top and curved braces are gold-covered, and the claws of the lion's feet are of silver.

The most unusual of the beds in its construction is King Tutankhamun's travelling bed, which is made to fold into a neat package (figs. 136, 137). In this piece we have a parallel again to English furniture of the eighteenth century, when mahogany travelling beds were made to fold into a similar package. In the Tutankhamun bed there are four pairs of legs and heavy bronze hinges between the three frames, the centre supports beneath relieving the strain on the hinges when the bed was opened out. The frame sections with their woven matting fold upon one another, the supplementary legs being hinged so they can be turned out of the way when the bed is folded. The three panels of the foot-board consist of plain wooden slats, and the frame is heavier than usual to stand the strain of folding and being moved about. All the wood parts, as well as the finely woven linen string web, had been painted white originally, although much of the paint has now worn off. The carved feet rest on bronze drums. Although this is the only bed of its type that has been found, the Metropolitan Museum has a miniature folding bed found in a private tomb of the Eighteenth Dynasty, which

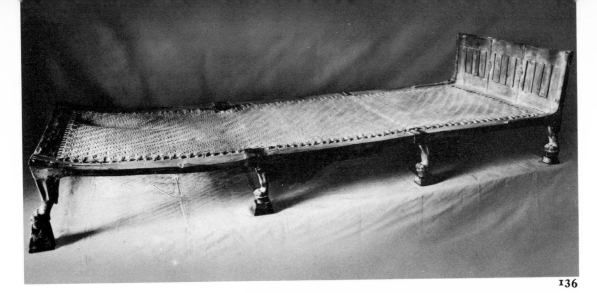

134 Solid ebony bed with string-mesh mattress. *Eighteenth Dynasty.*

135 Foot-board of the ebony bed. The cut-out figures, partly gilded, represent the household god Bes. *Eighteenth Dynasty.*

136 The travelling bed, unfolded for use. *Eighteenth Dynasty.*

137 The travelling bed, folded for transport. *Eighteenth Dynasty.*

136

137

suggests that, even if these were not common, other beds of this sort did exist.[7]

One other of the beds was also overlaid with gold (fig. 138), but in this instance with a thin gold-foil which is considerably more tarnished than that on the first bed illustrated. It is of the standard type, with carved animal legs and a three-panel foot-board, the panels being ornamented with the traditional figures of the god Bes and the goddess Thoeris modelled in low relief. The simplest of the five beds, which again follows the same general form, has plain slats in the foot-board panels and was originally painted white (fig. 139).

Tutankhamun's tomb also contained a number of head-rests. The rigid head-rest was one of the essential pieces of household equipment, and hundreds of examples still exist, scattered among the museums of the world. Most were carved pieces of wood supported by an oval or rounded column resting on a base, but occasionally they were made of stone or other material in more elaborate patterns. As befits a support made for the royal head, the head-rests of the king are of elegant design and workmanship. Some follow the conventional simple pattern of the wooden head-rests; others vary in their design and materials. One of the most exotic examples was probably made specifically for the tomb

138

139

rather than for practical use (fig. 140). Carved of ivory, the column represents the god Shu, supporter of the heavens, flanked on each side by *couchant* lions.

The second example has the face of the god Bes on the outside ends of the curved top and an engraving of a lotus design on the inside (fig. 141). The supports cross, as in the form of a folding stool, with duck-heads grasping the bottom rails with their beaks. Ivory is used for all parts of the head-rest, the upper section being stained in various colours while the runners are white. The third example is one of two of similar shape which were made of opaque turquoise-blue glass (fig. 142). A gold band, engraved with a running pattern of *ankh* and *was* symbols, covers the joint between the two separate parts of which this head-rest was made. Hieroglyphs giving the title of the king are incised on the face of the column.

Although the funerary couches of animal design would not have been used in the palace their inclusion here is justified, since they are made of wood and are in the form of beds, and are among the most spectacular objects in the tomb. In Napoleon's time beds of this sort were observed in the painted scenes on the walls of tombs, and drawings of them were made by the artists who accompanied him on his Egyptian campaigns and published in the great work entitled *La Description de l'Egypte*.[8] When first seen, these

140

141

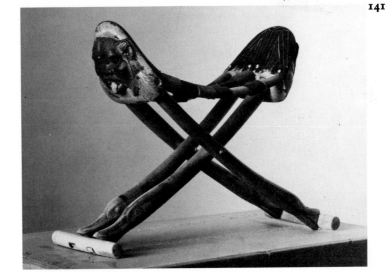

138 Gilded bed with figures of Bes and Thoeris on the foot-board. *Eighteenth Dynasty.*

139 Plain bed, painted white. *Eighteenth Dynasty.*

140 Ivory head-rest or pillow. The god Shu supports the curved rest, as he supports the heavens. *Eighteenth Dynasty.*

141 Head-rest in the form of a folding stool, with heads of Bes. *Eighteenth Dynasty.*

142 Turquoise blue glass head-rest made in two pieces joined by a wooden dowel, the joint being disguised by a gold collar. *Eighteenth Dynasty.*

142

representations were thought to be purely imaginary, and not until the discovery of the animal couches in the tomb of King Tutankhamun was there definite proof that such pieces had actually existed.

The sides of each couch consist of a pair of attenuated animals between which the bed frame with its cover of woven matting is suspended. The heavy timber of which the animals were constructed was first carved into shape and then covered with gesso over which a thin sheet of gold was applied. On this the details were carved and inlays inserted which give character to these strange beasts. Such couches were no doubt used primarily in the embalming and funeral rites and, as has been stated above, it is unlikely that they were ever part of the actual furnishings of the palace. However, one relief shows a similar couch with steps by its side which could have been for the owner's use, although this seems rather improbable.

The lioness couch, shown in its case at the Cairo Museum (fig. 143), is reminiscent of couches shown in *La Description de l'Egypte* where the deceased reclines surrounded by the deities of the afterlife (fig. 144). The form of the couch is somewhat different, but the boldly curving tail of the animal remains the same. The mane of the lioness in the Tutankhamun example is indicated by a short ruff, which, like the whiskers, is incised in the gold. The other details of this realistic head are described by Carter as follows: "the nose and eye frames are inlaid with dark blue glass; the eyes are of crystal with hazel irises and black pupils, the colours being painted on the gesso before the overlay of crystal was applied".

The spotted cow, with horns enclosing a disk, which appears on one of the beds, represents the goddess Hathor (fig. 145). Her body is described by Carter as "covered with an overall design of trefoils of dark blue sunk in the gold". Carter states also that the eye frames, brows and irises are of paste and that the whites of the eyes are gesso with red-painted corners. The foot-board, as in the other two beds, has three panels separated by gold-covered papyrus-shaped rods of the usual shape which is found on beds. Each panel is ornamented with a large hieroglyph modelled in low relief on both its face and back.

The third couch (fig. 146) is made to represent the goddess Thoeris, the protectress of childbirth, whose hippopotamus features appear frequently in the furniture of Yuia and Thuiu. The form of the body is similar to that of the other couches, but the head is rendered with great spirit with the whites of the eyes bloodshot around the edges (fig. 147). The teeth are of white ivory and the protruding tongue is of ivory stained red.

Apart from a few relatively unimportant pieces our intention has been to show the furniture found in the tomb of King Tutankhamun in its entirety, which has not hitherto been attempted. It seems unlikely that another such collection of furniture will ever be found. Although some important royal tombs remain undiscovered, few archaeologists believe that they were constructed in places where conditions favour the preservation of wood to the same degree as in the Valley of the Kings. And yet the Theban hills may still hold caches of royal furniture, saved from the plundered royal tombs of the New Kingdom. Meanwhile, the treasure of Tutankhamun remains unique. Some people are inclined to treat its design in a derogatory manner, comparing it unfavourably with Old

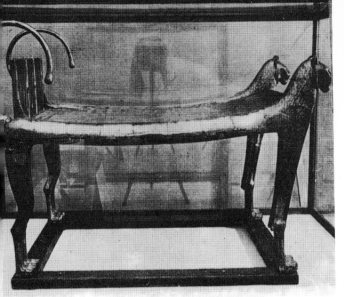

143

144

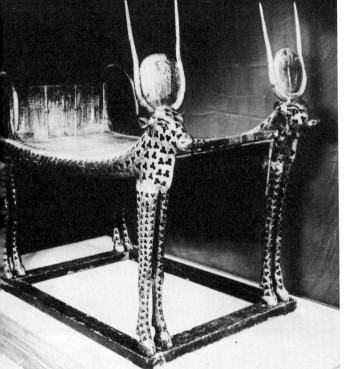

145

143 Ceremonial couch in the form of elongated lionesses. The parts are fastened together with bronze hooks and staples. *Eighteenth Dynasty.*

144 Lion couch in a scene showing the mystical union of Isis (as a falcon) and the revivified Osiris. *Roman Period.*

145 The Hathor couch. The markings are of dark blue glass inlaid in gold. *Eighteenth Dynasty.*

146 The Thoeris couch in the form of elongated hippopotamus bodies. Photographed at the time of excavation. *Eighteenth Dynasty.*

147 One of the Thoeris heads on the Thoeris couch. The teeth and tongue are of ivory. *Eighteenth Dynasty.*

147

Kingdom furniture, which is praised for its dignified restraint and classic simplicity. Taste, however, is an uncertain guide to judgment, especially in dealing with objects three thousand years old. The modern preference for functional design and simple ornament should not make us blind to the amazing achievement represented by the Tutankhamun furniture both for technical skill and for artistic conception.

5

THE EGYPTIAN VILLA AND ITS FURNISHINGS

The furniture of the upper-class home in ancient Egypt differed little in its range of types from that found in the Tutankhamun collection. The royal beds, chairs, stools, tables and chests had their counterparts in the homes of the well-to-do; but, as might be expected, the villa furniture was less ornate and, for the most part, strictly utilitarian. In general this simpler furniture has attracted little attention, but more than two hundred pieces, three thousand years old or older, still exist in a good state of preservation. Before considering the various individual types in detail, however, it may be well to look at the environment in which this more ordinary furniture was originally used.

As in all civilizations, the houses in ancient Egypt, as well as their furnishings, varied greatly according to the economic and social status of their owners. Consequently, in order to relate the furniture which is illustrated to the house in which it would be used, it is useful to select a specific type of dwelling as an example. Obviously the simple huts of the common people contained little or no furniture – at the most perhaps a stool or two, a rough table, and maybe a storage chest. Low benches of mud brick could in most cases serve the purpose of wooden furniture; spread with a woven mat, a bench of this kind also made a bed, raising the sleeping person above the floor. But even such simple mud benches were not always used. The ancient peasant, like the modern *fellah*, was accustomed to sit in a squatting position on the ground and so had no need of chairs. At the other extreme was the palace furnished with elaborate furniture like that of Tutankhamun. Between these two were the country villas and town houses of the nobles and officials.

Although there was, of course, no one typical house, the surviving evidence suggests that the dwellings of the well-to-do had much in common, whether in country or town. A model in the Cairo Museum, carefully constructed from archaeological evidence, shows what a noble's villa at El-Amarna looked like (fig. 148). Houses such as this with gardens could very well be built in the open plan of the new town of Akhenaten at El-Amarna, but they should, perhaps, be classified as country villas.

This type of dwelling, with a garden and a pond or lake, had its antecedents in the early years of Egyptian history; one of the earliest recorded dating from the time of King Sneferu, about 2600 B.C. Mention of this private estate occurs in the biographical inscription of Metjen, an official who rose to a high position and was eventually buried in the royal necropolis of Saqqara. In his description of the various favours he received he says: "A house, two hundred cubits long and two hundred cubits wide was built and equipped; fine trees were planted, a very large lake was made; fig-trees and vines were planted."[1] Some three hundred years later, Herkhuf, another successful official, who served the kings of the Sixth Dynasty, left the record of his achievements in his tomb at Aswan saying, among other things: "I built a house, I set up doors, I dug a lake, I planted trees."[2]

A rich source of information regarding early dwellings exists in the pottery model houses, known as 'soul-houses', placed in tombs of the Middle Kingdom. These 'soul-houses', coming mostly from the tombs of middle-class rather than noble owners, are crudely constructed with no attempt at refinement, but they incorporate a great variety of architectural detail. For the most part they have forecourts containing model offerings of food and drink, and their purpose was to provide a substitute in case the actual offerings ceased to be made. A considerable number of these 'soul-houses' exist in various museum collections, and in them we can see the precedents for the interior arrangement of the Amarna house, as well as details of doors, windows, porticoes and columns. Stairways leading to the roof – an important feature of houses in hot climates – are also indicated[3] (fig. 149).

Some idea of the exterior details of the house of a well-to-do Egyptian before the Eighteenth Dynasty can also be derived from the two models of the residence of the great noble Meket-Re, who lived during the late Eleventh Dynasty (about 2040 B.C.). These models, which are practically identical, were found in his tomb in Thebes; one is now in the Cairo Museum and one in the Metropolitan Museum (fig. 150). His house was built of mud brick with a columned portico facing the garden, and was set in a walled enclosure in which was a pool surrounded by trees. The models do not, however, tell us anything about the interior arrangement of the house, since they represent only the garden elevation.[4]

A great deal of knowledge, however, on the internal arrangements of a luxurious house of the Eighteenth Dynasty has come from the excavations at El-Amarna, and the details incorporated in the Cairo scale model are based on actual precedents from this locality. Similar arrangements of house and garden, as well as architectural details, are also portrayed in the rock tombs of El-Amarna, notably in the scenes in the unfinished tomb of the high priest Meryre.[5] Such houses were well suited to the hot climate, with thick walls of sun-baked brick, and a tall room in the cool central part of the house with clerestory windows high in the walls. The main doorway was usually capped with a cavetto cornice with a torus moulding – details we have seen repeated in furniture. In the model illustrated, this door opened into a porter's vestibule which led into the main part of the house. The roof was flat, as in most Egyptian houses, and was used for both living and storage purposes. Also, although it is not apparent on the model, the roof probably had a ventilator on top, called a *malqaf*, a hooded arrangement placed to catch the prevailing wind and direct it below. The most conspicuous element of the interior is the use of columns, usually of wood on stone bases, four tall ones for the central hall, and a varying number of lower ones in the principal other reception rooms.

The drawing of a floor-plan of a similar house given in figure 151 is based on the

148

evidence obtained by Dr Henri Frankfort from excavations at El-Amarna in 1929.[6] Although this includes characteristic details from several typical houses, it is based principally on one actual house which was located in the outskirts of the city and which, as the excavations revealed, was bounded by streets on two sides and by similar estates on the other two sides. The arrangement of the rooms is clearly shown in the plan, with an indication of their individual usage. The drawing also includes an interesting cross-section which shows several details of the interior, including columns with lotus capitals. The second storey represented in the front section of the house is based on the evidence of small column bases which had apparently fallen from above. Such had been found in similar locations in other houses, and it seems probable that, even if the roof did not carry a fully enclosed room as a second storey, it did have an open loggia with slender wooden columns there.

Traces of paint which remain in the interior indicate that the jambs and doors, as well as the wooden pillars, were painted bright red. The ceilings of the larger rooms were supported by brightly decorated main beams resting on the columns, and in one instance the smaller beams appear to have been painted pink with panels of white between. The central hall was apparently used as the principal living-room and for entertaining guests, while the long 'north room' and the smaller 'west room' comprised the formal reception areas. In the rear were the women's quarters and the master's bedroom suite. The furniture, consisting chiefly of stools, chairs and small tables, would have been moved about in the columned halls as needed. Such was the house of a wealthy man, but even the houses of people of lower estate retained the basic plan of living hall, or loggia, off which smaller rooms opened.

Furniture is portrayed very frequently in tomb paintings, but only rarely is there a scene where it is directly associated with the architecture of the house. One of the few scenes of this sort occurs in the tomb of Djehut-nufer at Thebes, showing three rooms in the town house of the deceased owner, one above the other (fig. 152).[7] In the lower room servants are busy at their occupations; the centre part represents an important room with four tall pillars; in the upper section there is a view of the private part of the house. The chairs represented are of the usual shape used in ordinary upper-class homes, as well as in the palace, but regrettably no other types of furniture are depicted. In another unusual scene from a Theban tomb, there is a row of four small cubicles, each of which has a bed (fig. 153).[8] Undoubtedly, however, the master bedroom of an important residence would contain other furniture also, such as stools and chests.

Colour plate VII. Detail from colour plate VI. The back panel of the golden throne.

149   150

149 Pottery model of a house (a 'soul-house') set in an enclosure. A staircase leads to an upper floor. *Middle Kingdom.*

150 View of the portico of the ancient model of Meket-Re's house. Note the water-spouts. *Eleventh Dynasty.*

151 Ground plan and section of a villa at El-Amarna. *Eighteenth Dynasty.*

152 Tomb scene showing a section through the house of Djehut-nufer. *Eighteenth Dynasty.*

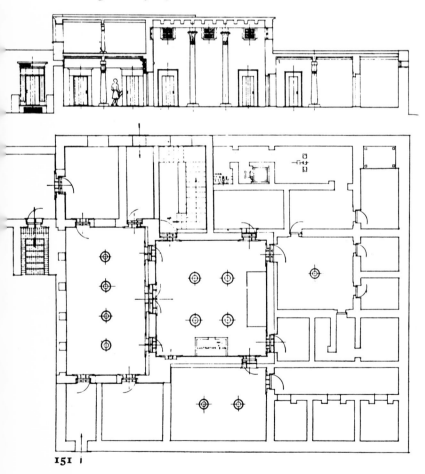

151

152

113

153

153 Tomb scene showing part of the house of Surer, with interesting small bed-cubicles. *Eighteenth Dynasty.*

154 Four stools with lattice design, two (a, b) with concave seats, and two (c, d) with double cove seats. *Eighteenth Dynasty.*

Furniture from the tomb of the architect Kha

In addition to chairs and beds, a well-furnished villa contained a variety of stools, tables and storage chests, all of which are well represented in a collection of household furniture that comes from a single source and undoubtedly is typical of what would be found in a comfortable house of its time. This remarkable collection, now in the Egyptian Museum in Turin, came from the tomb of the architect Kha, which was discovered in Deir el-Medina, a part of the Theban necropolis, in 1906 by E. Schiaparelli.[9] The furniture dates from approximately 1400 B.C. Individual examples of simple furniture had been discovered as early as the first part of the nineteenth century, and many others have been found since, but this is the largest and most varied collection ever found belonging to a single non-royal person.[10]

Kha, whose title is given as 'Overseer of Works', lived during the reigns of the kings Amenophis II, Tuthmosis IV and Amenophis III, about 1450–1375 B.C. Although he was not one of the most important officials, he no doubt lived in a comfortable house, to judge from the furniture which his tomb contained; and we may assume that his furnishings were typical of an upper-middle-class house. The El-Amarna house just discussed is perhaps fifty years later in date, but there is no evidence to suggest that any changes of consequence had been made in the manner of house building during the intervening period. It is quite possible, therefore, that Kha, as an official of the court, lived in a villa of a similar sort.

In total thirty-two pieces of furniture were found in the tomb, all of which were well preserved, and appear today much as they did thirty-four centuries ago, except for the deterioration in finish. The preponderance of stools and chests is immediately apparent. Except in the most elegant houses there were few chairs, and the stool was the popular sitting piece for all classes. Also, as we have noted before, the Egyptian house contained no wardrobes or cupboards for storage, and many chests were needed to hold linen and various other personal and household items. Tables, however, were perhaps more numerous than indicated, for they were easily moved and served various purposes. (The large dining table was unknown to the ancient Egyptians.)

Although there were only two beds, one for Kha and one for his wife, this does not

114

154a b
c d

155 Rough stool with solid construction for hard use. *Eighteenth Dynasty.*

156 Folding stool with traces of the original leather seat. *Eighteenth Dynasty.*

155   **156**

necessarily mean that his house contained no others. What was placed in the tomb, while reflecting the nature, quality and quantity of what Kha possessed in his lifetime, was nevertheless provided primarily to satisfy Kha's individual needs in the afterlife and did not necessarily include everything that he owned. The furniture in the funerary equipment, furthermore, consisted partly of pieces actually used during the life of the deceased, and partly of specially prepared items with inscriptions of funerary character painted and inscribed upon them. It seems likely, however, that pieces used in life may sometimes have been converted to funerary purposes by the addition of such inscriptions, and that, in general, the furniture in the tomb did not differ from furniture actually used.

Like most ordinary furniture, that of Kha was made of whatever local woods were available, with the exception of two of the stools which were constructed of a superior cabinet-wood probably imported from the Sudan. Most of the pieces had originally been painted, and in some instances they were decorated with patterns and motifs reproducing the designs of inlay work found on more elegant pieces.

The four stools of lattice design (fig. 154) are very much alike, but, since several would probably be included among the furnishings of a well-equipped home of the period, all four are illustrated to indicate the popularity of the type. They were originally painted but the paint has mostly disappeared. The upper two examples form an almost identical pair, each being rectangular in shape, with a well-preserved woven rush seat of concave shape. Both of the lower ones have deeply shaped double cove seats, that on the left having a seat constructed of wide wooden slats, while that on the right has a woven rush seat. Their design is similar to that of the stool from the tomb of Tutankhamun (fig. 101). The stools from Kha's tomb, however, were made almost one hundred years earlier, and it is evident that the type had been in use long before the time of King Tutankhamun. Kha's tomb also contained a rough stool of similar design, but much heavier in construction and evidently built for hard usage (fig. 155).

The other stools vary widely in their design. The most elegant is of the folding variety, having a cross-shaped base with supports terminating in carved duck-heads inlaid with ivory and ebony, the bills grasping the round stretchers below (fig. 156). The wood appears to be some imported variety, and pieces of leather still adhere to the curved seat-rails. Like the lattice stools, this type also has its counterparts among the furniture of Tutankhamun (fig. 103).

Another stool is quite different in design, with round legs and a double cove seat of leather which is torn, but otherwise intact (fig. 157). The legs give all the appearance of being turned, having fine lines ringing their lower parts, but there is no good evidence

116

that the wood lathe was known at this time (see page 304). Careful examination indicates that they were probably worked with hand tools such as light adzes, knives, chisels and stone rubbers. The four cross-stretchers flare at the ends where they join the legs. Like the preceding example, the stool is made of a fine dense hardwood, probably of tropical origin. One of the other stools has the traditional lion legs executed in simplified form (fig. 158). Its braided double cove seat is well preserved, but the wood parts are less well finished than in the two examples described above. The last stool illustrated, called a *panchetto a tre piedi* by Schiaparelli, is apparently a work-stool used in the workroom and domestic offices of a house. This type of stool, two of which were included in the tomb equipment, was made with heavy dished top and with three crude flaring legs, and is frequently illustrated in scenes showing craftsmen at work (fig. 159).[11]

From the evidence provided by scenes in tombs of the nobles of the Eighteenth Dynasty, it is clear that chairs were in fairly common use during the period; yet there was only one in the tomb of Kha (fig. 160). Its form is typical, but it is probably a funerary piece made specially for the tomb, rather than a piece of his own household furniture.[12] The legs and the back frame are painted black, no doubt to simulate ebony; some parts, such as the sides of the curved braces, are painted yellow to represent gilding, while the panel of the back, decorated with polychrome flowers on a yellow background, simulates the appearance of a gold-covered panel inlaid with glass, faience and semi-precious stones. The black and white framing lines on the back of the chair, and the black and white vertical lines within them, simulate inlaid strips of ivory and ebony. The faces of the curved braces are painted white, again to represent ivory, with black spots to indicate ebony pegs, while white dots on the sides of the legs represent ivory studs. Since chairs are represented so frequently in stelae and tomb paintings, one would expect to find several in Kha's villa, although they would doubtless have been less elaborate than the type simulated in his funerary chair. From the evidence of his tomb-equipment, however, it seems probable that Kha, not being among the first rank of officials, lived more modestly than the very great, and for the most part furnished his house with stools rather than chairs.

Of the five tables which are illustrated, the first is one of a matching pair (fig. 161). Both were originally painted white and carried a band of hieroglyphs at each end on their tops. The basic design is the same as that which appeared first in the Early Dynastic period, and which continues in use today in the form of the modern cocktail table. The rectangular shape and the square legs with stretchers differ only in proportion from those of the tables depicted in the scene from the tomb of Mereruka which dates from a thousand years earlier (fig. 52). The next three tables are made of reed with wrapped joints, exhibiting a method of construction still used for furniture made of similar materials today. Two are similar in design and height but vary in length (figs. 162a,b). Both are shown piled with offerings of food, as they were found when the tomb was opened. The third table is similar in construction but slightly taller than the preceding pair (fig. 163).

Although most of the pieces of household furniture so far discussed have been made of wood, the three tables just mentioned suggest that reed and other light materials were frequently employed. The actual evidence of pieces such as those of Kha is supplemented

157   158

by representations in tomb scenes. In the tomb of the high priest Meryre at El-Amarna, a painted scene shows tables of similar construction being used to carry food "from the king's kitchen" (fig. 164).[13] The advantages of furniture of this kind were numerous. Good wood for furniture was relatively scarce and costly; well-dried reed was plentiful, stout, very light and fairly rigid; what appear to be flimsy structures were in fact firmly strengthened with angle braces. Another table of informal type from the tomb of Kha, described by Schiaparelli as *il tavolino da giardino*, has heavy round splayed legs (fig. 165). Its open-framed top has cross-pieces spaced at intervals. The use to which this table was put is uncertain; it conceivably may have held jars of oil, or vases of flowers, of which the Egyptians were always fond.

In addition to the pieces already described, the collection of furniture from the tomb of Kha included a number of storage chests, some of which contained linen and various other personal effects when discovered. Others held alabaster vases originally filled with perfumed oils and other liquids; ordinary well-to-do individuals, as well as the king, took to their tombs for use in the afterlife whatever luxuries they could afford, as well as the necessities. Several of the chests were nothing more than plain boxes with flat tops, but the majority were fitted with gabled lids. Most had originally been painted white, the paint being applied directly to the native woods of which they were made – such as sycamore and acacia. That shown in figure 166 is one of the plainer examples of the gabled type; it is well constructed with substantial corner posts and cross-rails which frame wide board panels on each side. Traces of paint remain, and an inscription running from the fastening knob down the gabled top and the side contains an invocation for offerings on behalf of Kha. The lids of the gabled-top chests were joined to the chest by a variety of methods; in some cases the top was made in a single piece and was slid into position in grooves; in others the two halves of the lid pivoted where they joined the sides of the chest; but, whatever the method of joinery, the lids were secured with cords wound around the two large knobs provided for the purpose. A variety of ingenious joints were also employed in the construction of chests which will be described later (fig. 457).

Five of the chests found were elaborately decorated with painted patterns simulating inlaid work. Evidence is lacking as to whether these were made especially for the tomb or were actually part of Kha's household furniture. The absence of any apparent wear encourages the belief that they are funerary pieces, but it is curious that there are so many of an almost identical type; and there seems no logical reason why such painted ornamen-

118

157 Stool with double cove leather seat; the legs are not turned, but hand-carved. *Eighteenth Dynasty.*

158 Stool with lion's legs and well-preserved braided seat. *Eighteenth Dynasty.*

159 Three-legged stools with dished seats. *Eighteenth Dynasty.*

159

tation should not have been used on furniture of the home as well as the far more expensive marquetry. All five chests carry decoration consisting of geometric design (figs. 167, 168). Traditional patterns are used, carried out in red, blue-green, yellow and black. In addition, three of these chests have each one side decorated with a scene showing Kha and his wife receiving funerary offerings (colour plate IX). These charming, intimate paintings are executed in a manner less formal and accomplished than that employed for similar scenes on royal pieces, but have a special appeal because of their primitive quality. The texts which all five chests carry, as well as the painted scenes, are funerary in intent, and it is possible that they were all added to domestic chests when Kha's tomb-equipment was prepared.

A small vertical cabinet with a shrine-shaped top and cavetto cornice served as a wig box (fig. 169). Its interior was fitted with two transverse pegs on which was hung a wig which, according to the short funerary text on the front of the cabinet, was the property of Kha's wife Meryt. For some reason this cabinet was not fully finished, and its decorations were only partially completed. Apart from the small panel containing the funerary text, there are only the partial indications of a floral decorative pattern on the face and some incised cross-hatched lines on the back.

Two beds, apparently the ones used by Kha and Meryt during their lives, completed the equipment of furniture in the tomb (figs. 170, 171). Both were originally painted white, and most of the paint remains on the wife's bed. They were constructed in the usual manner of the times, with curving side-rails and carved legs of feline design. The workmanship is excellent, as can be seen in the smooth top joints between the side- and end-rails, and in the neat manner in which the latter are shaped to follow the line of the bed. The foot-boards of both beds are divided into three panels in the traditional manner, the panels being separated by slender rods of the usual type representing papyrus flowers meeting at their centres. As usual the foot-board is a separate framed construction added above the bed frame, and its union with the bed frame is strengthened by long curving braces made of bent wood or of pieces cut from the natural knee, or crotch, of a tree. The woven coverings are well preserved. But the bed linen which is shown on the wife's bed was not actually found in place when the bed was discovered; it was stored in some of the chests.

The question which is frequently raised concerning the comfort (or discomfort) of the Egyptian head-rest is perhaps partially answered by the one placed at the head of the wife's bed. Here a linen cloth wrapping has been added, undoubtedly to soften the hard

119

160

160 Chair with painted decoration simulating gilding and inlay-work of ebony, ivory, faience and glass. *Eighteenth Dynasty.*

161 Simple table with square legs and square stretchers, laden with ancient bread. *Eighteenth Dynasty.*

162a,b Two tables of reed construction with wrapped joints, bearing bread offerings. *Eighteenth Dynasty.*

163 Tall table or stand of reed construction. *Eighteenth Dynasty.*

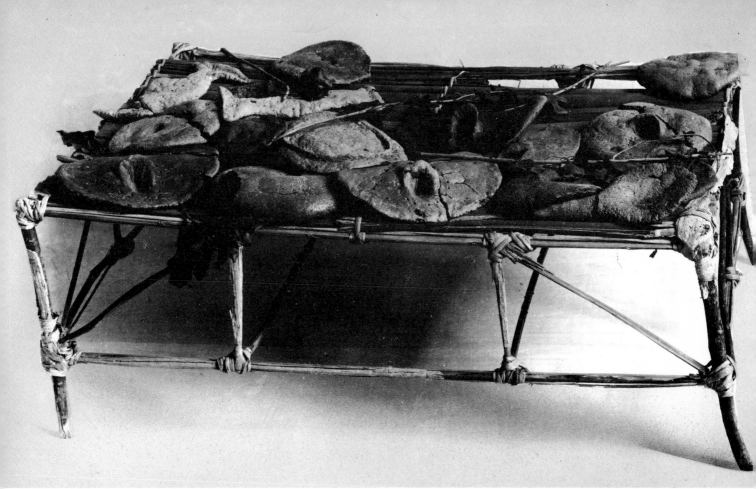

162a

b

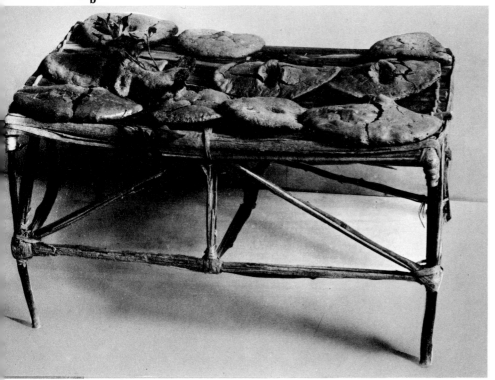

163

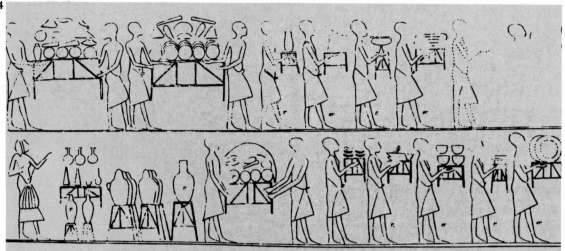

164

165

166

167

168

164 The use of lightly constructed tables and stands in a scene of presentation of gifts to Meryre. *Eighteenth Dynasty*.

165 A 'garden table' with slat top, splayed legs and lattice-bracing. *Eighteenth Dynasty*.

166 Wooden storage chest with gabled top. *Eighteenth Dynasty*.

167 Wooden storage chest painted elaborately to represent inlay-work. *Eighteenth Dynasty*.

168 Wooden storage chest with false inlay and marquetry work. *Eighteenth Dynasty*.

169 Tall chest with a shrine-shaped top, fitted internally to receive a wig. *Eighteenth Dynasty*.

170 Kha's bed of simple, white-painted wood. Note the neatness of the joints. *Eighteenth Dynasty*.

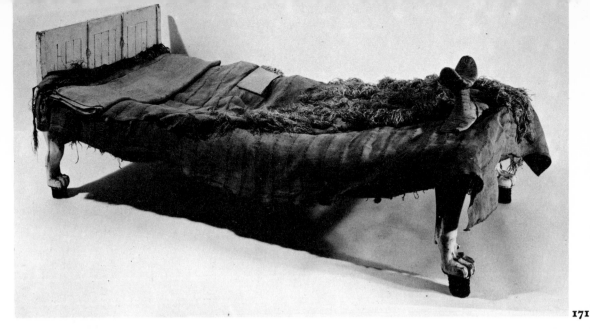

171 Bed of Meryt, Kha's wife. The linen was found in some of the storage chests. *Eighteenth Dynasty.*

172 Stela of Nen-waef showing chairs with the sloping back-rest and characteristic 'triangle' formed with the supporting struts. *Eighteenth Dynasty.*

surface of the wood. There is no firm evidence to support the view that padding was regularly added, although the Metropolitan Museum of Art also has a wrapped head-rest, but there can be no doubt that such a covering would be very much appreciated by the shaven-headed Egyptian, and it seems quite likely that this was a more frequent occurrence than the surviving examples would indicate.

It is apparent that we do not know for certain whether all the pieces found in the tomb were actually used by Kha during his lifetime. Nevertheless, they are unquestionably characteristic of what would have been found in an upper-middle-class house of the period, and in most instances the individual pieces have their counterparts in the examples of household furniture discovered elsewhere which will be considered in the next chapter.

6   HOUSEHOLD FURNITURE TYPES

Typical examples of all five of the usual categories of ancient Egyptian household furniture appear in the remarkable scene from the tomb of Ramose where they are represented being conveyed to the burial chamber (colour plate XA).[1] Since they were intended for the actual use of the spirit of the deceased in the hereafter, these were the familiar forms which he had known and lived with, and the painting no doubt accurately represents the furniture which was taken to his tomb (although none of these particular pieces was ever found). One attendant in the procession carries a cushioned chair on his shoulder. In the centre of the painting four other attendants bear shrine-shaped chests above their heads, while others carry a bed with mattress and head-rest, a lattice-type stool with concave

172

173 174
175 176

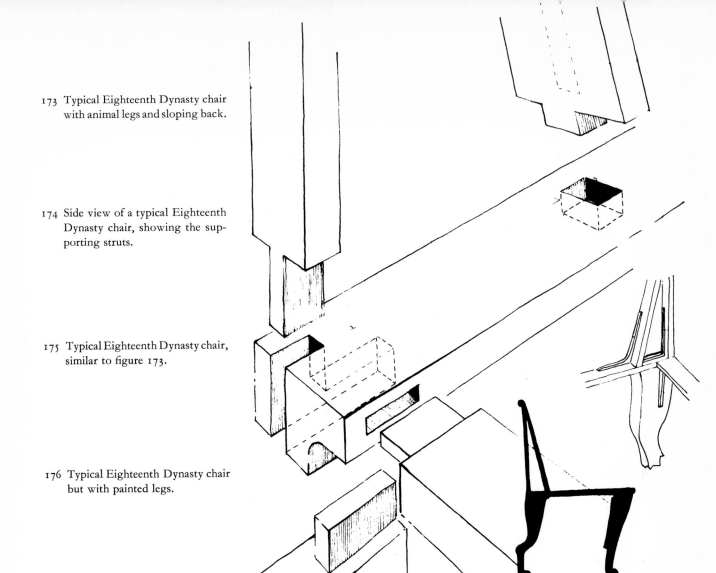

173 Typical Eighteenth Dynasty chair with animal legs and sloping back.

174 Side view of a typical Eighteenth Dynasty chair, showing the supporting struts.

175 Typical Eighteenth Dynasty chair, similar to figure 173.

176 Typical Eighteenth Dynasty chair but with painted legs.

177 Technical drawings of the Louvre chair showing details of construction (see fig. 176).

177

seat and four small tables or tabourets. Actual examples have been found elsewhere, however, almost identical to the pieces represented in the painting, and a number of these are included in the detailed discussion of household furniture types which follows.

Chairs

Chief among the various kinds of furniture was the chair, which in ancient times was an important status symbol and, as such, was representative of the best work of the ancient artisans. Unfortunately, no actual examples of the ordinary household chair have survived from periods antedating the Eighteenth Dynasty, and our knowledge of its origins and early development is almost entirely dependent on what can be learned from painting and sculpture.

127

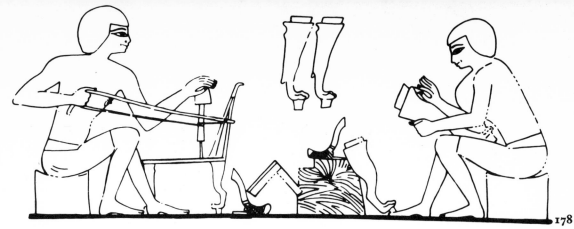

178 Scene of craftsmen at work making chairs. *Eighteenth Dynasty.*

In the first two chapters of this work we have discussed the chairs represented in the reliefs of the Early Dynastic period and Old Kingdom, and also the remarkable chair of Queen Hetepheres. These, however, were the chairs (or thrones) of royalty or other exalted persons, and it is unlikely that the chair with a back would be found in more ordinary households until some time in the Middle Kingdom. It is true that the paintings in the tomb of Hesy-Re (fig. 27b) show simple stools upon which open rectangular backs are superimposed and chairs of similar type dating from the Eighteenth Dynasty have been found, but we have no firm evidence that would indicate at what time such chairs were first used by middle-class persons.

During the Middle Kingdom, after the chair with the slanting back-rest was introduced, we see this represented in the stelae of well-to-do upper-class individuals as well as nobles. And by the early part of the Eighteenth Dynasty, judging by the frequency with which it is depicted, it has become the most popular type of Egyptian chair and an important item in the furnishings of upper-class homes. The close comparison between the chairs represented in the stelae and those actually found is well exemplified in an attractive early Eighteenth Dynasty stela in the Metropolitan Museum in which four chairs of this type appear (fig. 172).[2] The profile view, with the conspicuous triangular opening formed by the slanting back-rest and vertical bracing member, has already been commented on in discussing the chairs of Yuia and Thuiu (fig. 70). The chairs represented in the stela, however, are simpler versions of the type. Those in the upper register, on which Nen-waef, owner of the stela, and his wife are seated, are of approximately normal height, as indicated by the position of the sitters. The chair at the lower right, however, has a much lower seat and their young daughter who occupies it sits in a partly squatting position with one knee drawn up. Many of the ancient chairs actually found do not exceed nine or ten inches in height and probably were sometimes used in this manner by adults accustomed to squatting on the ground. Ordinarily, however, the sitter is portrayed in the normal sitting position, sometimes with knees drawn up at a sharp angle when the seats are low.

There are several well-preserved examples from the Eighteenth Dynasty of chairs such as those represented in the Metropolitan stela, one of the best being that in the Brooklyn Museum (figs. 173, 174). Made of a dense hardwood, this has the typical carved animal legs with a comfortable slanting and curved back. Its top and the vertical slats of the back panel are decorated with simple bone inlays – typical details not visible in the profile views. The woven seat was intact at the time of discovery around 1848 but was

128   Colour plate VIII. Stool. *Eighteenth Dynasty.*

sat on many times to demonstrate its strength while in use at lectures in the nineteenth century and as a result has been broken through (it has since been replaced). The Leiden Museum has an almost identical example with its inlays placed in the same position (fig. 175). A careful examination reveals slight differences in the carving of the legs and details of the back, but the chairs are apparently of the same period and may even have come from the same workshop. The Louvre also has a similar chair, but in this instance the legs are painted blue instead of being a natural wood colour like the rest of the chair (fig. 176). No other chairs have been found with painted legs, but scenes in the tombs of the nobles show legs represented in colours different from the rest of the chair (colour plate XB).[3]

The general structure of these chairs is clearly visible in the front and back view illustrations of the Brooklyn chair. The most important improvement over the straight-backed chair is the curved and slanting back-rest which has already been noted in the royal chairs of this period. Unfortunately, however, evidence is lacking as to when the curved feature was first introduced, the profile paintings and reliefs of earlier periods not indicating whether the back-rests are flat or curved, as has been mentioned before.

Although the technical discussion of joinery appears elsewhere in this book, it is interesting to note at this point how the ancient Egyptian craftsmen solved a practical problem in construction. The Brooklyn chair, unlike the modern chair which is customarily designed with a continuous back post, has separate legs, both front and back, which are fastened to the frame from below, and a back attached from above – as with most ancient Egyptian chairs. In order to achieve the necessary rigidity, the different parts are joined together by a series of mortise and tenon joints which pass each other in such a way as not to impair the strength of the heavy flat seat frame. This type of construction is, of course, more complicated than that in which a continuous back post is used, and the ingenious set of joints with which the chair is fastened together is illustrated in the drawing of a similar chair from the Louvre (fig. 177).[4]

In a detail from one of the painted scenes of artisans at work in the tomb of Rekhmire at Thebes we see workmen making chairs of this sort (fig. 178).[5] Spare legs are shown in the upper centre of the painting, while a workman at the right works on others. Even the tenons on the top of the legs are visible in this minutely detailed painting. At the left a workman is drilling holes with a bow-drill in the seat frame of an almost completed chair to receive the strands of the rush seat. The further details of this fascinating scene of woodworking in the Eighteenth Dynasty are discussed in the appendix on techniques.

A variation of the chair with slanting back-rest is seen in a Nineteenth Dynasty chair in the Cairo Museum from the tomb of Sennedjem (fig. 179). It is lightly constructed and crudely painted in patterns resembling marquetry and, like the painted chair of Kha (fig. 160), it is likely that it is a funerary chair rather than one that was actually used. Another version appears in the Metropolitan Museum sculpture which represents Yuny and his wife Renute, a priestess of Hathor, seated side by side in a double chair (fig. 180). Beneath the seat, on each side, is the lattice-type bracing which has been discussed previously and which is represented in Egyptian art as late as the fourth century B.C. (fig. 181).

179

179 Chair specially prepared for funerary purposes, painted with designs representing marquetry. *Nineteenth Dynasty.*

180 Pair-statue of Yuny and Renute showing a double chair with lattice bracing. *Nineteenth Dynasty.*

181 Chairs with lattice bracing in a scene on a ritual vessel (*situla*) of the Thirtieth Dynasty.

182 Squat chair with cut-out back, the design incorporating hieroglyphs and a figure of the god Bes. *Eighteenth Dynasty.*

183 Simple chair with the back made of plain slats. *Eighteenth Dynasty.*

180   181

182   183

One question not answered by the relatively few chairs found in the tombs is the extent to which they were actually used in ancient homes. Certainly chairs were far less numerous than stools and were probably a rarity except in the most affluent households. In one wall painting, however, from the tomb of Nebamun, fourteen chairs appear in a party scene in which women with wigs and scented ornaments on their heads and men with shaven heads are served by lightly clad young maidens (colour plate XB).[6] The side view of the chairs closely resembles those of the Brooklyn and Leiden chairs. It is essential to remember, of course, that scenes such as this were provided for the enjoyment of the deceased in his afterlife and, although they do not necessarily represent actual events, we may assume that formal occasions of this sort did occur in his life on earth.

Contemporary with the chairs with slanting backs illustrated above there are others with straight backs and low, broad seats. One of the best examples, now in the Metropolitan Museum, had belonged to Senenmut's mother, Hatnufer, and was found outside the doorway of her tomb (fig. 182). Senenmut, the favourite and chief official of Queen Hatshepsut, had two tombs at Thebes. His parents, Ramose and Hatnufer, who were not apparently of noble stock, were buried in a small tomb in front of the earlier of Senenmut's two tombs. Although the chair was broken into parts when discovered, the seat was intact and the chair has been re-assembled in its original shape. The legs are nicely carved in the usual feline design, and the frame of the back is mounted on the seat in the customary manner, reinforced with long bent right-angle braces. The wood is ebony, with three small panels of boxwood inlaid in the lower part of the back panel. In the upper section of the back there is a cut-out boxwood figure of the god Bes in the centre, and on each side are hieroglyphs *tyet* and *djed* alternately carved in ebony and boxwood. The seat was made of string mesh composed of triple strands of linen cord woven in a herringbone pattern.

184   185

A similar chair, although simpler, in the Metropolitan Museum, has a back panel consisting of five plain vertical slats (fig. 183). A third type of this general construction is included in the collection of ancient Egyptian furniture in the British Museum (fig. 184). The four vertical strips of ebony in the back panel are inlaid with small ivory ornaments and a line of ivory dots below. On the face of the top- and bottom-rails of the back appear rows of ebony pegs which were apparently intended to secure the tenons of the vertical slats. The seat, which is only eight inches high from the floor, still has its original covering of woven rush.

Most of the chairs which have been discovered, and all of those illustrated so far, have carved legs of animal form. The bull's leg appeared on furniture at the beginning of the First Dynasty and continued to be seen in the Old Kingdom period, but in later periods the lion's leg design was more commonly used. The earliest seats represented in Early Dynastic sculpture, however, had straight legs, and simple chairs of this construction continued to be made in the Eighteenth Dynasty. In its most elementary form, such as the example illustrated from the Berlin Museum, it resembles what today would be called a kitchen chair (fig. 185). A similar chair is shown later in a group photograph which illustrates a number of pieces discovered at Deir el-Medina (fig. 214).

Also straight-legged, but much more sophisticated in design, is a fine simple chair from the British Museum (fig. 187). The vertical back posts provided a rigid bracing to the sloping back-rest, which is curved for comfort. The front legs are rounded at the top and project slightly above the level of the seat. Differing in construction from the chairs where the seat frame is a separate unit and the animal legs are attached from below, the back post is one piece and the frame-rails are mortised directly to it. The straightforward simple design is more like that of William Morris than what is generally associated with Eighteenth Dynasty Egypt. There is also a marked resemblance to a hypothetical chair which illustrated a study of the modern chair in relation to human posture, made a few years ago at the Bauhaus in Dessau (fig. 186).

A chair in the Archaeological Museum in Florence is similar to the British Museum example above, but is rather more refined in its design and is constructed with its front

132

posts mortised into a heavy seat frame (fig. 188). The cutting away of the wood of the continuous back posts, where it projects above the seat, produces an open triangular space at this point like that in the profile view of chairs illustrated in the Metropolitan stela. Long curved angle braces between the seat and back-rest provide added strength at this point. In addition to front and back cross-stretchers, there are curved wooden brackets between the legs and seat-frame to prevent racking. The side view of the chair shows the curve of the top-rail, which is carved from one piece, with an interesting feature of design in the half-round moulding which curves around the top (fig. 189). Parts of the woven rush seat still remain. Simple as the Florence chair appears, it is one of the most interesting examples of ancient cabinet-making, and a measured drawing is included at the end of the book for the convenience of modern chair-makers who may be interested in its details (fig. 467).

One last type, appearing frequently in tomb representations but of which no example is extant, deserves a brief comment. The form, which obviously derived from the box-type seat of the Early Dynastic period, has a flush side panel elaborately decorated in a wide variety of designs (fig. 190). Usually there is a low back. Representations of these chairs in the tomb paintings were observed as early as the time of Napoleon's campaign, and coloured drawings of them were illustrated in the account of his Egyptian discoveries. Usually reserved for the gods, or the king in his divine role, they occasionally appear in less formal scenes. The great variety of patterns which appear in these brightly painted representations is interesting, but this type of seat, of course, does not belong in the category of household furniture.

Stools

The universal seating piece in ancient times was the stool. Although the chair was the formal seat for important occasions, stools were far more numerous and were used in the

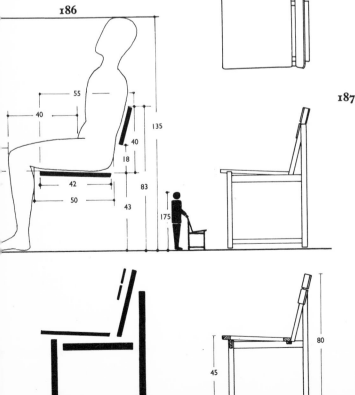

186

187

186 Drawing of a posture chair designed at the Bauhaus.

187 Side view of chair showing details of the construction of the back. *Eighteenth Dynasty.*

palace as well as in ordinary homes. In addition to the Turin stools from the tomb of Kha illustrated in the last chapter, a considerable number have been found in other locations and are widely distributed among other museum collections. There are approximately thirty in the Cairo Museum and many others in the museums of Berlin, London, Florence, New York, Brooklyn, Moscow and elsewhere.

The widespread use of stools in the Eighteenth Dynasty is apparent from the great variety of scenes in which they are represented. Among the most popular was the lattice type which appears in the relief of King Akhenaten and his family (fig. 86); and at the other end of the social scale a version of the same design is seen in the workshop scene in figure 191. The same type of stool often appears also in paintings from the tombs of the nobles in the Theban necropolis, sometimes in combination with chairs and stools with crossed legs, as in the intriguing party scene from the tomb of Nebamun and Ipuky (colour plate XI).

Several of the stools previously shown from the Kha collection have close parallels in the British Museum. The first of these, illustrated in figure 192, closely resembles the four stools with lattice bracing in Turin (fig. 154) and it is also almost identical with one of the same type in the Tutankhamun collection (fig. 100). Like the Tutankhamun stool, it was originally painted white over a gesso base. The rhythmic arrangement of its parts, combining delicacy with strength, fully justifies the popularity of this design, and a measured drawing is included at the end of the book for convenient reference by modern cabinet-makers (fig. 472).

Another British Museum stool, with rounded legs and a deeply curved seat with leather top, also resembles one of the Kha stools but is finer in its details and workman-

189

188 A very fine simple chair with curved and
    sloping back and curved brackets to
    strengthen the frame. *Eighteenth Dynasty*.

188

ship (fig. 193). The shape of the leg, with its narrow neck near the bottom which swells out again to form the foot, is one of the popular styles of the times. There are fine circular lines in the lower part of the legs, a characteristic detail also seen in several other stools of this type in the Cairo Museum. The legs are inlaid with ivory in typical patterns, and the stretchers are capped with ivory ferrules where they join the legs. The struts of the lattice bracing are also ivory.

An intriguing miniature piece with a woven top was perhaps intended as a child's bench (fig. 194). Its low height and general proportions suggest that it may have been intended for squatting rather than sitting in a normal position. The line of the bracket, or apron, which begins at the floor and continues in a curving line under the top is an attractive detail. The bench was originally painted white over gesso, most of which, however, has disappeared. Because of its woven seat, it is not likely to have been a foot-stool. (This is also represented in the measured drawings.)

Others of the British Museum stools are of the popular cross-legged type with carved and inlaid duck's heads joined to stretchers at the floor (figs. 195, 197). They are similar in principle to examples which have been illustrated in the palace furniture and also in the Kha collection, but are more slender and simpler in design. One of these has an unusual feature in the design of its stretchers, which have upward-curving duck's heads added at each of the ends (fig. 198).

Among the simpler designs is an example in the Berlin Museum which at first glance appears to be an ordinary camp stool but is actually a fine piece of craftsmanship (fig. 196). Instead of a plain joint between the stretcher and the leg, the wood of the lower part extends to meet the leg, which flares out at the end to make a flush joint. As a result, the

190

189 Side view of the chair in figure 188, showing the curved top-rail with moulding. *Eighteenth Dynasty*.

190 Box-shaped seat with solid sides decorated with a feather pattern. *New Kingdom*.

191 Scene of craftsmen making jewellery, seated on three-legged stools and four-legged stools with lattice bracing. *Eighteenth Dynasty*.

191

192 Stool with double cove seat and lattice bracing. *Eighteenth Dynasty.*

193 Stool with carved legs resembling turned work, ivory braces and inlay, and remains of a leather seat. *Eighteenth Dynasty.*

194 Low bench-like stool with a strengthening bracket running continuously from leg to leg. *Eighteenth Dynasty.*

195 Folding stool with legs terminating in duck's heads inlaid with ivory. *Eighteenth Dynasty.*

196 Folding stool with legs which flare out at the joints. *Eighteenth Dynasty.*

197 Folding stool with duck's heads used as terminals for the legs and stretchers. *Eighteenth Dynasty.*

198 Detail of duck terminals on the folding stool in figure 197.

195

196

197   198

parts appear to flow together like a natural growth, an effect which is accomplished by cutting away the wood of the stretcher so as to leave a smoothly carved extrusion where it joins the widened extremity of the leg. The technique involved extra work and served no structural purpose; but it was an attractive feature, and it demonstrates once more the conscious effort of the ancient Egyptian craftsman to achieve an aesthetic effect. A similar device adds interest to present-day chairs of the modern Danish school. The Metropolitan Museum also has an example of an ancient Egyptian stool with a well-preserved leather top which is made on the same principle although not quite so nicely executed as the stool in Berlin (fig. 199).

It is a curious coincidence that the only intact piece of wooden furniture of the Bronze Age ever discovered in northern Europe is similar in design (fig. 200). Discovered in Jutland and dated to approximately 1200 B.C., this is now in the National Museum in Copenhagen and raises the question as to whether there was some contact between Egypt and northern Europe at that time, or whether this is an independent creation and the resemblance only coincidental.

It is rather surprising that no example has been found of the stool with the bull's legs and projecting lotus-flower ornaments seen so often in reliefs of the Early Dynastic period and Old Kingdom and illustrated in Chapters 1 and 2. Considering the Egyptian adherence to traditional forms, it seems likely that these stools were used in the later periods also; but although they are an attractive and practical design they seem to have gone out of fashion in the Eighteenth Dynasty, and the chair has taken their place in the Middle and New Kingdom stelae. Stools with animal legs are found, but instead of the round projecting side-rails there is a framed seat and the legs are usually feline. One such stool has been illustrated in the Kha collection, and a number of others have been found, including one belonging to the Baker Museum for Furniture Research, which was originally covered in gesso and painted (fig. 201). The well-carved legs are braced with round stretchers; the covering, which was missing, has been restored in a similar material and woven in the same pattern as found in antique stools.

A similar stool in the Oriental Institute in Chicago has legs of a coarser design but with well-carved feet in which the claws are sharply outlined (fig. 202). In some instances,

137

199 **200**

however, the cruder stools merely suggest the shape of an animal leg, as in the example illustrated from Stockholm (fig. 203); the crude form, however, is not necessarily an indication of age, since well-carved animal legs were made long before this time. The form has special interest, nevertheless, because of its resemblance to the legs of tables found in an excavation at Jericho in Palestine which are dated approximately 1500 B.C. (Part II, Chapter 4). Examples similar to the Stockholm stool may also be found in both the Berlin and Cairo Museums.

Animal-type stools of later date occasionally have supports in the form of the fore and hind parts of a lion. One, which is in a private collection in the Netherlands, is elaborately carved and decorated (fig. 204).[7] The other, a partly restored example from the Saïte period, is in the Louvre and bears a resemblance to the Tutankhamun funeral couches in its use of the elongated animal body to form the sides (fig. 206). A carved support in the form of a lion with curved tail in the Brooklyn Museum was probably a part of a similar stool (fig. 205).

There were several versions of what we shall call the 'turned leg' type of stool, even though it is very doubtful whether the wood-turning lathe was actually in use in the Eighteenth Dynasty, as has been previously noted (see also page 303 below). A typical example, of which there are also a number in the Cairo Museum, is the one in the Metropolitan Museum with legs which are shaped inward in the lower section and flare out again at the bottom (fig. 207). This lower part is scored with fine lines which ring the turning, a feature found also in a squat heavy specimen from Berlin (fig. 208). The latter, however, has a bit of added interest in the flaring design at the ends of the stretchers where they join the legs. Much the same kind of stool, but with entirely plain round legs, was also made in this period. It was not until long after, however, during the Greco–Roman period, that the lathe and turned-leg furniture came into general use. Later, the designs are Grecian rather than Egyptian but, since they were actually found in Egypt and were no doubt made there, examples will be included. The members of the turnings are markedly different from the earlier shapes and resemble later European designs, as can be seen in the bench illustrated from Berlin (fig. 209) and in a well-preserved group of turnings of the second century B.C. from the Faiyum, now in the Kelsey Museum at the University of Michigan (fig. 210). A pair of earlier turnings of the usual type and some carved furniture supports in the Louvre (including a later carved Nubian figure) are illustrated in figure 211.

Among the stools that have survived are those that are strictly utilitarian of a rounded

138

201

202

203

199 An early example of a folding stool with flaring legs. *Twelfth Dynasty.*

200 Folding stool from Jutland. About 1200 B.C.

201 Stool with lion's legs, originally painted white. *New Kingdom.*

202 Stool with lion's paws with carefully carved claws. *New Kingdom.*

203 Stool with plain, shaped legs derived from an animal shape. *Middle Kingdom.*

shape. Some have heavy wooden tops supported by three roughly shaped out-curving legs like the work stools in the Kha collection and the example illustrated here from the Berlin Museum (fig. 212). There are others of this type also in the Cairo Museum. Another crude stool, with two thin pieces of wood in the shape of soles of feet attached to the top, apparently had a specialized function (fig. 213). The master in a rich household sometimes had a stone platform with a system of drains on which he stood while his servant poured water over him for a bath.[8] It appears likely that this wooden stand served the same purpose in a simpler home.

More often the ordinary ancient Egyptian stools have woven rush seats with square or rectangular legs like those on a plain low stool also in Berlin (fig. 215). Part of the woven seat still clings to its frame-rails. Sometimes the rectangular legs have a crude shaping, as in the Metropolitan example of the Seventeenth–Eighteenth Dynasty in figure 216, of which the coarse rush seat is almost intact.

A striking indication of the extent to which the simple rush-seat stool was used in the workshops and houses of the artisan class is seen in the photograph in figure 214. This well-preserved group of furniture was found by B. Bruyère in the tombs of the artisans at Deir el-Medina. In addition to two of the three-legged wooden stools and two crude chairs, there are seven simple rush-seat stools, probably the most widely used type of seating piece in the ordinary homes of ancient Egypt.

We should also comment on a type of cross-legged stool with carved feet frequently

204

205

206

207

204 Stool of late period with animal legs.

205 Furniture element carved in the form of a seated lion, possibly the leg of a stool. *New Kingdom* (?).

206 Stool with legs and side members in the form of complete lion bodies. *Twenty-sixth Dynasty.*

207 Stool with legs which give the appearance of having been turned. *Seventeenth–Eighteenth Dynasty.*

208 Squat stool with legs resembling turned wood. *Eighteenth Dynasty.*

209 Stool with turned legs of Greek character. *Ptolemaic period.*

210 Turned legs from stools of the Roman period in Egypt.

211 A group of legs from stools including two 'turned' pieces, with one in the form of a Nubian.

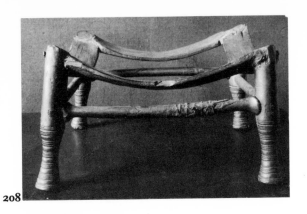

208

209

210

211

212

213

212 Rough three-legged stool with thick seat. *New Kingdom*.

213 Stool with special foot stands, possibly for use in a bath. *Late Period*.

141

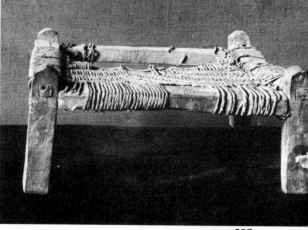

214 A collection of stools and a chair from the workmen's village and cemetery at Deir el-Medina. *New Kingdom.*

215 Simple stool with remains of the rush seat. *Nineteenth Dynasty.*

216 Simple stool with shaped legs and rush seat almost intact. *Seventeenth–Eighteenth Dynasty.*

represented in painted scenes in the tombs of the nobles, even though it is more elegant than most of the furniture included in this chapter. A similar stool has been illustrated in a relief from the Tutankhamun collection (fig. 104), but, although it is obviously a luxurious type, its use was not confined to the royal palace alone. That in figure 217 has special interest because of the close resemblance to the Chippendale ball-and-claw foot. No example of this type has survived, although they are often pictured, but, as has been noted earlier, what appears to be a ball is probably the end of the cross-bar ordinarily used on the cross-legged stools. The stool in figure 218 is similar in type, but somewhat more refined, and resembles the classic Greek stool in its proportions. The cushion in both cases is represented as a thin animal hide with the tail hanging over the edge of the seat.

Beds and chests

Beds and chests have been discussed in considerable detail in preceding chapters, and most of the usual types have been illustrated; so little more needs to be said. But although the beds shown come from various periods, covering nearly two thousand years, it should

217 218

217 Scene of a nobleman seated on a folding stool with animal legs. *Eighteenth Dynasty.*

218 Scene with a folding stool with animal legs, and covered with a hide seat. *Eighteenth Dynasty.*

219 Plain bed with linen coverings and a head-rest. Note the restored joint lashings. *Eleventh Dynasty.*

219

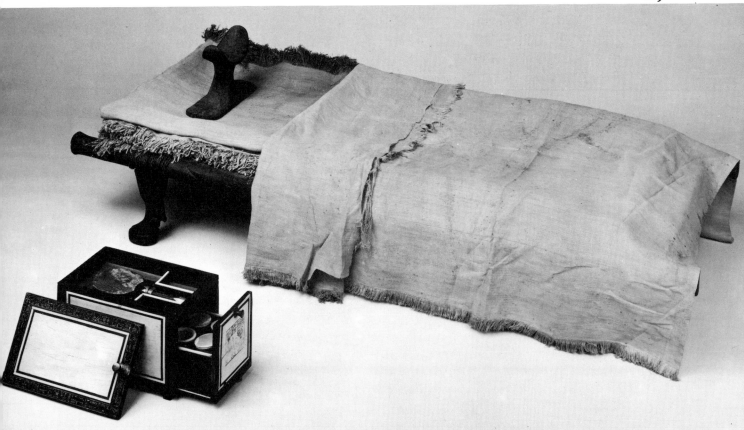

be noted that, with one exception, they all have animal legs. The exception is the representation of a bed with bent wooden supports in the drawings from the tomb of Hesy-Re (fig. 27c). Other types probably did exist but are not extant or represented in tomb paintings and reliefs.

During this long period, however, changes are apparent in the form of the animal legs used as bed supports. The earliest beds of which we have any record had heavy carved bull's legs. These were followed in the Third Dynasty by beds with legs of a more slender gazelle-like form with hoofs, judging from the Hesy-Re examples (fig. 27c). Soon after, in the Old Kingdom, the legs are of the feline type with a paw foot and claw (as has been noted previously in the bed of Queen Hetepheres and in that of Mereruka). From then on the lion's leg continues to be the type more generally used, as in the beds of Tutankhamun, although the primitive bull's leg also continues to appear until late in Egyptian history. An example in the Metropolitan Museum, New York, shows an Eleventh Dynasty bed which still has bull's legs and rounded rails, and is shown with contemporary coverings and head-rest (fig. 219).

There was little change in the general form of beds except that the foot-board is added in the Old Kingdom; and the rounded projecting side-rails of that time are replaced later by smoothly finished frame-rails of rectangular shape. The principal interest from the point of view of design occurs in the foot-boards, which vary in accordance with the amount of ornament and its character. An example from Kerma in the Boston Museum is interesting because of its unusual inlaid designs, characteristic of that part of Nubia in which the bed was found (fig. 220).[9] The foot-board is inlaid with three rows of small bone figures, of which a number of others were also discovered at the same location (fig. 221). It is not until much later, when the invention of the wood-turning lathe had brought turnings into common use, that beds with turned legs superseded the earlier types.

Two very simple storage chests are illustrated at this point, because of their personal associations and their contents (figs. 222, 224). These came from the tomb of Ramose and Hatnufer, the parents of Senenmut, favourite of Queen Hatshepsut, and architect of her great temple at Deir el-Bahari. One of the chests is a plain rectangular box with a flat lid made of heavy sycamore boards. The corners are dovetailed and there are sturdy battens underneath the bottom. The second has a double-pitched gable lid and stands on four short legs. Both chests were painted white and filled with sheets or bolts of linen, of which there were fifty-five, varying in length from fourteen to fifty-four feet, each folded in a neat rectangular bundle. The cloth varied from a coarse material like burlap, to a fine, filmy cambric, and ranged in colour from an almost pure white to medium brown. Clean, neatly ironed and folded, it most likely represented Hatnufer's supply of household linen. In spite of its thirty-four hundred years, it is so well preserved that it can still be folded and unfolded at will.

From these basic types an almost endless variety of chests was developed, many of which have previously been seen. Before we dismiss the subject, however, a few of the smaller boxes are shown which were used to hold the cosmetics essential to the toilet of the Egyptian lady as well as jewellery and other intimate possessions. Sometimes containing a mirror of polished metal, they held a variety of toilet necessities such as those found

Colour plate IX. Painted chest. *Eighteenth Dynasty.*

220

220 Bed from Kerma with an inlaid foot-board. *Twelfth Dynasty.*

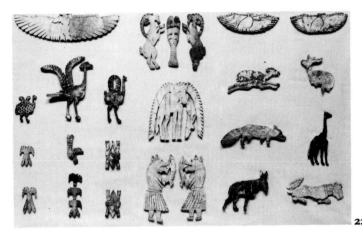

221 Ivory and bone inlays from the foot-boards of Kerma beds. They were partly cemented and partly pegged into position. *Twelfth Dynasty.*

221

in the well-preserved small chest on legs, originally from the tomb of Ani and now in the British Museum (fig. 223). This belonged to the lady Tutu, who lived about 1300 B.C., and some of the original contents can be seen in the photograph. The strange-looking apparatus at the top is a double-barrelled reed container for kohl, used freely as eye paint by Egyptian ladies. Below are divisions which hold jars of perfumed oils. The top and face of the chest have the usual knobs around which cords could be wound to make the lid secure. The design is slightly reminiscent of that of the simple chest with lattice bracing below already seen in the Tutankhamun furniture. Another small toilet chest is shown being carried to her mistress by a young servant girl (fig. 226).

Figure 225 illustrates a smaller painted box which is one of a pair discovered by Sir Gaston Maspero in 1886 in the tomb of Sennedjem and now in the Metropolitan Museum. One is inscribed for the "servitor in the place of truth"; the other is inscribed for his wife, the "house mistress Iy-neferti". The workmanship is rather careless and the painting hastily done, and it is likely that the boxes are funerary pieces painted to resemble inlaid work.

145

222

224

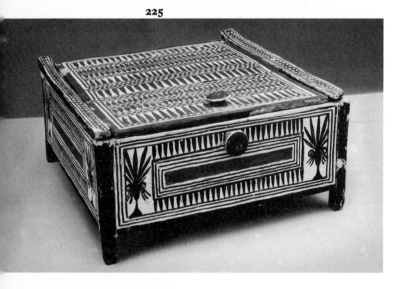

225

223

222 Storage chest with double pitched lid. *Eighteenth Dynasty.*

223 Tutu's toilet box of sturdy design and neat joinery. *Eighteenth–Nineteenth Dynasty.*

224 Rectangular storage chest of simple design. *Eighteenth Dynasty.*

225 Roughly constructed box painted to simulate inlay. *Nineteenth Dynasty.*

227

226 Figure of a servant girl carrying a storage chest on her head, the whole forming originally a cosmetic container. *Eighteenth Dynasty.*

227 Finely made fitted toilet casket with ivory and ebony veneer. *Twelfth Dynasty.*

226

The Louvre has an unusual example of a small chest or cabinet with a pair of hinged doors opening into a cupboard (fig. 228). Wooden bolts which slide through bronze loops are staggered above each other, a feature often pictured on the false doors of tombs but rarely seen on furniture. The legs splay out, a not unusual detail of Eighteenth Dynasty furniture, and the top has the traditional cavetto cornice and moulding. Two doors open from above to give access to the storage compartment.

It should be noted that besides jewellery and cosmetics the small boxes have yielded such diverse things as lichen, leaves, nuts, flint flakes, acacia thorns, scarabs, amulets, clay sealings, loose beads, shells, bits of resin, wax, pitch and pieces of aromatic wood – evidence that the urge to collect various odds and ends existed then as now.

Fortunately we are able to inspect two unusually fine toilet cases of the Middle Kingdom in the Metropolitan Museum. The first is the perfectly preserved small casket of the butler Kemu-ny, who lived in the time of King Ammenemes IV, 1796–1790 B.C. (fig. 227). It is constructed of many small pieces of cedar skilfully joined together and overlaid with panels of ivory and ebony. The lower part has a drawer divided into eight compartments to hold oil jars, and the upper section is fitted with divisions to hold Kemu-ny's mirror. As usual, the hieroglyphic text in the border of the top is not purely ornamental but is placed there to beseech favour for "the Real Familiar of the King, whom he loved, Royal Confidant in the Holy Place, giver of offerings to the Lord of the Two Lands, the Chamberlain and Butler Kemu-ny". The casket could be locked by means of a bolt that slides into a silver staple inside the drawer, in addition to being sealed

147

228

228 Storage chest with cupboard space below, the doors of which are fastened with bolts. *Late New Kingdom (?)*.

229 Reconstructed toilet casket of the princess Sit-Hat-Hor-Yunet, with fine panelled decoration. *Twelfth Dynasty*.

230 Shrine-shaped canopic chest with a sledge incorporated. *Eighteenth Dynasty*.

in the usual manner with cords lashed around the silver knobs on the lid and drawer front. The drawer construction with its overlapping front and narrower sides is a standard arrangement used today, and the workmanship is of the highest quality. The anhydrite jars illustrated at the side and bottom are also of the Twelfth Dynasty but come from another location.

Such cosmetic boxes were nearly always made of a fine grade of cedar, and sometimes veneered with ebony, ivory and boxwood. The finer ones are also decorated with faience, gold, silver or electrum. The second of the two Metropolitan examples contained the jewellery of the princess Sit-Hat-Hor-Yunet and more properly belongs to the category of palace furniture (fig. 229). Somewhat larger than the well-preserved casket of the butler Kemu-ny, this casket was mainly disintegrated when found, and what we see now is a restoration making use of the original ornamentation. Made in the traditional shrine shape, the piece was constructed of Sudanese ebony, adorned with elaborate panelling of ivory, gold, faience and cornelian, and mounted in gold and silver. Inlaid on the lid are four heads of the goddess Hathor, delicately outlined with gold and inlaid with faience and coloured stones. Originally there were four other small caskets belonging to the princess, two of which held wigs; the one illustrated contained most of her jewellery and also her mirror, her silver rouge dish and two sets of razors and whetstones.

Lest it be thought that all the cosmetic boxes in the Middle Kingdom in Egypt were so elaborate, it should be noted that the Metropolitan Museum alone has six undecorated boxes from middle-class tombs of the Eleventh to Thirteenth Dynasties at Thebes. These are nicely made of coniferous woods, sometimes covered on the outside with a coating of fine stucco. Space does not permit further pursuit of this subject, however, nor is there room to consider another somewhat related form of small box or casket – that used to contain the pieces used in the games of chance of which the Egyptians were very fond.

A third traditional box or chest is that provided in all important tombs to hold the

148

229   **230**

viscera of the mummy. Although these canopic chests were made only for funerary purposes, they exhibit features common to household cabinet-work. Consequently we show a typical canopic chest, which comes from the tomb of Ramose and Hatnufer (fig. 230). Since it is seldom possible to examine the small details of construction in these ancient pieces after they are safely locked in their museum cases, the interesting description of the intricate system of locking and other details by William C. Hayes, former curator of the Egyptian department of the Metropolitan Museum, is especially worthy of note.[10]

> Though uninscribed and undecorated, Hat-nufer's shrine-shaped canopic chest is one of the more interesting and certainly one of the best preserved examples of its time. A cubical wooden box one royal cubit, or about twenty inches, on a side, it is mounted on sledge runners and is topped by a shallow cavetto- and torus-cornice. To carry out its resemblance to a shrine the sides of the box slope very slightly inward and the lid has the rounded front and single pitch characteristic of shrine roofs. It is made throughout of heavy cypress planking and the corners of the box are dove-tailed. Ostensibly the lid was held in place by lashing the knob on its top to a similar knob on the front of the box. Actually it was locked in position by a concealed device involving projecting battens on the underside of the lid, L-shaped sockets in the tops of the box walls, and a self-operating tumbler lock near the front edge of both. The removal of what proved to be the outer lid of the chest revealed an inner lid set two inches below the rim of the box, and composed of two wooden valves, hinged vertically by means of cylindrical legs projecting from their outer edges into holes in the inner surface of the box walls. These two 'doors' rested on the two crossed partitions which divide the interior of the chest into four compartments, and were locked down by a boxwood bolt passed through wooden staples at the centres of their contiguous inner edges. The bolt is fitted with a small ebony tumbler which falls between the first and second staples when the bolt is shot home, thus preventing its removal. The chest is painted white inside and out, the paint on the exterior having been applied over a layer of fine linen cloth and stucco.

The last of the chests illustrated is made of reed and rush materials except for its knobs of ebony and ivory (fig. 231). Apparently this was a less expensive construction

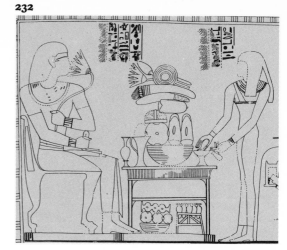

231 Toilet chest made of reed and rush, with elaborate lattice bracing. *Seventeenth Dynasty.*

232 Scene of offerings including a table, the top of which is in the form of a cavetto cornice. *Eighteenth Dynasty.*

than wood and was employed to a far greater extent in ordinary households than is indicated by the few examples illustrated. Woven baskets, also, were used for storage in place of the wooden chests, and small boxes of woven reed took the place of the more elaborate cosmetic chests of wood.

Tables

Next to the stool, the small table was probably the most common piece of furniture in ancient Egypt and is portrayed innumerable times in reliefs and paintings, usually holding food offerings. The ordinary person was content to squat on a mat after a hard day's digging in the field or working at his craft, but a crude box or table was no doubt used in quite simple homes for holding clay pots and other household utensils. But even though the table was commonly used in ancient times, relatively few have been found in tombs which have yielded a considerable number of chairs and stools. One reason so few have survived may be that the simple tables intended to receive offerings for the dead person were of necessity placed outside the inner burial chamber and consequently have disintegrated or were destroyed long ago. Fortunately, the few that do exist give proof that the representations in art are factual and not imaginary.

Dining in ancient times was very different from what it is today in the western world. There was no large central table at which people would be seated, and the custom then, as it is today in parts of the Orient, was to be served at individual tables, as seen in the painting from the tomb of Nebamun (fig. 232). Consequently, the tables were small and easily moved about. They seem also to have served the purpose of serving trays, as is indicated in the scene from the tomb of Meryre previously illustrated (fig. 164). In addition

233 Pair of Kha's rectangular tables. *Eighteenth Dynasty.*

234 Low rectangular tables with stretchers in a painting on a coffin. *Twelfth Dynasty.*

to their function as dining tables, they are often represented holding vases and jars and no doubt served many other household purposes.

Two types of tables emerge in the Early Dynastic periods. One, represented many times in Second Dynasty stelae, is the offering table with a round pedestal base and dish-like top, usually made of stone or earthenware. The other type, made of wood or reed, is rectangular in shape. In the Old Kingdom rectangular tables with straight legs and stretchers often appear in paintings and reliefs, as in tombs of Hesy-Re and Mereruka (see figs. 27 and 53), obviously the prototypes of the basic table still used today. These are represented innumerable times in later Egyptian art also, as in a painting dating from about 1900 B.C., the Twelfth Dynasty scene from El-Bersha in which they are depicted in varying sizes (fig. 234).[11] As is true of the household chair, however, our earliest actual examples of what was doubtless the most common form of table come from an Eighteenth

234

235   236

Dynasty tomb. One of a pair of such tables from the tomb of Kha has been illustrated in the preceding chapter, but because of the strong resemblance to those in the El-Bersha painting the two Kha tables are shown here together in a photograph taken shortly after the original discovery (fig. 233). The drawings in the painting resemble studies by a modern draughtsman, and the tables themselves could easily pass as cocktail tables used in present-day interiors. They are rough looking in their present condition, as will be noted in a more recent photograph (fig. 161), but when new and smoothly painted with bands of hieroglyphs on their tops, they must have appeared both functional and elegant.

More sophisticated but with a history almost as ancient is a type of table of which both the Brooklyn and Metropolitan Museums have good examples, with legs which splay out in a manner resembling the pylons flanking the gateways of Egyptian temples (figs. 235, 236). Another architectural feature, the cavetto and torus cornice, is a characteristic detail of Egyptian household furniture and frequently appears in the more elegant palace furniture as well. The Metropolitan table is skilfully made and joined together with pegged tenons, and an attractive detail is added in the form of thin strips of lighter coloured wood which run under the top-rails and along the edges of the legs, producing the appearance of a bead-moulding. The rounded corner where the leg and top frame meet is a feature which is sometimes repeated between the leg and stretcher also, and is one of the attractive details of Egyptian design. The resemblance of this table, and the one which follows, to those previously illustrated in the Mereruka reliefs is obvious (fig. 56). The well-preserved Brooklyn example is similar except that it does not have the curved bracket and the added strips of wood along the edges of the legs and underside of the aprons.

Among the variations found in this general type of table, those depicted in the rock tombs of El-Amarna are especially interesting. Drawings of a number of the tables represented here have been made directly from the tomb scenes by Davies, a few of the different types being illustrated in figures 238 a, b, c and d.[12] In each of the four in the upper part of the plate a centre leg is placed between the two outer ones. Since there was no practical need for this added support on a rectangular table, the natural inference is that the artist intended to represent round tables, unless it is another example of an Egyptian artistic convention in which the artist tried to convey an impression of two

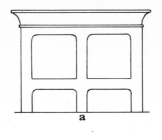
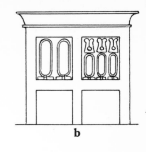

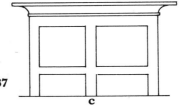
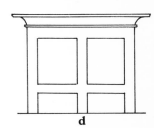

237

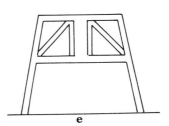
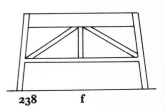

235 Table with splayed legs, in the form of a pylon. *Seventeenth–Eighteenth Dynasty.*

236 Pylon-shaped table similar to figure 235 but of simpler construction. *Eighteenth Dynasty.*

237 Three-legged table with painted top. *Eighteenth Dynasty.*

238 Types of table found in tomb scenes at El-Amarna. *Eighteenth Dynasty.*

238

sides. Evidence is lacking, however, of any such round tables of wood in Egypt. The other examples (figs. 238 e and f), with splayed legs and lattice bracing, are a type repeated many times in wall paintings and on papyrus rolls.

Two distinct variations in type are represented in a three-legged table and a small stand in the British Museum, each being a form of which we have no other examples. The table, which dates approximately to the time of the architect Kha, has the name of its owner Pa-per-pa inscribed on the top (fig. 237). Coated with gesso and painted, the top is decorated with a coiled figure of a cobra before an offering-table (the snake here represents the goddess Renenutet) (fig. 239). Underneath are two cross-battens and legs which splay outward, two at one end and a single leg at the other. Although the three-legged table does not seem to have been commonly used in Egypt, it had an advantage over the usual four-legged type, since it could stand firmly on uneven ground. Later, in the classic period in Greece, the three-legged table was the standard type used next to the banquet couch, and this British Museum example is significant as an early example.

The small stand mentioned has curving legs which open outwards at the top like petals to form a charming and unique holder for a small vase (fig. 241). Larger stands, or pedestals, were also used to hold single vases, as may be seen in another example in the British Museum (fig. 240). The latter type, which is one of the more frequently portrayed forms, is represented in the charming scene of the princesses from the tomb of Kheruef (fig. 243). These stands in the relief are more slender and the legs do not spread out as much, but the general design is similar. Like the British Museum stand, each is represented

153

239

239 Painting of the goddess Renenutet (represented as a cobra) with offerings and an offering-text on a table top. *Eighteenth Dynasty.*

240 Lattice-work pot stand, painted with bright colours. *Eighteenth Dynasty.*

241 Small stand with splayed members for holding a pot. *Eighteenth Dynasty.*

242 Lattice-work table in a tomb scene of the Twenty-sixth Dynasty.

240

241

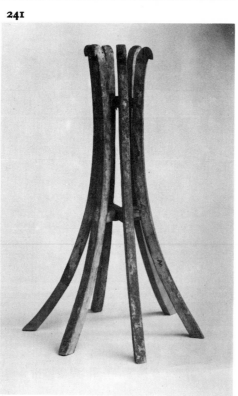

242

243 Tomb scene of princesses making offerings, including pairs of stands carrying vessels. *Eighteenth Dynasty*.

holding a vase. The use to which such tables are currently put can be seen in the Cairo Museum, where reproductions serve to hold the museum specimens of ancient ceramics. The table with splayed legs and a lattice-type of bracing is still represented late in Egyptian history, as is illustrated in the relief in figure 242 of the Saïte period (663–525 B.C.) from the Nelson Gallery, Kansas City.

155

During the early years of the nineteenth century, when interest in Egyptian sculpture and objects was aroused by illustrated accounts of travels in Egypt, Egyptian motifs were employed extensively in schemes of interior decoration, in garden ornamentation and, to a small extent, in furniture. This interest received a great impetus from Napoleon's expedition to Egypt, for it was from the time of this expedition that the country became readily accessible to European scholars. The resulting publications of Egyptian monuments and design details served as pattern-books and as the sources of inspiration for designers, and furniture was made incorporating Egyptian elements. Unfortunately, however, when carried to the extreme, the resulting work was sometimes flamboyant and vulgar – caricatures based on architectural and sculptural details rather than on actual pieces of Egyptian furniture. Some of these pieces of furniture are interesting as illustrations of the exploitation of a style, but as they are not unfamiliar to students of design, none will be illustrated here. Recently, however, a serious attempt has been made to adapt the ancient forms to modern use, as is illustrated in figure 245. Here the lattice-type framework, common in ancient Egypt for stools and tables, has been translated into metal and used for low tables, with considerable success. Although the design inspiration comes from ancient Egyptian furniture, the materials and technique are modern. As a result the presence of these adaptations in a modern building in Cairo does not seem incongruous, as can be seen in figure 244, which shows some of the furniture in its present setting.[13]

244

245

244 Tables and stools designed in the Ancient Egyptian style in a Cairo hotel.

245 A modern table based on ancient lattice-work tables.

PART II:
THE NEAR EAST

CHRONOLOGY—ANCIENT MESOPOTAMIA

The absolute chronology of Mesopotamia before *c.* 1500 B.C. is still a debated problem and several systems are concurrently used. It has been deemed convenient to follow in this book the system adopted by the Editors of the revised edition of the first two volumes of the *Cambridge Ancient History*, currently published in fascicules. This system is substantiated by M. B. Rowton in the chapter 'Chronology' (Vol. I, Ch. VI), Cambridge 1962, pp. 23 *ff*.

Proto-historic period:
3500–2800 B.C.

This comprises the archaeological building levels Uruk V, Uruk IV (which has yielded the earliest examples of written documents), Uruk III (also called Jamdat Nasr period), and Early Dynastic I.

Old Sumerian period:
2800–2370 B.C.

This comprises the Early Dynastic II and III periods and ends with the foundation of the first Semitic empire.

2680 Gilgamesh, king of Uruk.
2600 The Royal Tombs of Ur.
2550–2370 The dynasty of Ur-Nanshe at Lagash:
    2500 Eannatum, under whose reign, with writing now fully developed, historical records appear.
    2300 Urukagina, usurper and social reformer.
2370 Lugalzagesi of Umma and Uruk, last Sumerian king before the rise of the Akkadians.

Old Akkadian, or Sargonic, period: 2370–2230 B.C.

2370 Sargon I establishes Akkadian (Semitic) political supremacy.

2290 Naram-Suen, perhaps the first king to be deified during his lifetime, a practice which went on until the Old Babylonian period.
2250 Beginning of the Gutian invasion.

Neo-Sumerian period:
2230–2006 B.C.

2140 Gudea of Lagash, whose reign has witnessed a remarkable development of Sumerian art.
2120 Utu-hegal of Uruk puts an end to Gutian rule.
2113–2006 The Third Dynasty of Ur, the last manifestation of Sumerian political power:
    2113–2096 Ur-Nammu, founder of the dynasty and author of the earliest known code of laws.
    2095–2048 Shulgi, greatest of Sumerian kings.
    2047–2039 Amar-Suen.
    2038–2030 Shu-Suen.
    2029–2006 Ibbi-Suen, the last Sumerian king.

Old Babylonian period:
2017–1595 B.C.

2017–1763 Isin-Larsa Period:
2017–1794 Dynasty of Isin:
    1934–1924 Lipit-Eshtar, author of a code of laws.
2025–1763 Dynasty of Larsa:
    1822–1763 Rim-Sin, a king of Elamite origin and a rival of the great Hammurapi who finally put an end to his long, sixty-year reign.
1894–1595 First Dynasty of Babylon, also called the Hammurapi Dynasty:
    1792–1750 Hammurapi, the lawgiver.
    1749–1712 Samsu-iluna: beginning of the Kassite invasion.

1813–1781 Shamshi-Adad I, king of Assyria.
1595 Hittite raid of Babylon.

Middle Babylonian period:
1500–1000 B.C.

This period is dominated by the long rule of the Kassite Dynasty (1733–1157 B.C.).

Middle Assyrian period:
1500–1000 B.C.

Neo-Assyrian period:
1000–612 B.C.

883–859 Assurnasirpal II
858–824 Shalmaneser III
744–727 Tiglath-pileser III
726–722 Shalmaneser V
721–705 Sargon II
704–681 Sennacherib
680–669 Esarhaddon
668–627 Assurbanipal
612 Conquest of Assyria by the Babylonians and Medes.

Neo-Babylonian period:
1000–539 B.C.

728–722 and 688–648 Assyrian kings in Babylonia:
    728–727 Pulu (= Tiglath-pileser III)
    726–722 Ululaya (= Shalmaneser V)
    688–681 Sennacherib
    680–669 Esarhaddon
    668–648 Shamash-shum-ukin, rebel brother of Assurbanipal.
625–539 Chaldaean Dynasty:
    625–605 Nabopolassar
    604–562 Nebuchadnezzar II
    559–539 Nabonidus
539 Conquest of Babylon by the Persians.

Persian period: 539–331 B.C.

539–530 Cyrus II
521–486 Darius I
331 Conquest of Babylon by Alexander

I

SUMER: FURNITURE IN THE EARLY PERIODS
(c. 3100–c. 2370 B.C.)

The early history of civilization in the Near East, particularly in Mesopotamia, begins at about the same time as that of Egypt, possibly even earlier.[1] But unlike the Early Dynastic period in Egypt, from which actual examples of wooden furniture still exist, what remains of Early Dynastic Mesopotamian furniture is limited to a few fragments of ornamentation. In both cases furnishings were placed in the tombs of important persons at the time of the burials; but in Egypt the early tombs were protected by massive structures of masonry which still stand above the desert sand, whereas in Mesopotamia the tombs were constructed in a less permanent manner and the walls built of mud brick have mostly disintegrated and disappeared from the landscape. The rock-tombs which exist at Thebes and elsewhere in Egypt also had no parallel in Mesopotamia.

But there are other reasons to explain why no furniture has survived from ancient Mesopotamia, and chief among them is the difference in climate and natural environment. The tombs in Egypt were built beyond the reach of the annual flood waters of the Nile and were perpetually baked by the sun. In the Mesopotamian plain, on the other hand, the heavy annual rains brought about a dampness that caused the disintegration of the contents even though in some cases the tombs themselves have survived almost intact. Fortunately, however, our knowledge of ancient furniture in this area is not dependent on the few fragments that have survived. Even though actual examples of furniture are lacking, we have a vast number of representations of furniture in Mesopotamian seals and sculptures.

The ancient Near East (as the term is used here) includes Asia Minor, Syria, Palestine and Persia, as well as the Mesopotamian plain. Important discoveries pertaining to furniture have been made in all these areas, but, owing to the larger number of excavations in Mesopotamia and the great amount of material found there, our knowledge of the evolution of furniture design in the ancient Near East comes largely from this area. This presents us, however, with a much more varied and complicated picture than existed in Egypt. Unlike the Egyptians, who were united under the rule of a single king from the First Dynasty, the Mesopotamians and their neighbours congregated in cities with individual rulers who were frequently at war with one another, and political continuity was lacking. Mesopotamia also was dominated by a succession of peoples each of whom left its mark; nevertheless, in spite of this complicated ethnic and political background, there is a considerable continuity in the development of Mesopotamian design over a long period of time.

Chronologically, our discussion of the furniture of Mesopotamia, as well as of the other areas in the Near East, is divided into three main divisions: first, the Early Dynastic periods of Sumer, dating approximately from 3100 B.C. to 2370 B.C.; second, an era of about twelve hundred years, which begins with the Akkadian period and terminates with

159

the ending of the Kassite period about 1150 B.C.; and, third, the era which was dominated in turn by the Assyrians, the Babylonians and the Persians, and which may be considered to have ended with the invasion of Alexander the Great in 331 B.C. and the coming of the Hellenic influence.

Sumer, and the 'Royal Tombs' of Ur

The Sumerians were a non-Semitic people who, it is thought, probably some time during the fourth millennium B.C., moved into the southern part of Mesopotamia in an area called Sumer. There they developed a civilization centred in such important communities as Ur, Nippur and Lagash, which was a great advance over the primitive way of life that had previously existed. Sumerian civilization also flourished at Mari, in north-eastern Syria, although its population was not of Sumerian, but of Semitic stock. The art of writing was invented at an early date; temples and palaces were built; and furniture of reed and of wood appears to have been introduced at approximately the same date as that of the first furniture in Egypt. Shortly after the end of the First World War, British archaeologists began excavations at Ur in the area of ancient Sumer, and dramatic proof of the importance of this great early civilization came with the discovery of the so-called 'Royal Tombs' by Leonard Woolley in 1926–31.[2] It is true that these graves, some of which date from about 2600 B.C., yielded nothing comparable in the way of home furnishings to what was found in the tomb of Queen Hetepheres in Egypt, of about the same period, but they furnished scholars with sufficient new data to change the entire concept of the Mesopotamian past and have yielded tangible evidence of a high state of development of the arts and crafts of this ancient period in the Near East.

Although Egypt and Mesopotamia were geographically not far apart, there is no actual evidence of trade between them, and totally different cultures were developed. Nevertheless, the similarity of certain details in their furniture – such as the early use of the bull's leg as a design feature – indicates that some contact existed between the two areas even at this early period. This is, however, a subject for the archaeologist, and, regardless of what interchange of ideas actually did exist, the differences between their two cultures – not only politically, but also in the personal appearance of the people and in their arts – are more marked than the similarities. The Sumerians pictured in sculptures are very unlike contemporary Egyptians. The great beards, voluminous skirts and facial features of some of these early Mesopotamians appear strange compared with the Egyptians whose appearance is better known to us. Similarly, the art forms of the Mesopotamians are very different from those of the Egyptians, and in general are less well known in the western world.

Art objects revealed in the 'Royal Tombs' of Ur were unlike anything previously found in Mesopotamia – vessels of gold, silver and copper; jewellery; golden inlaid daggers; and head-dresses made of gold leaves and ornamented with lapis lazuli and cornelian. Among these treasures was a box-like object called the 'Standard of Ur', presumably carried in victory processions, which has a special interest for the student of ancient furniture (colour plate XII). In this there is a banquet scene of the 'king' and his

160   Colour plate X*a*. Procession to a tomb showing attendants carrying furniture. *Eighteenth Dynasty*.

b. Banquet scene. *Eighteenth Dynasty*.

246 Detail from the Standard of Ur, showing the king seated on a low back chair with animal legs. *Early Dynastic III*.

guests seated on stools with animal legs and entertained by two musicians. The animal legs are refined in design, and there is a well-balanced relationship between them, the vertical members at the side and the stretcher at the bottom. The seats probably were made of woven rush; the weaving of baskets was already well known, and cane and rush were frequently used in furniture. The 'king's' right arm appears to rest on a low back (fig. 246), whereas the seats of his guests are without backs. It is uncertain, however, whether this effect is intentional; the individual inlays are very small and this impression may be due to the difficulties of the restoration. The wooden background of the standard consisted of a panel about twenty-two inches long by nine inches high which had disintegrated entirely. Fortunately, the fact that the inlays of carved shell, lapis lazuli and coloured limestone had remained in their relative positions made possible the reconstruction of the mosaic, now one of the important treasures of the British Museum.

Various other articles made principally of wood had also been placed in the 'Royal Tombs', but the wooden parts of these had also completely disintegrated. There were traces of the 'queen's' bed, or bier, although the exact outline could not be discerned, and also of her clothes chest, about six feet long, which had been adorned with a mosaic in lapis lazuli and shell. Among the finer examples of the cabinet-maker's art were three harps of which it was possible to make restorations based on the ornamentation which remained. Although not furniture in the strict sense of the term, one is illustrated here because it represents a wooden piece of which the actual outlines could be discerned (fig. 248). The bull's head is covered with gold sheet hammered over a wooden core. The bandings on the side of the wooden sound box are of lapis lazuli, red limestone and shell. The wooden panels are of course restored but fortunately sufficient evidence remained to permit this to be done accurately. On the face of the sound box of one of the other lyres there were inlays of ivory which are of special interest as indications of the motifs used in the decoration of this period (fig. 247). Also found were two fine small lion heads in silver which Woolley surmised were ornaments of a throne, and a small set of mosaics which

161

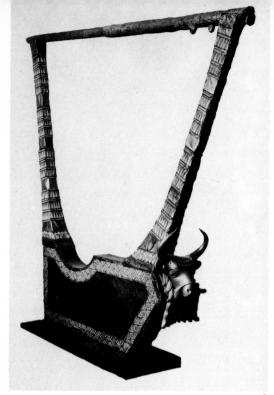

248

247 Ivory inlaid panel from the sound box of a harp. *Early Dynastic III.*

248 Gilded and inlaid harp from the 'Royal Tombs' of Ur. *Early Dynastic III.*

247

formed parts of a game box. Even though the finds that relate directly to furniture were few, they are indicative of the designs and materials used in ornamentation and are concrete evidence that a high degree of skill had been developed by the Sumerian craftsmen by the middle of the third millennium B.C.

Furniture depicted in cylinder seals

The discoveries made in the 'Royal Tombs' of Ur have been discussed first because they include the remains of actual furniture and related objects, as distinguished from representations in art. Dating from long before the time of these tombs, however, there are a large number of engraved cylinder seals on which representations of furniture of various sorts appear. These 'cylinder seals' are the most prolific source of knowledge we have of furniture of the early periods and convey a great deal of information, even though they are very small and the images are sketchy. Made of stone, and usually measuring between one and one-quarter to two inches long and approximately three-eighths to one-half inch in diameter (roughly the size of a little finger), the seals were skilfully engraved with religious and mythological scenes. Birds and beasts, as well as gods and human characters (often seated on chairs), are represented in considerable detail. As used originally, the seals were rolled on to the soft clay tablets bearing the cuneiform inscriptions, which served as documents, the resulting pattern serving as a personal signature.

249 Cylinder seal impression showing rectangular box-like stools. *Jamdat-Nasr period.*

249

250 Cylinder seal impression showing box-like stools with inner framed construction. *Jamdat-Nasr period.*

250

251 Cylinder seal impression showing a stool with animal legs. *Jamdat-Nasr period.*

251

252 Cylinder seal impression showing stool with straight legs and framed construction. *Early Dynastic III.*

252

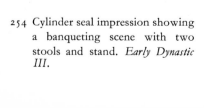

253 Cylinder seal impression showing a banqueting scene with three stools and a table. *Early Dynastic III.*

253

254 Cylinder seal impression showing a banqueting scene with two stools and stand. *Early Dynastic III.*

254

An amazing amount is told in these tiny engravings, and in them we have a history in miniature of furniture, particularly of seating pieces, from the prehistoric era in Mesopotamia to the late Assyrian period. It should be observed, however, that the original significance of the engravings was largely religious and social and that whatever they reveal of furniture is purely coincidental to the artist's primary intent. Great quantities of these cylinder seals survive from various periods within this era. For instance, the collection of the Morgan Library in New York, as illustrated in the work by Edith Porada, contains more than eleven hundred examples, of which about three hundred contain representations of some form of furniture.[3] A very large number of seals are included in the collection of the British Museum, and there are many more in the other museums.[4]

The seals which are illustrated, some twenty in all, have been selected to show the beginnings of furniture in the prehistoric era, from which no other representations exist, and to illustrate typical forms of the later periods. Exhaustive studies have been made by art historians of the engraving techniques employed and of the artistic and religious significance of the scenes portrayed, but to date no comprehensive study has been made of the furniture represented, and space does not permit this to be done here. There is a great deal of repetition in the forms of furniture depicted, but a definitive analysis of the entire corpus, made with this objective in mind, would no doubt throw further light on the question of chronological development.

Obviously these minute engravings do not give us a literal delineation such as we have in the Egyptian tomb paintings, which are factual representations. There can be no doubt, however, that they represented actual types, and the frequency with which chairs or stools appear would seem conclusive evidence that such seating pieces were in common use in Mesopotamia, at least by important people, from a very early period. Dating several hundred years earlier than the 'Royal Tombs' of Ur, the first of these seals comes from the later part of the fourth millennium B.C.

Among the most ancient of the cylinder seals are those in which 'pig-tailed figures' are portrayed. Dating from either the Jamdat-Nasr or the earlier Uruk period, these strange-looking figures are shown squatting or sitting on benches or stools of varying shapes and type of construction. The seals are roughly parallel in date to the beginning of the Egyptian First Dynasty (possibly earlier) and are evidence that in Mesopotamia, as in Egypt, the actual origins of furniture go back well before 3000 B.C. The earliest of these stools appear to have had a rectangular open box-like form (fig. 249) with the side sometimes filled in with a lattice construction. In a few instances there is an inner framed construction (fig. 250) where a cross-piece is indicated a short distance below the seat with short vertical supporting members between, a form repeated more clearly in seals of later dates.

A third of the 'pig-tail series' (fig. 251) shows the central figure seated on what Miss Porada describes as a stool with animal legs.[5] Although it may be argued that the image is too vague to permit such a conclusion, there are two things that support this assumption; first, the details of the legs of the stool resemble the legs of the animal at the right; and, second, the bull's leg was in common use by the end of the fourth millennium B.C. in Egypt, as is known from the carved ivory and wooden legs found in the excavations

255 Cylinder seal impression of the so-called 'temptation seal' showing two open frame stools. *Post-Akkadian.*

255

of tombs dating from the First Dynasty. And later, in Sumer, seats with bull's legs are clearly depicted in the mosaics of the 'Standard of Ur'. Although there may be a tendency to read into these early seals more than existed in reality, it is quite likely that they fail to represent adequately the variety of seating pieces that were in use by the beginning of the third millennium B.C. Unfortunately, however, no evidence exists in any other media from so early a period in the Near East.

The furniture and scenes depicted are more clearly defined in the seals which follow, dating from about 2600 B.C. In the first of these (fig. 252) the stool represented has a framed construction with straight legs and two horizontal stretchers, rather than an open box-like form usually seen in the early representations. Between the seat, which is curved and slopes downward, and the upper stretcher, there is a vertical supporting member. There is also the suggestion of a rudimentary back, and the design shows a considerable degree of sophistication. Even though there is no indication in these sketchy representations, it is quite likely that such pieces may have been well joined and smoothly finished. Probably the pieces intended for royal use would have been skilfully made, while the seats used by ordinary persons would have been more roughly constructed.

In an interesting Early Dynastic seal from the University Museum in Philadelphia (fig. 253) three types of stools are represented, as well as a table or altar. The furniture appears to be constructed of small branches of trees or roughly rounded pieces of wood; but the technique with which the seals are engraved may be responsible for this impression; it is hardly likely that so delicate an instrument as the large harp portrayed at the lower right would have been as crudely made as it appears to be. The two stools in the upper register have an interesting profile, with bowed stretchers on the side. (That at the left has two unidentifiable objects under the seat which give the illusion of the balls used to ornament English Regency chairs of the early nineteenth century, although the existence of such detail in this instance is, of course, most unlikely.) The altar, or table, at the lower left also gives the impression of naturally round pieces joined together, and representations in other contemporary seals indicate that this may have been so. The animal enclosures which appear frequently resemble the framework of the altar and are obviously constructed of small round poles.

A similar piece of furniture is shown in a convivial scene (fig. 254) where there are two facing seated figures, each raising a beaker, with an attendant between. Miss Porada has called this piece a sideboard,[6] and it appears that such pieces were used both for

165

altars and for household purposes. One of the stools has several vertical supporting pieces at the side – a detail which should be noted, since it is repeated many times in the seals and sculptures of later periods. The number of these vertical supports, as well as their arrangement, varies considerably, and in some instances they are placed so closely together that they appear to form a continuous side panel. The other stool in the engraving has a bracing of crossed pieces in the side, as does the table.

Occasionally the stools pictured have a plain square open frame, as in the famous 'temptation seal' from the British Museum (fig. 255).[7] Although this is dated eight hundred or more years later than the 'pig-tailed' seals, the stools depicted possibly represent the earliest primitive form. Usually, however, the open-frame stools shown contain lattice-work or other detail in the side panels that would serve as bracing as well as ornamentation.

Although some imagination is required to give substance to the rather impressionistic portrayals of furniture in the early cylinder seals, it is certain that the furniture-makers of the time had already developed a variety of seating pieces. The method of construction of these pieces, however, can only be a matter of conjecture for the present, since there is no direct evidence. Where cane and reed materials were used, one might logically expect to find wrapped or lashed joints or a woven construction, since the technique of basket-making was well known. In the case of wood furniture there is no reason to doubt that the mortise and tenon joint was known here as well as in Egypt, since the woodworking craft appears to have developed in the two areas at about the same time.

Furniture represented in sculpture

To supplement the evidence of the seals there are also a few sculptures of the period in which furniture is portrayed. Among these are two seated figures, dating from the first half of the third millennium B.C., which are part of the remarkable collection of sculptures in the round from Mari in the Louvre.[8] For the most part the sculptures from Mari are standing figures, but in a few instances the subjects are seated, as in the example (fig. 256) where a woman, perhaps a goddess, is depicted on a chair which rather resembles that of the 'king' in the 'Standard of Ur' (fig. 246). In each of the chairs there is an animal-type leg in the front with supporting vertical members at the side and a stretcher beneath. The front legs of the chair in the sculpture, however, are elongated so that they appear to serve as part of the arm-rests, and the seat is dropped below – an interesting feature of which we have no other example.

The second of the Mari sculptures illustrated represents a person known as the steward Ebih-il, who is depicted wearing a typical Sumerian fleece skirt (fig. 257). He sits on a slightly concave round hassock which is apparently a basket-like construction of woven reed, many varieties of which were available from the marshes of southern Mesopotamia. There is sound evidence that stools and chairs of reed or cane were made at a very early period, even if they did not precede those made of wood.

An interesting form of stool is represented in a white stone plaque of about 2700 B.C., from the temple of Inanna at Nippur, and now in the Iraq Museum in Baghdad (fig.

256 Stone statue of a woman seated on a chair with animal
legs. *Early Dynastic III.*

258). The stools pictured have heavy straight legs, with a vertical support of vase-like
shape between the cross-stretcher and the seat, all of which suggests a wood construction.
The harp represented is ornamented with a bull's head like that of the harp found in the
'Royal Tombs' at Ur. In another plaque, from Khafaji, we see a fierce-looking
personage seated on a stool with a series of narrow vertical strips on the side which
appear to support the seat (fig. 260). This form, which appears in Mesopotamia both in
seals and in sculpture, has an interesting parallel in an Egyptian stela of approximately the
same date, that of Menka-Heqet from Helwan (fig. 21). The vertical markings in the
Khafaji plaque appear little more than lines scratched in plaster, but a sculpture of later
date illustrated in the next chapter (fig. 272) suggests that the side of such a stool would
be composed of a series of narrow wooden strips.

In contrast to these simple forms there is the throne reserved for royalty and the gods,
which is ornamented with a lion in the side panel, and which is represented in the fine
statue of the goddess Inanna from Susa (fig. 259). Although this is dated rather later and
comes from south-west Iran rather than Mesopotamia proper, the costume of the goddess
is similar to those pictured in the preceding illustrations, and the sculpture comes from a
locality which had long been dominated by the Sumerians. It is interesting to note that
here again we have a parallel in Egypt, dating from about the same period, in the throne
of Queen Meresankh III (fig. 46).

Except for a few instances where a table appears in the scenes engraved on the cylinder
seals, the furniture portrayed in Early Dynastic Sumerian art consists almost exclusively
of stools and chairs. There is clear evidence, however, that other types of furniture
existed at an early period. Mention has previously been made of the traces of a bed and
a clothes-chest found in one of the 'Royal Tombs' at Ur, and beds, as well as other furniture, are mentioned frequently in the cuneiform records from this and later periods.

258

257 Stone statue of the steward Ebih-il seated on a hassock. *Early Dynastic III.*

258 Stone plaque showing a banqueting scene with two straight-legged stools. *Early Dynastic III.*

259 Stone statue of the goddess Inanna seated on a throne which is ornamented with a lion in the side panel. *Second half of 3rd millennium B.C.*

260 Fragment of a stone plaque showing a figure seated on a stool. *Early Dynastic III.*

257
259

260

2   FROM THE AKKADIAN PERIOD TO THE END OF THE KASSITE PERIOD

(c. 2370–c. 1150 B.C.)

The twelve centuries from *c.*2370 to *c.*1150 B.C. in the Near East, although considered together in this chapter, were characterized by numerous cultural cross-currents as a succession of invaders struggled for supremacy in the Mesopotamian plain. During this long era, which includes the Akkadian period, the Neo-Sumerian or Ur III period, the Old Babylonian period and the Kassite period, each group left its distinctive stamp on the period dominated by it.[1] In spite of these cross-currents, however, there is a recognizable continuity in Mesopotamian design throughout the era, for, while each of the dominant cultures introduced its own peculiar styles and customs, each also contributed to the perpetuation of the basic Mesopotamian motifs, in furniture as well as in the other arts.

Furniture represented in seals

As was true of the Early Dynastic Sumerian period, the cylinder seals are an important source of information regarding the various types of seating pieces in use during this period. The Sumerian influence continues to be seen in a high proportion of the seals, and the earlier traditional furniture forms are often repeated, but variations and new types also develop. Among the most numerous of the stools depicted in the Akkadian and Neo-Sumerian seals are those in which a box-shaped open frame has its side panel divided into smaller square or rectangular sections. These small sections vary in number and form a trellis-like design that was one of the most popular styles of the time, if one may judge from the frequency with which it is represented. Although only three examples are illustrated here, the type appears innumerable times in many variations.

The first of the lattice-type stools illustrated has six almost square sections in the side (fig. 261). In the second example, there are nine divisions (fig. 262), and in other instances four, twelve, or sixteen sections are indicated. Usually these sections are approximately equal in size, but in the third example illustrated the irregularity of the spacing

261 Cylinder seal impression showing a lattice-type stool with six sections in the side. *Old Akkadian period.*   169

suggests that such a stool would have been constructed of cane and reed, materials frequently used in the ancient world (fig. 263). In the case of stools depicted on other seals, where the parts are heavier and the sections are few, it seems probable that they were of a normal wood construction.

The seats with a grid pattern in their sides have especial interest, not only because of the frequency with which they appear in the seals of the period, but also because of the resemblance to a construction popular in Iraq today. This occurs in chairs called *kursi jireed*, which are often seen in the village coffee-shops near Baghdad and Babylon. These chairs are constructed from the spiny part of the fronds of date palm trees, which is strong and lends itself to a kind of cage construction. The smaller end sections of the spine are used for the vertical members and are inserted through holes in the heavier horizontal pieces. The latter come from the thicker part of the palm frond, and are only partially dried so that they tighten up on the vertical pieces as they dry out, and form a fairly rigid and durable construction. Crates to hold vegetables and fruit are made in the same manner and it seems likely that we have here an example of a craft that has continued with little change for more than four thousand years. The seats of the chairs are made of woven rush – a craft known from prehistoric times.

Among the other versions of the box-type seat are those with one or more inner rectangles, or squared arches, in the side panel (fig. 264), a form more fully developed in the sculptured stools such as those in figures 274 and 277. There is also the formal throne with the lion motif in the side panel, of which we have an example in the seal which portrays a goddess, possibly Ishtar (fig. 265). This somewhat resembles the Sumerian throne illustrated in the preceding chapter (fig. 259), but here there are two lion figures depicted back to back in profile. The lower part of the frame extends forward as if to form part of a dais, a feature frequently seen in the more formal seats.

Among the Akkadian seals are two which are of especial interest as an indication that the cross-leg stool was known at this early period (figs. 266, 267). The question might be asked, because of the condition of the seals, whether these are factual representations. Later, however, in a clay plaque of the Old Babylonian period, a similar form of stool is clearly depicted (fig. 279), and it appears that the prototype for this form of seat dates to the Akkadian period. If so, it is possible that the use of this form in Mesopotamia antedates its appearance in Egypt, where it does not appear to have been used until the Middle Kingdom. Also, in one of these seals (fig. 267) we see the forerunner of a table later to become the most popular type of the Assyrian period.

The chair in the Akkadian seal illustrated in figure 270 is one of the earliest examples in which the curving back appears, used here in association with the lattice-type base. The roll at the top is a typical Near East feature seen more fully developed in a plaque of a later period (see fig. 275). A similar curve of the back in an exaggerated form occurs in the chair represented in figure 271, but the combination of detail in this piece is so bizarre it seems likely that this is the product of the artist's imagination rather than a realistic representation of a form that actually existed. Another curious feature in this strange-looking chair is the placement of the heavy carved bull's leg at the back of the seat, without a corresponding carved leg in front. Regardless of how factual the portrayal

262

263

264

265

266

267

268

269

262 Cylinder seal impression showing a lattice-type stool with nine sections in the side. *Old Akkadian period.*

263 Cylinder seal impression showing a lattice-type stool with irregular sections in the side. *Old Akkadian period.*

264 Cylinder seal impression showing a box-type seat with squared arches in the side panel. *Ur III period.*

265 Cylinder seal impression showing a goddess, perhaps Ishtar, seated on a throne with heraldically crossed lions on the side panel. *Old Akkadian period.*

266 Cylinder seal impression showing a cross-leg stool. *Old Akkadian period.*

267 Cylinder seal impression showing a cross-leg stool and a cross-leg table. *Old Akkadian period.*

268 Cylinder seal impression showing one stool with rounded legs and a single stretcher, and another stool without a stretcher. *Old Akkadian period.*

269 Cylinder seal impression showing a stool with a fringed cushion. *Old Babylonian period.*

270 Cylinder seal impression showing a curved back chair with lattice-type base. *Old Akkadian period.*

271 Cylinder seal impression showing the King Ur-Nammu seated on a curved back throne. *Ur III period.*

may be, however, it gives evidence of the use of two typical Mesopotamian details – the bull's leg and the sharp turn which terminates the chair back.

In the seals of the Old Babylonian period the simple wooden stool with rounded legs and a single stretcher appears so frequently it seems probable that this was the seat most generally used at this time, although it also appears on seals of an earlier period, such as figure 268. The stool which is pictured at the left, in a well-preserved engraving, has legs which swell out at the top and bottom, with a slender neck between. The other stool in this scene has heavy plain legs without a stretcher. In a number of the seals what appears to be a cushion with a deep fringe or woven skirt is added to the conventional plain wooden stool (fig. 269).

Furniture represented in sculpture

Although sculptured representations of furniture are not numerous in this era, the ones that we do have give valuable information about the development of traditional types, and also present some new forms. In a relief of the early second millennium B.C. the Sumerian influence is clearly apparent in the series of vertical strips which form the side of the stool (fig. 272). In most instances where this motif has been seen previously, as in the relief from Khafaji (fig. 260), there is no indication of the construction that may have been used in the pieces represented. In this example, however, the details of the relief suggest that the seat is supported by narrow wood pieces joined tightly together in some manner.

172

Mention has also been made previously of the box-type seat seen in the seal engravings which has one or more inner rectangles or squared arches. The ultimate development of this form appears in the fine stela of Ur-Nammu, the first king of the third dynasty of Ur (c. 2113–2096 B.C.), now in the University Museum in Philadelphia (fig. 274).[2] The king stands before the god, who sits on a handsome throne with a concave seat, its side-rail terminating at each end in a sharp curve, or finial. On the side of the seat there is a series of rectangular arches, one inside the other, which is possibly intended to represent the recessed entrance of a palace façade of the period.

A very different type of stool from anything seen in the earlier examples is represented in the well-known statue of Gudea, the ruler of Lagash during part of the twenty-second century B.C. (fig. 273).[3] This impressive sculpture, one of the remarkable collection in the Louvre portraying this ruler in various poses, shows him seated on a stool with a thick seat supported by heavy rounded splay legs joined by a strong stretcher. The same form of leg which curves outwardly and swells at the bottom continues to be seen in Meso-potamian furniture as late as the Assyrian and Neo-Babylonian periods.

The chair with a back, of which we have seen a suggestion in the cylinder seals, also appears in the sculptured reliefs of the late third millennium B.C. A relief which dates from about the time of Gudea in the Neo-Sumerian Period depicts a low-back chair ornamented with a carved lion's head (fig. 275). The side-rail of the seat dips slightly in the centre and curves up in a smooth line to join the back, and the seat-rail and legs appear as if they may have been tenoned together. The Egyptian chairs of this period were constructed with mortise and tenon joints, and it would seem certain that the Meso-potamians were familiar with this construction also, in view of other similarities that appear in the furniture of the two areas. The lion's head which ornaments the top of the front leg is obviously akin to what appears in contemporary Egyptian design, and this resemblance suggests that the head was carved of wood and gilded as in the Egyptian examples. It is possible, however, that such an ornament may have been made of metal, since similar ornamental parts of silver and gold were found in the 'Royal Tombs' of Ur, and many made of bronze have been found from later periods. Whether the leg itself was straight or carved in the form of an animal leg (as seems more likely in this instance) is, unfortunately, only a matter of conjecture, since this part of the relief is missing.

Less sophisticated in design, but important as one more example of a conventional chair, is the one that appears in a small plaque (fig. 276) of approximately the same date as our last example. The shape of the back is reminiscent of the curving backs seen in the seals, and the plaque gives additional evidence that the chair with the back was already fully developed, even though the stool was the seating piece most commonly used.

There is a repetition of what may be called the architectural motif in the stool depicted in the stela of Hammurapi, King of Babylon in the eighteenth century B.C. (c. 1792–1750), in which he is portrayed receiving his famous code of laws from the seated god (fig. 277).[4] Here we have again a series of squared arches, diminishing in size, as was previously seen in the more elaborate seat of Ur-Nammu (fig. 274). Also from approximately the same period come three interesting and attractive plaques which depict more ordinary kinds of stools.

Although the cross-leg type of stool is suggested in the earlier seals, it is much more

272 Stone relief showing a stool with vertical strips on the side. *Old Babylonian period.*

273 Diorite statue of Gudea seated on a stool with splayed legs. *Gutian period.*

274 Stela of Ur-Nammu showing a throne with squared arches. *Ur III period.*

272   273

274

clearly portrayed in the Old Babylonian plaque illustrated in figure 279. In this instance the stool on which the harpist is seated obviously represents the folding type, as is indicated by the rope stretched between the bottom of the legs to keep them from spreading farther. The resemblance between this piece and the cross-leg stools of the Eighteenth Dynasty in Egypt is not unexpected, perhaps, but an extraordinary resemblance also exists to a folding stool dated about 1200 B.C. that was found in Jutland – the only intact ancient wooden piece of this era ever found in Northern Europe, and now in the Copenhagen Museum (fig. 200). In both the Babylonian and the Jutland pieces the legs swell out in the centre where they cross and also again at the bottom. In the Jutland stool, however, there are runners beneath as in the ancient Egyptian stools, whereas in the Babylonian plaque the legs of the stool rest directly on the ground, the rope probably being attached to cross-stretchers.

174

A unique plaque which represents a carpenter at work is especially interesting from the woodworking point of view (fig. 280). Using an adze, the universal woodworking tool of antiquity, he is working on what appears to be a roughly shaped piece of wood. He sits on the typical plain stool with cross-stretcher, and the seat, probably made of rush, is framed within heavy rounded rails. The legs, which are likewise rounded, have a larger square section or knob at the top where the side-rails join. In another plaque, which portrays a seated harpist, a similar stool appears with markings on the side-rail where the strands of the woven rush seat would be attached (fig. 281). Although ordinarily the simple four-legged stool is represented with a stretcher, in rare instances it is omitted.

The repetition of traditional forms which we see in the art of this period continues until late in Mesopotamian history. But, although we may conclude that certain types of furniture remained popular over long periods of time, it is also evident that in some instances the repetition of a traditional form is symbolic and probably has little or no relationship to the furniture actually used at the time.

A conspicuous example of such a repetition occurs in a stone tablet of *c.* 870 B.C. which commemorates the restoration of the temple of Shamash at Sippar (fig. 278). Chronologically the sculpture does not belong in this chapter, but the sun-god and his costume, the ring-and-staff symbols and the bull-men on the side of the throne are all archaic features characteristic of the third millennium B.C. The frame of the throne shows the influence of the later period, but the general form is similar to that of the throne of the goddess in figure 265, while Shamash and his symbols are almost the same as they appear in figure 274, where Ur-Nammu stands before the seated god.

As in the Early Sumerian period, the furniture types represented in sculptures and seals of this era consist chiefly of stools and chairs, and only rarely is there a suggestion of a table, even though tables were commonly used. But although beds are not ordinarily depicted in these media, tomb excavations have uncovered a considerable number of small clay models of beds such as that of the Old Babylonian period (fig. 282). These give us little specific information regarding design, but the markings on the top indicate the pattern of the matting or cording that was used. Other such models include one from Ur. The terracotta model of a bed (fig. 283) and the clay model of a chair (fig. 284) were both found in an unstratified area of Ur, but it is probable that they date from the Isin–Larsa period (*c.* 2017–1763 B.C.). The ornamentation of the chair back is of especial interest.

In the literature of the era, however, there is ample evidence of the existence of beds, together with specific references to their materials and decoration. For example, *a bed of boxwood with slender claw feet* is mentioned in a list of household objects from the pre-Akkadian period (about 2380 B.C.);[5] *a bed of apple-wood with (legs) ending in bull's feet (and) copper mountings* is listed in an inventory dating from the Neo-Sumerian period (about 2100 B.C.);[6] and *one bed of boxwood, overlaid with silver, one bed likewise of boxwood* is listed in an inventory of the Middle Babylonian period (about 1400 B.C.).[7]

Many similar references to beds and other pieces of furniture occur, and recently a comprehensive study of the literature referring to furniture in Ancient Mesopotamia has been published by Professor Armas Salonen of the University of Helsinki.[8] In one of the

275   **276**   **277**

275 Fragment of a terracotta plaque showing a woman seated on a chair with curved back. *Ur III period.*

276 Small plaque showing a chair with curved back. *Ur III period.*

277 Stela of Hammurapi showing the sun god seated on a throne with squared arches in its side panel. *Old Babylonian period.*

278 Stone tablet showing the sun god seated on a throne with heraldic bull-men on the side panel. *Neo-Babylonian period.*

279 Terracotta plaque showing a harpist seated on a cross-leg stool. *Old Babylonian period.*

280 Plaque showing a carpenter using an adze. *Old Babylonian period.*

281 Fragment of a terracotta plaque showing a harpist seated on a stool with woven rush seat. *Old Babylonian period.*

278

279

280

281

charts in this scholarly work fifty-five individual pieces of furniture are listed according to the materials of which they were made, mostly cited from documents of the Ur III period at the end of the third millennium B.C. In addition to the woods previously mentioned in the quotations above, tamarisk, plane tree, citron, apple and other varieties, including imported woods, are listed. It is also noteworthy that, in this list, beds outnumber the other types of furniture.[9] Elsewhere, in the many other ancient documents quoted by Professor Salonen, there are references to gold, silver, bronze, lapis lazuli, ivory and other materials used as furniture ornamentation, as well as materials used for cushions and bed coverings.

177

282

283

284

282 Clay model of a bed. *Old Babylonian period.*

283 Terracotta model of a bed. *Isin–Larsa period*

284 Clay model of a chair. *Isin–Larsa period.*

Although the comparative numbers of the different types of furniture mentioned in this chart do not mean that these types actually were used in this same proportion, it is interesting that twenty-seven beds are listed as compared with eighteen stools and ten tables. The predominance of stools and chairs in the scenes in the seals and sculptures is due, of course, to their function as seating pieces for the gods and personages portrayed. It is only in the first millennium B.C., when the rulers of Assyria and Babylonia wished to make a record of the tribute received from their conquered enemies, that furniture was depicted for its own sake.

As to the design changes that occurred in the Kassite period, the record is obscure. The furniture represented in the cylinder seals is mostly a repetition of that seen in the Old Babylonian and earlier periods, and representations in sculpture are so rare that no valid conclusions can be drawn as to what may have been the prevailing fashions of the time. But even though the traditional forms doubtless continued to be used, it is probable that the increased contact with Egypt and Syria largely influenced the changes which occurred during this period.

Strong as was the influence of tradition in Mesopotamia, it did not dominate furniture design to quite the same extent as in Egypt, and as a result there is rather more variation in the details of the furniture depicted in the arts of the early periods in Mesopotamia than in Egyptian furniture prior to the New Kingdom, judging by the seating pieces which are represented. This variety is somewhat obscured, however, because of the different media in which the stools and chairs chosen for illustration were originally depicted. Consequently, in order that the different forms developed in Mesopotamia can be compared more readily, a number of the pieces previously illustrated are rendered in line drawings, to approximately the same scale, and arranged in chronological sequence (fig. 285). Although not all-inclusive, this chart will serve both as a summary of the more prominent types of seating pieces that existed before the Neo-Assyrian period and as an introduction to those that followed.

178

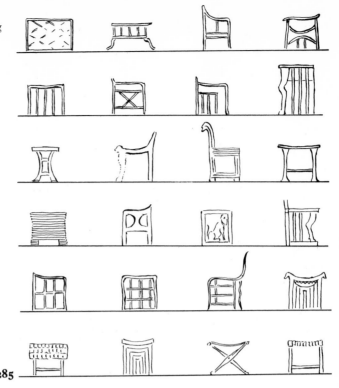

285 Chronological development of the seating
piece in Mesopotamia.

285

3   THE ASSYRIAN AND NEO-BABYLONIAN
PERIODS IN MESOPOTAMIA
(c. 1350–539 B.C.)

During the course of the Assyrian era new types of furniture appeared, particularly in the
Neo-Assyrian period of the ninth to seventh centuries B.C. when the kings of Assyria
were at the height of their power. But although we call this furniture Assyrian, its design
was the result of various cultural influences as was true in the earlier periods. The
Kassites continued to rule southern Mesopotamia, including Babylonia, for two hundred
years after Assur, the homeland of the Assyrians, asserted its independence in the north,
about 1350 B.C.,[1] and Babylon remained the spiritual and cultural centre of Mesopotamia
for a long period of time. And even after the Assyrians established their supremacy over
Mesopotamia and the surrounding areas, they were in frequent conflict with the Babylonians until, in turn, the Babylonians and their allies conquered Nineveh in 612 B.C.
In spite of their political difficulties, however, the two countries exerted a strong cultural
influence on each other; and, in addition to the Babylonian influence, the furniture depicted in Assyrian art reflects the exposure to the arts of Syria and other neighbouring
countries.

The first five hundred years of independent Assyrian history are what may be called

179

the dark ages as far as factual representations of furniture are concerned. We have incontrovertible evidence, however, from an outside source, that the furniture of contemporary Egypt was not unknown in Mesopotamia, at least in Babylon, in the fourteenth century B.C. The rulers of Babylon had received gifts from the kings of Egypt consisting of chairs and beds of ebony ornamented with gold, which are described in the cuneiform tablets found at El-Amarna in Egypt (see pp. 60–61). Elaborate furniture of this sort was certainly known to the Assyrians, and we may assume that the craftsmen who were capable of building and adorning the great palaces of Mesopotamia were also able to build suitable furniture of their own.

What effect this Egyptian furniture may have had on the design of Assyrian furniture is not apparent; possibly it was considered a 'foreign style' and had little or no stylistic influence. Probably the furniture taken as booty by the Assyrian kings or received as tribute from neighbouring nations had a more direct effect, and it seems appropriate first to take note of some of the written records in which furniture received as booty or tribute is mentioned. Assurnasirpal (883–859 B.C.) gives a list of spoils taken to his palace, among which are "chairs of ebony and boxwood".[2] Elsewhere, referring to tribute received from the land of Bit Adini in Syria, he mentions "chairs of ivory overlaid with silver and gold".[3] Sargon II (721–705 B.C.), in the account of his campaign against Urartu to the north, gives a list of the booty taken, among which is "one bed (with) silver frame, the god's own resting place, set with precious stones and gold".[4] Frequent mention is also made in the kings' lists of ivory furniture and furniture inlaid with ivory received from Syria.[5]

Such furniture no doubt became part of the palace furnishings, but to what extent furniture from abroad affected the design of that actually made in Assyria it is not possible to state precisely, and the influence of Assyrian design on the peripheral areas was probably far greater. Obviously the pieces referred to specifically, such as the ones above, are those that were considered most valuable. Likewise, most of the furniture that appears in the palace bas-reliefs is that considered worthy of being recorded for posterity. But, even though the emphasis is on the more elaborate furniture, inferences can be drawn about changes in furniture in general.

Signs of these changes occur also in the cylinder seals of the Assyrian and Neo-Babylonian periods, but it is not necessary to rely on the seals for evidence to the same extent as in the earlier periods, since more realistic representations of furniture are available in the bas-reliefs. One noticeable difference from the earlier seals is the more frequent appearance of tables in the ritual scenes (fig. 287). These vary in shape, some appearing like open pedestals or 'whatnots' (fig. 286), broader at the base than at the top.[6] Others have a box-like top supported by in-curving legs which may simulate animal legs (fig. 288).[7] The most common type portrayed, however, is the table with crossed legs and animal feet. Not that the cross-leg design is something new – we have already seen the suggestion of such a table in the seals of the Akkadian period – but apparently it now came into more general use, with legs or feet of animal type.

Two general types of the cross-leg table appear, those with legs which terminate in pad feet, usually in the shape of lion's paws, as in figure 290, and those with an angular section at the bottom in the shape of a goat's leg and hoof, as in figure 289. Very similar

286 Cylinder seal impression showing a table or stand with splay legs. *Neo-Assyrian period.*

287 Cylinder seal impression showing a table in a ritual scene. *Neo-Assyrian–Babylonian period.*

288 Cylinder seal impression showing a table with incurving animal legs. *Neo-Assyrian period.*

289 Cylinder seal impression showing a cross-leg table with goat's leg and hoof. *Neo-Assyrian period.*

290 Cylinder seal impression showing a cross-leg table with animal feet. *Neo-Assyrian period.*

286

288

290

289

287

examples appear in the bas-reliefs also (figs. 333, 334), indicating again the relationship of the seal engravings to the styles in current use. The highly stylized design of the table with goat's hoofs is of special interest, both because of the introduction of a form not seen in the earlier seals, and because of the close resemblance to the stools with crossed legs and goat's hoofs seen later in Classical Greece. (See fig. 435.)

Among the most typical pieces of the time is the straight high-backed chair which appears with the tables illustrated above, and is represented many times in the cylinder seals. These chairs differ considerably in the design of the base, some constructed with a single stretcher, as in figure 289, and others with a varying arrangement of stretchers and detail in the side-panels, similar to what we have seen in stools of the early periods. The tall stiff back, however, is characteristic of all these representations. But although there are signs of change in the details of the chairs, as well as in other pieces represented, for the most part the furniture presented in seal engravings is a repetition of forms seen previously.

The most important source of information, however, relating to furniture is found in the bas-reliefs from the excavations of the royal palaces at Nineveh, Nimrud and Khorsabad.[8] The emphasis is obviously on palace furniture, but there are also some representations of more ordinary furniture, and it is therefore convenient to discuss them under the two separate headings.

Palace furniture in Assyria, 883–612 B.C.

A succession of Assyrian kings, beginning with Assurnasirpal in the ninth century B.C., built great palaces and lined the walls with bas-reliefs commemorating their conquests. Fortunately, however, these reliefs also present a vivid picture of the palace furniture of the period. The palace walls constructed of mud brick have crumbled away for the most part, but, buried deep in the soil, the great winged beasts of stone that guarded the gates and the bas-reliefs which decorated the walls have survived to give a priceless visual record of the time. They were first brought to the attention of the western world in the 1840s by Austen Henry Layard of England and Emile Botta of France, and the greater part of the reliefs found in these early years are now in the collections of the British Museum and the Louvre. But although a great deal of attention has been given to their historical importance, relatively little note has been taken of the furniture that is represented in them.

The earliest of the reliefs illustrated, dating about 870 B.C., comes from the palace of Assurnasirpal at Nineveh, and depicts the king sitting on a backless throne with his feet resting on a foot-stool and an attendant standing behind him (fig. 291). The design of the throne, more clearly shown in the detail (fig. 292), is highly sophisticated and shows a marked departure from what has appeared hitherto. Although the frame appears to have been made of wood, it seems likely that the feet and stretcher may have been made of bronze, since similar metal parts have been found in various excavations (figs. 326–8). The small heifer's heads which ornament the seat appear to be an integral part of the rail and may have been carved out of wood and gilded, but it is possible that these also were

291 292

291 Stone bas-relief showing Assurnasirpal (883–859 B.C.) seated on a backless throne with foot-stool. *Neo-Assyrian period.*

292 Detail of a bas-relief showing design of Assurnasirpal's backless throne. *Neo-Assyrian period.*

made of metal since similar ornaments made of bronze or gold have been found in the excavations. The feet of the throne are in scale to its weight and height, and the details of the ornamentation suitable. The edges of the legs are relieved with a beading, and the stretcher ornamented with double volutes. On the slightly curved seat is a cushion, and beneath is what appears to be a valance similar to the fringe on the king's robe. Dignified and elegant, the throne of Assurnasirpal, our first example of distinctly Assyrian design, conveys an impression of splendour well befitting this great oriental ruler.

The next throne relief illustrated comes from the palace of Tiglath-Pileser III (744–727 B.C.) at Nimrud and is now in the Leiden Museum (fig. 293).[9] Dating from the later part of the eighth century B.C., the throne on which the king is seated is obviously the prototype of Sennacherib's throne in figure 299, the principal differences being in the feet, which are more slender in the earlier throne, and in the treatment of the stretcher. In each case the frame is plain; but the possibility must be considered, since this is the king's throne, that it may have been covered with gold, judging by the many written records in which gold ornamentation is mentioned. A cloth is draped over the seat and a long cushion hangs over the back, as almost invariably appears on the royal thrones.

A century later Sargon II (721–705 B.C.) built his palace at Khorsabad from which have come some of the finest of the reliefs in which furniture is depicted. Assyria was then the dominant nation of the Near East, and, in spite of continued wars, this was a period of prosperity and the building of great palaces. One of the earliest to be discovered,

183

293 Stone bas-relief showing Tiglath-Pileser III (744–727 B.C.) seated on a throne. *Neo-Assyrian period.*

294 Stone bas-relief showing attendants carrying furniture. *Neo-Assyrian period.*

Sargon's palace city, 'Dur Sharrukin', has been the most thoroughly excavated and studied of all the Assyrian palaces.[10] This covered a large area, with extensive residential quarters, and the pride of the king in his great palace is expressed, in the typical Assyrian manner, in an inscription discovered in the excavations.

> Sargon, king of the universe, has built
> a city. Dur-Sharrukin he named it. A
> palace without a rival he built therein.[11]

Among the reliefs found in the great courtyard of the palace are four slabs, now in Baghdad, which portray pieces of furniture being presented to the king by attendants, probably as gifts or tribute from a conquered monarch. Unlike the better known Assyrian reliefs in the British Museum which were discovered a century or more ago, these were not found until the Oriental Institute of Chicago began new excavations at Khorsabad in 1929, and are part of the finds that remained in Iraq. Carefully restored and effectively displayed in the new building of the Iraq Museum in West Baghdad,[12] they are dramatic evidence of the esteem in which fine furniture was held by the Assyrian rulers.

As was appropriate for Sargon's great palace, the furniture depicted is elegant in design and finely carved. Each of the four pieces – two tables, an arm-chair, and a foot-stool – is sculptured in something more than full scale, following the heroic proportions of the attendants portrayed (the slabs are nearly ten feet high). The details are meticulously

184

rendered, and, being modelled in relief, these portrayals give us an excellent idea of what the actual appearance of this furniture must have been. (See colour plate XIII.)

Each table is made in two parts, the upper section having feet in the form of lion's paws. This in turn rests on a frame, or shelf, which is supported by feet in the shape of cedar-cones pointing downward, supposedly due to the belief that cedar-cones in this position possessed a magic power to ward off the attacks of the earth genii and to keep away their evil influences.[13] At any rate, the inverted cedar-cone used as a foot was a detail of design frequently seen not only on tables but on other furniture as well.

The more elaborate of the two tables shown (fig. 294) has a carved stretcher with a running pattern consisting of pairs of the letter C back to back resembling the volutes of the 'Cypriot' capital, similar to the ornaments on the stretcher of the throne of Assurnasirpal (figs. 291, 292). Under the top there are three vertical pieces carved with the sacred tree motif, reminiscent of the honeysuckle design of Classical Greece. At the corners of the top, and of the frame underneath, are small ornaments in the form of ram's heads. The corner posts consisted of slender carved figures which repeat the figure of the king as he is portrayed elsewhere in the Khorsabad reliefs, except that his crown is omitted. The details of the large relief are carefully reproduced in these small figures, including the flowers held in the king's hand. In spite of the large amount of ornamentation, however, the table has a refined elegance and is a nicely balanced piece of design. Quite possibly the slender frame and the small delicately carved ornaments may have been made of ivory, since this material was freely used in the furniture of this period.

The second table (fig. 295) is similar in plan but has a heavier frame and a flush top which appear to have been made of wood. Its heavy claw feet, however, are rather clumsily inserted between the upper and lower sections, which suggests that they were made of bronze, since similar bronze feet have been found in excavations elsewhere. Two figures with raised hands support the top, and, like the lions' feet, were most likely made of some other material than wood – probably either bronze or ivory. (Although this has the appearance of a table, it should be noted that it is described as a 'seat' in the Iraq Museum records.)

The chair or throne (fig. 296) has cedar-cone feet and a stretcher with double volute ornamentation like that of the first table, but the double base construction is omitted. Between the arm and the seat there are four small standing figures, and a larger one stands on top, presumably part of the back-rest. But although it seems likely that these small parts may have been made of metal or ivory, it should be observed, again, that in Egypt it was customary to carve in wood and then gild – sometimes in instances where the designs were of the utmost delicacy – and the Mesopotamian craftsmen may also have carved and gilded small figures such as these. Small pieces of gold sheathing from this period, around the edges of which were holes pierced for nails and which could have been used for just such a purpose, have been found at Ziwiye, a site in Iran.[14]

The small stool in the fourth relief has details similar to those of the other pieces except the projection of the posts above the top (fig. 297). There seems to be no practical reason for such a projection unless it served to hold a cushion; a similar feature appears often in the foot-stools of the period. The second attendant in this scene is carrying a small

295

296

297

298

295 Stone bas-relief showing attendants carrying a table with heavy
   frame and flush top. *Neo-Assyrian
   period.*

296 Stone bas-relief showing attendants carrying a chair with back-
   rest. *Neo-Assyrian period.*

297 Stone bas-relief showing attendants carrying a small stool. *Neo-
   Assyrian period.*

298 Stone altar from Khorsabad. *Neo-
   Assyrian period.*

299 Stone bas-relief showing Sennacherib (704–681 B.C.) seated on a
   nîmedu-throne.

model which represents a section of the walls of a fortified city, possibly as a token of fealty to accompany the gifts.

Outside the gates of the citadel at Khorsabad two stone altars of particular interest were found, one of which is now in the Oriental Institute in Chicago and the other (fig. 298) in the Iraq Museum in Baghdad. Although the altars differ from the usual concept of traditional Assyrian design, the inscription is evidence that the altars were contemporary with the sculptured slabs from the palace: "To [the god . . . has Sargon, king of the world, king of Assyria, governor of Babylon, king of the land of] the Sumerian and the Akkadian, set up and presented [this altar]."[15] Probably derived from Egyptian sources, the design is suggestive of later Greek and Roman furniture in the round top and the three legs terminating in lion's feet. And even though this particular altar was made of stone it is quite possible that wood pieces of similar design may have been made in Assyria at this time.

The bas-reliefs from the palace of Sennacherib (704–681 B.C.) at Nineveh, particularly those which commemorate his campaigns in Palestine and Syria, are among the most interesting for both furniture and Biblical history. As usual, these deal with the serious business of war and conquest, which remained the constant preoccupation of the Assyrian rulers, but royal thrones are also depicted, as well as a number of pieces of more ordinary furniture which were spoils from a conquered city or used as camp equipment. Layard made a remarkable series of drawing at the time of the discovery, about 1849, which are illustrated since they give a clearer delineation of the furniture than photographs of the reliefs in their present condition.[16]

Not only did Layard depict the furniture shown in the reliefs in careful detail in his drawings, but also, in his popular two-volume work on the discoveries at Nineveh and Babylon published in 1853, he describes the finding of the remains of a royal throne and foot-stool in the excavations of the palace at Nimrud.[17] This account includes a direct reference to the 'chair of state' of Sennacherib, and since it is a first-hand report in a work long out of print, it is quoted verbatim.

In the further corner of the chamber, to the left hand stood the royal throne. Although it was utterly impossible, from the complete state of decay of the materials, to preserve any part of it entire, I was able, by carefully removing the earth, to ascertain that it resembled in shape the chair of state of the king, as seen in the sculptures of Kouyunjik and Khorsabad, and particularly that represented in the bas-reliefs already described, of Sennacherib receiving the captives and spoils, after the conquest of the city of Lachish. With the exception of the legs, which appear to have been partly of ivory, it was of wood, cased or overlaid with bronze, as the throne of Solomon was of ivory, overlaid with gold. The metal was most elaborately engraved and embossed with symbolical figures and ornaments, like those embroidered on the robes of the early Nimroud kings, such as winged deities struggling with griffins, mythic animals, men before the sacred tree, and the winged lion and bull. As the woodwork over which the bronze was fastened by means of small nails of the same material, has rotted away, the throne fell to pieces but the metal casing was partly preserved. Numerous fragments of it are now in the British Museum, including the joints of the arms and legs; the rams' or bulls' heads which adorned the end of the arms (some still retaining the clay and bitumen with the impression of the carving, showing the substance upon which the embossing had been hammered out), and the ornament scroll-work of the cross-bars, in the form of the Ionic volute. The legs were adorned with lion's paws resting on a pine-shaped ornament, like the thrones of the late Assyrian sculptures, and stood on a bronze base. A rod with loose rings, to which was once hung embroidered drapery, or some rich stuff, appears to have belonged to the back of the chair, or to a frame-work raised above or behind it, though not I think, as conjectured, to a curtain concealing the monarch from those who approached him. In front of the throne was a footstool, also of wood overlaid with embossed metal, and adorned with the heads of rams or bulls. The feet ended in lion's paws and pine-cones, like those of the throne. The two pieces of furniture may have been placed together in a temple as an offering to the gods, as Midas placed his throne in the temple of Delphi. The ornaments on them were so purely Assyrian that there can be little doubt of their having been expressly made for the Assyrian king, and not having been the spoil of some foreign nations.

Among the best known of the scenes portrayed on the walls of Sennacherib's palace are those which commemorate the capture of the Biblical city of Lachish – after Jerusalem, the largest city in ancient Palestine. On the relief which Layard mentions in the quotation above, the inscription states: "Sennacherib, King of the World, King of Assyria, sat upon a *nîmedu*-throne and passed in review the booty (taken) from Lachish" (fig. 299).[18] Although none of the furniture probably seized as booty is depicted in this scene, we have

300 Drawing showing detail from the *nîmedu*-throne of Sennacherib (704–681 B.C.).

301 Drawing from a bas-relief showing Sennacherib (704–681 B.C.) seated on a throne without arm-rests.

302 Drawing from a bas-relief showing Sennacherib (704–681 B.C.) seated on an unornamented throne with pine-cone feet. *Neo-Assyrian period.*

a detailed representation of the king's throne, which presumably had come with him from Nineveh. Foreign campaigns such as this sometimes lasted for months or years, and the throne traditionally accompanied an oriental king as a sign of rank.[19] The frame of the throne has an unusual design, vaguely resembling bamboo (fig. 300). There are the usual Assyrian inverted cedar-cones for feet and ornamented stretcher with arm-rests which curve downward. The triple row of figures with uplifted hands on the side panel were quite likely made of bronze or ivory like those shown in figure 296. As is customary in the Assyrian thrones represented, the seat is high and the king's feet rest on a foot-stool with lion feet on a pine-cone base.

In another of the campaign bas-reliefs, Sennacherib is represented seated within the walls of a city after its capture. The throne has no arms and is quite different from the one illustrated above, which is typically Assyrian, and it is possible that this had been captured from the enemy (fig. 301). The bull's legs which rest directly on the floor and the freely shaped apron of the stool are details which vary from the usual Assyrian types. A third drawing shows the king sitting on a plainer throne, unornamented except for the carved pine-cones which form the feet (fig. 302).

While thrones are being discussed, it should be noted that Assurbanipal (668–626 B.C.) describes in detail a throne, as well as a bed, which he carried off from Babylon to Assyria and which he dedicated to the god Assur:[20]

189

6⅔ cubits, in the (royal) cubit, is the length of the sideboard, 3⅓ cubits, in the royal cubit, is the front; 12 posts (?) of gold are on the long side of the bed, 6 ditto on the broad side. The top-end of the side-boards are (in the form of) a dragon; . . . -ornaments of obsidian, carnelian, and lapis lazuli surround the . . . -mattresses. Upon the lower mattress are golden (ornaments representing) water. The legs are (in the form of) female genii; beneath the female genii are . . . -claws. 8 female genii are (depicted) on the two rungs on (either) side (of the bed), and one female genius on each . . .; (ornaments representing) water surround the female genii. The rungs are plated (?) with (ornaments representing) water. 1⅔ cubits, in the royal cubit, is the leg of the bed.

3⅓ cubits, in the royal cubit, is the length of the throne, 1⅔ cubits is the width. (Ornaments representing) water surround female genii. 4 female genii are (depicted) on the two rungs on (either) side, 2 ditto on the front: all that on the throne. 1⅔ cubits is the length of the . . . -stool, ⅔ cubit the height, ⅔ cubits the width of the . . . up to the dragon (of the bed).

The description of the throne corresponds in some respects with the impression of a throne of which the outlines could still be seen in the clay floor of the temple of Marduk at Babylon when it was excavated. From the description of the bed, which is given in somewhat more detail than that of the throne, it would seem that there was a carved dragon, the sacred animal of the god Marduk, at the top of each of the bed posts. The female genii, mentioned as legs and ornaments, were the traditional female creatures with bodies of winged beasts, often represented in Assyrian and Babylonian art.

Among other interesting pieces of furniture depicted in the bas-reliefs of Sennacherib's palace are a bed and a table, the latter resting on the bed (fig. 303). The bed with its curved head-board is a type frequently shown in bas-reliefs of the period, but the design of the table (or perhaps it is a stool) differs from the usual forms seen in the Assyrian reliefs. It is possible, of course, that this piece, which is apparently booty from Babylon, is not typical of that ordinarily used in Nineveh. It is significant, however, that this shape, which generally is associated with Greek and Etruscan furniture, is represented in Mesopotamian art at this early period.

King Assurbanipal, also, left the record of his victories sculptured in bas-reliefs on his palace walls, and in one of the most famous scenes, now in the British Museum, several Assyrian pieces of furniture are depicted. In this scene the king is shown feasting with his queen in the royal gardens, after his defeat of King Teumman of Elam.[21] The palm trees, birds and hanging vines suggest a romantic environment, but a grim note is added by the severed head of the defeated king which hangs in a tree. Furniture, including a bed, a throne and foot-stool, and tables of two different sizes, has been moved into the garden for the comfort of the royal couple (fig. 305).

Although the table beside the bed is heavier in scale than those in the Khorsabad reliefs, the details are similar in several respects – notably in the use of a separate base with inverted cedar-cone feet on which rests an upper section with claw feet. The couch on which the king reclines has heavy elaborately carved legs which terminate in pine-cones, and a sharply curved head-board within which is a bolster. The curved head-board is a characteristic feature of beds of the period, but the royal couch depicted is, of course, far more elaborate and ponderous than the ordinary beds of this type (fig. 335). Besides the usual details in the feet and carving, the upper section of the heavy bed post is ornamented on its face with two small figures which were probably of metal – probably bronze but presumably gold.

The queen sits, facing the bed, on a tall chair of the usual royal type with a cushion draped over the back and her feet resting on a foot-stool. The extreme height of the royal chairs distinguishes them from ordinary seating pieces as a mark of dignity, and here seems also to serve the practical purpose of enabling the queen to converse more easily with the king on his high couch (fig. 304).

In addition to the large table beside the bed, one of smaller size appears at the right of the scene. They are alike in detail, having the typical double base construction, but different in height, and the lower table is much lighter in scale. The same general form is seen again in the high table or altar in the relief which depicts Assurbanipal pouring a libation over lions slain in a hunt, as he makes an offering to the gods (fig. 308). This

303

304

303 Bas-relief showing table (or stool) resting on bed with curved head-board. *Neo-Assyrian period.*

304 Detail showing the royal furniture used by Assur-banipal (668–627 B.C.) and his Queen. *Neo-Assyrian period.*

305 Stone bas-relief showing Assurbanipal (662–627 B.C.) and his Queen feasting. *Neo-Assyrian period.*

305

306 Ivory panel showing a table. *About eighth century* B.C.

307 Drawing from a bas-relief showing a convivial scene with stools and a table. *Neo-Assyrian period.*

308 Stone bas-relief showing Assurbanipal (668–627 B.C.) pouring a libation in front of an offering table. *Neo-Assyrian period.*

Colour plate XI. Banqueting scene with guests on stools and chairs. *Eighteenth Dynasty.*

interesting relief is one of a series dealing with hunting which lined the walls of a gate-house by which the hunting train left and entered the palace grounds. The table is considerably more elaborate than the two shown above, with an ornamented vertical member in the upper panel and the small figure of a man in the bottom panel. The square legs of the frame are worked with a kind of cross-ribbing. Since the sculptures are somewhat limited in the fine detail ordinarily represented, it is interesting to compare the tables above with one depicted in a small ivory panel from Ziwiye, which although found in Iran is Assyrian in design (fig. 306).

It should be noted that whereas in ancient Egypt most tables were very low, seldom over fourteen inches in height (except for the round pedestal offering tables represented in stelae), in the Near East they varied considerably. For instance the tables most commonly depicted in the Assyrian reliefs are apparently twenty-six to thirty inches high, about the height of tables used today for tea or dining. This seems to be true also of the cross-leg tables seen in seal engravings. Although these tables are usually depicted as individual tables, since the dining table seating several persons did not come into general use until much later, four Assyrians are shown seated around a single table in a unique convivial scene from the Khorsabad reliefs, drawn by Botta at the time of discovery (fig. 307).[22] The table has the usual combination of an upper section with claw feet and a separate base, with a dish-shaped top over which a cloth is draped. The four men, probably warriors toasting a victory with rhytons raised high, are seated on stools ornamented with bull's heads on the seat and a double volute design on the stretcher. Rather than the pine-cone feet, however, which commonly appear on the base of pieces of this sort, the feet are worked with a series of rings.

Ivory and bronze ornamentation in palace furniture

One of the puzzling questions that arises in analysing the ornamentation of the furniture represented in the Assyrian reliefs is whether certain parts were carved in wood or if they were made of ivory or metal of some sort. Archaeological and written evidence make it clear that the use of ivory was common practice in the more elegant furniture, but there is no implicit evidence of this in the reliefs. The small ornamental figures of the thrones and tables depicted could certainly have been made of ivory; but what has survived in the way of bronze parts suggests that metal was more likely in elaborate thrones such as that of Sennacherib (fig. 300), at least in the heavier sections such as the bronze feet and stretchers. In spite of the dearth of evidence in the reliefs, however, it is certain that ivory, as well as gold, silver and bronze were freely used in the ornamentation of the palace furniture of this period.

Carved plaques and other furniture parts of ivory have been found in various places in the Near East, but the most important discoveries have come from the excavations at Nimrud, located on the Tigris about twenty miles south of Nineveh, where quantities of ivories were first found by Layard in the 1840s.[23] Within the last few years new discoveries of great importance have been made in the same locality by Professor M. E. L. Mallowan.[24] These ivories, which are believed to have ornamented the palace furniture, were

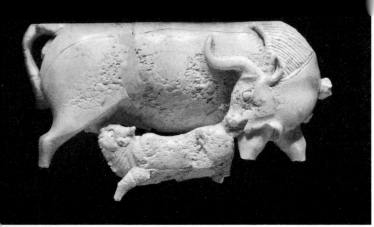

309a   b

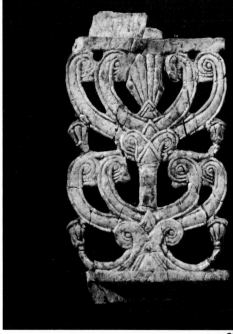

310   311   312

309a Ivory furniture ornament showing a cow suckling a calf. *About
eighth–seventh century* B.C.

b Reverse of an ivory furniture
ornament in 309a showing
method of attachment. *Eighth
century* B.C.

310 Ivory furniture ornament showing an animated ibex. *About eighth–
seventh century* B.C.

311 Ivory furniture ornament showing a rampant goat. *About eighth–
seventh century* B.C.

312 Ivory furniture ornament in the
shape of a sacred tree. *About
eighth–seventh century* B.C.

313 Ivory furniture ornament showing two sphinxes.
About eighth–seventh century B.C.

mainly found in the ruins of residential quarters presumed to have been occupied by high officials. Of North Syrian workmanship, the carvings date from the eighth and early seventh century B.C., and apparently are the remains of furniture stripped of its gold and left behind when the palace buildings were sacked by the Medes and Babylonians in 614–612 B.C. In these ivories, more than in any other form of art, the decorative motifs of the period are revealed.

The plaques were usually attached by means of tenons, which may be seen in most of the illustrations. An interesting example from the Metropolitan Museum, however, is cut out in the back to provide for a slotted key type of joint so it could be attached to the face of a flat surface. The design represents a cow suckling a calf (fig. 309a), and on the reverse side the method of attaching the plaque is clearly apparent (fig. 309b). A wide variety of subjects are portrayed in these ivory ornaments including conventional patterns like that of the sacred tree in figure 312, and animal and mythical scenes. The fragment of a plaque illustrated in figure 310 contains the animated figure of an ibex. In another example a rampant goat nibbles the top of a stylized tree or vine (fig. 311). As a contrast to these rather charming and whimsical carvings, the traditional Assyrian spirit is apparent in the scene where winged beasts trample the prostrate enemies (fig. 313); and in another example (which has two intact tenons) the figure of a man is portrayed in the Phoenician style (fig. 315). Altogether, a considerable number of plaques have been found and are now in various museum collections; but although, as decoration, they may properly be considered an integral part of furniture design, a detailed study belongs in the province of the art historian.

Occasionally a piece of furniture is depicted in these ivory carvings, as in the scene where a woman is portrayed sitting on a tasselled throne with her feet resting on a footstool (fig. 314). Although it is obvious that the intent in this instance was to indicate a cushion with a fringe, it seems reasonable to assume that other details represent ivory ornamentation. In another of the carvings a chair with rounded back is depicted, resembling the modern wicker chair in its shape. The arched framework at the side, however, appears to be inlaid with ivory (fig. 317).

A third plaque in which chairs are depicted is Egyptian in its arrangement and in the design of the chairs, even though Syrian in workmanship (fig. 318). This also was found in the palace at Nimrud, but the details of the figures and the chairs suggest that it comes from an earlier period. Chairs of this type are often represented in Egyptian art of the Eighteenth Dynasty but those which appear in this plaque are especially interesting because of the open-work pattern of the sides.

Most extraordinary from the furniture viewpoint are the larger panels discovered by Mallowan which formed parts of chairs and beds and are direct evidence that not only the ornamentation but also complete pieces of furniture were made of ivory. The chair back in figure 316, now in the Metropolitan Museum, is curved and three open-work panels are framed between the four flat vertical stiles. These are ornamented at the sides with delicate open-work stars and apparently were originally backed with wood. It seems quite probable that in between the half-cylinders of ivory on the top-rail there were ornaments of gold or silver which were torn off at the time of the sack of the palace. Another large panel, now

314 Ivory plaque showing a woman seated on a tasselled throne. *About ninth–eighth century* B.C.

315 Ivory furniture ornament showing a Phoenician. *About ninth–eighth century* B.C.

316 Ivory chair back with open-work panels. *About ninth–eighth century* B.C.

317 Drawing of an ivory plaque showing a man seated in a chair with rounded back. *About ninth–eighth century* B.C.

318 Ivory plaque showing chairs in Egyptian style. *About ninth–eighth century* B.C.

319 Carved ivory bed panels. *About ninth–eighth century* B.C.

320

in the British Museum and presumed to have been in the head-board of a bed, contains six vertical carved panels, the outer ones representing the tree of life, the inner panels depicting bearded warriors and clean-shaven youths (fig. 319). The frame was made of plain ivory but it seems likely that an elaborate bed such as this would also have had an ornamentation of precious metals.

Although ivory furniture, as distinct from ivory ornamentation applied to wood furniture, is only indirectly related to our main subject, we would be remiss if we failed to include three remarkable furniture panels from the Iraq Museum, recently published for the first time in Professor Mallowan's definitive work on the discoveries made at Nimrud (figs. 320, 321, 322). The extraordinary carvings in these panels will not be discussed in detail, but the two centre small panels in figure 320 should be especially noted. The female figure at the left is seated on a tasselled seat resembling that in one of the plaques previously shown (fig. 314); the seat at the right is plain with straight legs. In both instances a companion foot-stool is represented on which rest the feet of the seated person. It is to be hoped that further research will disclose the precise use of such panels. The form, as seen in the illustration (fig. 318), suggests the side-panel of a chest, but no indication exists of the other parts that would be required to complete a chest, and it seems probable, as is assumed above, that these formed the back-panels of couches and chairs. Other structural parts of ivory have also been found at Nimrud such as the ivory sphinx, lion's leg and carved foot illustrated, which were supports for ivory or wooden furniture (figs. 323, 324, 325). But even though a relatively large quantity of ivory carvings and other fragments of furniture survive, there is little apparent relationship between them and the furniture represented in the bas-reliefs.

The bronze parts that have been found, however, can be more directly related to what appears in the representations. In Layard's description of the remains of the royal throne

320 Ivory panel showing two seated women and two standing men.

321 and 322 Ivory panels with relief carving.

323 Carved ivory furniture support in the shape of a sphinx. *Thirteenth–twelfth century* B.C.

at Nimrud (quoted previously) he mentions overlays, "engraved and embossed with symbolical figures and ornaments", "ram's and bull's heads which adorned the end of arms", "the ornamental scroll-work of the cross-bars", and what he calls "the joints of the arms and legs", all made of bronze. Eugène Flandin, who accompanied Botta in 1843, wrote: "I found among the ruins small bull's heads of copper, repoussé and carefully chased, inside of which a few fragments of dried wood still remained."[25]

In addition to the discoveries at Nimrud and Nineveh, other bronze furniture parts, much like those described by Layard, have been found to the north of Assyria near Lake Van in what was the ancient country of Urartu (now eastern Turkey). These date approxi-

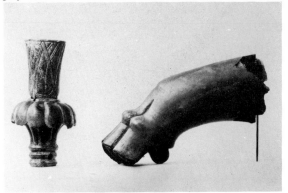

324 Carved ivory furniture support in the shape of a lion's foot. *About ninth–eighth century* B.C.

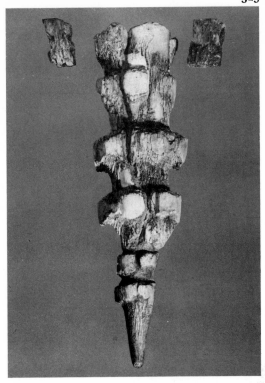

325 Carved ivory foot. *About ninth–eighth century* B.C.

mately to the time of the conquest of Urartu in 714 B.C. by Sargon II, who, in his account of the treasures of Musasir, expresses the amazement of the victorious Assyrians at the skill of Urartians in the arts of metal-working. Obviously a strong Assyrian influence was already present, apparent in the massive elaborate feet, the *lamassu* and other mythological and human figures, as well as in other details. Not enough pieces remain to permit a complete reconstruction of a throne such as that of Sennacherib, although a suggested arrangement of the parts found appears in Dr Barnett's discussion of the excavations at Toprak Kale (Urartu).[26]

Among the more interesting of the bronze structural parts is an ornamented corner section now in a private collection in Paris (fig. 326). The other bronzes illustrated are from the British Museum. The first of these is a companion piece to the one above with a similar pattern in its sides (fig. 327). It is obviously an angle piece made to receive the ends of wooden frame-rails such as that found by Layard, which had sockets on the top to receive the tenons of an ornament or upper section. The round holes were perhaps intended to receive semi-precious stones or some similar ornamentation. The inner faces of the angle pieces are ornamented with a well-drawn palmette design which seems superfluous since normally these faces would be hidden.

The traditional foot with lion's paws is represented in another of the bronzes, with a double line of decoration at the side (fig. 329). Here again it is probable that the open spaces at the top were intended to receive some kind of ornamentation. The female centaur, presumed to be part of a throne, is also typically Assyrian, with the upper part of a human figure combined with the winged bull (fig. 328).

199

327

326

329

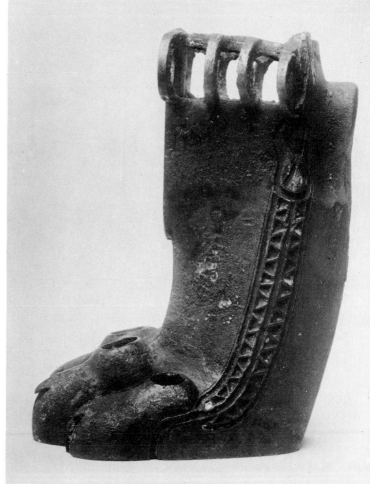

328

326 Bronze corner section of a piece of furniture. *About eighth–seventh century* B.C.

327 Bronze angle piece. *About eighth–seventh century* B.C.

328 Bronze part of a throne in the shape of a female centaur. *About eighth–seventh century* B.C.

329 Bronze furniture support in the shape of a lion's paw. *About eighth–seventh century* B.C.

330 Bronze end sections of a table and stand.

331 Bronze stand from Cyprus showing Mesopotamian influence.

Although the Urartians seem to have specialized in the casting of bronzes, it should not be inferred that Assyria was lacking in fine metal-work. Bronzes for all kinds of purposes, useful as well as decorative, were also made in Assyria and special note should be made of the fine bronze reliefs from the gates of Shalmaneser[27] at Nimrud which depict scenes from the king's campaign in Syria (about 850 B.C.). In these reliefs, stools, tables and a couch are depicted, all very much like the furniture represented in the later stone bas-reliefs of King Sennacherib (figs. 332–5).

Besides the smaller parts, some entire sections of bronze furniture have been found in the Near East. Like ivory furniture, however, bronze furniture as such is incidental to our main subject of wood furniture design. Nevertheless it is significant for the light it throws on the design details of the furniture represented in sculpture, particularly since all wooden furniture of the period has vanished long ago. For instance, the table-end from the British Museum (fig. 330) includes several of the most typical features – a lion's paw foot, ornaments in the form of ram's heads and a stretcher with double volutes. In contrast to these often repeated details the more delicate design of a small stand is unusual (fig. 330). Although the last of the metal pieces illustrated was found on the island of Cyprus rather than on the mainland, it is included here since it dates from approximately the same time as the other bronzes and is definitely Mesopotamian in design (fig. 331).[28] The harp-player and the stool on which she sits bear a striking resemblance to those shown on the plaques of the Old Babylonian period (figs. 279, 280).

Ordinary household furniture

Because the palace bas-reliefs present the most comprehensive picture of the furniture of the late Assyrian period, there is a tendency to over-emphasize the royal furniture. As in all periods, however, there were varying grades of rank and wealth, and by far the largest

201

332

proportion of furniture that existed was doubtless that used outside the royal palace itself. In a few instances, fortunately, the reliefs also contain scenes in which the simpler types appear, and they give us an indication of the furniture generally used in this period.

The reliefs showing a file of Assyrian soldiers carrying furniture seized as booty from a captured city (fig. 332) are the most informative. These drawings, made by Layard from the reliefs as originally found in Sennacherib's palace, and seldom illustrated, are worthy of careful study from the furniture viewpoint. The city from which this booty was taken cannot be positively identified (quite likely it was situated in North Syria), but the furniture shows a marked Assyrian influence in its design, even though it was not made in Assyria proper.[29] In these interesting reliefs we see ten individual pieces of furniture, each different in design, being transported by the soldiers along the river and through the palm trees on the way back to Nineveh. But although this was furniture deemed worthy of being brought back to the palace along with other spoils of conquest, the forms are simpler than the elaborate royal furniture portrayed in the bas-reliefs, and are doubtless more typical of the more ordinary furniture in Assyria at this time.

Eight tables, a chair and a bed are represented in these reliefs. The bed resembles that of King Assurbanipal in the garden scene (fig. 305), in that it has a high sharply curved shape at the head end; but, unlike the king's bed with its elaborate decoration, this is plain and rests on simple tapered legs with a long straight stretcher between. The straight high-back chair is perfectly plain also except for what appear in the relief to be

202   332 Bas-relief showing soldiers carrying off furniture as booty.

cedar-cone feet with an ornamented stretcher. The tables are the most interesting of the pieces, and being shown side by side to the same scale provide a unique opportunity for comparison.

Three of the tables are simplified versions of those previously illustrated from the palace reliefs and rest on the typical inverted cedar-cone feet. They vary considerably in proportion and design, one of the tops being rounded on the under-side, possibly indicating a dished surface above. Another of the tops is ornamented with the traditional ram's head terminals. All of the other tables, with the exception of one of the cross-leg type, have straight legs. These also vary from one another, the legs terminating in bell feet in two of the tables, flaring outward in another, and running straight to the floor in another. Heights and widths also vary. The single example of a table of the cross-leg type has plain legs, instead of terminating in animal feet as is often depicted, and at the point where the legs cross a pin is clearly indicated. Instead of having a rectangular top, however, as the other tables appear to have, the three crossed legs suggest that in this instance there is a round top and a tripod base.

This, of course, is not furniture that would have been used in the mud huts of the common people, but evidence that such furniture was in fairly general use appears in the campaign reliefs. For instance, glimpses of similar furniture appear in a relief from Nineveh which portrays the circular wall of a fortified camp, within which there are four vignettes of interiors (fig. 333). Two of the tables and the stool are simple versions of

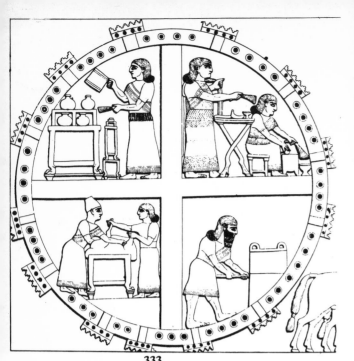

333   334

types that have previously been noted in the palace reliefs. The third table, with crossed legs and animal feet, is likewise a familiar type, represented in the seals illustrated at the beginning of this chapter (fig. 290), as well as in the stone reliefs.

Similar small scenes appear in the remarkable relief from Sennacherib's palace in which the king is portrayed sitting on his throne and receiving a deputation within the walls of a fortified city or camp (fig. 334). In the lower part of the scene there are six beehive-shaped structures, probably representing officers' tents, each of which contains one or more pieces of furniture. It might be inferred, since this is one of the Sennacherib campaign scenes, that this furniture, like that carried away by the file of soldiers illustrated above, was booty seized from some captured city. During these long campaigns, however, since the army sometimes settled down for long periods in fortified camps when besieging a city, it seems likely that the furniture represents part of the regular travelling equipment of the officers.

Containers to hold water can be seen hanging from the centre poles of these tent-like structures, and the scenes give us an impressionistic view of domestic activities, as well as glimpses of a variety of furniture. In the bottom scene an attendant lifts a mattress on to a bed with a curved head-board, similar to the bed shown in figure 332. A cross-leg stool with a cushion appears in one scene where two men sit on hassocks conversing with each other; and in the other interiors typical Assyrian tables are depicted, two of them having crossed legs with animal-type feet. A puzzling feature of these small scenes is that usually one and not more than two pieces of furniture are portrayed in any single interior. Obviously this would not be true in the ordinary household, but it appears that here the separate tents were devoted to different purposes. At any rate the scenes display a representative group of plain furniture.

In another campaign relief, now in Berlin, an officer is depicted returning to a tent within which his bed is being made ready, while meat is being prepared in the adjoining tent (fig. 335).[30] Like the bed in the previous scene, this has the characteristic curved head-board of the period.

335

333 Bas-relief showing vignettes of furniture in a fortified camp. *Neo-Assyrian period.*

334 Bas-relief showing Sennacherib (704–681 B.C.) receiving a deputation inside a fortified camp. *Neo-Assyrian period.*

335 Bas-relief showing a bed being made ready for an officer. *Neo-Assyrian period.*

The kings of Assyria obviously were fond of luxurious furniture, judging by their records and the detail in which it is portrayed in the bas-reliefs. It is also probable that less important persons equally treasured the simpler furniture which they possessed. But, although some of the pieces of the period are attractive in their design and ornamentation, in general there is a rigidity in the furniture portrayed, particularly in chairs, that perhaps reflects the severity of the people who owned it. Long before this time Egyptian chairs were made with a sloping back-rest curved to fit the body. Such chairs must have been known to the Mesopotamians, but they are missing from the furniture portrayals of this period in Mesopotamian art. Instead, there are tall straight chairs on which the occupants sit bolt upright. It is not until later in Classical Greece that the chair with the curved back appears in general use again and the person seated leans back taking his ease.

4   # THE PERIPHERAL REGIONS
(*c.* 1600–500 B.C.)

Around the borders of Mesopotamia were countries with differing cultural backgrounds but all influenced to a greater or lesser extent by Assyrian–Babylonian design.[1] To the west was Syria, whose craftsmen were skilled workers in ivory and gold, and, judging by the Alalakh tablets (see page 208), also produced wood furniture in considerable quantities; and to the south-west was Palestine, extending below Syria and Phoenicia. To the north, in the kingdom of Urartu, the Urartians were noted as metal-workers, making bronze fittings and ornaments such as those we have seen in the last chapter. In Asia Minor (Anatolia) were the Hittites, who, before the invasion of Syria and Palestine by the Assyrians, left their mark on the arts of the Levantine area. And to the south-east, in an area once Sumerian in culture, was the country of Persia, which, to some extent, retained its own individual art forms even though overshadowed by Mesopotamian influences

336

337

for long periods. Although these countries each played an important part in the history of the Near East, the continuity of an art tradition such as existed in Egypt and Mesopotamia is lacking. This lack of continuity is especially apparent in the few representations of furniture that survive, but they do serve to give some indication of the variety of styles that existed in the peripheral regions during this period.

ANCIENT SYRIA

The contribution of the Syrians and Phoenicians to the history of ancient furniture lies principally in their ivory work, of which quantities were exported to Mesopotamia. Syria had long been the principal source for ivory, which was a favourite material in the ancient world for the decoration and making of furniture, and large quantities of ivory and ivory goods were sent to Egypt in the Eighteenth Dynasty period. The Nimrud ivories (figs. 319–25) were probably made for the most part by the north Syrian craftsmen; and evidence that they also made complete pieces of furniture constructed of ivory appears in the annals of the Assyrian kings as well as in the actual finds that have been made. In the accounts of tribute and booty from Syria, Assurnasirpal (883–859 B.C.) lists, among other pieces of ivory, "*ivory couches overlaid with gold*", "*ivory tables*" and "*chairs of ivory overlaid with silver and gold*", as well as "*many tables of ivory and boxwood*".[2] Other Assyrian kings have also left lists of ivory goods and furniture received from Syria, and some few small pieces, almost complete, have survived.

Although the furniture represented in the Syrian reliefs illustrated may possibly have been ornamented with ivory, the structure and design indicate that these, like the pieces in the Assyrian reliefs, would have been constructed mostly of wood. In the first of the reliefs, a stela from Ras Shamra dating from about 1300 B.C., the Egyptian influence is strongly evident in the chair, although the workmanship of the relief is Syrian (fig. 336). This dates from shortly after the period when the rulers of Egypt had conquered northern Syria, and the chair legs of animal design which face forward and rest on round drums

206

336 Stela from Ras Shamra showing a chair with Egyptian influence. *About thirteenth century* B.C.

337 Sarcophagus of Ahiram showing a throne of lion design. *About thirteenth century* B.C.

338 Stela showing a chair with slanting back and a cross-leg table. *Eighth century* B.C.

338

are typically Egyptian, as is the low back-rest. Underneath the seat, however, is an ornamental design which seems to be a regional variation and may have been made of ivory. In the second relief illustrated, which is part of the sculptured ornamentation of a thirteenth-century B.C. sarcophagus found at Byblos, the Egyptian influence is apparent in the formal scene but the design of the throne is distinctly Syro-Palestinian (fig. 337). The lion has been a well-recognized motif in the design of royal thrones, both in Egypt and Mesopotamia, since early times, but the figure is rendered differently here and somewhat resembles that in the ivory plaque from Megiddo in Palestine (fig. 349). The table, with its boldly curving legs, is typically Near Eastern.

Dating from the eighth century B.C., a stela from Zinjirli is distinctly Mesopotamian in character (fig. 338). The table, with crossed legs and feet in the form of animal hoofs, is similar to those in the Assyrian reliefs. On the other hand, the chair differs somewhat from those usually portrayed; its straight legs, rest and stretcher are not unusual, but there is a concession to comfort in the slanting back and cushioned seat that is not ordinarily seen in Mesopotamian furniture. Even more strictly Assyrian in design are the throne and foot-stool of King Bar Rekub represented in a relief from Zinjirli, dating shortly after the conquest of Syria by Sargon II (721–705 B.C.) (fig. 339); and the chair

207

339 Relief showing Bar Rekub seated on a throne with foot-stool. *Eighth century* B.C.

and table which appear in the stela of the priest Agbar from Nerab (fig. 340) are simplified versions of those depicted in the Nineveh reliefs. In the last of the Syrian reliefs illustrated, a stela from Ras Shamra, there is a table with a slender pedestal supported by splayed legs which are braced by a stretcher – apparently intended to represent a tripod base (fig. 341). The type of the base is Mesopotamian, but the deep frieze of the top suggests (even though the details are obscure in the sculpture) that this may be a Syrian detail consisting of an ornamental band of ivory.

Some significant data of earlier date regarding the relative quantities of different types of furniture made in the ancient Near East appear on cuneiform tablets found at Alalakh (now in Turkey), dating about 1400 B.C. Alalakh was possibly a woodworking centre, and, although it was located in Syria rather than in Mesopotamia proper, it appears that the furniture in the two areas was similar. Since these tablets give valuable information on the furniture production, as well as use, of this period in the Near East, several of the texts which refer specifically to furniture are noted below.[3]

No. 417 lists furniture and other items of wood made "by seven carpenters of the woman Zazi. Fourteen tables, two made by each workman, twenty-one chairs and twenty-one footstools, three by each craftsman."

No. 419 lists "twenty tables, thirty-two chairs and thirty-five footstools belonging to the house of Irihalpa" who was a court official of the time of Niqmepa (about 1400 B.C.).

No. 420 is a receipt for "twenty-one chairs and four tables given by Ibrihuta to Hauheya".

No. 424 tells how fourteen pine-logs were cut up to make, among other things, eleven chairs.

Colour plate XIIa. The 'Standard of Ur'. *Early Dynastic III.*

b. Detail from colour plate XIIa. The 'king's' seat.

No. 227 gives an account of "sixteen houses (firms) of joiners who made sixteen tables, eighty stools, five couches with sides, four couches *ša wizzae* (an unknown type) and two footstools for a couch". The text also states that these were manufactured within a certain length of time, but, unfortunately, the exact interval is not clear.

Except for the pieces described as belonging to Irihalpa, which were probably part of the furnishings of a great house, or palace, the lists quoted above apparently refer to ordinary furniture made on order or for sale in the regular course of business. Doubtless, a considerable quantity of ordinary furniture was required by the palaces with their many rooms for court retainers, in addition to the more elegant palace furnishings, but it seems likely that most of the furniture in these lists was destined for use in more moderate dwellings. This is suggested, not only by the rather large quantity produced by the individual cabinet shops, but also by the records which appear in other of the Alalakh tablets. One of these (No. 421) lists furniture according to the individual owners, each of whom has a varying number of pieces such as would be suitable for ordinary domestic use; and in another (No. 114) there is an indication that the average prosperous household would have approximately three chairs, three foot-stools, three tables and one or two couches.

From the few isolated furniture representations available to us it is obviously not possible to conclude that Syria had a distinctly individual style of its own. It is indicated however, from the quantities of furniture listed in the Alalakh tablets quoted, that north Syria was an important furniture manufacturing area, and it is probable that, after the time of Assurnasirpal, Assyrian influence in design predominated. Other representations in Syrian seals and sculpture throw little additional light on the question of the prevailing

340 Stela showing the priest Agbar seated on a chair and facing a table, both of Assyrian design. *Fourteenth century* B.C.

341 Stela showing a pedestal table. *Fourteenth century* B.C.

furniture types. It should be recognized, however, that the furniture portrayed as booty "from a conquered city" in the reliefs from Sennacherib's palace (fig. 332) most likely came from Syria. Should this be so, it is then reasonable to assume that the chairs, tables and bed depicted in these reliefs are typical of the furniture made and used in Syria during the Late Assyrian period.

ANCIENT PALESTINE

Located between the desert and the sea, Palestine constituted the bridge between the two great civilizations of the ancient world. Separated from Mesopotamia only by Syria and exposed to Egypt on its southern border, it was subject to frequent invasion, and as a result its arts reflect the influence, first of one, and then of the other, of its powerful neighbours. During the latter part of the second millennium B.C. the dominant influence was Egyptian. Later, during the Assyrian and Neo-Babylonian eras, the Mesopotamian influence is more apparent. Being a comparatively poor country, Palestine could not rival the great nations in the luxury of its palaces and their furnishings, but a number of references to its furniture occur in Old Testament and other contemporary records, and there is some evidence of the furniture of the early periods in engravings and sculpture. Also, in recent excavations at Jericho, important finds of the remains of ancient wood furniture have been made, dating from the middle of the second millennium B.C.

Written evidence

We first hear of furniture from Palestine in the records left by the Egyptian king Tuthmosis III, who conquered Palestine and Syria in his campaign to the east early in the New Kingdom, about 1500 B.C. In the description of the loot taken from the captured city of Megiddo (Armageddon) in northern Palestine, nineteen pieces of furniture are mentioned: "six chairs of the enemy, of ivory, ebony and carob wood, wrought with gold; six footstools belonging to them; six large tables of ivory and carob wood; a bed belonging to that enemy of carob wood, worked with gold and every costly stone."[4]

Later, when Sennacherib attacked Palestine, his campaigns were commemorated, and the booty taken was portrayed in the sculptures of Nineveh and described in the records of the time. In the relief in which the king reviews the booty taken from Lachish (fig. 299 and p. 188), furniture is not pictured, but it is likely that here, as in other instances, furniture was included in the spoil taken from a captured city. For example, in the annals of his campaign against Jerusalem (701 B.C.), Sennacherib tells of couches, chairs and rare cabinet woods received from Hezekiah as tribute:

As to Hezekiah, the Jew, he did not submit to my yoke, I laid siege to forty-six of his strong cities, walled forts and to the countless small villages in their vicinity, and conquered them. . . . Hezekiah himself, whom the terror-inspiring splendour of my lordship had overwhelmed . . . did send me, later, to Nineveh, my lordly city, together with thirty talents of gold, eight hundred talents of silver, precious stones, antimony, large cuts of red stone, *couches (inlaid) with ivory, nîmedu-chairs (inlaid) with ivory*, elephant hides, ebony wood, box wood, (and) all kinds of valuable treasures. (Italics added by author.)[5]

Numerous Old Testament references to furniture also exist, some in considerable detail, which tell of the furniture of the Hebrews in Palestine, beginning with the time of the Exodus, about 1300 B.C.[6] In the Book of Exodus 25 : 23–8 we read of Moses receiving a commandment from the Lord on Mount Sinai:

And you shall make a table of acacia wood; two cubits shall be its length, a cubit its breadth, and a cubit and a half its height. You shall overlay it with pure gold, and make a moulding of gold around it. And you shall make around it a frame a handbreadth wide, and a moulding of gold around the frame. And you shall make for it four rings of gold, and fasten the rings to the four corners at its four legs. Close to the frame the rings shall lie, as holders for the poles to carry the table. You shall make the poles of acacia wood, and overlay them with gold, and the table shall be carried with these.[7]

Detailed instructions for the making of the tabernacle are also given, and a direction that acacia wood be used and that the parts be fitted with tenons set into sockets of silver (Exodus 26 : 15–30).

Later there is the account of the making of King Solomon's throne in the year he was visited at Jerusalem by the Queen of Sheba, about 900 B.C. (2 Chronicles 9 : 17–18).

The king also made a great ivory throne, and overlaid it with pure gold. The throne had six steps and a footstool of gold, which were attached to the throne, and on each side of the seat were arm-rests and two lions standing beside the arm-rests.

Obviously these Old Testament accounts refer to furniture made for the temple and the palace, but from them we may assume that the craftsmen of ancient Palestine were well able to make the furniture ornamented with ivory and gold mentioned in the accounts of Tuthmosis III and Sennacherib. It is worthy of note also, that in Palestine, as in ancient Egypt and Mesopotamia, "lions standing beside the arm-rests" continued to be used as symbols of royalty in the king's throne.

The mention of the "ivory throne" of Solomon, in addition to other Biblical references to the material, indicates that ivory was an accepted medium for the making of fine furniture in Palestine as it was in Syria. It would not, of course, be used in the making of ordinary household furniture, but one reference at least indicates that ivory furniture was not uncommon. In the warnings to the people of Israel, in the book of Amos, mention is made of those who take their ease and "lie upon beds of ivory and stretch themselves upon their couches" (Amos 6 : 4). No complete pieces of ivory furniture remain from ancient Palestine, but ornamental plaques used for decoration have been found, and in a few instances furniture is portrayed in the scenes engraved on ivory panels (see fig. 349).

As is true elsewhere in the Near East, most of the furniture described in the written records is the elaborate type intended primarily for palace or temple. Occasionally however we find a Biblical reference to furniture that evidently served a more utilitarian purpose. For instance, there is the description of the furniture with which "the Shunammite woman" furnished a room for the prophet Elisha. In all probability this is simple furniture – not elaborate furniture inlaid with ivory and gold: "Let us make a small roof chamber with walls and put there for him a bed, a table, a chair, and a lamp, so that whenever he comes to us, he can go in there" (II Kings 4 : 10). We have no direct evidence as to what these particular furnishings looked like but recent excavations at Jericho have brought to light for the first time the remains of simple wooden furniture from ancient Palestine. This furniture long antedates that of the Shunammite woman, but styles did not change often, or rapidly, and it is possible that the same types were still in use. These finds will be discussed in detail later (see p. 218).[8]

Seals

Relatively few representations of furniture in art have been found in Palestine. Furniture appears only rarely in the early Syro-Palestinian cylinder seals and when it does appear it is usually similar to that represented in the Mesopotamian seals. Since visual records of furniture are so sparse from Biblical Palestine, two seals found recently at Tell es-Saʿidiyeh (near the Jordan river midway between the Lake of Tiberias and the Dead Sea) are of particular interest (figs. 342, 343). These were discovered in 1964 by an expedition sponsored by the University Museum of the University of Pennsylvania, under the direction of Dr James B. Pritchard, during the first season's excavations of this relatively neglected locale. Although influenced by the styles of other Near Eastern centres of seal engraving, these seals dating from the eighth century B.C. appear to be the work of native seal cutters, and it seems a reasonable assumption that the chairs depicted represent types which were in use in Palestine at the time.

The chair with the tall straight back and turned legs resembles chairs seen in contemporary Assyrian seals, and the seated figure faces a low table of similar design. This type of simple chair appears to have been popular throughout the ancient Near East, and it is noteworthy that very similar chairs are still found in the country styles of Europe and the Americas twenty-seven hundred years later. Then, as now, the seats were made of woven rush.

The other chair, which today we would call a 'ladder-back', has a sharply curving back with four cross-slats. As far as I know, this example is unique but the construction is logical and practical and it seems likely that other chairs shown only in profile may have had similar cross-slats. The curving back is, as we have noted before, a feature seen quite often in Early Mesopotamian chair representations.

342
343

342 Cylinder seal impression showing chair with straight back and turned legs. *Eighth century* B.C.

343 Cylinder seal impression showing a 'ladder-back' chair with curving back and four cross-slats. *Eighth century* B.C.

344

344 Drawing of two scarabs showing high-back chairs. *Late 2nd millennium* B.C.

Two unusual scarabs which date from the second millennium B.C. also depict chairs with curving backs, perhaps suggesting that this may have been a traditional feature of chairs in Palestine (fig. 344).[9] Minute as they are, these little pictures give us some idea of the details of the chairs. One of the chairs has animal-type legs in front and back which face forward as in the Egyptian chairs of the period. In both chairs, however, there is a marked curve backward at the upper part of the back-rests – a feature not found in Egypt, except where this appearance is simulated by the drape of the cushions.

345

345 Statue of a man seated on a stool. *Middle of the 2nd millennium* B.C.

213

Sculpture

Although extremely archaic in appearance, two commemorative sculptures found in Palestine are illustrated since they also represent both Egyptian and Mesopotamian characteristics. In spite of the impression of great antiquity, the sculptures probably date to approximately the middle of the second millennium B.C. They were found recently by Dr Yadin of the Archaeological Service in Israel[10] at the site of Hazor, which was one of the important cities of ancient Palestine and which is mentioned by Joshua in describing his conquest of the "northern cities". The stool, on which the person portrayed sits in a squatting position, is Mesopotamian in appearance, with heavy stretchers (fig. 345). The chair in the other sculpture is Egyptian in type, with forward-facing animal legs, but the features of the dignified person who occupies the chair are more Semitic than Egyptian in appearance (fig. 346).

The conspicuous rarity of sculptured figures seated on thrones, or of other representations of furniture from the Assyrian and Neo-Babylonian periods, raises the question of whether this may not be due, in part at least, to the strict injunction in the Hebrew religion against the making of "graven images". The decalogue forbade not only the making of gods but also the "likeness of anything that is in the heaven, or that is in the earth beneath" (Exodus 20 : 4). Although in fact this injunction was not always strictly obeyed, pictorial representations of all sorts are conspicuously lacking from the period when the Assyrian kings are portrayed so frequently, sitting on their thrones, in the sculptures of Nineveh and Khorsabad.[11]

346 Statue of a man seated on a chair. *Middle of the 2nd millennium* B.C.

Carved ivories

What is possibly the earliest example of ivory carving from ancient Palestine in which furniture is represented, appears on the lid of a small box found at Tell-el-Farah on the southern border near Egypt (fig. 347).[12] Probably the person seated was the Egyptian governor, who wears a robe of the period of Sethos I (about 1300 B.C.) and sits on a chair of an Egyptian type. The sweep of the back and sharply curved finial, however, suggest a Near Eastern influence. The lion's feet are also more Mesopotamian in character than Egyptian, but the general form of the chair is typical of chairs of the New Kingdom in Egypt, as is the cushion of an animal skin with the tail of the hide hanging down.

Most of the ivory panels found in Palestine, however, have come from Megiddo, whose ivory workers were rivals to those of Syria. For the most part the carvings

347 Engraved lid of an ivory box showing an Egyptian-style chair. *Fourteenth century* B.C.

348 Drawing of an ivory plaque showing a throne decorated with a sphinx. *Thirteenth–twelfth century* B.C.

349 Drawing of the side-panel of an ivory box showing stools and tables with Mesopotamian influence. *Thirteenth–twelfth century* B.C.

347

348

349

350

351

350 Carved ivory furniture ornament showing the god Bes. *Thirteenth–twelfth century* B.C.

351 Carved ivory furniture ornament showing a sphinx. *Thirteenth–twelfth century* B.C.

352 Carved ivory box with Assyrian winged lions. *Thirteenth–twelfth century* B.C.

352

relating to furniture are ornamental plaques, but occasionally pieces of furniture are depicted. A banquet scene with furniture appears on a narrow ivory panel with dove-tailed ends (probably late second millennium B.C.) which is one of four that formed the sides of a shallow box (fig. 349). The panel is only two inches high, and the figures accordingly are in miniature, but the individual pieces of furniture are rendered in detail. The three stools with heavy legs and the table with boldly curved animal-shaped legs

216

resemble other Near Eastern furniture, but no close parallel to the small stand exists in the other representations which we have. In another scene of about the same period, celebrating a victorious homecoming (fig. 348), a prince sits on an elaborate throne which, although ornamented on its side with a sphinx instead of a lion, is reminiscent of the description of the throne of King Solomon.

The carved ivory plaques from Megiddo, like those from Nimrud, seem to have been intended for furniture ornamentations, two of which are illustrated here. In one of these the Egyptian influence is apparent in the representation of the god Bes who holds the Egyptian symbols of life (fig. 350).[13] In another the figure of a sphinx is represented with the body of a lioness and the head of a woman, Syro-Palestinian in type (fig. 351). On each of these two plaques the tenons with which they are attached are clearly visible in the photographs. Typical Assyrian winged lions stand by the side of a small square open box (fig. 352), the shape of which resembles the socket of an elaborate piece of furniture. Complete pieces of ivory furniture were probably also made by the craftsmen of Megiddo, as in Syria, judging by the written records previously quoted.

Furniture from the Jericho excavations

Although there had been many finds of furniture in Egypt, dating from about the same period, it was not until the comparatively recent excavations at Jericho that remains of furniture from ancient Palestine have been discovered. This important project which was initiated by the British School of Archaeology in Jerusalem (Jordan) in 1952 was shared in by several other archaeological institutions and carried on under the direction of Kathleen M. Kenyon. Giving us our only actual evidence of furniture in ancient Palestine, these excavations are of particular interest.

Remains of wooden furniture were found in at least ten of the Early Bronze Age tombs and present a unique record of the ordinary furniture of this period in Palestine – probably dating two hundred or more years before Joshua "blew down" the walls of Jericho. It is curious that wood should have been preserved here, when elsewhere in the ancient tombs of Palestine it had almost entirely disintegrated, and it has been suggested in the report of the excavations that there may have been an accumulation of gas, due to unknown causes, that killed the organisms causing decay.[14] Not that any of these pieces of furniture were found intact; unlike the well-preserved furniture of Egypt, what was found here consisted of fragments only, but enough remained, fortunately, to give an idea of its original appearance. Remains of tables were found in most of the tombs. There were also fragments of several stools and benches, but only one bed was clearly identifiable. This was discovered in the largest and most important of the tombs and undoubtedly indicates that the ordinary people slept on rush mats, such as those on which the bodies had been placed. It might be assumed, in view of the quantity found, that tables were the most commonly used types of household furniture, but this does not necessarily follow, since tables served a double purpose in the tomb furnishings – to accompany the deceased in the afterlife, and to hold the offerings placed in the tombs.[15] Probably stools were actually more numerous in the Palestinian household of the period, as they were in Egypt.

Laboratory studies made by the Jodrell Laboratory, Kew, indicate that the woods used in these pieces were tamarisk, willow and a wood resembling cherry.[16] One interesting feature mentioned in the excavation reports is the extreme shrinkage which had taken place in the wood parts – in contrast to the Egyptian furniture in which the dimensions of the wood has remained remarkably stable. Judging by comparison with the bone ornamentation, which retained its original form, the reports state that wood had shrunk 25 per cent across the grain and 16 per cent in length.[17] Whether or not these percentages are subject to correction in further tests, the change in dimension suggests that green wood was used in the making of the particular piece tested, and that it is eventually dried out in the fluctuating moisture conditions of Palestine.

Enough remained of several of the pieces of furniture to permit accurate reconstructions, one of the best preserved examples being the large bench of which the fragments found are illustrated in the drawing in figure 353. Included in the drawing is a perspective of the bench as it would appear with the parts assembled. The plain flat leg, with rounded foot and a shaped inner edge, obviously derives from the carved animal-type supports and closely resembles the legs found in simple Egyptian stools (figs. 195–204). In this instance, however, the legs turn inwardly towards each other rather than facing in one direction as was customary in Egyptian stools. It is important to note, however, that in an Eleventh Dynasty model from a boat from the tomb of Meket-Re there are miniature models of chairs and a long table (or bed) which closely resemble these pieces from Jericho, and have scroll legs which turn in towards each other (fig. 463).

A simple stool with turned legs[18] also resembles Egyptian types, but it differs from those we have seen in the shape of the turnings as well as in the four rounded stretchers which hold it together. As in the illustration of the bench, a drawing shows both the fragments found and a sketch of the stool as reconstructed (fig. 354). The round legs project above the seat and are rounded at the top. (It should be noted in the sketch that where the lower part angles out on one leg, this is due to the warping of the wood.) Parts of another stool were found near by with a leg intentionally shaped with an outward curve at the bottom and decorated with incised rings.

Each of the tables was made with three legs, two at one end and one in the centre of the top at the other end. Although the table with three legs was apparently not in common use in ancient Egypt, this was also the arrangement of all those found at Gordion in Anatolia (fig. 372) and was customary at a later date in Greece. The tables in the Jericho tombs varied in size from approximately thirty-four to sixty inches in length. They were narrow in relation to the length, apparently varying between ten and sixteen inches in width, and were very low, approximately ten to twelve inches high.

The long tables are especially interesting, since nothing similar exists in the ancient furniture found elsewhere. One of these was provided with a round sunken place in the centre, cut out from the thick plank from which the top had been fashioned, similar to the hollowed-out section illustrated in figure 355. This cut-out part somewhat resembled that of a 'cobbler's bench', but the purpose is unknown; it may perhaps have been used to hold tools or utensils, or possibly food. On the underside of this same long table top there were three round protrusions into which the legs were tenoned, these projecting

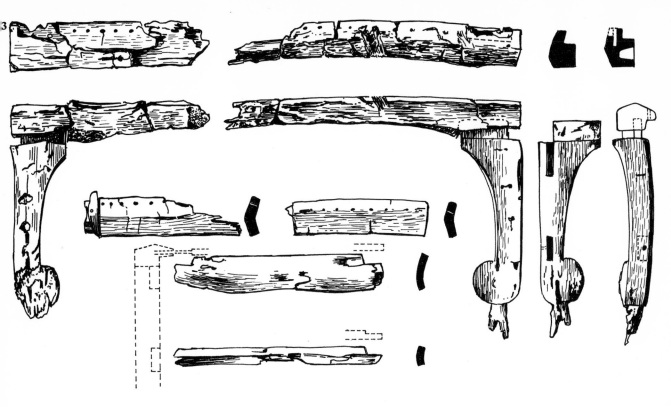

353 Drawing of fragments of a wooden bench. *About 1600* B.C.

354 Drawing of fragments of a wooden stool. *About 1600* B.C.

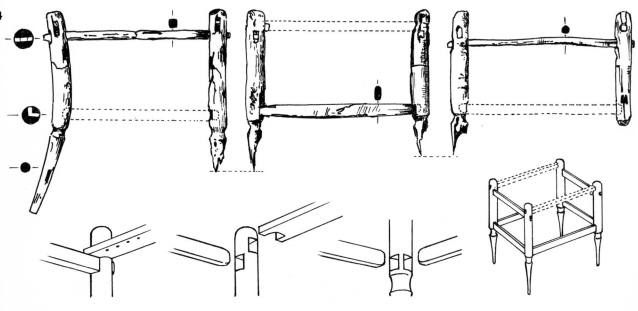

355 Drawing of fragments of a wooden table. *About 1600* B.C.

parts being part of the original thick plank. The surplus wood remaining was cut away (fig. 356b). Obviously this represented a great deal of work with the crude adzes and chisels that were available; Ricketts states that in one instance the plank was approximately four-and-a-half inches thick, twelve-and-a-half inches wide, and fifty-five inches long.[19] Another of the table tops was enclosed in a frame, forming a border, mitred at the corners and mortised into the sides of the plank (fig. 356a).

The shape of the table legs varied. Although the majority of the fragments of legs found are round, a long table from Tomb H18 had the same shaped legs, facing inwardly towards each other, as those of the bench illustrated above. The large number of fragments found makes it unpractical to discuss them all in detail but the shorter table of which the remains of the top have been illustrated in figure 355 is worth mentioning. In this instance almost the entire top is covered with a dished-out section. At one end, between the two mortise holes cut for the legs, is a shallow socket cut in from the top, apparently for something to be attached to the surface of the table. The break in the centre of the other end of the top suggests that the mortise hole to receive a single end leg was placed at this point.

Some fragments which appear to be those of a bed were found in Tomb J, but the only parts that could be definitely identified as belonging to a bed were those found in Tomb H18. The frame was a simple rectangular construction consisting of squared pieces of wood, with five cross-pieces tenoned into the long rails. The small holes bored in the long rails and the cross-pieces indicate that there were five separate panels formed of woven rush, some of which still clung to the side-pieces – a construction that would seem very uncomfortable for a bed, unless covered with a heavy mattress. Judging by the fragment of the bed leg that was found, the legs of the bed were six to eight inches in height and were shaped like those of the bench and long table.

The natural inference from the fragments that were found is that this furniture was crudely made; the thirty-five hundred years that have elapsed have destroyed any traces of fine workmanship or elegance that may have existed. It is only in the remains of the toilet boxes that there is evidence of ornamentation. There were a number of these, but

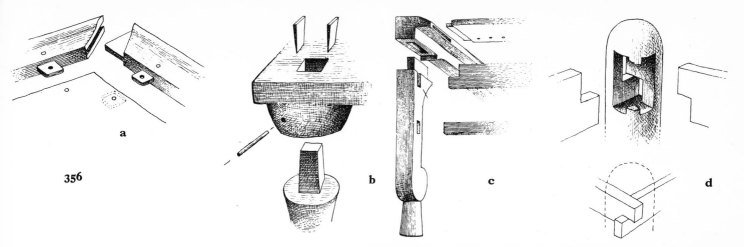

a

356

b

c

d

356 Drawing of construction details of the Jericho furniture. *About 1600* B.C.

357 Panel of a bone inlaid toilet box. *About 1600* B.C.

357

not enough remained of any single box to permit a reconstruction. It was obvious, however, that, like their Egyptian counterparts, a great deal of care had gone into their construction and ornamentation. The method of fastening – with cords laced around knobs placed in the cover and on the face – was the same as that used in Egypt. The joinery was also similar, but we find a stylistic difference in the bone inlays which were used for ornamentation (fig. 357).

For the most part, the question of joinery details has been left for the appendix (page 297). In this instance, however, we are including the construction drawings made by Michael Ricketts, draughtsman of the expedition, since they relate directly to the pieces found in the Jericho excavations.[20] Figure 356a shows the corner section of the frame of one of the long tables. The mitred rails are fitted with a tongue-and-groove joint, and they are fastened to the centre section of the table top with small tongues of wood. These were mortised, both into the frame-rails and into the top, and further secured by small

221

pegs inserted from the top. Figure 356b gives details of the method of attaching a round leg to the plank top of a table. The round projection below the top is that previously described as having been cut from the solid wood. In this instance it appears that the tenon of the leg tapered and was tightly fixed in the mortise by two wedges driven from above.

The most elaborate of the joinery, and that for which there was the most evidence, was found in the bench with woven top. Figure 356c gives a partial view of the construction. Two mortises were cut into the side of the leg to receive the tenons of the lower stretcher and an upper cross-stretcher which was placed under the seat-rail. At the top of the leg a third tenon was fitted into a mortise on the under-side of the short seat-rail. The section at upper left represents one of the short seat-rails with a rabbet on its inner edge to receive the strands of the woven seat, and has a socket at the end to meet the corresponding tenon of the long seat-rail. Figure 356d illustrates the construction detail of a stool of which nothing remained but the leg, the lower part of which was ringed with incised lines. Unlike the stool in figure 354, in which the seat-rails are placed at

358

359

358 Reproduction of wooden bench from Jericho with woven top. *About 1600* B.C.

359 Reproduction of wooden table from Jericho. *About 1600* B.C.

360 Reproduction of wooden stool from Jericho with woven top. *About 1600* B.C.

361 Reconstructed bronze and wooden stool. *Sixth–fifth century* B.C.

362 Reconstructed bronze and wooden bed. *Sixth–fifth century* B.C.

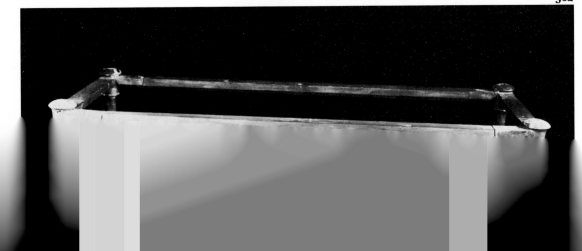

different heights, the rails met each other at the same level where they entered the post, and were fitted with halved mortise and tenon joints.

Although drawings are essential to an understanding of the construction details of this furniture, its actual appearance when new can be better visualized from the reproductions on display in the Royal Ontario Museum in Toronto, which institution was one of the sponsors of the Jericho excavations.[21] These conform in size to the measurements of the original pieces and closely follow the drawings made by the expedition staff. Included in these reproductions is the large bench with a woven covering (fig. 358) and also the small stool with woven top and turned legs which could pass as a present-day provincial type (fig. 360). Similarly the long table which has been reproduced has a modern look in its proportions (fig. 359). A reproduction was also made of the bed, based on the fragments that were found. Except that it is longer, with the top divided into smaller panels, it closely resembles the bench with woven top.

Dating about a thousand years later than these discoveries in Jericho, furniture fragments found at Tell-el-Farah reflect a very different design influence. These consist principally of the bronze fittings of a bed and stool, now in the Palestine Archaeological Museum in Jordan, of which the reconstructions are illustrated (figs. 361, 362).[22] Although probably fifth century B.C., this use of metal in connection with wood parts is similar to what we have seen in earlier Assyrian furniture. This is particularly true of the corner angle pieces of bronze used to join the wooden frame pieces of the bed, which in principle are the same as found at Nineveh dating from the eighth century B.C. In the shape of the legs, however, we see reproduced the form of turned wooden legs which became increasingly popular in the sixth and fifth centuries B.C.

ANCIENT PERSIA

Of the various peripheral countries only Persia, although dominated for long intervals by the Mesopotamians, was considered by Frankfort to have had an individual style which was never entirely lost.[23] Unfortunately, however, as in Syria and Palestine, the few representations which we have of furniture only complicate the question of what may have been the special characteristics of the native furniture design. The furniture depicted in the earlier seals and sculptures from this area displays no marked individuality, but a chair represented in a twelfth-century B.C. sculpture from Susa differs somewhat from the usual Mesopotamian types (fig. 364). The relief has special interest also as one of the rare instances where furniture of the Middle Assyrian period is represented, when the Persian area was still ruled by the Kassite Dynasty. Seated on the chair is the goddess Nanay, before whom appear the king, Meli-Shipak, and his daughter. The lion's claw feet are, of course, a common feature of Mesopotamian furniture, as is the slender rounded pedestal, on which rests the sacred cone, but the vertical ornamental pieces of a rope design between the seat and the base, and the rope design of the stretcher, are unusual details.

Another relief from Susa, perhaps of the ninth century B.C., portrays a woman who is seated with her feet doubled under on a low, clumsy stool (fig. 363). The heavy feet of lion's claw design resemble the bronze work of Urartu, but a stool or table of this

363

363 Bas-relief showing a woman seated on a low clumsy stool. *About ninth century* B.C.

364 Stele showing the goddess Nanay seated on a throne with ornamental pieces of a rope design. *Twelfth century* B.C.

365 Relief showing Darius the Great seated on his throne. *About 524* B.C.

364

365

sort made entirely of bronze would be exceedingly heavy, and it is likely that the major part of such a piece, if not all, would have been made of wood. The seat-rail projects at the back, as in early Egyptian stools, and on top of the seat is what appears to be a cushion made of a heavy woven fabric. The dish-like top of the table with a rounded section below is a feature seen fairly often in Mesopotamian seals, but the heavy rounded legs and the wide carved band between display local characteristics.

Furniture representations from the following periods in Persia are rare, but sculptures in which Darius the Great is portrayed on his throne, dating from the sixth century B.C., indicate a marked difference between furniture design of this period in Persia and that which was portrayed in the Assyrian reliefs (fig. 365). Almost precisely this same relief is repeated many times on the walls of the great palace of Darius at Persepolis, but unfortunately no other furniture is pictured there to permit further comparison. Not only is the design of his throne a marked contrast to that of the thrones of the Assyrian kings, but the architecture of the palace also exhibits a marked departure from the traditional architecture of Mesopotamia. The great hall is a forest of columns – a feature common in Egypt but not seen in Assyrian and Babylonian palaces – superficially resembling the Ionic columns of Greece, but with elaborately carved capitals and ornamental details that are distinctively Persian.[24]

The king's throne and foot-stool indicate the increase in the use of turnings that occurred at about this time[25] and exhibit some other distinctive features. Not only the legs and feet, but also the stretchers are turned. The foot of the throne has a beaded bell-shaped member, the upper part of the leg has a series of four turned rings, and in between is a carved section.

The period of Persian rule – from the conquest of Babylon by Cyrus the Great in 539 B.C. to the defeat of the Persians by Alexander the Great in 331 B.C. – is roughly contemporaneous with the Late Archaic and Classical periods in Greece, but the representations of furniture in painting and art that are so abundant in Greece during this period are almost entirely lacking in the art of the Near East.

ASIA MINOR – GORDION AND ALTINTEPE

There are but few visual records of furniture from ancient Anatolia and there would be little reason to treat this area separately at this time except for recent discoveries of the remains of ancient furniture made at Gordion, located approximately seventy miles southwest of modern Ankara. Gordion was the capital of ancient Phrygia, the Anatolian kingdom ruled in the eighth century B.C. by King Midas, the legendary 'king of the golden touch' celebrated in Greek myths. Greek colonies were being established on the coast at about this time and doubtless there was some contact between the Archaic Greeks and the Phrygians, but to what extent this was reflected in the furniture of inland Anatolia, if at all, is uncertain. It seems more likely that the furniture of the East still influenced that of Greece during this period.

These important discoveries at Gordion were made in 1956 and 1957 by an expedition under the direction of Dr Rodney Young of the University Museum of Philadelphia.[26]

226

366 Back-rest for a throne of carved openwork.
Eighth century B.C.

367 Fragments of furniture from Gordion.
Eighth century B.C.

A number of burial mounds were excavated, some of earlier periods and others contemporary with the Late Assyrian period, and in two of the latter, dating about the time of Sargon II (721–705 B.C.), were found the remains of a considerable amount of wood furniture. One of the mounds contained the tomb of a young child with whom had been buried toys and a great deal of household furnishings. There were also a large number of fragments of wooden furniture, carved and decorated, which would not be expected in an ordinary grave and which consequently suggest that this was the ritual burial of the child of an important family – perhaps a young prince of the royal family.

Among the remains of furniture found in this tomb was an elaborate open-work carved panel which it was first surmised had formed the back of a chair or throne (fig. 366). Its actual function in a piece of furniture is still uncertain, but obviously it represents a complicated piece of cabinet-work and a sophisticated concept of design. In addition, there were found the remains of the child's bed, parts of two or more chairs, pieces of foot-stools, traces of a wooden chest and various fragments of tables. Apparently one of the tables had a round top, while the others were rectangular. The lower frame of one end of the bed was better preserved than most of the furniture parts, and revealed a rounded cross-rail which had been joined to rounded legs with mortise and tenon joints. Carved and inlaid fragments which had formed parts of the head-board were also identified. But although the members of the excavation staff were able to ascertain the types of furniture placed in the tomb from the fragments remaining, it has not been possible as yet to reconstruct satisfactorily any of the individual pieces. There is sufficient evidence to encourage attempts at reconstruction, but for the most part the many fragments, such as those in figure 367, present an unsolved puzzle.

When the largest of the Gordion tombs (called the 'Royal Tomb') was opened in the following year, the remains were found of nine tables, two inlaid screens or throne backs and a large poster bed, as well as the unidentifiable fragments of several other pieces of furniture. These had been placed in a chamber measuring about seventeen by twenty feet inside and built of squared beams of pinewood mortised at the corners. The tumulus mound above had been raised to a height of about two hundred feet. Evidently the burial place of an important person, even if not the legendary King Midas himself (as was once suggested), it dates to the most flourishing period of Phrygian history, about 725 B.C. In addition to the other furnishings there were one hundred and seventy bronze vessels of varying shapes and sizes, most of which were apparently of local manufacture. Some had been hung on the walls of the tomb, and others had been placed on the tables, which had collapsed under the weight of the metal as the wood became weakened with age.

A large four-poster bed had been placed in one corner to receive the body of the deceased, as can be seen in the drawing which shows the contents of the tomb as they were originally found (fig. 368). The bed rested on four large square corner blocks, above which were corner posts into which the foot-board and head-board were dowelled. In his report of the excavation Rodney Young surmises that there were two end panels, each convex in shape with scrolled designs at the outer corners, and long rails constructed of contrasting light and dark wood.[27] The platform of the bed was made of wooden planks laid lengthwise, suggesting that it was intended especially for funerary use, as it seems likely that beds intended for sleeping would have had a more resilient base. A pile of bed-clothing had been placed on top at the time of burial, consisting of twenty layers of linen and wool cloth in various colours.

Leaning against the east wall of the chamber were the remains of two screens, one of which is illustrated in position as found (fig. 370). (The rosette-like object resting on the floor at the lower right part of the photograph is one of the many ornamental bronze

368

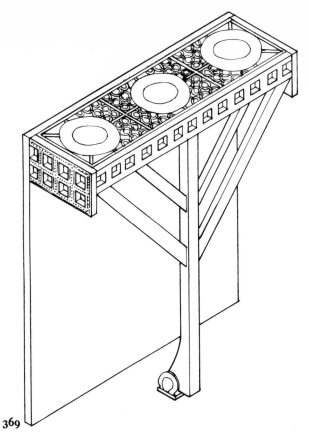

369 Drawing of the reconstructed standing screen, showing reverse of panel. *About 725* B.C.

370 Inlaid wooden screen from Gordion. *About 725* B.C.

369

vessels found in the tomb.) These screens were similar in size to the large carved panel found in the child's tomb and probably served the same purpose. Their ornamentation, however, is different; those in the 'Royal Tomb' are inlaid with boxwood and yew, instead of being carved and decorated with bronze studs. These later discoveries were also better preserved and more complete and seem to answer the previously unanswered question as to the probable use of such screens. When the various parts are fitted together, as in the drawing by Dorothy Cox (fig. 369),[28] they form a free-standing unit that could easily be moved about and apparently formed the back-rest for either a low throne or a hassock. Although this is only conjecture, the latter seems a likely assumption, as the hassock is still a popular seat in the Near East, and there were probably innumerable bright-coloured cushions available to add to the comfort and oriental splendour. As long before as the New Kingdom in Egypt, hassocks are portrayed in the tomb paintings,[29] and cushions had been used from a very early period.

The different parts of the screen were fastened together by tenons fitted into sockets, and further secured by small pegs run through the parts joined and the tenons. Its face is elaborately decorated with patterns composed of dark pieces of wood inlaid into a lighter ground, probably boxwood. The workmanship is so exact that, rather than interfere with the regularity of the design, the inlays are even inset into the ends of the pegs which secure the tenons wherever the pegs appear on the surface. The cut-out sections into which the

368 Drawing of the contents of the 'Royal Tomb' at Gordion. *About 725* B.C.

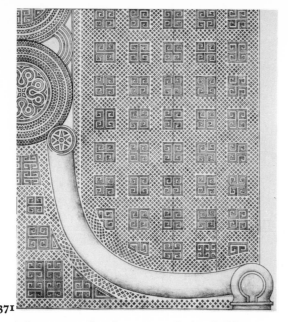

372

371 Drawing of the face of the standing screen. *About 725* B.C.

372 Drawing of a simple three-legged table from Gordion. *About 725* B.C.

inlays were fitted were made by drilling straight rows of small holes and then cutting away the remaining wood with some kind of a tool. The geometric patterns of the design, which can be seen more clearly in the drawing in figure 371, bring to mind the Byzantine motifs of a much later period.

Slightly below the centre of the screen panel there is a round medallion, below which are curved pieces of wood resembling table legs running to the lower corners at each side and terminating in scroll feet. Fitted to the back of the screen at its upper edge there had been a shelf, with three cut-out carved circles, and aprons decorated with inlay patterns similar to those of the face of the screen. Under the shelf a back leg was attached which was braced on each side by two wooden pieces running diagonally upwards and fastened at their upper ends with tenons fitted into sockets. Curious as this structure appears to our modern eyes, the parts which were found in the tomb indicate that the reconstruction in the drawing illustrated is essentially correct.

All of the tables were three-legged, an arrangement which kept them steady on an uneven floor and which was to become customary later in Greece. Of the nine tables found, one was extremely elaborate; the other eight were simple and alike in design (fig. 372). The tops of the plainer tables are rectangular with rounded corners, with the surface worked down so as to leave a raised rim, and the edges are rounded a bit underneath, thus giving a dished appearance. The wood of the tops was partly decayed, but enough remains to show that it was a straight-grained, soft, brown variety, although the exact species is uncertain. The legs, which are rounded and curve outwardly at the bottom, were attached to the top by tenons which projected through the wood to the upper surface. There were two legs at one end, the third leg being placed in the centre of the top at the other end. They were made of a harder, lighter-coloured wood than the tops, and are better preserved. The grain of the wood follows the curve of the legs, suggesting that they were bent before shaping, although it is possible that naturally

230

curved pieces of timber had been made use of. Where the legs join the top a thick cushion-like ring of contrasting wood had been placed around the tenon, which in turn was locked into place by a horizontal peg. Although the design and construction of these tables was clearly visible, unfortunately none was sufficiently well preserved to permit being re-assembled.

The most extraordinary piece of furniture in the tomb, however, was the so-called 'pagoda table', which was found in a jumbled heap (fig. 373). This elaborate concoction was constructed with three legs and was made of the same basic woods as the simpler tables, but here the similarity ceases. Some distance below the top there was a frame consisting of a wide band ornamented at intervals with finely carved and inlaid square medallions. Between this frame and the top there were delicate vertical supports, four on the ends and three on the face, which terminated in double dowel-like members fitted into holes in the underside of the top. At the front, the corners of the lower frame were connected to the feet with lacy, open-work carved 'draperies' of wood that might have been intended to give some bracing to this complicated structure, but more probably were purely ornamental. In the back there are wooden vertical strappings between the frame and the two back feet. The legs, which are round and curve outward at the bottom, are ornamented with two carved rings and a beaded bulbous section in between, and terminate in curious hooded shoes. At the four corners appear carved handle-like pieces which might have served as handles with which to lift the table, but their light construction suggests that, like the 'drapery' in front, their principal function was ornamental. The medallions of the frame and the decorated sections of the drapery and of the handles are inlaid with dark wood on light in geometric designs. The reconstruction, as illustrated in a drawing by Dorothy Cox (fig. 374), portrays the fantastic construction of this curious piece, which resembles nothing else in either ancient or modern design. But regardless of how we view this table as a matter of taste or good design, it presents striking evidence of the technical skill of the cabinet-makers of the time.

Although these remains of wood furniture from Gordion are unimpressive compared with the perfectly preserved pieces from ancient Egypt, they are important in that they give us a glimpse of the furniture of a virtually unknown culture that existed in Asia Minor about three hundred years before the Classical era in Greece. Furthermore, the design motifs of the Gordion pieces, even though they may not be considered beautiful, differ radically from what we have seen from the other countries of the Near East. During the time when this furniture was made, Phrygian design seems to have been relatively free from the influence of Mesopotamia, if we may judge by the Gordion finds. What remains to be answered, however, is whether, and to what extent, the Gordion pieces are typical of the Anatolian furniture of that time.

Since the ancient arts of Asia Minor have not as yet received the amount of study and exploration given to the antiquities of Mesopotamia, additional important discoveries can be expected in this area. Recently, in Turkey, at Altintepe, the tomb of a Urartian prince has been discovered in which there were the remains of a considerable amount of wood furniture dating from the end of the eighth or first quarter of the seventh century B.C. Built of well-dressed stones, the tomb contained three chambers, in two of which a

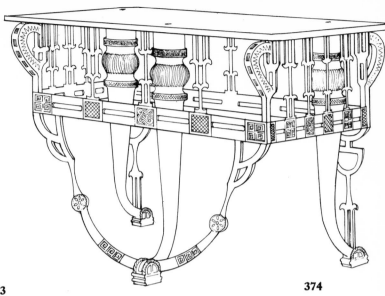

373   374

373 The 'pagoda table' in situ at Gordion. *About 725* B.C.

374 Drawing of the reconstructed 'pagoda table' from Gordion. *About 725* B.C.

number of stools and tables had been placed at the time of burial.[30] In the third and smallest chamber were found remains of a wooden couch 'reinforced' with eight bronze rings[31] and a large table decorated with silver.

Although information is not available as to whether complete reconstructions will eventually be possible, the fragments that have been published clearly show that the furniture resembled that shown in the Assyrian reliefs. The corners of tables and chairs were decorated and strengthened with metal corner-pieces, and the wooden stretchers had been sheathed in bronze with a running design of double volutes. Some of the pieces had the familiar Assyrian construction consisting of an upper section with legs terminating in lion's claws, which rested on a platform-base supported by ornamented round feet. The legs which rested on the ground were mostly silver plated while the animal-shaped legs above were sheathed in bronze. Most of the wood had disintegrated, except for some parts protected by metal, as in other Near Eastern tombs, but the fragments found indicate that part, if not all, of the furniture had been decorated with geometric patterns incised or in relief.

Even though this furniture does not appear to be as novel in design as was that found at Gordion, its discovery will help to fill in the gap that exists in our knowledge of the furniture of this area. The report of the expedition also points out that the owners of the tombs lived in a Urartian town within a large citadel on the summit of Altintepe, and that the contents of some of their houses and palaces might still be preserved and await discovery. Excavations are continuing at Altintepe, and it is to be hoped that these and further discoveries will reveal furniture that will throw further light on what existed in Asia Minor during the Assyrian–Babylonian period.

232

PART III:
THE AEGEAN

Chronological table of the Aegean Bronze Age and later periods.

Date (B.C.)	CYCLADES	CRETE	GREECE	EVENTS, ART, etc.
3000	EARLY CYCLADIC	EARLY MINOAN	EARLY HELLADIC	Cycladic idols
2000				
1900	MIDDLE CYCLADIC — I, II, III	MIDDLE MINOAN — I, II, III	MIDDLE HELLADIC	First Cretan Palaces
1800				
1700				
1600				Second Cretan Palaces — Shaft Graves Mycenae; Throne of Minos; Linear B Knossos
1500	LATE CYCLADIC — I, II, III	LATE MINOAN — I, II, IIIA, IIIB, IIIC	LATE HELLADIC II *or* MYCENAEAN — I, IIIA, IIIB, IIIC	
1400				
1300				Trojan War
1200				Linear B Pylos
1100				Dorian Invasion
1000	DARK AGES			
900				
800				Homeric poems, final form.
700	ARCHAIC PERIOD			Hesiod
650				Sappho. so Ion
600				
550				Pindar
500	CLASSICAL PERIOD			Persian Wars (490–479)
450				Parthenon (447–432)
400				Peloponnesian War (431–404)
350				Alexander the Great (356–323)
300				

Although not a geographical entity like the Nile Valley or Mesopotamia, the islands and coastal lands of the Aegean area are joined together by the sea which, instead of being a barrier, formed a highway that served to bring about a common culture in the ancient world. But in contrast to Egypt and the Near East, where the history of furniture design can be traced from the earliest beginnings in an almost direct line for more than two thousand years, the early record in the Aegean area is obscure, and the line of development is sharply broken at the end of the Mycenaean period.

Visual evidence of furniture is sparse until the seventh and sixth centuries B.C., when representations of furniture in sculpture and painting become abundant in Greece and a distinctly Greek character emerges. But although the record from the earlier periods is fragmentary it has significance in its relationship to the furniture of the other peoples of the ancient world, and also as the prelude to later Greek design – even if little or no direct influence is apparent. These early periods fall into three divisions, the first of which comprises the third millennium B.C., from which come the earliest signs of furniture in the Aegean area. The second consists of the Minoan era, more particularly that part dating from 2000 to 1400 B.C., when great palaces were built and the Minoan culture reached its peak on the island of Crete. The third division encompasses the Mycenaean period, dating roughly from 1600 to 1200 B.C., during which time the cultural focus shifted to the mainland of Greece, and is popularly symbolized by the great citadel of Mycenae and the 'golden treasure' in the National Museum in Athens.

After the mysterious destruction of the Mycenaean cities there comes a long gap in the history of art known as the 'dark ages', followed by the period designated by art historians as the Archaic period in Greece. Although called 'archaic', this was a great creative period during which the new Greek forms of art and architecture emerged after the long 'dark period' that preceded. This was also the time when the motifs of furniture design borrowed from Egypt and the Near East were beginning to be replaced by classical types of Greek furniture. Then came the Classical period and the great flowering of Greek art.

Our survey of ancient furniture in the Aegean ends with the furniture of the Archaic period in Greece, or, as we have chosen to call it, the Early Greek period, since the furniture which followed in the Classical, Hellenistic and Roman periods belongs to the 'classical' world rather than to the 'ancient', in the strict sense of the term. Many of the more familiar types of classical furniture, however, are derived from prototypes of an earlier date, the more important of which will be noted in our limited survey of Early Greek furniture. For the definitive study of Greek, Etruscan and Roman furniture reference should be made to Gisela M. A. Richter's scholarly work, which is being republished.[1]

Archaeological research has revealed that trade between Crete, the Near East and Egypt existed from an early age,[2] and in general the cultural movement was from east to west until the time of the Greek ascendancy. This influence can be seen in the arts of Crete

376

375 Terracotta seated figure, from Thessaly. *About 3000* B.C.

376 Terracotta model of a table, from Attica. *About 3000* B.C.

and Mycenae; and Egyptian and Mesopotamian details are also clearly apparent in the furniture of Archaic Greece. But, in spite of what exposure there may have been to the arts of these older and richer civilizations, the 'peoples of the seas' developed their own distinctive forms and decorations. Unfortunately, as in Mesopotamia, no wooden furniture has survived from these early periods in the Aegean world; climatic conditions on the islands and on the mainland of Greece are not conducive to the preservation of wood. The finds that have been made, however, of stone statuettes, terracottas and seal engravings in which furniture is represented – from the Cyclades, from Crete and from Mycenaean sites – give us some clues as to the appearance of the furniture that existed in the Aegean area during the third and second millennia B.C.

2   # THE EARLIEST FURNITURE
(3000–2000 B.C.)

Signs of a primitive culture appear in the islands and on the mainland of Greece early in the third millennium B.C., or somewhat before, expressed in pottery, small idols or figurines, and other objects of clay or stone. By the middle part of this period a considerable degree of skill had been achieved, and the sequence of development of styles in pottery can readily be traced. No comparable evidence exists, however, relating to the development of furniture, and what knowledge we have from this time is largely dependent on a few Cycladic statuettes of seated figures in which stools and chairs are represented.

A suggestion of furniture appears in two small terracottas found in Thessaly and Attica, dating from about 3000 B.C., and now in the National Museum in Athens (figs. 375, 376),[1] but the most significant evidence of furniture in the Aegean from this early period is seen in the intriguing marble statuettes of harp players found in the Cycladic Islands, dating approximately 2500 B.C. The first of these illustrated is one of two very similar figures found on the island of Thera and now in the museum in Karlsruhe (fig. 377).[2] In the other of this pair, most of the harp has been broken away; in both statuettes the harp player is seated on a primitive stool with heavy, partially rounded legs. There is of course no positive evidence in these small sculptures that a wooden stool is represented, but the resemblance to the stools of other early civilizations, and the extreme weight, if made of stone, suggest a seat made of wood. A similar stool is also represented in a rather badly mutilated statuette from the island of Naxos in the National Museum in Athens. Only the torso of the seated figure remains, but the outlines of the seat are clearly the same as those of the examples from Thera (fig. 378).

More revealing from the viewpoint of furniture, however, are two remarkable marble statuettes of harp players seated on chairs with backs, one of which is in the Metropolitan Museum in New York, and the other in the National Museum in Athens. In the Metropolitan example (fig. 379), the lower part of the chair has heavy legs like those of the stools, with a slightly rounded outline in the angle where the legs join the seat. The two projections at the rear of the seat seem quite definitely to represent the extension of wooden seat-rails (fig. 380). The back is a separate construction which would quite likely have been attached to the seat with tenons, as was done in Egyptian furniture, and both the dip in the top of the frame and the arched panel in the centre show a rather sophisticated sense of design.

Even more unusual is the chair in a statue in Athens which was discovered on the island of Keros, near Amorgos (fig. 381). The legs of the chair rest on runners which curve upwards and meet beneath the centre of the side-rail of the seat. At the outer side of the back legs there are two buttons (clearly visible in the rear view – fig. 382) at the point where the seat would naturally be joined, and which are rather strong evidence that a chair made of wood is represented, joined together with dowels or tenons.

Recently another striking example of these interesting seated harp players has come to light, reported to have been found in the Southern Cyclades which is now in the Virginia Museum of Fine Arts (fig. 383). The pointed arch at the top, repeated just above the seat, is reminiscent of the example in Athens, and also is faintly suggestive of the lines of the later 'throne of Minos'. The under section, however, is unique. There seems no valid reason why a marble model should have so elaborate a bracing, except that here again a wood prototype is represented. The back tapers to form a pointed arch, and an arched slat is inserted a short distance above the seat to form a back-rest. In total, the chair represents a concept of design that has, as far as I know, no parallel.

377

378

379

380

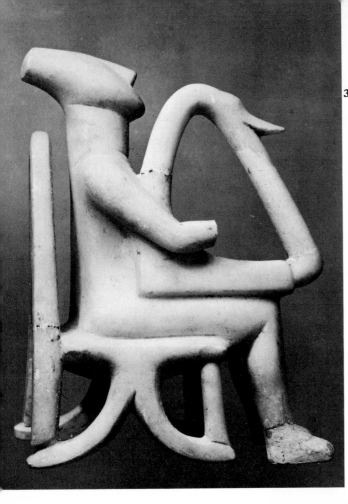

381

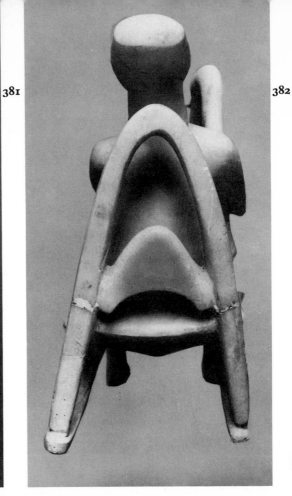

382

377 Marble statuette, from Thera. *About 2500* B.C.

378 Stone statuette, from Naxos. *About 2500* B.C.

379 Marble statuette, from the Cyclades. *About 2500* B.C.

380 Back view of figure 379.

381 Marble statuette, from Keros. *About 2500* B.C.

382 Back view of figure 381.

383 Marble statuette, from the Cyclades. *About 2500* B.C.

383

But even though there are resemblances in style between the three statuettes, and all come from the Cyclades, there are some interesting variations. The back of the Athens chair is formed by the extension of the rear legs, whereas in the Metropolitan example the back frame is separate – a basic difference. The seated figure in the latter example is heavier, and placed tightly against the chair back, with the lower part of the harp merged with the torso, while in the Athens statuette the musician sits free of the back with a lighter and smaller harp resting on his lap.

From the historical viewpoint, the three chairs represented present an interesting problem, since they have no apparent relationship to what we know of Mesopotamian or Egyptian furniture that existed at this same period. This is true also of the decorated pottery of which a considerable quantity has been found in the Cyclades, particularly on Amorgos, Thera and the other southern islands of the group. These are the closest of the islands to the south-western coast of Anatolia, and it seems likely that peoples from this area moved into the islands by sea at an early period and developed their own art forms. But even if we conclude that this furniture was an independent development, it cannot be assumed that it is representative of an extensive woodworking craft. The Cycladic Islands were small and limited in economic resources, and it was not until there was a concentration of wealth and power on Crete during the Middle Minoan period, that a luxurious civilization developed in the Aegean area.

3 THE MINOAN ASCENDANCY
(2000–1400 B.C.)

By the early part of the second millennium the Minoans in Crete had developed an advanced civilization and had become the great maritime power of the Aegean. But although palaces and towns had been built at Knossos and elsewhere on the island, they were destroyed by earthquake and fire about 1700 B.C., and nothing remains to tell of their furnishings. What evidence has been found of the furniture of the Minoans dates mostly from the Late Minoan period in the fifteenth century B.C., and comes principally from the 'Palace of Minos' at Knossos, which had been rebuilt after the first great earthquake and restored once more after another earthquake which occurred about 1570 B.C.

Excavations were begun here by Sir Arthur Evans shortly before the beginning of this century and, except for the interruption of the First World War, were continued under his direction until 1932, when he returned to England to complete the last volume of his monumental work, *The Palace of Minos*.[1] It was Evans who named the people responsible for this civilization 'the Minoans', after the mythical king Minos; and, thanks to his colourful restoration of the palace, as well as to the spectacular discoveries that were made, widespread interest has been stimulated in what has been called the first civilization of the European world.

Surrounding the ruins of the palace were the remains of fine town houses and villas as well as quarters for the artisans who supplied the necessities and luxuries for this highly

240   Colour plate XIII*a*. Bas relief showing servant carrying chair. *Neo-Assyrian period.*

b. Detail of colour plate XIII*a*.

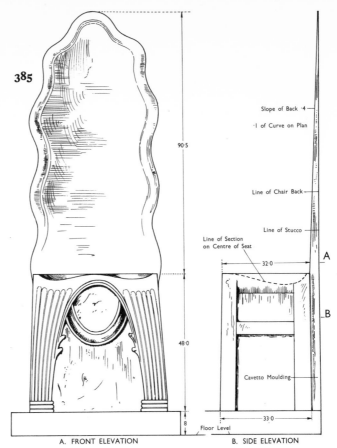

384 Replica of throne from Knossos.

385 Drawings of throne (fig. 384).

Labels in fig. 385: Slope of Back ·4 / ·I of Curve on Plan / Line of Chair Back / Line of Stucco / Line of Section on Centre of Seat / 90·5 / 32·0 / A / 48·0 / B / Cavetto Moulding / 8 / 33·0 / Floor Level / A. FRONT ELEVATION / B. SIDE ELEVATION

developed urban life. Among these requirements were certainly furnishings for the palace and houses of the well-to-do, since there is no reason to doubt that beds, stools, chairs, tables and storage chests were in use here as in contemporary Egypt and Mesopotamia.

Other important palaces have been excavated at Mallia and Phaistos, and a smaller one at Gournia. In the latter, which evidently had been a small industrial centre, were found various workshops. In one building, which apparently had housed a carpenter's shop, were found a saw, several chisels, an awl, a drill and some other tools. Another building had been used as a bronze factory and contained moulds for casting double axes, chisels and similar implements. Excavations are continuing at other sites, and in 1962 Nikolaos Platon of the Greek Archaeological Service discovered the foundations of an important palace near Zakro. So far about forty-five rooms have been unearthed, and it is stated there may have been as many as one hundred and fifty. Among the more recent finds made at this site in 1964 were three large saws and other carpenter's tools, probably used in the reconstruction of the palace.[2]

Minoan art had its own individual characteristics – different from what had preceded, and destined to have a direct effect on Mycenaean art. This was not, however, because of lack of contact with the other contemporary civilizations. Ships capable of sailing to the nearby coasts are pictured on Minoan seals dating about 2000 B.C.,[3] and there is ample evidence of trade with the Egyptians and the Phoenicians in the Minoan pottery found in their tombs. Naturally the trade was reciprocal and, in addition to native Minoan characteristics, the influence of Egypt and the Near East can be seen in the arts and furniture of Crete. It also seems quite likely that the techniques of woodworking that

241

were highly developed in Egypt would have been known in Crete, and not impossible that some pieces of Egyptian (or perhaps Syrian) furniture may have been imported.

Many archaeologists have contributed to our knowledge of the Minoans, and there is a large bibliography of both popular and scholarly works relating to the discoveries that have been made.[4] From the excavations of palaces and tombs have come frescoes, jewellery, pottery and other finds that give a good picture of Minoan art and some idea of the people and life of the period, but unfortunately it cannot be said that the excavations have yielded a comparable knowledge of the Minoan furniture. We must, however, examine the evidence that does exist.

The fires that accompanied the destruction of the palaces consumed whatever wood furniture there was, but in the palace of Minos the king's throne, made of stone, was left intact and now stands before the colourful frescoes restored by Evans.[5] The details of the throne, however, are more clearly apparent in the replica in the Ashmolean Museum (fig. 384), and in the drawings which appeared in Evans' *Palace of Minos* (fig. 385),[6] than in any photographs available from Heraklion.

Although contemporary with the early part of the Eighteenth Dynasty in Egypt, the design of the throne is a different concept from that of Queen Hatshepsut (fig. 66), or King Amenophis III (fig. 67), or the slightly later throne of King Tutankhamun (figs. 89, 90, colour plate VI). The wavy outline of the back, somewhat resembling an oak leaf, and the arched and fluted front legs with a swag between are unique and combine to form an attractive and dignified design. The shaping of the upper surface of the seat, similar to what appears today on wooden seated chairs, is interesting, and the introduction of a side-stretcher between the legs further suggests that a wooden structure served as a model. Certainly such a stretcher would serve no purpose in a stone chair. Evans mentions the remains of a thin plaster coating that once covered the stone, and traces of white and red wash, with lines for guiding the artist in painting his design.

In another part of the palace, in a mass of melted gypsum plaster, Evans found the impression of a second throne, apparently made of wood, since the material of which it had been constructed had vanished completely. The impression was not sharply enough defined for the design of the throne to be ascertained, but with it there were the outlines of a wooden canopy with 'fluted columns' of which there were some carbonized remains.[7]

Among the other finds that relate to furniture are a number of terracotta sarcophagi, or burial chests, rather like household storage chests and often brightly decorated. A considerable number of these are in the Heraklion Museum. One in the Ashmolean Museum, found by Evans at Knossos, has attractive ornamentation (fig. 386). Others of the sarcophagi have gabled tops, instead of flat lids, as in another example in the Ashmolean Museum (fig. 387). Of higher quality is a stuccoed limestone sarcophagus in Heraklion, from Hagia Triada (colour plate XIV). It clearly represents a wooden form of chest, and is ornamented both with formal motifs of circles and scrolls and with a typical Minoan scene in the panel. It has been suggested that the clay chests found in Crete may actually have been used for household storage before serving the purpose of sarcophagi. Although this seems quite possible, the wooden chests from Egypt suggest that a wooden construction was probably also used in Crete.

386 Terracotta sarcophagus from Knossos. *About 1400* B.C.

387 Terracotta sarcophagus from Knossos. *About 1400* B.C.

387

Although in some instances we see a foreign influence in Minoan furniture, a form of table or altar which appears on several seals seems to be a distinctly Minoan invention. As represented in the engravings, these altar-tables appear sufficiently large to permit an entire bullock to be placed on the top. In one example the table is represented with four legs, two to a side, and the projecting end poles suggest that it was intended to be used as a carrying table (fig. 388a). In the other example illustrated, which appears in an impression from a stone seal, the table has four legs on each side with additional supports between (fig. 388b).

Such altar-tables were doubtless intended for use in the sacrificial rites, and it is impossible to state what relationship they may have had to ordinary household furniture. The more elaborate example, however, exhibits a distinctive and rather attractive design in its broad tapering legs with flat arches between. There is no evidence to warrant such a conjecture, but it is tempting to surmise that a similar design may have appeared in the palace furniture.

Some representations of stools have also been found. In one clay seal impression, in which a woman pouring liquid into a large jar is portrayed, a stool with straight legs and a stretcher appears (fig. 388c). This is drawn rather carefully by the artist, and the angle pieces that are indicated between the legs and cross-rail apparently represent braces such as were commonly used in Egyptian furniture. The stool itself is not unlike the basic Egyptian stool. Another type of stool, reminiscent of the folding stools of Egypt and Mesopotamia, is represented in what Evans called 'the camp-stool frescoes'. The lower parts of the legs are not visible in the fragment illustrated (fig. 388d), but a cushion seems to be indicated on the seat. A more clearly delineated view of a folding stool is seen in the intriguing seal impression entitled 'the Young Minotaur' in which the waving tail looks much like a chair-back (fig. 388e). What might be a leather seat appears to be stretched between the upper part of the legs, which are tied together at the bottom in a manner reminiscent of a Babylonian stool previously illustrated (fig. 279).

243

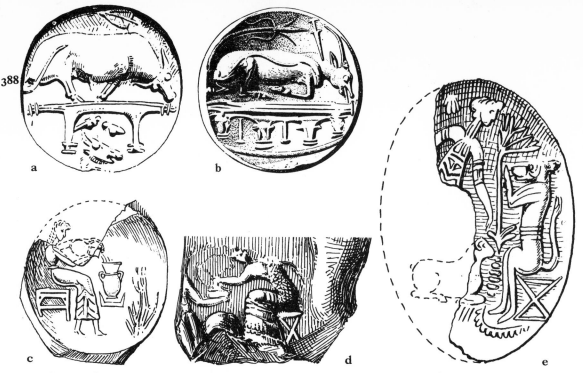

388 Minoan seals showing: (a) altar-table, (b) altar-table, (c) woman seated on a stool, (d) woman seated on a stool, (e) seated Minotaur.

Among the discoveries relating directly to furniture is the unique terracotta model of what appears to be a carrying chair, also found at Knossos, dating from the Middle Minoan II period, probably about 1750 B.C. (fig. 389). The lattice design has not appeared in our other representations of Minoan furniture, and it is unsafe to draw any conclusions from this isolated example, but it suggests a practical construction that may have been used in other furniture.

Several actual examples of small low stands or tables made either of stone or clay have come from Minoan tombs and, although it is unlikely that much the same forms were made in wood, it seems certain that small wooden tables would have been part of the ordinary household furnishings, judging by the long time they had been used in Egypt. The stone table illustrated, called by Zervos a 'table tripod', displays an extraordinary detail in its legs, which are in the form of half-rosettes (fig. 390).[8] But, interesting

389

as this is, it is possibly an artist's idea of something to be carved in stone rather than a form that would have been executed in wood. Most of these small tables, however, have plain straight legs, sometimes three and sometimes four. In the terracotta example shown (fig. 391) the top is channelled for ritual purposes, but usually the tops are flat to receive a bowl or other objects.

Because of the limited evidence that survives from Crete as compared with the many representations in art as well as actual furniture from Eighteenth Dynasty Egypt, it is difficult to make any valid comparison as to the standard of living that existed in these contemporary civilizations. The Egyptian culture was, of course, far the older, and its traditions were firmly established long before the development of the Minoan civilization. But although there is no counterpart on Crete to the great temples and monumental structures of the ancient Egyptians, the remains of the palaces and royal villas on the island bear comparison with those of Thebes and El-Amarna. The palace of Minos at Knossos near Heraklion is visited by many thousands of tourists each year, but the impressive ruins of the palaces at Mallia and Phaistos and the royal residence at Hagia Triada are as yet less well known.

Since there is no direct evidence of a wide variety of luxurious furniture such as we have from Egypt, we can only surmise what the furnishings of the palaces and the fine villas of the nobles were like. Their modern conveniences, however, in the way of light-wells, bathrooms, and drainage, as well as plastered walls with dadoes and brightly painted frescoes, make it a reasonable assumption that their interiors contained a range of furniture comparable to that used in Egypt, even if not as luxurious as that of the pharaohs. Naturally the houses of the towns would have had less luxurious furnishings. Their façades, however, as they are represented in the remarkable faience plaques found at Knossos (fig. 392) display a considerable degree of sophistication, a fact which suggests that their interiors must have contained much more than the crude furnishings of a peasant's hut. [9]

The destruction of Knossos about 1400 B.C. marked the end of Minoan power. Its decline had set in some time earlier when the Mycenaeans began to assert their supremacy over the Aegean area, and for our next record of furniture we must look to mainland Greece. But although the centre of power now moves from Crete to Mycenae, the influence of Minoan art lives on in that of the Mycenaeans.

389 Terracotta model of carrying chair, from Knossos. *About 1750* B.C.

390 Stone table, from Knossos. *About 1500* B.C.

391 Terracotta table, from Knossos. *About 1500* B.C.

390

391

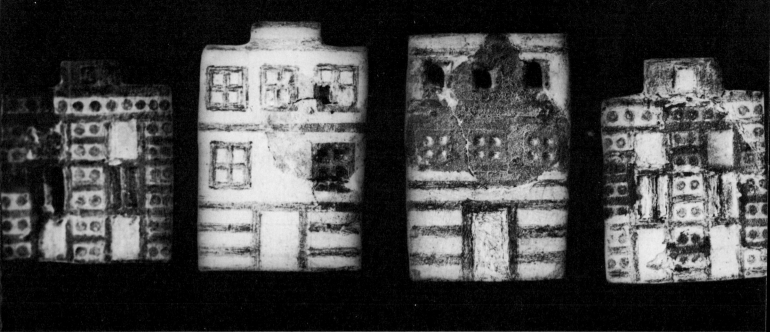

392 'Town mosaics' from Knossos. *About 1750* B.C.

4   THE MYCENAEAN PERIOD IN GREECE (1600–1200 B.C.)

Unlike Crete, where the palaces and towns were built without fortifications, the rulers of Mycenaean Greece built their palaces within Cyclopean walls of powerful citadels, like Mycenae and Tiryns, where defence against the enemy was the first consideration. Such an environment does not suggest a life of pleasure and luxury like that which existed at Knossos and Hagia Triada but, in spite of this forbidding aspect, a wealth of gold and other treasure has been found in the tombs of Mycenae. These, and other finds of the Mycenaean period, are assembled in the first large room of the National Museum in Athens, where they form an impressive introduction to the wonders of the Greek civilization displayed in this great museum. But although the Mycenaean collection includes many objects of gold, ivory and bronze, as well as pottery, there is no direct suggestion of furniture except in a few miniature terracotta models and fragments of ornamentation.

Our knowledge of furniture in Mycenaean Greece would still be largely dependent on such bits and pieces were it not for the written records found at Pylos, which have only recently been deciphered. New light has now been cast on the question of whether any furniture existed that was comparable in elegance to the treasures that had been discovered. For this we are indebted to the discoveries of the 'Pylos tablets' made by Professor Carl W. Blegen in his excavations of the Palace of Nestor, and to Michael G. F. Ventris, who, in 1952, first deciphered the Linear B script in which these records were written.

These discoveries, however, form only one more chapter – even if an important one –

in the long record of discoveries from earlier excavations which had established the groundwork for what is known of Mycenaean history and art. The romantic story of Heinrich Schliemann, who came to Mycenae in 1876 to prove his theory that the heroic tales of Homer were based on historic fact, and that this was Agamemnon's city "rich in gold", is one of the best known episodes of archaeological history.[1] His discovery of the Grave Circle, and the finding of fabulous treasures of gold in the royal graves, caused a great sensation and was a landmark in Greek archaeology. Even if he had not found the actual tomb of Agamemnon, as he thought, he had opened the vista to a new civilization hitherto unknown.

Following Schliemann, the excavations at Mycenae were carried on by C. Tsountas of the Greek Archaeological Society, who uncovered the remains of the palace on top of the acropolis, as well as the foundations of several houses within the citadel walls, and excavated a number of important tombs. Since the beginning of the present century many new discoveries relating to the Mycenaean civilization have been made – and continue to be made – not only in mainland Greece, but also in Cyprus, in Rhodes and in other localities influenced by this widespread culture.[2] Our specific interest lies, of course, in those discoveries which help to answer the question of what kind of furniture existed at this period, especially on the mainland of Greece. Of these discoveries the finds made by C. W. Blegen at Pylos and carved ivories from houses excavated by A. J. B. Wace at Mycenae have particular interest.

Pylos, like Mycenae and Tiryns, is located in the Peloponnese, but is situated on the south-west coast about one hundred miles distant and is separated from them by a rugged terrain. The palace, built on a hill-top a short distance from the classical Pylos, lacks the great fortified walls of these other more famous strongholds, but the precipitous sides of the hill formed a natural protection, and a mountain barrier arises to the north and east. Partly, no doubt, because it does not have the grim surroundings of Mycenae and Tiryns, the remains of the palace, now completely revealed, give a somewhat more luxurious impression. The general arrangement of the living quarters, however, is similar.

The first discoveries at the site were made by Blegen in 1939. After the war, he resumed his excavations in 1952, and they were carried on annually until 1961. Much of the site has been cleared, and an excellent description of the palace is now available.[3] The columned central hall of the king's apartments, with its frescoes reminiscent of those of the palace of Minos, and the other important rooms of this complex of buildings once formed a suitable background for luxurious furniture. The only semblance of furniture that remains, however, is the stone bench, originally plastered and decorated, that stood against the wall in the waiting room. But although probably fiction rather than fact, it is interesting to note that in his tale of the visit of Telemachus to the palace of Nestor, Homer says, "Nestor of Gerenia bade Telemachus, the dear son of divine Odysseus, to sleep there on a corded bedstead under the echoing portico."[4]

Early in the course of the excavations a store of clay tablets inscribed in what was termed Linear B was found. Luckily the fire that destroyed everything consumable in the palace served only to bake and harden the clay. It was surmised that they were domestic accounts, but the tablets remained meaningless until they were finally deciphered by

393a Linear B tablet from the Palace of Nestor. *About 1200* B.C.

b Inscriptions on tablet in figure 393a describing tables of ebony, ivory and yew.

Michael Ventris, and it was revealed that among these priceless records of Mycenaean life were inventories of furniture and other household equipment (fig. 393a, b).[5]

The tablets referring directly to furniture are included in what is known as the TA series, of which eight are inscribed with detailed lists of various pieces of furniture and their ornamentation. In all there are listed five chairs, fifteen foot-stools, and eleven tables. The importance of these records in the early history of Greek furniture can hardly be overestimated, as we have no other contemporary written descriptions, and the few crude representations of furniture in contemporary art give us little actual information.

How these lists happened to be made is a question that has not been answered satisfactorily. There is no direct evidence that they refer to the palace furnishings, nor, it would appear, to 'burial furniture' in the same sense as in Egypt, where it accompanied the pharaoh to the tomb to be sealed up and left undisturbed for ever. An interesting discussion of the different suppositions occurs in the recent study of the Pylos tablets by Professor L. R. Palmer.[6] But regardless of why these inventories were made, the minute descriptions of material and ornamental details are of great value.

Although some differences exist between scholars as to the exact translation of these texts, the basic interpretations remain much the same.[7] The Palmer translations are among the more recent, and consequently have been used for reference. They are also quoted in full below, since the texts are brief and give a striking word picture of this extraordinary amount of Mycenaean furniture.[8] (The italics are given as they appear in the published account.)

TA 707. Chair, ebony, with gold birds on the back (sides?), and a footstool inlaid with ivory *rosettes*. Chair, ebony, with back (sides?) of ivory . . . worked with a pair of *stag's* heads and the figure of a man and heifers. Footstool, of ebony, inlaid with ivory *rosettes*.

TA 708. Chair, ebony, with the back (sides?) inlaid with ivory. Chair, ebony, with the back (sides?) of ivory; they are worked with stag's heads and figures of men. Footstool, ebony, inlaid with ivory figures of men and lions.

TA 714. Chair, crystal, inlaid with cyanos and *tin* and gold on the back (sides?); they are inlaid with golden human figures and a pair of *stag's* heads and golden (bull's heads?), and with golden palm trees, and with palm trees of cyanos. Footstool, inlaid with cyanos and tin and gold and with golden *cross-bars*.

TA 721. Footstool, inlaid with ivory rosettes and spiral *flower-bud*. Footstools, inlaid with ivory *rosettes* and *flame-pattern* and spiral, footstool, inlaid with ivory *rosettes* and *flame-pattern*, footstool, inlaid with ivory *rosettes* and *flame-pattern*, footstool, inlaid with ivory rosettes.

TA 722. Footstool inlaid with ivory man and horse and polypod and palm trees. Footstool inlaid with ivory lion's heads and with *flame-pattern*. Footstool inlaid with ivory *flower-buds*. Footstool inlaid with ivory *flower-buds*.

TA 642. Table, stone, crystal, *inlaid* with *undulations* of cyanos, *tin* and gold, with nine feet. Table, stone, (some other material), *inlaid* with ivory, it is worked with *rosettes* and helmets. Table, stone, splay-legged, with nine feet, with feet and support of ivory; and it is worked with a spiral.

TA 713. Table, stone, with supports of ebony and ivory, splay-legged, with nine feet, worked with spiral. Table, of ivory, with marble shaft, feather pattern, with six feet, worked with spiral. Table, ebony, with ivory supports, splay-legged, with nine feet, shell pattern.

TA 715. Table, ebony, with ivory supports, splay-legged, with nine feet, shell pattern. Table (of ?? wood) ivory, splay-legged; table (of ?? wood) ivory, with marble. Two tables of yew-wood, splay-legged, with box-wood e-ko-s, with nine feet, spiral pattern, inlaid with tin.

Among the questions raised by Palmer in his parenthetic insertions (given above as they appear in the published version) is whether 'back' should read 'sides'. At first glance this seems unlikely, but the ornamentation in the form of animals, which appears on the sides of chairs represented in Early Greek painting, indicates that the latter version is not unreasonable (see colour plate XV). Either interpretation can be fitted into the context.

Unfortunately, however, these descriptions give but few clues to the actual appearance of this furniture. One associates it immediately with the inlaid chairs and foot-stools that were found in the tomb of King Tutankhamun, dating not far from the same time (see Part I, Chap. 4). It seems quite natural that there should be some resemblance, for at this time the Mycenaeans controlled the trade route to Egypt that was once dominated by the Minoans. It cannot be expected, however, that the furniture of King Nestor or King Agamemnon could rival that of the great pharaohs of Egypt, who were not only kings but considered also to be gods.

But even if there were resemblances between the furniture described and that found in Egypt, especially in the chairs and foot-stools, we cannot assume that the forms were the same, since the Mycenaeans were more directly influenced by the culture of the Minoans, and the ornamentation described is mostly Minoan–Mycenaean in character. The running spiral was known in Egypt and is conspicuous on one of the Tutankhamun pieces (fig. 105a); but this design was presumed to have been imported into Egypt from Crete, and most of the other motifs described, such as the sea-shell, the octopus (polypod), the helmet and the flame pattern, are distinctly Minoan or Mycenaean. There are, however, other suggestions of Egyptian and Mesopotamian influence. The descriptions of foot-stools inlaid with ivory figures of men bring to mind the Tutankhamun foot-stools on the top of which are the carved or inlaid figures of captives. The 'gold birds' on the back of the chair listed in TA 707, on the other hand, are more reminiscent of the finials seen in Near Eastern furniture representations.

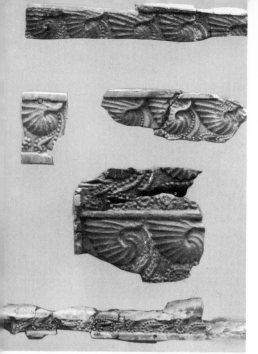

394a   b   c

It is difficult, however, to associate the description of the tables with any known Egyptian or Near Eastern prototypes. Several tables are described 'with nine feet', and two 'with six feet'. Exactly what is meant by these descriptions is unknown, and differing explanations have been given. It has been suggested that the figures refer to measurements, although it is difficult to rationalize this with what would have been the probable dimensions. Another supposition is that the multiples of three feet have reference to tripod bases, or to platforms, each supported by three animal feet, above which there would be a column or other upper supports. Unfortunately, however, there is no record of such a feature being used at this period.

Descriptions of the shapes of the tables are also confusing, but presumably those called 'projecting' were made to stand against the wall, while others were free standing. The term 'splay-legged' may be presumed to refer to legs which curve out, such as those on the Eighteenth Dynasty table from Egypt (fig. 165), and which were commonly used in later periods in Greece. The 'ivory supports' mentioned in the Palmer quotations may refer to legs made of ivory imported from Syria, but it should be noted that in the original Ventris translations this word is interpreted as 'strutting' instead of 'support'. The final determination of the exact meanings of terms about which there is doubt must of course be left to the philologists, and it is to be hoped that further discoveries will answer the unsolved questions which remain.

In an interesting study of the archaeological background of the Pylos furniture tablets, Reynold Higgins of the British Museum lists a variety of ivory ornaments found on different Mycenaean sites.[9] These include inlays "in the form of helmeted heads, argonauts, murex shells, lilies, ivy-leaves and dolphins". Also included are ivory objects to be attached in the form of "bull's heads, spiral patterns, cockles, helmeted heads, figure-of-eight shields (very frequent), architectural columns and capitals, and the so-called triglyph pattern", as well as "elaborate scenes carved in ivory". From this it would appear that the decorative designs in use were even more varied than those listed in the Pylos tablets.

250

e   f

394 Ivory decoration for furniture, from Mycenae. *About 1250* B.C.

Among these finds are a number of carved fragments discovered in the excavations of two houses located outside the citadel walls at Mycenae. The location of these rather important houses (named the House of Sphinxes and House of Shields, because of finds that were made in them) suggested to Wace that they were probably built during a period of peace, and he surmised that the ivory fragments found in the basement of the House of Sphinxes were furniture ornaments which had fallen down from the upper floor when the house and furniture were burnt.[10] Included in these remains were fragments of a running design which may have formed borders, a number of carved cockleshells, miniature columns of architectural design which Wace suggests were also furniture ornamentation, and plaques with a sphinx motif (fig. 394).[11] Wace mentions 'flame ornaments' also, as well as other motifs not illustrated, and comments on the small holes drilled in plaques for the insertions of pegs so they could be attached.

It is impossible, of course, to visualize the furniture listed in the Pylos tablets from a few fragments of ivory. And after the elaborate descriptions we have read, these few pieces of furniture ornamentation come as an anti-climax. They are of especial significance, however, since they express a distinctly Minoan–Mycenaean concept of ornamentation opposed to the traditional motifs of Egyptian and Mesopotamian designs. It must be recognized, however, that the furniture described in the Pylos tablets was doubtless royal furniture, and it is most unlikely that such furniture existed except in the royal palaces.

Simple, crude-looking chairs are represented occasionally in miniature terracotta models found in graves, like the three now on display in a case near the entrance to the Mycenaean gallery in the National Museum in Athens (fig. 395). To what extent these models are realistic it is not possible to say, since they are unlike the chairs represented later in paintings and sculpture. The central example, however, exhibits a practical design for a wooden chair in the horizontal curved slats of its open back, the vertical bannister in the centre, and the outer supports which could form arm-rests. The legs are broad at the top and taper downward – a convention found in most of the chairs represented. The chair at the right is more puzzling from the viewpoint of wood construction, although it

251

395

is a type frequently seen in such terracottas. The shape of the back is not unlike some that are used today made of moulded plywood, but it is difficult to associated it with any ancient wood construction that is known.

Quite similar in style but with a different painted ornamentation is a terracotta miniature chair found near Argos (fig. 397). The most curious feature of all four chairs is that in each case there are only three legs, one broad leg being placed in the centre of the back, whereas no such arrangement is pictured in later paintings or sculpture.

A few models of beds have also been found of which an example discovered near Corinth is illustrated (fig. 396).[12] The bed is painted with ornamental designs like the chairs, and it should be noted that where seated figures appear their costumes are also painted with similar designs. The significance of the many small terracotta figures that have been found in the tombs is uncertain, but although they are crudely modelled it is probable that they reflect something of the furniture of the time.

Mention should be made also of fragments of small stone or clay tables that have been found, but these seem to be objects commonly made of such materials rather than forms with wooden prototypes. Representations of what were undoubtedly wooden pieces appear on seals, but unfortunately such examples are extremely scarce. The best of these is seen in the impression of a large gold signet-ring from the 'Tiryns hoard', said to have been discovered in a bronze cauldron at Tiryns (fig. 398a). In the enlargement of the section with the chair, the crossed legs of the chair and its back are clearly shown (fig. 398b).

In its general concept this chair is reminiscent of the ceremonial chair of King Tutankhamun in which a tall back is mated to a campstool type of base (fig. 91). This is, of course, a somewhat far-fetched comparison, as in one case we have an actual chair, elaborately inlaid and carved, while in the seal only an outline appears. It gives us, however, the outline of a chair that might have been ornamented with ivory and gold as described in the Pylos tablets, and have been used in the Mycenaean religious rites. The curve of the chair back is reminiscent of Near Eastern design.

There is no intimation in these inadequate representations of the elegance of the

252

395 Terracotta models of chairs, from Mycenaean graves. *1400–1200* B.C.

396 Terracotta model of a bed, from near Corinth. *About 1350* B.C.

397 Terracotta model of a chair, from near Argos. *About 1350* B.C.

397

furniture described in the Pylos tablets, nor a suggestion of the wealth represented in the gold treasures now in the Athens Museum. Consequently, rather than conclude our discussion of Mycenaean furniture on this note, reference should be made to the beautiful hexagonal gold-covered box found in a shaft-grave at Mycenae. Finely fitted together, and beautifully engraved, this is quite likely an example of the workmanship in wood and gold that is described in the records from the palace of Nestor (fig. 399).

We should consider also the descriptions which Homer has given us of furniture of the time when Agamemnon ruled in Mycenae. Although not finally written down until several hundred years after 'the heroic age' (perhaps in the eighth century B.C.), these descriptions may have had a basis of fact, as did others of the Homeric legends that once were considered only myths. In the *Odyssey* Homer writes of Penelope's "chair inlaid with spirals of ivory and silver, which of old the craftsman Icmalius had made and had set upon it a footstool for the feet",[13] and he also gives a detailed account of Odysseus constructing his bed:

> I cut away the leafy branches of the long-leaved olive, and, trimming the trunk from the root, I smoothed it round with the adze well and cunningly, and made it straight to the line, thus fashioning the bed post, and I bored it all with the auger. Beginning with this, I hewed out my bed, till I finished it, inlaying it with silver and ivory, and I stretched on it a thong of oxhide, bright with purple.[14]

398a

b

398a Gold signet-ring, from Tiryns.
　　About 1400 B.C.
　b Detail of figure 398a.

399 Wooden box with gold covering,
　　from Mycenae. *About 1550* B.C.

399

Later, in the Archaic and Classical Greek periods, scenes from the Homeric stories are depicted innumerable times in vase paintings, and a large number of these scenes contain furniture. The characters are portrayed in the 'modern dress' of the time of the painting – a common convention in the art of all periods when ancient events are depicted – and we must conclude that this is also true of the furniture, which represents that with which the artist was familiar. It is interesting, however, to see how these artists visualized the furniture of the glorious age of Mycenaean history. In one of these imaginary scenes Penelope is pictured on her bed surrounded by the suitors, who try to protect themselves from the arrows of Odysseus by using a typical three-legged Greek table as a shield (fig. 400).

Following the abrupt ending of the Mycenaean civilization and the burning of the palaces in the twelfth century B.C., the next five hundred years is an almost complete blank as far as the archaeological record of furniture is concerned.[15] This was the 'Dark Age' of Greek history and art, and it is not until the late eighth century B.C. that furniture begins to be represented in works of art and we again pick up the thread of history of the ancient furniture of Greece.

THE EARLY GREEK PERIOD
(750–475 B.C.)

5

The period preceding the Classical period in Greece is usually called the Archaic period in art histories. In our survey of the furniture of this time, however, the term Early Greek has been used instead to denote the period from about 750 to 475 B.C.[1] This avoids the use of the word 'archaic', with its connotation of crudeness, as applied to an entire period, and clearly refers to the furniture of the Greeks whose culture supplanted that of the Mycenaeans, with whom they apparently had little or nothing in common.[2] It should be noted, however, that wherever the designation 'Archaic' appears in the text, in reference to sculptures or paintings, it is used in the technical sense to denote the period to which they belong.

From the viewpoint of furniture history, this was a transitional period of great importance. The record for the eighth century B.C. is extremely limited, and consists chiefly of a few small terracotta statuettes in which primitive-looking chairs are

400 Vase painting: slaying of suitors. *About 450 B.C.*

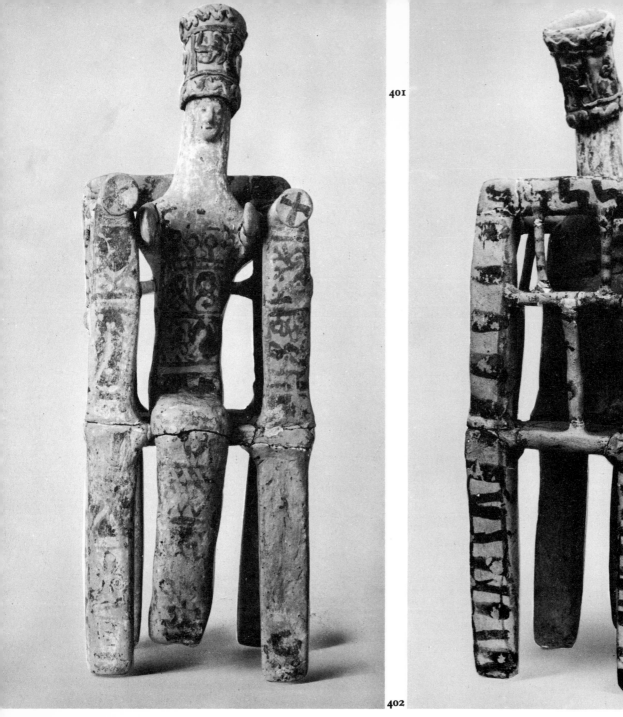

401 Terracotta seated figure, from Boeotia. *Late seventh or early sixth century* B.C.

402 Back view of figure 401.

represented and crude paintings on 'geometric' vases. But although interesting archaeologically, they reveal little in the way of actual details. By the late seventh and early sixth century B.C., however, furniture of considerable sophistication of design appears in the representations in sculpture and painting; and by the beginning of the fifth century B.C. most of the basic forms of Greek furniture are established.

Previously, in our discussion of the furniture of the Minoan and Mycenaean periods,

256   Colour plate XIV. Painted limestone sarcophagus. *About* 1400 B.C.

because the record is so sparse it has been necessary to grasp at every scrap of evidence. The problem now, however, is one of selection from the many sculptures and vase paintings in which furniture is depicted; and, since it is not possible to illustrate all the variations that occur, it has been necessary to restrict our selection to those examples that are most significant from the viewpoint of design development. These serve, however, to show the relationships that existed to the designs of Egypt and Mesopotamia, and the emergence of distinctly new Greek forms of furniture.

The terracottas

An interval of several hundred years intervenes between the date of the Mycenaean terracottas illustrated in the last chapter and those that appear at the beginning of, or just before, the Early Greek period. These are an indication of the stirring of the creative instinct which occurs toward the end of the Dark Age, but, since they are followed soon by more explicit representations of furniture, only a few examples of these terracotta figurines are shown.

In most instances, the chairs depicted in these miniature models have little relationship

403

403 Terracotta seated figure. *Eighth century* B.C.

404 Terracotta seated figure, from Boeotia. *About 580* B.C.

404

405

405 Terracotta model of a table, from Cyprus.
About eighth century B.C.

to furniture represented in other media. For example, the chair in a rather charming figurine from Boeotia, now in the Athens Museum, has arms of exaggerated height that terminate in decorated disks (fig. 401). This is a conventional detail that appears in other figurines (as does the head-dress of the seated person) and in monumental sculpture, but is not known to have existed in actual wooden furniture. Also, between the arm and seat, there is an open-work lattice-pattern that has no counterpart in other representations (fig. 402), although this dates perhaps from the beginning years of the Early Greek period.

In an eighth-century B.C. terracotta, however, now in the Metropolitan Museum, a resemblance to later Greek furniture can already be seen in the broad horizontal slat at the top of the back, curved to fit the figure (fig. 403). Also a conventional construction with four legs is now represented, instead of three legs as in the Mycenaean examples illustrated. A terracotta of the early sixth century B.C. from the British Museum gives but little of the detail of the chair, but the sharply curved back legs and the posture of the sitter suggests the sweep of the back of classic chair design (fig. 404). In an interesting Cypriot miniature model from the Metropolitan Museum, a three-legged table is represented which clearly shows the form of the popular table of the Classical eras (fig. 405). Other terracottas of both earlier and later dates might also be illustrated, but it seems best at this point to consider the Archaic sculptures in which chairs are depicted in more realistic detail.

Furniture in Early Greek sculpture and reliefs

The sculpture and reliefs which follow date from about 650 B.C. to 500 B.C., mostly coming from the latter half of the sixth century B.C.; but it is possible, of course, that the types of chairs and stools represented date from a somewhat earlier time. These sculptured representations are shown separately from the furniture of the same period depicted in paintings. This is not because there is a difference in the types represented – actually the forms portrayed are the same in comparable periods of design – but because of the advantage in being able to make direct comparisons between examples represented in the same art medium (which in the case of sculpture has the added advantage of being three-dimen-

258

sional). And this also facilitates comparison with the Near Eastern sculptures and reliefs which were illustrated in the last section.

Chronologically, the Early Greek examples which follow come from the end of the Assyrian–Babylonian period, and the majority date from approximately the time of the Persian conquest of Babylon. (The palace bas-reliefs of Assurnasirpal, Sargon, Sennacherib and Assurbanipal date from about 850 B.C. to 650 B.C.) But though a few resemblances in detail can be detected, there is a striking difference between the furniture popular with the Assyrians and that of the Greeks. Naturally the small city states of Greece with their ideals of democracy provided a very different background from that of the rich Oriental civilizations of Mesopotamia ruled by warlike kings, and the difference in the two cultures is apparent in the furniture that evolved.

Among the earliest of the life-sized sculptures in which furniture appears is the headless statue of a seated figure in the National Museum in Athens, dating from the middle of the seventh century B.C. (fig. 406). The front legs of the seat terminate in lion's paws which face forward in the traditional Egyptian manner (fig. 407), and on the top of the foreleg on the right side the remains of a carved lion's head can be seen – also a typical Egyptian ornamentation. The combination of the fore and hind legs of the animal, however, which is so characteristic of Egyptian design, is a feature that is rarely seen in Greek design although it occurs in what are known as the 'hero reliefs' from Sparta and vicinity (fig. 408).

The appearance of Egyptian and also Near Eastern motifs in Early Greek design

406

406 Marble statue, from Arcadia. *650–640* B.C.

407 Detail of figure 406.

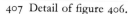

407

260

408 Limestone relief, from Laconia. *About 550* B.C.

409 Marble relief, from Paros. *About 550* B.C.

409

naturally brings up the question of how and when they came to Greece. The use of the animal-type leg dates, of course, to the earliest beginnings of furniture history, and occurs in Egypt and Mesopotamia at least two thousand years before the Early Greek period. It is generally assumed that the appearance of these foreign motifs in the design of the Archaic Greek period was due principally to exposure to the contemporary arts of Egypt and the Near East. By the seventh century B.C. Greek colonies were widely established throughout the Mediterranean, and no doubt the Greeks had direct knowledge of the arts of the peoples to the south and east. It is curious, however, that there are no signs apparent in Early Greek furniture of the styles developed during the height of the Late Assyrian period (850–612 B.C.) (see Part II, Chapter 3), and the possibility should be considered

261

that these foreign influences may have been transmitted in an earlier period. Nothing exists in the way of actual evidence to prove that they came by way of the Mycenaeans, but it is tempting to assume that some vestiges of earlier design motifs may have persisted in the workshops of the Dark Age, even if proof of such continuity is lacking in the arts of painting and sculpture.

Mention has been made above of the 'hero reliefs' from the region of Sparta in which chairs with animal-type legs are represented. These somewhat uncouth sculptures date from the middle part of the sixth century B.C., and the chairs display a number of unusual motifs. In the example illustrated the lion's legs are carved in a grotesque manner quite unlike the earlier prototypes, but the Egyptian influence is clearly apparent. The other details – the inward curve of the chair back and the design of the carved finial at the top, the turned support of the arm and the disk-like knob at its end – are distinct departures from earlier traditional types. These, however, were monumental sculptures, and it does not follow necessarily that they are faithful representations of existing furniture.

What no doubt is more closely related to the type of chair in actual use is that represented in a fine sculptured relief of the middle sixth century B.C. found in the island of Paros, and now in the Berlin Museum (fig. 409). At first glance the chair appears to have plain straight legs, but closer examination reveals that lion's paw feet are indicated, facing in opposite directions in the Greek fashion. Other typical Early Greek details also appear in the stump of the arm, in the ornamentation between the stretcher and seat, and in the inward curve of the slanting back.

In a series of marble reliefs from what is known as the Harpy tomb several pieces of furniture are depicted which, judging by their resemblance to other pieces depicted elsewhere, probably represent contemporary styles.[3] Special interest attaches to these sculptures, not only because of the furniture represented, but also because of the locale in which they were found. Although Greek in their style and execution, they came from a tomb discovered in Xanthus on the south coast of Asia Minor opposite Rhodes. Their date is contemporary with the Persian conquest of Babylon, but here, as in the other Greek coastal settlements, the designs of Greece have usurped those of the local culture.

These reliefs, now in the British Museum, are weather-worn, but the outlines of the furniture are sufficiently clear to give a good idea of its design. Dating from the end of the sixth, or early part of the fifth century B.C., they doubtless represent styles that were well established in the sixth century B.C. Exact dates for the introduction of a new style, however, cannot be determined from the time when it is first depicted in art; for though sometimes a newly popular fashion may be represented, in other instances a long established style is probably portrayed.

Two of the chairs in the Harpy reliefs have turned legs, which came into general use, both in the Near East and in Greece, following the invention of the wood-turning lathe (see Techniques, p. 303). The turnings, however, have taken on a Greek look, and the chairs could not be mistaken for either Near Eastern or Egyptian. In the first of the reliefs illustrated (fig. 410), a woman is represented sitting on a well-proportioned small arm-chair, with her feet on a foot-stool. The arm of the chair is supported by the carved figure of a sphinx, and terminates in a small carved ram's head – both familiar details in

410

411

410 Marble relief, the Harpy tomb.
Late sixth century B.C.

411 Marble relief, the Harpy tomb.
Late sixth century B.C.

412

412 Marble relief, the Harpy tomb.
Late sixth century B.C.

Near Eastern design, but now, also, established motifs in Greek furniture. The second of the turned-leg chairs has carved feet, resembling what was known in the Chippendale period as the 'ball and claw' design (fig. 411). A distinctly Greek motif appears in the arm supports carved in the form of the sea god Poseidon.

In the preceding examples the relationship to traditional forms is apparent, but in the third arm-chair (fig. 412) the base of the chair represents a uniquely Greek contribution to design, and one that is frequently portrayed in sixth-century B.C. vase paintings. This will be discussed more in detail later, but note should be taken here of the flat, rather broad legs with double volute capitals and the suggestion of shaping at the sides. With this distinctly different form, however, we see represented a traditional foot-stool with heavy lion's feet and stretcher, and the chair has a curving back with a finial, both features being reminiscent of Near Eastern design, while the seated figure is pictured in the traditional Egyptian pose of smelling a lotus flower.

The personage depicted in the fourth of the Harpy reliefs is seated on a stool with turned legs and a cushion (fig. 413). Such simple four-legged stools are among the most common forms of ancient seating pieces, but the style of the turnings marks this example as a definitely Greek type. The shape of the turning, which has a swelling near the top with a narrow neck above, and a long plain shaft below, is a form that is frequently pictured in paintings and sculptures, and that continued to be popular in the Classical period. It seems likely, however, that this particular shape was not generally used until the latter part of the sixth century B.C., since we have no earlier representations, and it is interesting to contrast it with the leg of the stool that appears in an earlier statue from Tripolis in Arcadia which dates from the seventh century B.C. (fig. 414). In the latter there is an almost square section at the top of the leg where the seat-rails join, and a long rectangular part below which tapers upwards.

The refinement of the two stools pictured in the intriguing scene called 'the cat and dog fight' suggests that they belong to a later date (fig. 415). Notwithstanding their finished appearance, however, they come from the Archaic period. This marble relief, now in the National Museum in Athens, was found embedded in the ruins of the 'long wall' built by Themistocles in 478 B.C. to defend Athens against its enemies, but the sculpture itself is ascribed to 510 B.C. The stool depicted at the left, with turned legs and a cushion, is similar to the stool represented in one of the Harpy reliefs. The one at the right is a sophisticated version of the cross-leg stool which we have seen represented frequently in the art of Egypt, the Near East and Crete; and its finely proportioned design suggests that in Early Greece, also, such stools were in use some time before the date of this sculpture. The legs, which are rounded and subtly tapered, are ornamented with rosettes where they join the seat. But instead of turning outward, as was customary in the Egyptian cross-leg stools with carved lion's feet, here the feet turn inward toward each other.

Other sophisticated examples of Early Greek design are represented in the finely modelled terracotta plaques which have come from Locri, a Greek colony in the south of Italy. Dating from the first part of the fifth century B.C., they are further evidence of the widespread existence of Greek furniture designs throughout Magna Grecia. Even if somewhat elaborate in its ornamentation, the seat on which Pluto and Persephone are

413 Marble relief, the Harpy tomb. *Late sixth century* B.C.

414 Limestone statue, from Arcadia. *About 630* B.C.

415 Marble relief, from Athens. *About 510* B.C.

416 Terracotta relief, from Locri. *470–460* B.C.

417 Terracotta relief, from Locri. *470–460* B.C.

418 Vase painting, couches and tables. *625–600* B.C.

portrayed is an elegant piece of design, with slender legs, fluted and tapered, which terminate in nicely carved lion's feet (fig. 416). The back has a graceful curve and ends in a swan's neck finial, and the chair is well balanced in its proportions. It is not a form, however, that continued into later Greek design. In one of the other Locrian plaques a woman is represented placing a folded garment in a small chest on legs which is unique in both its form and decoration (fig. 417). (Restored details of the chair are doubtful.)

Furniture in Early Greek painting

Until this point, only the limited range of furniture represented in sculptures and reliefs has been considered. The examples illustrated are by no means all-inclusive, and like the sculptured representations of other early civilizations they are confined principally to stools and chairs. In the vase paintings of Early Greece, however, a much wider range of furniture is depicted. The pottery of Attica and other centres was widely distributed throughout the Greek world, and many fine examples have also been discovered in the tombs at Cervetri and elsewhere in Etruria.

Mythological characters and scenes of daily life replaced the 'geometric' ornamentation of an earlier period, and in this painted decoration all the usual types of Greek furniture are clearly pictured. So vast a number of these vase paintings still exist – from the Early Greek and later periods – that it is possible to show only a small fraction of them here. In most instances, the examples shown date from the sixth and early fifth centuries B.C., and, except for a few cases where it seems advisable to clarify a point of design, paintings of the Classical period are not included.

Because these paintings are strictly decorative art and the medium is more flexible, they give a much more informal and romantic view of the furniture portrayed than do the sculptured representations. Banquet scenes are among the more popular subjects, one of which is pictured in the earliest of the paintings illustrated (fig. 418). Here the banquet couches are portrayed in their usual position, end to end, with a table holding food and wine by the side of each couch. More will be said later about the tables (which look surprisingly 'classical' for so early a date), but special attention will be given to the couches at this point.

The couch in ancient Greece served a double purpose: it was not only a bed to sleep on, but also a couch on which to recline when dining. Possibly this was a custom imported from the Near East; Assurbanipal is depicted reclining on a couch while he feasts in the garden (Part II, fig. 305). Regardless of what its original intention might have been, however, this was the universal custom on festive occasions throughout Greek and Roman times, with the couches lined up sideways against the walls of the room.

The banqueting couch depicted in the painting illustrated opposite, judging by the age of the Corinthian vase on which it appears, dates to the latter part of the seventh century B.C. If the legs of the couch were the only examples of their kind depicted in Early Greek art, one would be tempted to think that the shape was imaginary. A similar form occurs rather frequently, however, in other Archaic examples, although the sides of the heavy section are often straight, rather than concave. The recently invented wood-turning lathe encouraged the turning of a variety of shapes, and it is surmised that these legs were turned, since other shapes that are obviously turned appear soon after. If they were not turned, it has been suggested that this curious design was cut out from a thick rectangular piece of wood. No other structural details are shown, but the bed is covered with a mattress and is equipped with a cushion on which the reclining person rests his elbow.

This particular design of leg did not continue in fashion in the later periods, and was superseded in the sixth century B.C. by legs of rectangular shape, deeply incised at the sides and usually ornamented with painting or carving. Countless examples of banquet couches with this sort of leg are represented in the paintings of this and later periods. Most of the usual features of the type appear in the example represented in figure 419, but rather close scrutiny of the illustration is required to distinguish the finer details of the design. In a second example of the same type, the cut-out section of the leg is clearly delineated, as is also the raised head-rest and other details of design (fig. 420).

A characteristic feature is the double volute ornament which forms a capital at the top of the leg. In some instances this appears at the head of the couch only, and in other examples at both ends. The same motif has been noted previously on one of the chairs depicted in the Harpy reliefs (fig. 412). When it appears in sculpture, the capital is carved, but in the painted examples the details of the design appear to be ornamentation applied to a flat surface. In any case, there is a considerable variation in the actual details. Usually a palmette ornament occurs above and below the incised portion of the leg with a rosette

419

419 Vase painting, couches and tables. *520–510* B.C.

420 Vase painting, couch and table. *530–510* B.C.

or other ornamentation above. In the present example the volute capital appears only at the head, where there is a low back-rest on which the cushion is placed. The long rail is decorated with rosettes and swastika-like designs, and on the upper face of both legs at the foot of the couch, the end of a tenon is indicated where it would logically be joined to cross-rails. The pattern of the fabric with which the cushion is covered and the edging of the mattress are indicative of the textile designs in vogue.

Chairs also are depicted with similar incised and painted legs. The *thronos*, or seat of honour, on which Zeus is seated in figure 421 is exaggerated in height, however, and apparently lacks the usual incised sections. A particularly fine example of the throne with cut-out legs is illustrated by a drawing, rather than a photograph, in order to facilitate a better examination of the details (fig. 422), and the close resemblance of the design motifs to those of the couches is apparent by comparison with the couch illustrated (fig. 420).

Obviously it lessened the strength of the leg to cut away so much of the wood, but the aesthetic effect is rather pleasing, and it may be that this was done in order to lessen the feeling of weight. If the leg were cut from a heavy plank, the part that remained would have sufficient strength, and the knobs left at each side of the narrow point served to lessen the feeling of structural weakness. It would have been a simple job for the craftsman to cut out the surplus wood with a narrow fine-toothed saw, and smooth the opening with a rasp.[4]

Although the throne on which Poseidon is seated in figure 421 does not have a back,

420

421

there is a rail which serves the purpose of an arm-rest, supported by the volute capitals which crown the legs. On the edge of this rail, and also on the edge of the seat-rail and the stretcher, are painted designs resembling mouldings, while between the stretcher and the seat there is a lyre-shaped ornament. The total effect is that of a handsome and dignified seat of state, distinctly Greek in design. It presents an interesting contrast to the throne of Assurnasirpal previously illustrated (fig. 291), which is similar in its proportions and is also an impressive and well-designed seat of state, but very different in its design details.

Considerable emphasis has been placed on the custom of cutting out a section of the leg in this type of design, since this is a peculiarly Greek innovation. Occasionally, however, couches and chairs of similar design are pictured with the sides of the legs straight, but retaining the same motifs of decoration. Such a leg is represented on the chair in the drawing illustrated in figure 423. In this instance the semblance of a chair back appears, resembling a staff with a palmette finial. In other examples, more conventional backs appear, with or without the cut-out feature in the legs.

In some instances a piece of furniture that appears to be purely imaginary is pictured in the mythological scenes. In one of the more curious examples a chair is depicted with ornaments in the form of the fore-part of a horse, with his legs projecting behind (fig. 424). The shape of the base is not unusual, although the cut-out section of the legs is exaggerated, but it seems unlikely that such a chair could actually have existed. It is, however, reminiscent of the descriptions in the Pylos tablets (see p. 248), and for that reason this rather improbable piece has been included. In these descriptions, animals of different sorts are described, 'worked' or 'inlaid' on the sides, and figures of men are also mentioned.

422   423

The possibility that some vestige of the Mycenaean tradition is represented here is an intriguing speculation.

More attention has perhaps been devoted to this specific type of Early Greek couches and thrones than might be expected in a general history of ancient furniture. They represent, however, an interesting phase of design, and the couches, particularly, continue to be seen in the sculptures, as well as the paintings, of the Classical, Hellenistic and Roman periods. Almost the same design also appears in Etruscan art. The sculptures give a more realistic view of these couches than the paintings, since they are three-dimensional, but the characteristics of the style have already been rather fully discussed, and consequently the representations in Greek sculpture will not be illustrated here. Special note should be taken, however, of the fine terracotta sarcophagus from Cervetri in the Louvre (dating from 525 B.C.) (fig. 426), and other Etruscan sarcophagi in the Villa Giulia in Rome, which are very similar to the Early Greek couches in design.[5]

Mention was made earlier of the tables that almost invariably are portrayed beside the banquet couches. Those which appear in figures 418 and 419 are similar in design, although their proportions are different, and there is also a considerable difference in the date of the paintings in which they are depicted. The same type also appears in the scene previously illustrated where one of Penelope's suitors uses a table as a shield to protect himself against the wrath of Odysseus (fig. 400). Some other types of tables are occasionally represented, but special attention will be given to this particular design, since it is not only a style pictured very frequently but is also one of the most important examples of Early Greek design.

271

424 Vase painting, chair. *About 540* B.C.

Only the side view of the tables is given in the paintings, and the plan is not shown, but there seems to be no question, judging by small bronze and terracotta models that have survived, that the majority of these tables were constructed with three legs (fig. 425). The Greek word for table, *trapeza*, suggests such a construction, although the written records also mention tables with four legs as well as three.[6] The three-legged table was known in Egypt but was not generally used there, although an unusual example exists in the British Museum collection of ancient Egyptian furniture (Part I, fig. 237). It was a practical arrangement, however, as it enabled the table to stand evenly on a rough floor, and three-legged tables were found both in the excavations at Jericho (Part II, figs. 358, 359) and at Gordion (Part II, figs. 372, 373).

A close scrutiny of the tables pictured will indicate that a front view of a leg attached to the side is shown at one end, and a side view of another leg at the other end. The explanation is simple. There were two legs at the end where the face view is portrayed, one at each side, with the top projecting beyond; while the leg shown in profile is a single leg facing in the other direction, placed in the centre and flush with the table end. Tables of almost exactly the same appearance are portrayed many times in the banquet scenes, but rather than illustrating another of these conventional scenes, an unusual view is shown of a slave carrying a typical table (fig. 427). These were moved about as needed, since the ancient Greeks, like the Egyptians, did not have large dining tables, and small tables were used for dining, and placed wherever needed.

The legs of this type of table are often fluted on the face, and taper downwards to a carved lion's foot which turns sharply outwards. Dowels are almost always indicated on the face of the side leg at the points where they would serve to join the parts together. In the last example there are three dowels indicated – two where they would probably be

Colour plate XV. Vase painting of Zeus on a chair. 550–525 B.C.

425 Bronze model of table. *Etruscan, 525–500* B.C.

426 Terracotta sarcophagus, couch. *Etruscan, about* 525 B.C.

425

attached to the edge of the top, and one where the leg would be attached to what was presumably a cross-brace beneath the top (not visible in the painting). In most cases there is a long stretcher, which would logically be fitted at one end into a short stretcher placed between the side legs, and tenoned at the other end into the single leg placed in the centre.

Usually a bracket which would fit under the table top is pictured on the back of the single leg. This is indicated only vaguely by curved lines in the table carried by the slave, but usually it is clearly pictured as an integral part of the leg. In the example previously illustrated in figure 419, what appears to be a bolt to attach the table top to the bracket is indicated. There is a natural inclination to ask how factual the representations of these legs may be. Fortunately some ancient table legs in bronze of very similar design have been found, although of somewhat late date. Examples exist both in the Palermo Museum and in the Louvre, one of which is illustrated in figure 428.

The question will be raised, of course, whether this means that the legs of this style were usually made of metal rather than wood. Apparently, bronze legs must have been used at times, but it seems likely that such legs would ordinarily have been constructed of wood. Judging by the paintings, the tables were easily moved about, and doubtless wood was less expensive and more plentiful than bronze, as well as lighter in weight. The problem of carving such legs in wood would be simple for the sculptors and artisans of ancient Greece who have left the record of their skill in marble.

Another table of the same general type is pictured in a scene on a vase from the

426

Ashmolean Museum, which depicts a boy carrying both a couch and a table over his shoulder (fig. 429). The table is loosely drawn but obviously is intended to represent the same sort as those above. Its top does not project beyond the legs at one end in the usual manner but this can perhaps be explained by carelessness on the part of the artist. The scene has especial interest, however, because of the unusual couch that is represented. The turnings of the legs are similar to those pictured on stools and chairs, but the curved wooden head-rest is an unusual and attractive feature. With the increased use of turnings in the fifth century B.C., beds with turned legs are represented more often, and the curved head-board and foot-board are first introduced at that time. Since this type of couch has become an accepted symbol of Greek design, a unique scene in which such a couch appears is illustrated, even though it is of somewhat later date than the other furniture included in this chapter. Led by a piping satyr, a donkey lightly carries on his back a comfortable couch on which Dionysus and Ariadne are pictured taking their ease (fig. 431). But although the piece itself is a later creation the turnings obviously derive from those of the Early Greek period.

Couches with animal legs of the Egyptian type also appear occasionally in the paintings from the early years of the Archaic period, but they too are seldom represented in later paintings and in general represent no unusual features. In a unique example of the late sixth century B.C., however, portrayed in a painting on a *kylix* in the Villa Giulia, we have an intriguing design unlike anything seen in Egypt or on Mesopotamian furniture (fig. 430). The goat's leg had been used often before on furniture in both Egypt and Mesopotamia, but not in the same manner, and this small couch with its gracefully curved head-board is a distinctly Greek creation. Beside it stands the usual table on which is a bowl of wine. The goat-like character with the lyre, and the goat lying below, are also unmistakably Greek. It seems rather unfortunate that we have no other examples of such a couch, for its graceful lines are prophetic of future design.

The stools pictured in Early Greek paintings show a closer relationship to the tradi-

427 Vase painting, slave carrying table. *About 470* B.C.

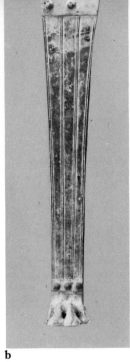

428a   b   429

tional Egyptian and Near Eastern types than do the couches and tables. But in the stools also, as in the other pieces, a definitely Greek character emerges. For instance, in the turned-leg examples, of which two are represented in the sculptures previously illustrated (figs. 413 and 415), the shape of the legs is distinctly Greek, and other characteristic forms were developed later. A more obvious difference is apparent, however, in the stools with cross-legs of which a great many are pictured.

The cross-leg stools are derived, of course, from the early camp-stool type of seat, and in the tomb paintings of the Eighteenth Dynasty the cross-leg stool with lion's feet is portrayed quite frequently (Part I, figs. 217, 218). A conspicuous change occurs, however, in the Early Greek version, already apparent in the stool portrayed in the 'cat and dog fight' relief from Athens (fig. 415). Instead of the feet facing outward in the traditional manner, they turn in sharply toward each other, as was noted in our discussion of this example. Many of this type are represented in the paintings, with slight differences in details. The legs, however, are usually more angular than in the above example, with an abrupt turn at the knee (fig. 432). (In this painting there is also depicted a box-type seat with a rectangular opening in its side, not a usual type but one that appears occasionally.)

In other examples, a circular ornament is indicated at the top of each leg, and also at the point where they cross, suggesting that this may have been a gilded or painted decoration, or possibly an ivory inlay (fig. 433). And in the lively scene illustrated in figure 434, the rail of the stool has a running scroll design, with a decorated rosette at each end. While some of the cross-leg stools were intended to fold, others, like this example, had a fixed seat, which is indicated not only by the rail, but also by the plate at the junction of the legs, which apparently was applied to give rigidity.

In contrast to the legs with claw feet which usually turn in, when the goat's leg motif appears the hoofs face outward. In the former, also, only the claw feet are represented, whereas the entire lower part of the goat's leg is depicted in a realistic manner, joined by the knee to the upper straight section of the leg. One of the earliest examples, dating from

428a, b Bronze table leg. *First century* B.C.   275

429 Vase painting, boy carrying couch and table. *500–475* B.C.

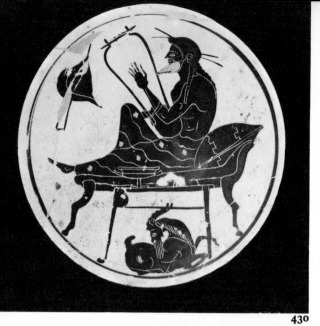

430 431

430 Vase painting, couch. *Late sixth century* B.C.

431 Vase painting, couch on donkey. *Late sixth century* B.C.

432 Vase painting, stools. *515–510* B.C.

433 Vase painting, stool. *550–525* B.C.

434 Vase painting, stool. *500–475* B.C.

434

432

433

the middle of the sixth century B.C., is portrayed together with an early chair (fig. 435).
A somewhat similar design feature was used earlier by the Assyrians in their cross-leg
tables (figs. 289, 290), but its adaptation as a base for stools seems to have been a Greek
innovation, and these seats represent one of the most interesting Greek types. In order
that its outlines can be seen more clearly a typical example of the type is illustrated in the
line drawing in figure 436.

The chair in early Greece went through a more complete evolution than the stool,
beginning with those in which a foreign influence is apparent and ending with a distinctly
Greek creation – the 'classic chair'. Mention has been made previously of the seat with
bull's legs, resembling Egyptian prototypes, which appeared in early sculpture, and we
have observed that this was soon superseded by the chair with a straight leg and claw
feet – a type seen likewise in the paintings of the period as in figure 437. In chairs
with turned legs also, a change soon occurs, the legs represented in the Harpy chair reliefs
being replaced by turnings of various shapes, usually without a stretcher. A typical

435 Painted terracotta plaque, stool and chair. *About 550* B.C.

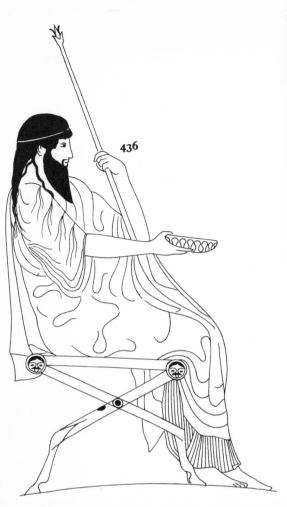

436

437

438

436 Vase painting, stool with goat's legs. *About 450* B.C.

437 Vase painting, chair. *About 550* B.C.

438 Vase painting, chair. *About 450* B.C.

example occurs in the painting which portrays King Midas (fig. 438), with his oriental head-dress. The development of the greatest importance, however, is the one that leads to the *klismos*, which we will call the 'classic chair'. This was the favourite chair of classical Greek artists and is portrayed innumerable times in their paintings, but it was conceived in the earlier period.

An intimation of the flowing line of the classic chair that is to come a little later is seen in the chair pictured on a fine Archaic vase in the British Museum, dating about 540 B.C. (colour plate XV). The straight legs of the Locri chair are replaced by legs that curve out slightly, and the back curves up and outward in a subtle line; the carved claw feet and other traditional features are still present, but a general softening of the outline of the chair is evident. The carved animal ornamentation between the stretcher and the seat seems extraneous, but there is some evidence that such ornamentation was actually used; a number of other examples very similar to this one exist in the paintings, and, as we have previously noted, the descriptions in the Pylos tablets mention animals 'worked' on the sides.

In the next stage of development the claw foot disappears; the legs acquire a more pronounced outward curve, and the back sweeps upward in a continuous line, although the vestige of a swan's neck finial still remains (fig. 439). Not long after, sometime in the early part of the fifth century B.C., the chair acquires a broad horizontal back slat at the top that encircles the shoulders of the seated person, and a fixed form for the classic chair is established.

No exact date can be ascribed for the time when the chair in its final form was first actually made, since there is no evidence to link the date of the evolution of the chair and its exact representation on the vase paintings. One of the earliest examples pictured of the chair as finally developed occurs on a vase painting of the first quarter of the fifth century B.C., illustrated in figure 440. But in the prosperous period that followed the defeat of the Persians in 479 B.C., this became the most popular of all Greek chairs – judging by the frequency with which it is portrayed. For this reason the form is naturally associated with the Classical period, although its antecedents and development stem from the earlier period.

The many variations in design of this chair that followed cannot be illustrated here. The backs of some chairs sweep back in an exaggerated curve, as in figure 441, while others are straighter; legs vary in their curves, and differences occur in other details. It is possible, however, to study its basic features in hundreds of examples – for instance, in the graceful chair pictured on a vase in the Ashmolean Museum (fig. 442). The deep outward curve of the front leg is balanced by that of the back leg, which continues upward in a graceful line, while the upper part of the front leg projects forward, terminating in a sharp point.

A good idea of the construction of the chair can also be obtained from these pictorial representations. The projection of the curved back slat at the top is clearly rendered in the example above, as well as the side-rail of the seat, with the tenon protruding through the back leg. Quite often, also, the ends of dowels that would be used to fasten the legs to the front and back seat-rails are indicated on the sides of the legs. In other examples (not

441

440

439 Vase painting, chair. *515–510* B.C.

440 Vase painting, chair. *500–475* B.C.

441 Vase painting, chair. *500–475* B.C.

442 Vase painting, chair. *About 450* B.C.

442

444

443 Vase painting, satyr carrying a chair. *About 450* B.C.

444 Lead model of chair. *Uncertain date.*

445 Vase painting, chair and small table. *475–450* B.C.
(See colour plate XVI.)

446 Vase painting, carpenter at work. *500–475* B.C.

443

illustrated), the weaving of leather thongs around the side-rail to form a seat is portrayed. But although a general idea of the construction can be obtained from the profile views, it is not necessary to depend on these alone. The actual construction details are more clearly indicated in a unique scene where a satyr carries a chair rendered in pseudo-perspective (fig. 443). A vertical banister in the chair back can also be seen, not visible in the side views. The front-rail and its method of attachment are shown, and a woven seat is depicted.

A few small models and representations in sculpture also exist which give information as to the shape of the back and other details that are not apparent in the paintings. Among these is a lead miniature model in the British Museum (fig. 444). The legs do not have the sweeping curves of the typical classic chair, but the broad curving back and the vertical slat are characteristic of the type.

Usually the classic chair is associated with more elegant scenes, but it appears also in a painting which portrays a vase painter seated at his work, from a fine vase in the Torno collection in Milan (fig. 445, and colour plate XVI). The chair is an interesting variation of the type, and beside it stands a small table with outward curving legs which repeat the lines of the chair legs. On the table is placed the painter's bowl of colour. Not only is the scene of interest because of the furniture depicted – it presents a striking example of the high esteem in which the artist was regarded in Ancient Greece.

Technical details of the construction of ancient Greek furniture will not be mentioned here except briefly, but the boldly curving legs of the classic chairs present an interesting problem, and one that was not present in the rigid forms of ancient Egypt and Meso-potamia. It is possible, of course, that the curved parts were shaped from a large plank,

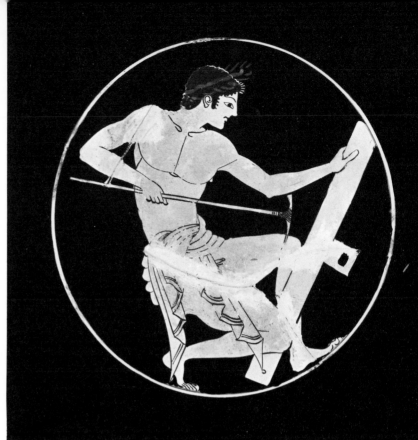

445   446

but this would present a serious danger of breakage at the point where cross-grain occurs. A more likely answer is that the wood was first steamed and then bent into shape. It seems probable that bending was employed to form the braces used in reinforcing the joints of ancient Egyptian furniture, and there is good evidence that the technique of bending was well understood in ancient Greece.[7] In the other problems involved in cabinet-making – the seasoning of the wood, the joinery, and the finishing – there seems no doubt that the methods used by the ancient Egyptians continued with little change in ancient Greece. For instance, in a Greek vase painting of the fifth century B.C. which depicts a carpenter at work (fig. 446) he is using an adze which is much the same as that employed in Egypt two thousand years before – although probably made of iron instead of copper or bronze.

In the writings of the ancient authors, particularly Pliny and Theophrastus, mention is often made of furniture and woodworking, as well as the woods used in cabinet-making.[8] But although a great deal of interesting and valuable information can be derived from these accounts, unfortunately little actual furniture has survived from ancient Greece to permit an actual examination of the joints and methods used.[9] For this reason we have turned back to Egypt for more precise knowledge of the techniques used by the woodworkers of the ancient world. These methods are clearly revealed in the many examples of ancient Egyptian furniture that still exist, and in contemporary scenes of craftsmen at work. This knowledge of woodworking was presumably shared by the other advanced civilizations of the ancient world, and, consequently, the detailed discussion of ancient Egyptian methods of woodworking which appear at the end of this work will be considered relevant also to the furniture of ancient Greece.

283

With the ending of the Early Greek period and the beginning of the Classical era we have come to the halfway point in furniture history. Twenty-five hundred years have passed since furniture was first made in Mesopotamia and the Nile Valley, and another twenty-five hundred years must elapse before we reach the present time. But although this halfway point marks the limit established for our present survey of ancient furniture, it does not mean that there was suddenly a marked change. It is rather that once again, as had happened in Egypt where traditional forms of design endured for more than two thousand years, a design tradition had become established that was to have a long-lasting influence.

The Classical period, as defined by archaeologists, lasted less than two hundred years (475–330 B.C.). But in a broader sense, the Classical era, as it pertains to furniture and

447

447 Part of east frieze of Parthenon. *About 445* B.C.

448 Gravestone of Demetria and Pamphile. *About 325* B.C.

448

architecture, continued without a break in Greece and the Roman world until the time of Constantine; and, although interrupted for long intervals, its influence has continued until today. The endless variety of furniture represented in the art of the Greek and Roman world is outside the scope of this work; but the persistence of the earlier styles in the Classical period should be noted.

To a large extent the furniture of Classical Greece represents the refinement of types established earlier. For instance, the stools on which Poseidon and Apollo are seated, sculptured on one of the slabs from the frieze of the Parthenon, do not differ radically from those we have seen in the Archaic reliefs, but the mark of the Classical period is apparent in the refinement of line (fig. 447). Also, although the chair portrayed in the stela of Demetria and Pamphile employs traditional motifs, the total ensemble suggests a classic sense of proportion (fig. 448). And in the many sculptured and painted representations of the classic chair, the *klismos*, we see the finest expression of ancient Greek furniture. Most famous of these examples is perhaps the perfectly proportioned chair in the stela of Hegeso (fig. 449).

Although probably Hellenistic rather than earlier, it seems that we would be remiss to omit what is generally considered to be the only complete piece of Pre-Christian Greek furniture which has survived (fig. 450), now in the Musées Royaux d'Art et d'Histoire in Brussels. It was obtained at Luxor in Egypt and presumably was made by Greek artisans in Egypt, if not imported from Greece itself. The round top and three boldly curving

285

449 Gravestone of Hegeso. *About 400* B.C.

449

legs terminating in goat's hoofs, resemble the details of similar tables in classical Greek paintings, and also the bronze tables which have survived from Pompeii.

The influence on design of the Christian era

Up until now we have considered Greek furniture against the background of the past, but, since it represents the continuance of the chain of development that began in prehistoric times, it seems fitting that we should also look briefly at the way classical furniture has influenced the designs of later periods.

About a thousand years after Constantine's time, during the Renaissance, there came a great revival of classical design. But although the Greek forms of architecture (as they had been interpreted by the Romans) appear in profusion, it cannot be said that the forms of Greek furniture are directly reflected in the furniture of the Renaissance. There is an indirect influence in types inherited from the Roman period, but the close relationship that we see in architecture does not exist in furniture. For instance, the outstanding example of Greek furniture design – the classic chair – is not seen in Renaissance times. A new phase of furniture design appears, instead, in the application of columns, pilasters and other classic architectural motifs to credenzas, large bookcases and other pieces that did not exist in Greek times, and in the use of columns for furniture supports.

Again, in the eighteenth century in Western Europe it is through architecture that

286

the Greek classic themes of design achieve a new popularity, and the stage is set for the Greek Revival in furniture. Gentlemen architects, like Lord Burlington who visited Venice, were enamoured with the villas designed by Andrea Palladio, which dotted the Venetian countryside; and the great Palladian houses of England and Ireland were the result. The proportions and details of classic architecture were reproduced also in the smaller Georgian houses; and on the Continent, likewise, there was a great surge of interest in classic architecture.

With this vogue for the classic look in architecture there came a parallel interest in furniture which displayed a classic theme in one way or another. The rediscovery of the ruins of Pompeii and Herculaneum in the middle of the eighteenth century came at a psychological moment, and the Greek motifs that were repeated in the frescoes, art objects and furniture found in these excavations, greatly influenced later eighteenth-century design and decoration. At the same time the travellers who visited Greece on the 'grand tour' (a necessity for every eighteenth-century gentleman) brought back souvenirs and an enthusiasm for everything Greek. Reflecting the enthusiasm of the period, classic motifs appeared in the furniture of Sheraton, Hepplewhite, and other furniture designers in England and their contemporaries on the continent.

It was not until the early years of the nineteenth century, however, that the Greek Revival came into full swing. Thomas Hope in England and Percier and Fontaine in France produced books of furniture design, adapting classical motifs, that became the pattern books for the cabinet-makers of the time. Napoleon I, in the furnishings he commissioned for Malmaison, gave his artists and artisans unlimited scope in the carrying

450

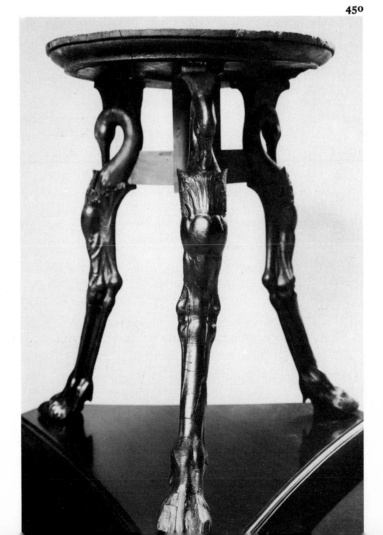

450 Three-legged carved wooden table. *Hellenistic*.

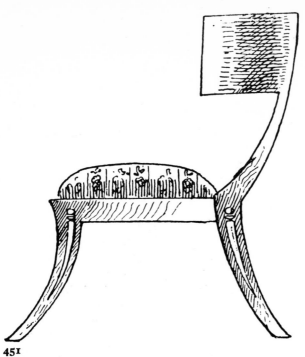

451 Classic chair; eighteenth-century English.

451

out of the popular classic style. In America, Thomas Jefferson followed the design of Palladio's Villa Rotonda in the building of Monticello; and houses, usually of wood, that looked like small white Greek temples were built everywhere throughout the United States. Duncan Phyfe's delicate furniture displayed classic inspiration, as did the heavy furniture of mahogany resembling French Empire styles, but without ornamentation, that is sometimes called (rather inappropriately) 'Colonial'.

There are hundreds of books on the subject of eighteenth- and early nineteenth-century furniture and it need not be discussed in detail here. It should be noted, however, that, although for a time ancient Greece provided the inspiration, only rarely was there an attempt to follow the actual forms of Greek and Roman furniture as they were known from painting and sculpture. Such efforts were mostly limited to pieces like the famous couch of Madame Récamier and the neo-Classic chair, the latter being directly inspired by the classic chair like the one in the Hegeso stela. For the most part the classic motifs were applied to new forms of furniture that appealed to the taste of the times, or to functional pieces like bureaux and cabinets that were unknown in the ancient world.

In the case of the classic chair, however, efforts were occasionally made in the Napoleonic era to approximate the appearance of the ancient prototype, as can be seen in an example in the Baker Museum which still has its original upholstery with the gold-embroidered Napoleonic bees (fig. 453).[1] In England we see a close approximation of the Hegeso chair in a drawing by Thomas Hope (fig. 451), and in Germany also, similar chairs were made at this time (fig. 452). But usually, even though the inspiration is apparent, the designers of the Directoire, Regency, and Empire periods used the classic chair only as a starting point and from this developed their own distinct styles, as illustrated in two examples chosen from the hundreds that exist (figs. 454, 455).

288   Colour plate XVI. Vase painting of chair and small table. 457–450 B.C.

452

453

452 Classic chair; nineteenth-century German.

453 Classic Napoleonic chair.

454 Chair of Empire style; French.

455 Chair of Directoire style; French.

454

455

The popular enthusiasm for the 'Greek fashion' died out toward the middle of the nineteenth century. But even today, in this period of eclecticism, the influence of the Classical era is still apparent. In Greece, at the present time, accurate reproductions of the *klismos* and other ancient pieces, as they appear in Greek paintings and sculpture, are being made.[2] And in both Europe and America, period furniture, in the spirit of Palladio, continues to be popular alongside the modern designs of today. More than any other individual piece of Greek furniture, however, it is the classic Greek chair that has had the most lasting and direct influence; only its immediate antecedents have been traced in detail, but in a broader sense its ancestry can be traced to the chairs of ancient Egypt and Mesopotamia, and it remains a conspicuous symbol of the continuing influence of the past upon the present.

APPENDIX

The considerable amount of furniture that has survived intact from ancient Egypt has made possible a direct examination of the methods and materials employed at this early period. Similar opportunities do not exist elsewhere, since the furniture of the other countries of the ancient world, except in rare instances, has perished long ago, but it is reasonably certain that methods were similar. At any rate, we see exhibited in ancient Egyptian furniture principles of woodworking that were established more than four thousand years ago and are still in use today.

One of the first writers to inquire into the making of Egyptian furniture was a British scholar, Sir J. Gardiner Wilkinson, who was one of the early explorers of the Theban tombs. In 1837 he wrote a popular three-volume work entitled *Manners and Customs of the Ancient Egyptians*, in which he discussed at some length the furniture which had been discovered in the tombs.[1] Several of the pieces which he described and illustrated at that early date can still be seen in the British Museum, and for the most part his assumptions made more than a century ago have been proved to be valid.

At the beginning of the present century, following his epochal discoveries of furniture from the First Dynasty, the distinguished archaeologist W. M. Flinders Petrie published a small volume on the arts and crafts of ancient Egypt. In this he stressed the importance of the woodworker in early Egypt and discussed some of the details of ancient Egyptian woodworking.[2] Most important of the modern scientific works in which methods are discussed is that by A. Lucas entitled *Ancient Egyptian Materials and Industries*, first published in 1926 and now in its fourth edition.[3] Mr Lucas was Honorary Consulting Chemist, Department of Antiquities, Cairo, formerly Director of the Chemical Department, and assisted Howard Carter in analysing the finds from the tomb of Tutankhamun.

A comprehensive up-to-date summary of the information relative to ancient woodworking as well as other crafts is available in *A History of Technology*, published in Oxford in 1954. The chapter on woodwork, by Mr Cyril Aldred, Keeper of the Department of Art and Archaeology, Royal Scottish Museum, Edinburgh, contains much useful information and some drawings of constructional details.[4] A short discussion of cabinet-making in ancient Egypt may also be found in the *Introductory Guide to the Egyptian Collections in the British Museum*, published by the museum in 1964, in the chapter on arts and crafts by A. F. Shore, Assistant Keeper of Egyptian Antiquities.

Woods and their seasoning

Petrie states that, although not plentiful, timber was probably less scarce in ancient Egypt than it is today; but in any case the local supply was supplemented from very early times by imports from abroad – such as ebony from the south and cedar from Syria. Many different varieties of wood are mentioned in the ancient written records, but only actual laboratory examination can determine the exact species of ancient wood used in any individual instance (with the possible exception of ebony). For the most part, where specific woods have been mentioned earlier in this work, the commonly accepted opinion has been followed, since the exact variety is not vital from the viewpoint of design. It must be recognized, however, that in many instances the designation is uncertain where it has not been verified by microscopic analysis.

Rather than list the Egyptian woods as they appear in the ancient records, we have included only those which have been identified by laboratory examination. It does not necessarily follow, however, that all or even most of these varieties were used by the joiners in making furniture. Some of the specimens examined came from coffins, chariots, or other objects that can hardly be considered furniture as such.[5] Also, some varieties are too soft or fibrous to be suitable for good cabinet-work, but the relatively long list will at least refute any idea that only a limited selection was available.

Native woods included acacia, almond, carob (locust-bean), fig (*Ficus arica*), date palm, dom palm, persea, sidder, sycamore fig, tamarisk, willow and poplar. The individual characteristics of some are of interest only to wood technologists, but a number of the species, some unknown to our present-day cabinet-makers, were used for making furniture. For instance, acacia, which was used in ship-building in ancient Egypt and is still employed for this purpose there and elsewhere in the Mediterranean, has a dense texture and served also as a cabinet-wood.[6] Carob wood also was considered desirable for furniture, although this appears to have grown more freely in Syria than in Egypt. Tuthmosis III mentions furniture made of carob wood taken as booty from Megiddo in Palestine (see Part II, p. 210). The wood of the dom palm, unlike that of the date palm, is compact and hard and is said to have been employed for making the feet of couches; and the strong, black wood of the persea tree is said to have been used for making beds and tables. The sycamore fig, not to be confused with the sycamore of northern climates, and the sidder were two of the more ordinary and useful varieties. There were several species of the latter, of which the most common in Egypt is called the *nabk* and bears a light yellowish-coloured fruit like a cherry. At best, however, none of these woods was really a fine cabinet-wood, and some were used only for rough work.

Supplementing these local varieties, foreign timbers were imported in order to obtain wide boards or planks not obtainable from the smaller trees of Egypt, and to supply the craftsmen with choice wood such as ebony and cedar, which did not grow in Egypt. One of the reliefs on the walls of Queen Hatshepsut's temple at Deir el-Bahari shows the return of the ships from Punt bringing rare tropical woods as well as treasures from the South.[7] In an Assyrian relief from Khorsabad we see small ships towing logs, quite likely cedar logs from Syria such as were imported by the Egyptians (fig. 456). Byblos, located on the Phoenician coast in an area famous for its cedars, was long dominated by the Egyptians and was an important centre of trade between ancient Syria and Egypt. A little farther north, about seventy miles from modern Beirut, still stand, under the protection of the Lebanese government, four hundred of the majestic cedar trees, which are probably the grandchildren, if not the children, of the trees imported by the Egyptian pharaohs.

The list of non-native woods identified by laboratory examination includes ash, beech, box, cedar, cypress, elm, fir, juniper, lime, maple, oak, pine, plum and yew (most of which

294

456 Assyrian relief from Khorsabad showing towing of logs.

probably came from Syria and neighbouring areas) and, most important and finest of all the imported cabinet-woods, ebony from the Sudan. Ebony was frequently inlaid with ivory or ornamented with gold, and the value placed upon it is indicated by the special mention of chairs and beds made of ebony ornamented with gold sent by Amenophis III and Akhenaten to the kings of Babylon (see Part I, p. 60). Probably most of the non-native varieties were not available to Egyptian craftsmen in usable quantities, and the most plentiful and most desirable, with the exception of ebony, was the cedar of Lebanon, of which the sides of the great Tutankhamun shrines appear to be constructed.

After the selection of a suitable wood, the next essential step in the making of fine furniture is the proper seasoning of the green timber so that excessive shrinking, splitting and warping is avoided in the assembled piece of furniture. Even though climatic conditions were unusually favourable in Upper Egypt, it would seem, judging by the condition of the fine pieces found in the tomb of Tutankhamun, that the wood must have been properly dried before it was made into furniture. Otherwise, if green wood or improperly seasoned wood had been used, joints would have opened up when exposed to the almost bone-dry air, and other signs of 'movement' of the wood would have been seen. As it is, the joints of the furniture are practically as tight as when originally fitted, and the solid wood sides of the great gilded shrines show but few signs of checking.

We may therefore assume that the ancient Egyptians were sufficiently familiar with the properties of wood to take steps to remove the moisture and sap from the freshly cut timber before using it, although no records exist that tell us exactly how this was done. Doubtless the woodworkers understood that it was necessary to cut the timbers into planks or boards before the wood could be properly dried. In modern production the lumber would be placed in courses, with 'stickers' between, so that air could circulate and the lumber be 'air-dried' before being placed in a dry-kiln to complete the process. (In some instances today lumber is taken almost directly from the saw and dried in scientifically controlled dry-kilns.) It is unlikely, however, that any artificial means of seasoning was employed in ancient Egypt, although covering with manure is said to have been done in ancient Greece,[8] and logically only ageing and exposure to air could be relied upon. Possibly the boards and planks were piled in layers with air space between, but it seems rather more likely that the Egyptian craftsmen would have stood their timber on end in courtyards as is done in small cabinet shops in Italy and elsewhere on the Continent today.

The climate of Upper Egypt created a natural dry-kiln, and when exposed to the hot dry air for a few months green lumber would become almost bone dry. It would have been most important, however, to prevent the wood from drying too rapidly, with resultant checking if exposed directly to the dry air and burning sun, and it has been suggested that a covering of matting may have been used to avoid this.[9] Once the properly seasoned wood was incorporated into furniture, it remained in a permanent state of equilibrium as long as it was kept in this climate. The problem of widely varying conditions of humidity to which furniture is exposed in Europe and America did not exist in the area around Thebes from which most of the surviving examples of ancient Egyptian furniture have come. The rainfall at Cairo rarely exceeds two inches a year.[10] At Luxor in Upper Egypt

   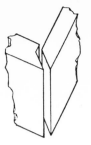  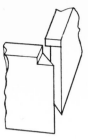 

BUTT JOINT   HALF JOINT   SIMPLE MITRE   SHOULDER MITRE   DOUBLE SHOULDER-MITRE   MITRE HOUSING   DOVETAIL HOUSING MITRE

457

457 Joints used in Egyptian cabinet-making; examples drawn from Old Kingdom coffins.

458 Carpenter's tools, including saws, adzes (used instead of planes), a bow-drill with bits, chisels, an oil-horn and hone. *Eighteenth Dynasty*.

458

(ancient Thebes) the rainfall is negligible, and the rare showers that occur at long intervals have no appreciable effect on the humidity. But, even though the stress to which this furniture was exposed remained nearly constant, it was important that there be a preliminary seasoning. (In America or England, after wood is made into furniture, its moisture content will vary from very little to as much as twelve per cent, depending on where the furniture is used and the time of year.)

The requirements for the making of elegant palace furniture were of course more exacting than for the manufacture of common furniture or burial coffins, but even in coffins we can see evidence that the handling of wood was well understood. The sides and ends are often two or more inches thick, and sometimes very wide pieces of wood are used, as in the extraordinary Old Kingdom coffins now in the University Museum, Philadelphia. The workmanship exhibited in ancient Egyptian coffins varies widely in

296

quality, of course, but some of the finer ones in the British Museum, dating from about 2000 B.C., show relatively little checking, and in one instance where cracks appear on the exterior the highly decorated surfaces on the inside remain almost as smooth as when originally painted. Tops are sometimes from three to as much as six inches thick. The wood used in a box construction such as this, however, where the grain runs in the same direction, would not require the same attention to its seasoning as that used for fine cabinet-work.

Joinery and woodworking tools

Since coffins exhibit in simple form many of the woodworking principles used in furniture, their joinery will be considered first. Various methods were employed in the edgewise joining of the planks used in their construction. Sometimes the planks are joined by dowels or tongues of wood fitted into sockets. In other instances 'butterfly' cramps are inset in the surface. In some early examples where straight, long wood was apparently not available, small irregular pieces were fitted into one another, both edgewise and endwise. And in an extraordinary coffin from the Step Pyramid at Saqqara, dating about 2700 B.C., six thin layers of wood were applied on top of each other and fastened with wooden pegs – constituting perhaps the first example of plywood.[11] These veneers, if they may be so called, were each a little less than a quarter-inch thick, the grain of the alternate layers running in opposite directions as is the case in modern plywood construction. Most of the Middle Kingdom coffins, however, are constructed of solid planking and in some instances exhibit a good quality of cabinetry.

The joints used at the corners of these ancient burial coffins are worthy of note because they represent a variety of types used also in furniture. The most common, except for a plain butt joint, is the mitre joint secured by round dowels inserted into holes exactly as is done today. Other more complicated joints were also used, including shoulder-mitres, double shoulder-mitres, dovetails, dovetail-mitre-housings, and halving joints. Describing the varied individual joints is of little practical use, however, since pictures convey far more clearly the different methods of fitting. Consequently the reader is referred to figure 457, in which the different joints used are represented, together with their names.[12]

Even if there were no other evidence except the scenes of joiners at work depicted on the walls of tombs, of which illustrations follow, we would still be fairly well informed about the tools and methods used by the ancient Egyptians in the making of furniture. Although the basic principles of joinery did not differ greatly from those used in the coffins, finer workmanship was of course required and, in the early periods, was dependent on the use of tools made of copper, a relatively soft metal. Previously, in the first part of this book (page 24), we have noted the large number of copper tools found by Emery in a single tomb of the First Dynasty. Many tools of later dates have also been found, such as the set made of bronze which is now in the British Museum which was discovered stored in a basket in a Theban tomb of New Kingdom date (fig. 458).[13] Until the Middle Kingdom (about 2000 B.C.) tools were made of copper. During the Eighteenth Dynasty

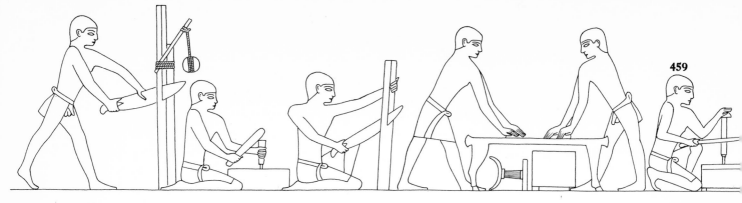

459 Joiners at work. In this scene from the Tomb of Ti craftsmen are shown using saws, adzes, the bow-drill and rubbers. *Fifth Dynasty*.

460 Cabinet-making in a scene from the Tomb of Rekhmire. On the right can be seen craftsmen working on the fretted details of a chest ornamented with amuletic patterns. *Eighteenth Dynasty*.

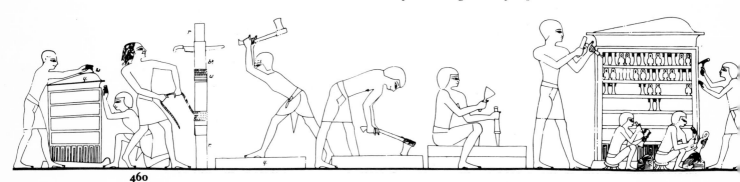

460

woodworking tools of bronze came into common use and their harder cutting edges facilitated the making of fine furniture.

The most important of the tools was perhaps the adze, with a bronze or copper cutting blade lashed to a wooden haft. This was the universal tool used for hewing and trimming the rough timbers as well as for shaping and smoothing the surface. In the hands of the skilled craftsman it was a versatile and effective tool, with blades varying from five to eleven inches in length. For finer work the ancient artisan employed a variety of chisels, holding the chisel in one hand and striking it with a wooden mallet with the other. Other essential tools were the saws used for cutting timber, the awls used for punching small holes, and the bow-drills with which holes were cut to receive the strands of linen cord or rush which formed the seats of chairs and coverings of beds. Knives used as scrapers were apparently responsible for the final smoothing of the wood, and their marks are apparent in the shaping of edges. But even though tools of copper and bronze were now available, the primitive tools of flint were still used for some purposes until the time of the Eighteenth Dynasty.

The use of the various tools employed in the making of furniture is pictured in the realistic woodworking scenes carved and painted on the tomb walls, one of the earliest being that found in a tomb at Saqqara, of about 2500 B.C. (fig. 459).[14] Two of the men in this scene are sawing rough wood, using the ancient Egyptian pull-saw which required the major effort to be exerted on the pulling stroke; consequently, the cutting edge of the teeth is set towards the handle. Seven of such copper saw blades dating about 3000 B.C. were found by Emery in the First Dynasty tomb previously mentioned, their lengths

461 Furniture-makers in the Tomb of Rekhmire. Two craftsmen are shown using a bow-drill to drill the holes in a bed-frame to take the strands of a woven mattress. *Eighteenth Dynasty*.

varying from about five to fifteen inches. The large piece of wood being cut at the left is lashed to an upright post, the standard procedure for sawing the larger timbers. The smaller piece being cut by the other man is held with one hand while he saws with the other. One of the workmen squats while he chisels a block of wood, using a club-shaped mallet to strike the chisel; and two men working together smooth the upper surfaces of a bed frame, using what are presumed to be rubbing blocks of sandstone. The comparison of the design of the bed with one in the Mereruka reliefs is interesting, since both are of approximately the same period (fig. 53). Underneath the bed is a head-rest and a small chest, probably awaiting finishing. At the extreme right of the scene a workman is using a bow-drill, the tool used in ancient times instead of an auger and bit.

The same types of tools were still in use a thousand years later, when the furniture of Tutankhamun was made, as is evident in the intriguing scene from the tomb of Rekhmire at Thebes, dating about 1460 B.C. (fig. 460).[15] (See also fig. 178.) Twelve men in all are at work. Two workmen in the upper register are engaged in the making of the typical Theban chairs. At the left in the lower part of the scene a piece of timber is being lashed to a standing post in the traditional manner before being sawed, while two men in the centre are splitting other pieces with axes. At the right the recesses to hold inlays are being chiselled in the sides of a shrine, while another craftsman strikes a chisel with his mallet.

Other woodworking scenes also appear in these remarkable paintings. In one (fig. 461) the manner of using the bow-drill is very clearly indicated, although in this instance there are two men working together instead of one as in the scene previously mentioned. The drill is probably heavier, and the second man presses down on the hollowed dom-nut in which the top of the wooden shaft revolves, as the hole is bored in the heavy wood of the bed-frame. The bow which the workman at the left 'saws' back and forth is sharply delineated, as is the string wound around the shaft of the drill to cause it to rotate. The separate cutting bit of bronze is also apparent, and no doubt this, like the other tools made of this soft alloy, would have needed frequent sharpening. Tools made of iron did not come into use until considerably later. Underneath the bed is a small inlaid chest

461

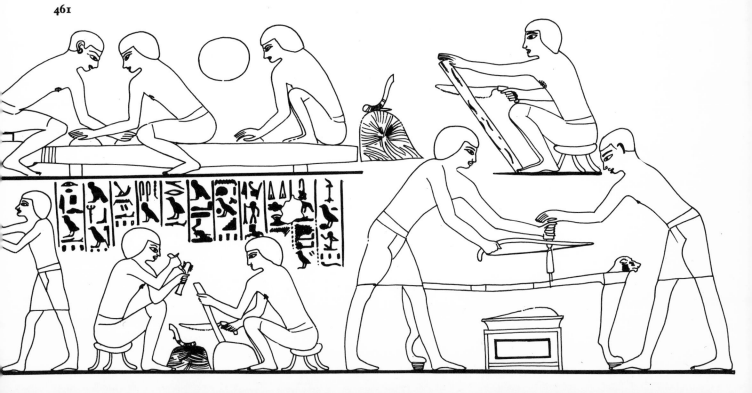

462

with a shrine-shaped lid, and the workmen sit on three-legged stools, which, like the bed and the chest, are typical pieces of the Eighteenth Dynasty.

Before discussing the third of the Rekhmire paintings, it is interesting to compare the two illustrated above with an ancient model of a carpenter shop (fig. 462). Dating from the early Middle Kingdom (about 2020 B.C.), this is one of the remarkable group of three-dimensional models found in the tomb of Meket-Re at Thebes.[16] Although paintings representing daily activities were more common, they were sometimes supplemented at this period with three-dimensional models. Besides the carpenter shop, models of Meket-Re's villa with its walled garden and pool had been placed in the tomb, as well as models of a butcher's shop, a weaving shop, a brewery and bakery, a granary and a cattle stable, which, together with models of the boats used by Meket-Re on the Nile, presented in total a unique and factual picture of the life of the period.

Although a rougher kind of work seems to be indicated in the Meket-Re model than in the Rekhmire paintings, the same basic methods are seen in the hewing of a large timber with adzes and in the cutting of a thick piece of wood with a pull-saw. The workman in the centre, who is about to strike his chisel with a wooden mallet, presents a realistic picture of how mortise holes were cut, probably following the same method that was used as long ago as 3100 B.C., when the mortise and tenon joint was first invented (see pp. 21–25), and which is still used today five thousand years later. In the background is a large chest, painted white.

Inside one of the Meket-Re boat models there were miniature models of furniture which quite likely represent the kind of full-sized furniture that was made in a carpenter shop like the one illustrated. These were the furnishings of the cabin (fig. 463a, b, c, d). The crude legs derive, no doubt, from the traditional carved animal legs, but instead of facing in one direction in the customary manner they face toward each other – a feature

462 Model of a carpenter's shop with men using saws, chisels and adzes. *Eleventh Dynasty.*

seen only rarely in Egyptian design. This same feature appears in the furniture found at Jericho in Palestine, and the model of the long table or bench bears a striking resemblance to one of the Jericho pieces (fig. 353).

Veneering and inlaying

One of the interesting details in the third of the Rekhmire scenes illustrated (fig. 464) is the pot beneath which a fire is flaming, probably in the process of cooking glue. When animal glue was first employed, however, is uncertain.[17] There is no firm evidence of its

463 a

b

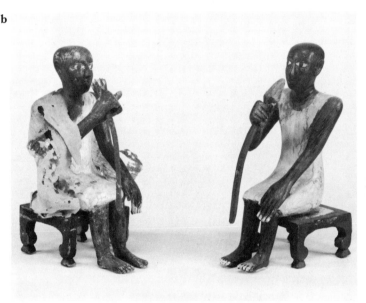

c

d

463 Miniature furniture from model boats found in the Tomb of Meket-Re. *Eleventh Dynasty.*

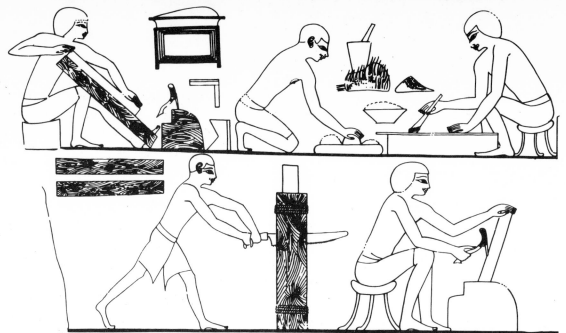

464

being so used in the Old Kingdom (joints in this period were usually drawn tightly together by thongs threaded through holes); but by the time of the Eighteenth Dynasty, from which this painting comes, glue was in common use, both as an adhesive and for mixing with whiting to make gesso. Made of animal parts containing gelatine, the glue used by the Egyptians of this time was not essentially different from the animal glue used today.

The actual use being made of glue in this scene, however, is not certain. It looks a little as though the man with the brush may be applying a coating of gesso, in which glue would need to be mixed. Normally, however, the gesso would not be applied on a piece of furniture until it was assembled, and the other parts of the scene suggest that the workman is spreading glue on a thin piece of wood – possibly a strip to be inlaid. The small chest in the picture appears to be ornamented with inlaid strips of ebony, and the workman at the left appears to be gluing woods of different species together. Although not apparent in the black and white illustration, the upper piece of wood is coloured reddish in the original painting, probably to represent a superior cabinet-wood, while the lower piece is yellowish and marked with a coarse grain to represent a more ordinary variety like the block on the floor into which a workman has struck his adze. But it is not necessary to depend on such scenes for evidence of veneering in the Eighteenth Dynasty. Numerous actual examples from this period can be seen in the extant furniture.

The use of inlay and veneer dates back to the First Dynasty, but the type of adhesive used in the early periods is not known. No traces have been found of animal glue, and probably gums of various sorts were used. One of the chairs and the curtain box of which the remains were found in the tomb of Queen Hetepheres (dating about 2600 B.C.) were elaborately inlaid (figs. 30, 35), but the extent to which inlaying and veneering were used in ancient Egypt can best be seen in the furniture of Tutankhamun. Faience, coloured stones, opaque coloured glass, ivory and ebony were all employed for inlays, apparently fastened into place with animal glue. Veneering in the modern sense where a choice wood or other valuable material is applied over a more ordinary wood for the sake of appearance is also seen, ebony and ivory being used most often for the faces. Both Lucas and Aldred

464 Scene of furniture making in the Tomb of Rekhmire. In the upper register one man is shown applying glue from a pot heating on a fire. *Eighteenth Dynasty*.

cite individual examples[18] in which a thin veneer is held in place with glue, or thicker pieces are attached with small wooden pegs. Mention has been made earlier of the veneers used on the chairs of Yuia and Thuiu, and conspicuous examples of inlaying and veneering are to be seen in the chests from the tomb of King Tutankhamun.

Turning and bending

What later became one of the most common and useful tools, the wood-turning lathe, does not appear to have been known to the Egyptians of the Eighteenth Dynasty, although round legs which have the semblance of being turned occur quite frequently in the stools of this period. Some of the legs even have the series of fine rings characteristic of turned work, as in the stool in the British Museum which has been illustrated in figure 193. The pivot-holes normally found at each end of turned stock are lacking, however, and it has been concluded by Lucas,[19] as well as by Petrie,[20] that the legs of this and similar stools were not turned but were hand-worked.

Opinions differ regarding the time when the wood-turning lathe was first used. Pliny states that the lathe was invented by Theodorus of Samos, who lived in the seventh century B.C.,[21] but this is doubtful evidence, since in the same sentence Pliny also says that the saw and the carpenter's axe were invented by Daedalus (a mythical character of the time of King Minos, about 1450 B.C.). As we know, these tools were in use in Egypt more than a thousand years before that time. It is not impossible, of course, that the true turning-lathe may have been invented by the Greeks; but what appear to be turned legs are often portrayed in Mesopotamian art, and it has also been suggested that the lathe may have originated in the heavily wooded and furniture-making area of Syria. The principle of the bow-drill and the revolving motion in shaping wood and pottery had long been known in Egypt, however, and I am inclined to believe that this principle was applied in some way in the making of the round legs used on Egyptian stools, even if the true wood-turning lathe had not yet come into general use. At any rate, it was not until about the seventh century B.C. that there was a marked increase in the use of turned legs.

Another technique of which the origin is not known is the bending of wood into curved shapes by artificial means. Wooden angle-braces to strengthen the joints between the legs and frames of tables and stools are represented in the scenes previously illustrated (fig. 27b) from the tomb of Hesy-Re (about 2660 B.C.), but none of the brackets pictured have survived to indicate whether they were of natural growth or artificially bent. In later times the curved bracket became an element of design as well as serving a useful purpose. A number of examples may be seen in the furniture previously illustrated and a typical application appears in the measured drawing of the chair from the Archaeological Museum in Florence (fig. 469).

Some of the braces appear to be natural growth, but, since quite a good many of such pieces were used, it is possible that the naturally curved pieces available were supplemented by pieces of wood grown into shape. I am not aware of any analysis that has determined whether or not some of these curved forms were bent into shape, but this is a simple process, and since the Egyptians were well acquainted with the structure of wood it seems probable that artificial bending was resorted to at an early period. By the time of the Greeks it seems certain that bending was used to form the sharp curves of the *klismos*, the popular chair of the Classical era.[22]

Construction details

A surprising variety of joints were used by the early Egyptian cabinet-makers. The sophisticated joints used in the construction of the Queen Hetepheres canopy have been illustrated earlier (fig. 34), as well as the detail drawing of a typical Theban chair (fig. 467). These only suggest, however, the many refinements and intricate details of the ancient joinery. It is not possible to illustrate all the variations that exist, but a number of studies made under the direction of M. Garnier of the Collège Technique Boulle, Paris, directly from furniture in the Louvre are helpful in visualizing how the different parts are fitted together.[23] The drawings are self-explanatory to those familiar with the finer points of woodworking and will mean little to anyone else, but will serve to illustrate the variety of joints that existed (figs. 465, 466).

Intricate locking joints were also constructed so that a series of tumblers fell into place when the doors of a shrine were closed, presumably never to be opened again, and there was a variety of methods used in fitting the lids of storage chests. These were usually secured by cords wound around two knobs, one on top and one on the end, and then sealed with the owner's mark so that any tampering was immediately apparent. This required the top to be fastened at the other end in some manner, and sometimes it was hinged with copper hinges very like those of today. More often, though, there was some kind of a wooden joint which prevented its being opened without the seal being broken. One method was to slide the top into a section fitted into a groove so that the top could not be lifted off; in other examples the end of the top opposite the seal was shaped with a pattern that fitted into a corresponding grooving cut into the inside face, and served the same purpose as a hinge.

There were various other niceties. One device frequently used was the insertion of small pins through the mortise and tenon joints to keep them in place. Where dowels came to the surface in finely finished furniture, the dowel ends were often capped with ivory or ebony; in gilded pieces the ends were covered with pieces of gold-leaf or capped with gold buttons. Where small knots appeared in ebony, they were drilled out and neatly patched with wood of the same colour, and in more ordinary wood the large defects were filled in with a kind of stucco and grained. Scarf joints were employed in the joining of small pieces of wood. Nicely fitted wood or metal bolts running through staples were used when such a fastening was required.

Finishing

A high percentage of the pieces of ancient Egyptian furniture which have been found were originally painted. In some instances only traces of paint remained, and in others the paint was still in a good state of preservation when found. The plainer pieces were

465 Detail drawing of furniture joinery.

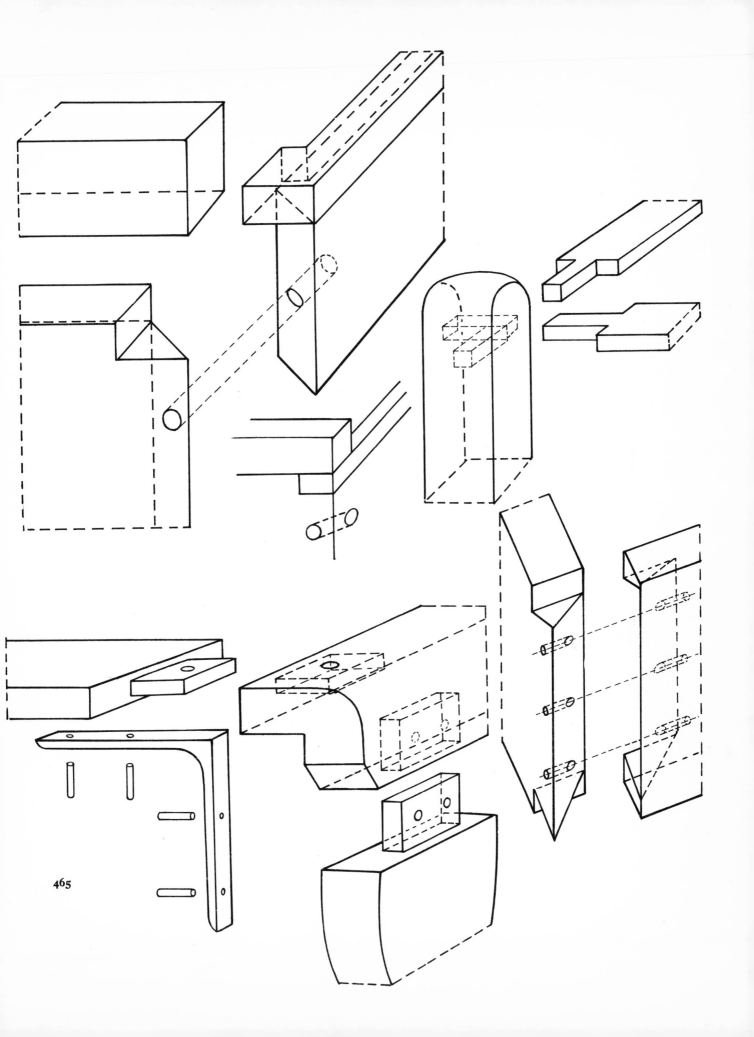

465

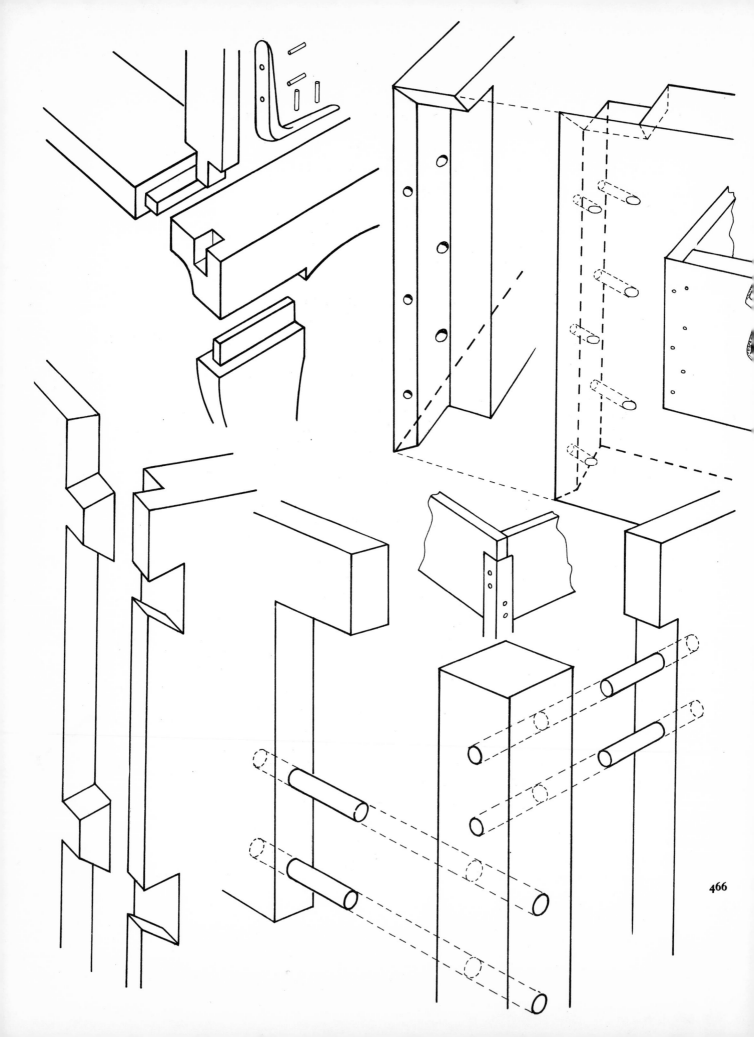

466

ordinarily painted in a single colour, usually white, brownish-yellow, or red, while the more elaborate furniture was decorated or gilded when it was not inlaid. Paint was sometimes applied directly to the raw wood, but it was customary to apply it over a gesso base in the better quality work. Many examples exist of painting on gesso, one of the most outstanding being the chest from the tomb of Tutankhamun which is decorated with brightly coloured fighting and hunting scenes (figs. 112, 113).

The use of gesso deserves particular notice, since it was employed both as a ground for painting and as a base for gilding. Although usually gesso is considered to be a mixture of glue and whiting, the term is somewhat ambiguous and is loosely used to indicate any kind of a gypsum plaster mixed with size.[24] Frequently a layer of coarse woven linen was applied between the wood and the gesso in ancient Egypt, probably with glue as an adhesive, in order to bind the coating more firmly and reinforce it with the tough linen fibres. Exactly the same procedure is still followed in the cabinet shops of Florence, Italy, where fine painted furniture is produced using the ancient techniques. In some instances, where carvings were not cut in the wood, the effect of raised carving was obtained by modelling the gesso in low relief, which was done with great delicacy and skill and then covered with gold-leaf.

Of the other materials used in finishing furniture, only varnish, which came into use in the Eighteenth Dynasty, can definitely be identified. Its composition is in doubt but presumably a resin base was used. Both a colourless clear varnish and a glossy black varnish were used, the former frequently as a coating over painting. The Tutankhamun chest mentioned above, for example, had been coated with a transparent varnish over its decorative scenes, which like all ancient Egyptian paintings were painted in tempera, not in oil. The varnish had apparently turned yellowish with age, since it seems that these coatings were originally colourless. Various authorities have observed that where varnish had been applied over a white surface there are now sometimes unsightly and irregular edges, and that, presumably, these areas would not have been finished so carelessly unless the varnish used was originally transparent and without colour.[25]

Black varnish, however, was opaque and served as a finish in the place of black paint. It had been used on several wooden chests and boxes found in the tomb of Tutankhamun, and was also applied on the heavy framed bases on which the three animal couches stood. The canopic chests and some other pieces from the tomb of Yuia and Thuiu had also been finished with this material, and it has been surmised that the intent may have been to simulate ebony.[26] The few instances in which it occurs, however, indicate that it was not customarily employed on furniture used in the home.

Both gold-leaf and the thicker sheet-gold were freely used for covering the wooden surfaces of the royal furniture and shrines, as well as a highlight for carvings. Much of this applied gold is still bright and in good condition, and quite a good many specimens of gold-leaf have been examined. Although not as thin as modern leaf, its thickness was apparently about the same as that used in Europe during the eighteenth century.[27] The leaf was ordinarily applied over gesso, being attached with a sizing or other adhesive much as is done today. Very thin leaf was sometimes used over carved gesso ornamentation and has lost some of its brightness, but the heavier leaf has kept its metallic lustre.

466 Detail drawing of furniture joinery.

The thicker sheet-gold was applied directly on the wood surface and fastened with small gold pins or studs; if the wood was shaped or carved, the gold was hammered into shape.

Identification of the finish used on cabinet-woods that were not painted presents a special problem. Whatever may have been applied originally has either vanished completely or disintegrated to the point where laboratory tests are not conclusive. The problem is further complicated by the fact that a treatment of some sort has usually been given to the wood since its discovery. Consequently, examination of the pieces in their present condition cannot always be depended on although the patina of the wood can suggest what might have taken place.

Crude pieces of furniture like those from the cemetery at Deir el-Medina (fig. 214) were apparently left in the raw wood unless they were painted, although often some faint traces of paint can be seen on pieces that appear to have no finish. But fine cabinet-woods like ebony were no doubt given a finish to preserve the colour and brightness of the wood. After the wood was smoothed by the craftsmen with sandstone rubbers, the normal procedure would have been to polish it with abrasives and linen pads, and then finish with natural oils, gums and resins, all of which were available. The effect of oil on wood certainly would have been noted at an early period, in kitchen use if nowhere else, and a thin coating of resin varnish (absorbed by the wood long since) could have provided lustre. Beeswax also, frequently used as a protective coating over painted surfaces and for other purposes,[28] was available, but no positive statement of the methods and materials employed in wood-finishing can be made until further proof is available.

Upholstery

'Upholstered' furniture, in the modern sense, was not known in ancient Egypt, but cushions were draped over the backs and seats of chairs from a very early period. One of the earliest known examples where a chair with such a cushion is depicted appears on a carved stone relief from Saqqara, dating about 2800 B.C. (fig. 24). The back of this rather modern-looking chair is straight and the cushion would no doubt have added considerably to its comfort. Similar use of a cushion draped over the back frequently appears in the Old Kingdom reliefs, particularly on low-backed chairs. In the Eighteenth Dynasty cushions were in common use, but there was less need for a back cushion with the curved and slanting back-rests that were introduced during the Middle Kingdom and that replaced the straight back in the finer chairs.

Cushions were usually covered with a woven linen fabric. In some painted reliefs of the Old Kingdom the dress worn by the seated person and the cushion on his stool are both represented in pure white, suggesting that they were made of the same white fabric (see colour plate II). The art of weaving and dyeing linen was known from a very early period, and until late in Egyptian history flax fibres were used almost exclusively in the making of cloth. The technical details of the craft as practised in ancient times are clearly portrayed in painted scenes and in three-dimensional models (like the one found in the tomb of Meket-Re). Most of the fabric actually found in the tombs consists of linen-sheeting. Quantities were used for wrapping mummies – sixteen layers in the case of

Tutankhamun – and, in addition, long lengths were sometimes folded neatly and stored in chests so they would be available for the use of the spirit of the deceased in the after-life. Fragments of more heavily woven coloured linen have also been found in Eighteenth Dynasty tombs, and a complete cushion covered with a pinkish woven linen was discovered near one of the chairs in the tomb of Yuia and Thuiu.

Although no separate cushions covered in leather have survived, many other evidences of its use on furniture have been found. The tanning of leather, like the weaving of fabric, had been practised by prehistoric man, and raw-hide thongs were used to lash joints together long before glue was used in joinery. Interlacing straps of leather were employed as an alternative to woven rush on beds and stools of the First Dynasty (before 3000 B.C.), as has been described in the first chapter where the important discoveries of Petrie and Emery are discussed (pp. 19–25).

Numerous examples of stools which once had hide-leather seats have also been found, often with fragments of leather still adhering to the seat-frame, and occasionally with the seat almost intact as in the stool illustrated from the Metropolitan Museum (fig. 199). The strong and flexible leather was particularly well suited for use on folding stools of this type. Cow-hide was most commonly used but goat-skin has also been identified. We know also from the painted scenes that wild animal skins, probably imported from abroad, were sometimes used for cushions. What appear to be leopard skins are depicted, as in the banquet scene from a Theban tomb where one of the stools has a spotted cushion with the tail of the animal hanging at the side (colour plate XI). The same effect is simulated in an intriguing manner in an ivory inlaid stool from the tomb of Tutankhamun (fig. 102).

When separate cushions were used some filling material would of course be required. The Cairo Catalogue describes the cushion found in the tomb of Yuia and Thuiu as filled with pigeon feathers. In the revised edition of Wilkinson's work it is stated that "mattresses and couches seem to have been padded with feathers of the water-fowl".[29] The British Museum also has an Eighteenth Dynasty cushion stuffed with what are described as water-fowl feathers. Its linen cover is faded to a plain drab shade but probably was once brightly coloured. But when thicker mattresses or cushions were used, such as that portrayed on Mereruka's bed (fig. 53), it would seem more likely that a firmer material would have been employed as a filling – probably straw or other fibres that could be easily obtained in quantity.

Except for the stools covered with leather, most of the seating pieces which have been found had woven seats of rush or linen cord. The making of baskets and matting was one of the first arts known to prehistoric man, and much the same methods were employed in the plaiting and weaving of seats. Petrie found traces of woven rush covering on beds of the First Dynasty excavated at Tarkhan (Part I, pp. 19–25), and stools with woven seats are clearly depicted in Second Dynasty stelae (dating c. 2800 B.C.). A diagonal pattern of weaving is indicated on one of these early reliefs (fig. 19), and various other patterns can be seen in the actual stools and chairs which have been found. In the cruder examples the rush is wound around the seat frame; in the more sophisticated pieces, where a finer weave is used, the strands are inserted through small holes in the upper surface of the frame and consequently are not visible in an elevation view. Many of these ancient woven seats were still in good condition when found, and the woven coverings of the beds found in the tombs of King Tutankhamun, Yuia and Thuiu, and the architect Kha are all very well preserved. Until recently the hand-weaving of rush seats was widely practised wherever chairs were made, but of late mechanically woven cane has largely taken its place, either because of cost or because craftsmen who know the art are no longer available. Fortunately, however, hand-weaving still continues in some parts of the world, perpetuating a useful craft that is more than five thousand years old.

Measured Drawings

MEASURED DRAWINGS

Since it is only rarely that a practical woodworker can have direct access to original ancient pieces so that measurements can be taken and accurate working drawings made, a small selection of measured drawings of Egyptian pieces by M. McDonald-Taylor has been included for the benefit of those directly interested in woodworking. The pieces selected for illustration are the simpler plain ones which are less well known than the spectacular furniture from the tomb of King Tutankhamun, and which can be rendered in small-scale drawings more satisfactorily than can the elaborately carved and inlaid royal furniture.

The lowness of some of the seating pieces will be immediately noticed by reference to the scale. This does not mean, however, that they were intended for child's use, since the early Egyptians were of small stature and also sometimes used their chairs sitting in a squatting position. Seats of the chairs of royalty were more nearly the same height as those now used. It should be noted that in order to portray the details more clearly the smaller pieces are rendered in a larger scale than the full-size chairs. Comparative sizes can be determined by the scales superimposed on the drawings.

CHAIR

FRONT ELEVATION

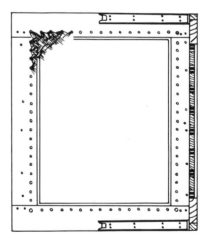

SIDE ELEVATION

BACK ELEVATION

PLAN of SEAT

Of acacia wood: back inlaid with ivory
and ebony. Seat of plaited string (much worn)
From Thebes. New Kingdom—c. 1250 B.C.
Overall Dimensions
Height: 2' $\frac{7}{16}$"
Width: 1' 6$\frac{7}{8}$"
Depth: 1' 4$\frac{7}{8}$"
From British Museum No. 2480

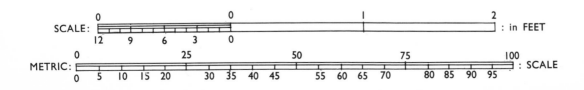

SCALE: 0   0   1   2   : in FEET
12   9   6   3   0

METRIC: 0   25   50   75   100   : SCALE
0   5   10   15   20   30   35   40   45   55   60   65   70   80   85   90   95

CHAIR

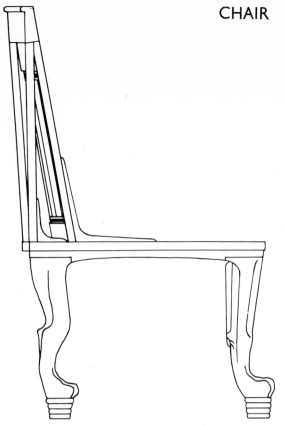

SIDE ELEVATION

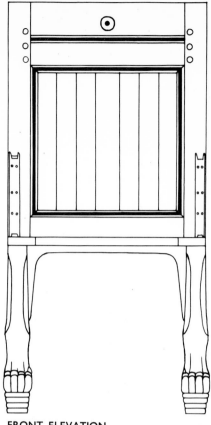

FRONT ELEVATION

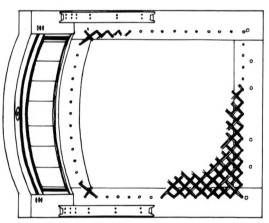

PLAN OF CHAIR FROM ABOVE

BACK ELEVATION

From Thebes—c. 1400 B.C.
Dynasty XVIII
Of unidentified wood, decorated with strips of
darker wood and circular inlays of bone .
Now in Brooklyn Museum, N.Y.
Overall dimensions:
Height: 2′ 11$\frac{13}{16}$″
Width: 1′ 5$\frac{7}{8}$″
Depth: 2′ 0$\frac{5}{8}$″

314

CHAIR

FRONT ELEVATION

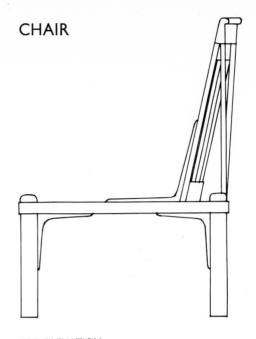

SIDE ELEVATION

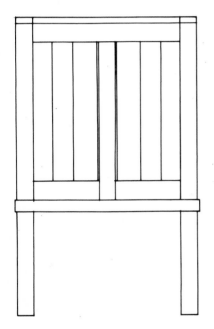

BACK ELEVATION

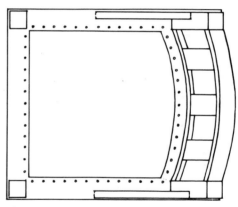

PLAN looking down on SEAT

Overall Dimensions
Height: 65·50 cm.
Depth of Seat: 48·60 cm.
Width of Seat: 42·25 cm.
Of cedarwood
Egyptian—c. 1500 B.C.
(Museo Archaeologico, Florence, Italy)

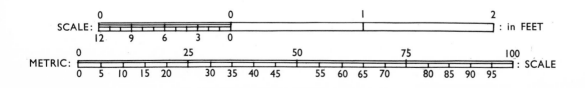

SCALE: 0   0   1   2   : in FEET
      12 9   6   3   0

METRIC: 0   25   50   75   100 : SCALE
        0 5 10 15 20 30 35 40 45 55 60 65 70 80 85 90 95

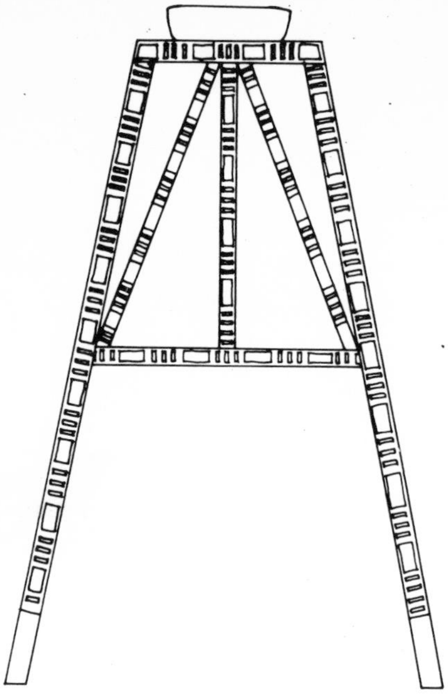

ELEVATION

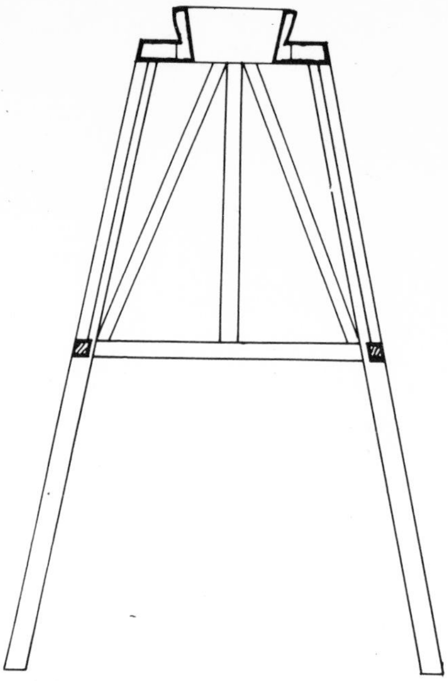

SECTION

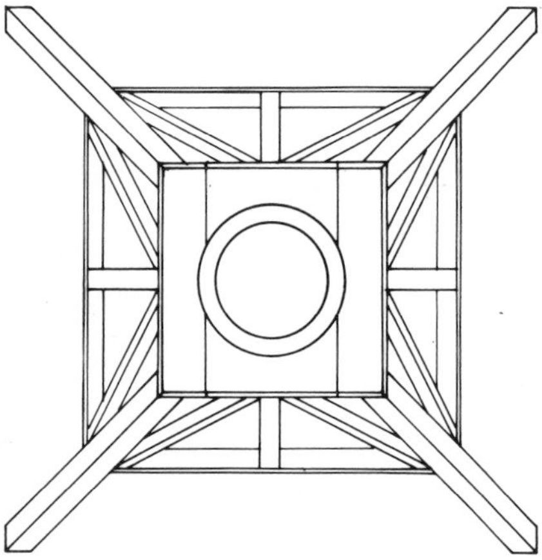

PLAN of TOP & SUPPORTS

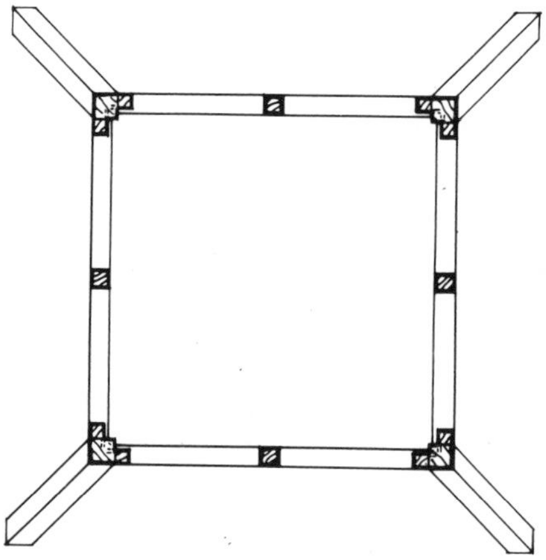

PLAN at STRETCHER LEVEL

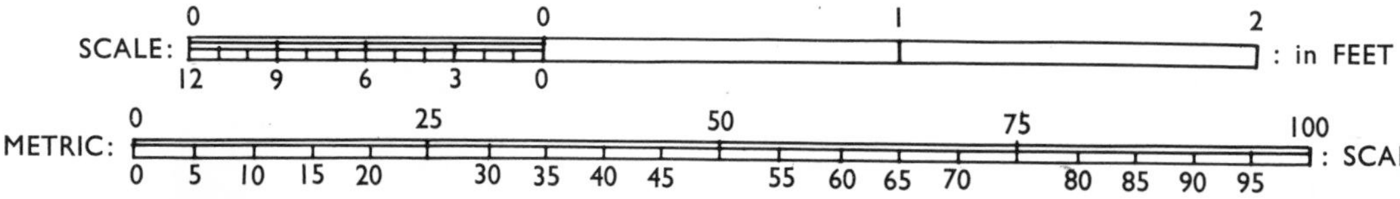
SCALE:
0 0 1 2
12 9 6 3 0
: in FEET
METRIC:
0 25 50 75 100
0 5 10 15 20 30 35 40 45 55 60 65 70 80 85 90 95
: SCALE

JAR STAND

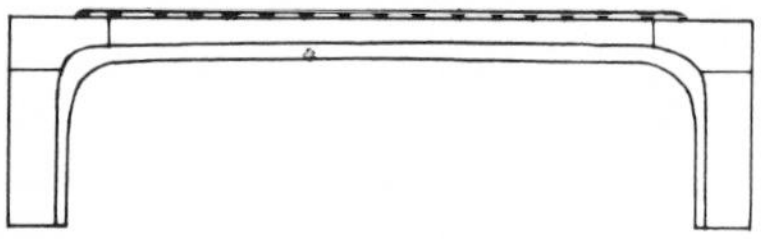

LONG ELEVATION

A (above) JAR STAND
British Museum No. 2470
Overall Dimensions:
Height: 2′ $3\frac{1}{8}$″
Length:
Width: 1′ $6\frac{1}{2}$″

STOOL

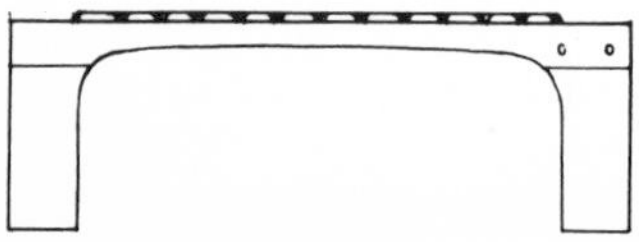

SHORT ELEVATION

B (lower) STOOL
British Museum No. 46705
Overall Dimensions:
Height: $4\frac{1}{2}$″ + $\frac{3}{16}$″ String
Length: 1′ $4\frac{7}{8}$″
Width: 1′ $2\frac{1}{8}$″

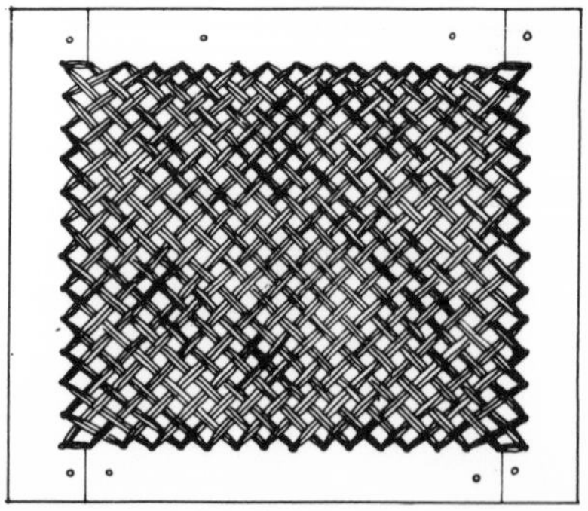

PLAN of SEAT

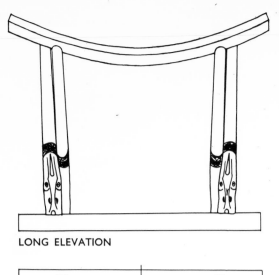

LONG ELEVATION

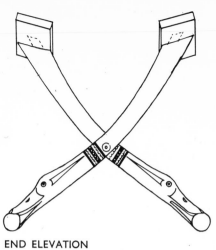

END ELEVATION

FOLDING STOOL

Leather seat (perished)
British Museum No. 2477

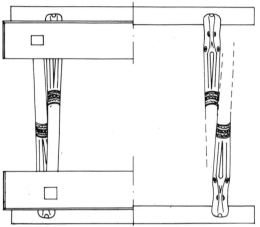

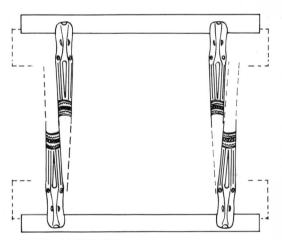

Overall Dimensions:
Height: 1′ 6$\frac{7}{8}$″
Length: 1′ 11$\frac{3}{8}$″
Width: 1′ 6$\frac{3}{4}$″

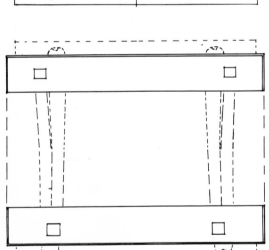

PLAN of SEAT

Top

PLAN of SUPPORTS

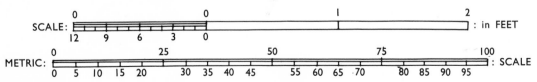

SCALE: |0   0   1   2| : in FEET
12 9 6 3 0

METRIC: |0   25   50   75   100| : SCALE
0 5 10 15 20 30 35 40 45 55 60 65 70 80 85 90 95

317

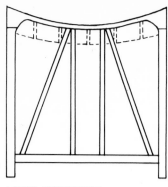

LONG ELEVATION

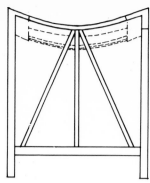

SHORT ELEVATION

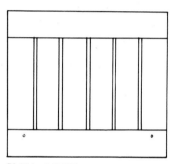

PLAN of SEAT

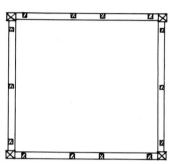

PLAN of STRETCHERS

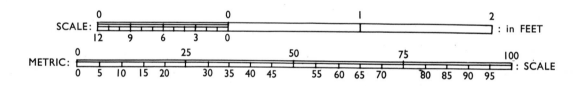

SCALE: : in FEET

0   0   1   2

12   9   6   3   0

METRIC: : SCALE

0   25   50   75   100

0 5 10 15 20   30 35 40 45   55 60 65 70   80 85 90 95

Overall Dimensions
Length: 1′ 2½″
Width: 1′ 0⅝″
Height: 1′ 2¾″

STOOL

British Museum No. 2476

318

LONG ELEVATION

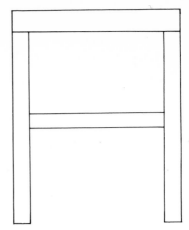

SHORT or END ELEVATION

PLAN of TOP

TABLE

ONE OF A PAIR, PAINTED WHITE

Overall Dimensions
Length: 75 cm.
Width: 38 cm.
Height: 47·50 cm.

In Museo Egizio, Torino, Italy
Museum No. Supp. 8257

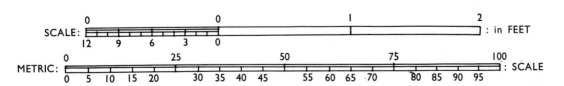

SCALE: in FEET

0   0   1   2

12   9   6   3   0

METRIC: SCALE

0   25   50   75   100

0   5   10   15   20   30   35   40   45   55   60   65   70   80   85   90   95

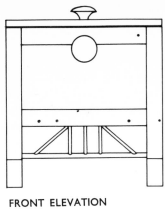

FRONT ELEVATION

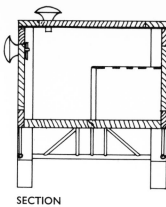

SECTION

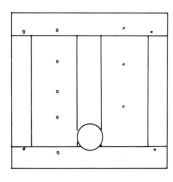

PLAN of LID

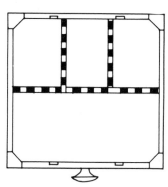

PLAN of INTERIOR

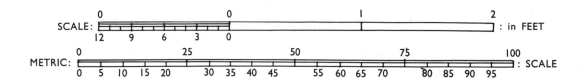

SCALE: [0 ... 0 ... 1 ... 2] : in FEET
12 9 6 3 0

METRIC: [0 ... 25 ... 50 ... 75 ... 100] : SCALE
0 5 10 15 20 30 35 40 45 55 60 65 70 80 85 90 95

Overall Dimensions
Length: 1′ 2⅛″
Width: 1′ 1⅜″
Height: 1′ 2½″

TOILET CHEST

British Museum, London No. 24708

320

NOTES

INTRODUCTION

1 Recognition should also be given to the earlier work on this period by Caroline L. Ransom, *Couches and Beds of the Greeks, Etruscans and Romans*, the University of Chicago Press, Chicago, 1905. Although begun as the first of a series of studies in ancient furniture, unfortunately no other volumes followed. More recently a book entitled *Furniture of Classical Greece* by T. H. Robjohn Gibbings and C. W. Pullin has been published in New York (1963) which illustrates a number of pieces of classical and archaic furniture together with reproductions made by E. Saridis of Athens.

2 We are advised by the art division of the New York Public Library that of the estimated total of 1400 titles on furniture, more than half are in languages other than English. A number of these deal with the furniture of Greece as well as other individual areas, including limited studies of ancient Egyptian furniture (particularly in German) but no general comprehensive study of ancient furniture is included in these foreign works.

3 When this book was in the planning stage this question was discussed in detail with several authorities in this field. Laurence Sickman, Director of the William Rockhill Nelson Gallery of Art, Kansas City, kindly gave me a detailed list of all known furniture objects of the Han period, consisting chiefly of lacquered tables, toilet boxes and a carved wooden chair. He has also pointed out several pieces from Changsha illustrated in a Communist Chinese publication, now in the Peking Historical Museum. Since all of these are of considerably later date than the period covered in our book, however, it has been thought best to omit entirely the subject of Far Eastern furniture. There can be no question, however, but that furniture existed in China at an early date, as in other ancient countries.

PART I: EGYPT

Chapter 1: The Early Beginnings: Dynasties I, II and III

1 A. Lucas, *Ancient Egyptian Materials and Industries*, (4th ed.), London, 1962, p. 200.

2 The principal accounts of these discoveries are contained in E. Amélineau, *Les nouvelles fouilles d'Abydos*, 3 vols. Paris, 1899–1905; W. M. F. Petrie, *Royal Tombs of the First Dynasty*, 2 vols. London, 1900–1 (vol. II is entitled *Royal Tombs of the Earliest Dynasties*); id., *Abydos*, 3 vols. London, 1902–4.

3 Petrie, *Tarkhan I and Memphis V*, London, 1913; id., *Tarkhan II*, London, 1914.

4 Full details of his finds are to be found in W. B. Emery's *The Tomb of Hemaka*, Cairo, 1938; *Hor-aha*, Cairo, 1939; *Great Tombs of the First Dynasty*, 3 vols. Cairo, 1949, London, 1954, 1958. See also Emery, *Archaic Egypt*, London, 1961.

5 Emery, *Great Tombs of the First Dynasty*, II, p. 7, pls. 6, 7.

6 *Cf*. G. Elliot Smith, *The Ancient Egyptians*, London, 1923, p. 56.

7 The evidence for the use of glue in securing joints is largely negative in the Early Dynastic period. *Cf*. Lucas, *op. cit.*, p. 3. For the evidence on the use of leather, see Techniques, p. 309.

8 Emery, *Great Tombs of the First Dynasty*, I, p. 62 (no. 578).

9 Petrie, *Tarkhan I*, pp. 23–4, pls. viii, ix. Narmer, whose name was found on objects associated with some of the early burials at Tarkhan, was a king who is sometimes identified with Menes, to whom is credited the unification of the land of Egypt at the beginning of the First Dynasty, about 3100 B.C.

10 Petrie, *Tarkhan I*, p. 24.

11 Emery, *Great Tombs of the First Dynasty*, I, p. 13. I am grateful to the author for permission to use quotations and drawings from this volume.

12 *Ibid.*, p. 57, fig. 28.

13 *Ibid.*, pp. 57ff.

14 A. Scharff, *Die Altertümer der Vor- und Frühzeit Ägyptens*, Pt. 2, Berlin, 1929, pl. 34, nos. 292, 293.

15 Emery, *Great Tombs of the First Dynasty*, II, p. 43, no. 95, pls. 18*a*, 31*a*.

16 For examples of inlays of wood, faience, ivory and bone, see Petrie, *Royal Tombs of the First Dynasty*, I, pl. XXXVII; II, pls. XXXIV*ff*. On the discovery of jewellery in early tombs, see W. S. Smith, *The Art and Architecture of Ancient Egypt*, London, 1958, p. 27.

17 Z. Y. Saad, *Ceiling Stelae in Second Dynasty Tombs from the Excavations at Helwan* (Supplement to *Annales du Service des Antiquités de l'Egypte*, Cahier 21), Cairo, 1957.

18 Emery, *Great Tombs of the First Dynasty*, III, pls. 23*b*, 39, p. 30*f*.

19 Emery, *Archaic Egypt*, London, 1961, pl. 32(a).

20 J. E. Quibell, *Archaic Mastabas* (*Excavations at Saqqara, 1912–14*), Cairo, 1923, pl. 26.

21 Quibell, *The Tomb of Hesy* (*Excavations at Saqqara, 1911–12*), Cairo, 1913.

22 *Ibid*. For the paintings of furniture, see pls. XVI–XXIII.

23 It is generally thought that the complex of buildings contained within the great enclosure wall surrounding the Step Pyramid reproduces the complex which made up the royal palace area in Memphis. The palace buildings, built largely of mud brick, were copied in stone at Saqqara. For a description of the many ingenious architectural features found there, see I. E. S. Edwards, *The Pyramids of Egypt* (rev. ed.), London, 1961, pp. 53*ff*.

24 J. H. Breasted, *A History of Egypt* (1st ed.), London, 1905, p. 39.

Chapter 2: The Old Kingdom

1 G. A. Reisner and W. S. Smith, *The Tomb of Hetepheres* (*A History of the Giza Necropolis*, II), Cambridge, Mass., 1955.

2 *Ibid.*, p. 29.

3 'Composition' is a more correct term to describe an ancient Egyptian material made of powdered quartz frit, moulded and glazed. It is often called for convenience 'faience', although this term is strictly incorrect when used to describe such material; see Lucas, *Ancient Egyptian Materials and Industries*, pp. 156*f*.

4 See Reisner, *A History of the Giza Necropolis*, I, Cambridge, Mass., 1942, pp. 350–1. A similar scene of a bed under a canopy occurs in the *mastaba* of Ankhmare at Giza, *cf.* W. S. Smith, *A History of Egyptian Sculpture and Painting in the Old Kingdom*, London, 1946, p. 189.

5 Note in particular the form and detail of the falcon with down-stretched wings in an attitude of protection; here the god Horus is protecting the name and titles of the king. Sneferu's principal name is contained in the oval cartouche in fig. 33c; his Horus or throne name is placed in the rectangular box in fig. 33b; this box incorporates, at the bottom, an architectural façade, probably representing an early palace; it is surmounted by a falcon wearing a double-plume head-dress with ram's horns.

6 The reconstruction, carried out under Reisner's supervision, was made by Mr Bernard Rice, and is described in detail by Smith in *A History of the Giza Necropolis*, I, pp. 23*f*.

7 Royal head-rests of later periods were often very elaborate; *cf.* those from the tomb of Tutankhamun, figs. 140, 141 and 142.

8 The open papyrus flower is bell-shaped; the open lotus flower is triangular.

9 The reconstructed items are all shown together in a special room in the Cairo Museum. This room opens from the gallery containing funerary furniture from the tomb of Tutankhamun, and near by are shown the objects from the tomb of Yuia and Thuiu (see chapter 3). The juxtaposition of this material from widely separated periods is particularly instructive, and underlines the remarkable achievement in design and decoration reached during the early Old Kingdom.

10 *Illustrated London News*, 28 November 1959.

11 Great quantities of gold were used in Egypt in antiquity. Much was obtained from mines within Egypt, but more from Nubia and elsewhere. On sources for gold, see Lucas, *Ancient Egyptian*

Materials and Industries, pp. 224*ff.* Many texts list gold-embellished furniture and other objects used in temples, e.g. the Karnak inscription of Amosis I (*cf.* Breasted, *Ancient Records of Egypt*, Chicago, 1906, II, § 32); gold was also used for architectural decoration (*cf.* Breasted, *op. cit.*, II, § 155).

[12] Giza *mastaba*, no. 5080, mostly published by H. Junker, *Giza*, III, Vienna, 1938, pp. 187*ff.* The unfinished scene is published in Smith, *A History of Egyptian Sculpture and Painting in the Old Kingdom*, p. 291, fig. 141.

[13] Giza *mastaba*, no. 6040; see Smith, *op. cit.*

[14] Part of the decoration from the *mastaba* of an official named Djadjaemankh (possibly to be read Tepemankh) of Fifth Dynasty date.

[15] Reisner and Smith, *A History of the Giza Necropolis*, II, pl. 11.

[16] *Cf.* C. Aldred, *Old Kingdom Art in Ancient Egypt*, London, 1949, pl. 16.

[17] The plant of Lower Egypt in this heraldic composition is regularly the papyrus; the plant of Upper Egypt is sometimes the lily, sometimes the lotus, sometimes indeterminate. The design is fully discussed by H. Schäfer, "Die 'Vereinigung der beiden Länder'", in *Mitteilungen des Deutschen Instituts für ägyptische Altertumskunde in Kairo*, 12, Berlin, 1943, pp. 75*ff.*

[18] Cairo Museum, nos. 9 and 13; *cf.* L. Borchardt, *Statuen und Statuetten von Königen und Privatleuten im Museum von Kairo*, I, Berlin, 1911, pls. 3, 4.

[19] Smith, *A History of Egyptian Sculpture and Painting in the Old Kingdom*, pp. 257–8.

[20] E. Naville and H. Hall, *The XIth Dynasty Temple at Deir el-Bahari*, I, London, 1907, pls. 19, 20.

[21] Cairo, no. 1536, of Sixth Dynasty date.

[22] Aldred, *Old Kingdom Art in Ancient Egypt*, pl. 10.

[23] This tomb has been finely published by the Oriental Institute of the University of Chicago: P. Duell (ed.), *The Tomb of Mereruka*, 2 vols. Chicago, 1938.

[24] Examples of later date are to be found in the Cairo Museum.

Chapter 3: Palace Furniture of the Eighteenth Dynasty

[1] The time between the end of the Old Kingdom (about 2180 B.C.) and the beginning of the Eighteenth Dynasty (about 1567 B.C.) includes two 'dark' interludes, the First and Second Intermediate Periods (about 2181–2050 B.C. and about 1786–1567 B.C.), when Egypt politically disintegrated; finds of importance from these periods cannot be expected. Between them came the Middle Kingdom (about 2050–1786 B.C.).

[2] S. Mercer, *The Tell el-Amarna Tablets*, I, p. 17, Letter 5, lines 18–24, 30.

[3] *Id.*, pp. 47, 49, 51, Letter 14, col. II, lines 19–21, 26, 63, 64.

[4] On gold-leaf and gold-foil, see pp. 307–8 below.

[5] Torgny Säve-Söderbergh, *Private Tombs at Thebes*, Oxford, 1957, Tomb of Amenemhet, called Surer, plate xxx. See also Smith, *Ancient Egypt*, Boston, 1960, fig. 75, for a suggested restoration of the chair using the arm-panel in the museum collection.

[6] T. M. Davis, with G. Maspero and P. E. Newberry, *The Tomb of Iouiya and Touiyou*, London, 1907; the objects from the tomb were later republished in a volume of the general catalogue of the Cairo Museum: J. E. Quibell, *The Tomb of Yuaa and Thuiu*, Cairo, 1908.

[7] See Quibell, *op. cit.*, pls. 14, 15.

[8] See Quibell, *op. cit.*, pl. 28 (no. 51108).

[9] See Quibell, *op. cit.*, pls. 51–6.

Chapter 4: The Furniture of King Tutankhamun

[1] The principal publication is H. Carter and A. Mace, *The Tomb of Tut·Ankh·Amen*, 3 vols. London, 1923–33. There are good illustrations in P. Fox, *Tutankhamun's Treasure*, Oxford, 1951, and superlative coloured illustrations in C. Desroches-Noblecourt, *Tutankhamen*, London, 1963.

[2] The representation of Queen Nefertiti is also very informal – much more so than in the case of the well-known sculptured head in the Berlin Museum

(see, e.g., K. Lange and M. Hirmer, *Egypt* (2nd ed.), London, 1957, pl. 181); in both cases the queen is shown wearing the same head-dress.

3 Many of the technical observations embodied in Carter's notes are due to the examinations of objects by Arthur Lucas, a chemist who worked for the Egyptian Antiquities Service from 1923 to 1937. Results achieved from his work are embodied in his standard handbook *Ancient Egyptian Materials and Industries*.

4 Traditionally the foreign enemies of the Egyptian king were symbolized by nine bows, usually shown beneath the feet of the monarch. Occasionally, as here, the enemies were personified, actual figures of foreigners replacing the symbolic bows. Nine remained the number of traditional enemies, but they were not given specific identifications until a late period.

5 E.g., N. de G. Davies, *The Tomb of Two Sculptors at Thebes*, New York, 1925, pl. 7.

6 A fine facsimile copy of the paintings on this chest has been published by Nina de G. Davies and Sir Alan H. Gardiner, *Tutankhamun's Painted Box*, Oxford, 1963.

7 Illustrated in W. C. Hayes, *The Scepter of Egypt*, II, New York, 1959, fig. 118, p. 203.

8 Published by the Commission des Monuments d'Égypte, and fully entitled *Description de l'Égypte, ou Recueil des Observations et des Recherches qui ont été faites en Égypte pendant l'Expédition de l'Armée française, publié par les ordres de Sa Majesté l'Empereur Napoléon le Grand.* Paris, Imprimerie Impériale, 1809–28. Two beds with animal designs are shown in *Arch.*, Vol. II, pl. 44.

Chapter 5: The Egyptian Villa and its Furnishings

1 The inscriptions from the Tomb of Metjen were formerly in the Berlin Museum (nos. 1105, 1106). This passage is published in K. Sethe, *Urkunden des Alten Reichs* (2nd ed.), Leipzig, 1932, p. 4, lines 10–14.

2 For the Egyptian text see Sethe, *op. cit.*, p. 121, lines 13–16.

3 See A. M. Badawy, *A History of Egyptian Archi-*

tecture, I, Giza, 1954, pp. 55 ff.; many illustrations of soul-houses are given in W. M. F. Petrie, *Gizeh and Rifeh*, London, 1907, pls. 15–22.

4 Full descriptions and illustrations of these model houses are contained in H. E. Winlock, *Models of Daily Life in Ancient Egypt*, Cambridge, Mass., 1955, pp. 17–19, pls. 9–12, 56, 57.

5 See N. de G. Davies, *The Rock Tombs of El Amarna*, II, London, 1905, pl. 36.

6 The house, as reconstructed, is fully described by Seton Lloyd, 'Model of a Tell el-Amarnah House' in *Journal of Egyptian Archaeology*, XIX (1933), pp. 1–7.

7 See N. de G. Davies, "The Town House in Ancient Egypt", in *Metropolitan Museum Studies*, I, New York, 1929, figs. 1a, 1b, pp. 236–40.

8 From the Tomb of Amenemhet, called Surer; see Torgny Säve-Söderbergh, *Four Eighteenth Dynasty Tombs*, Oxford, 1957, pl. XXXVII, p. 40.

9 The objects, now in the Turin Museum, are published in E. Schiaparelli, *La tomba intatta dell'architetto Cha*, Turin, 1927.

10 By the kind permission of Dr E. Scamuzzi, the director of the Egyptian Museum at Turin, the whole collection was removed from its cases for examination and photography.

11 E.g., N. de G. Davies, *The Tomb of Rekh-mi-ré at Thebes*, II, New York, 1943, pls. 53–5.

12 This is the view of Dr S. Curto of the Turin Museum, from whom also come the detailed description of colour given here and the measurements of the individual pieces.

13 N. de G. Davies, *The Rock Tombs of El Amarna*, II, pl. 36.

Chapter 6: Household Furniture Types

1 Ramose was vizier at the end of the reign of Amenophis III and at the beginning of that of Akhenaten (about 1385–1370 B.C.). His tomb has been fully published by N. de G. Davies, *The Tomb of the Vizier Ramose*, London, 1941.

2 Stela of Nen-waef and his wife Irenena, who are

shown in the upper register; their son Meru and daughter Demi-wedja are shown in the lower register; see Hayes, *Scepter of Egypt*, II, p. 168, fig. 93.

3 It seems possible that the legs of the Louvre chair may be additions made after the original discovery, but this possibility has not been checked by close examination.

4 The drawings reproduced here are owing to the kindness of M. Garnier of the Collège Technique Boulle in Paris.

5 Rekhmire was a vizier under Tuthmosis III. His tomb, one of the best preserved in the Theban necropolis, is published by N. de G. Davies, *The Tomb of Rekh-mi-rē at Thebes*, 2 vols. New York, 1943.

6 British Museum, no. 37986, a fragment from a tomb identified probably as belonging to an official named Nebamun, of late Eighteenth Dynasty date, possibly of the reign of Amenophis III.

7 Mr J. Möger of Soestdijk kindly gave his permission to publish this piece.

8 See T. E. Peet and C. L. Wooley, *City of Akhenaten*, I, London, 1923, pp. 45–6.

9 See Smith, *The Art and Architecture of Ancient Egypt*, p. 120.

10 Hayes, *Scepter of Egypt*, II, pp. 226–7.

11 Smith, *Ancient Egypt*, pl. 50. The tables depicted on this fine painted coffin from El-Bersha in the Boston Museum resemble the renderings of a present-day modern designer.

12 N. de G. Davies, *The Rock Tombs of El Amarna*, 6 vols. London, 1903–8.

13 A view of the main hall of the Nile Hilton Hotel in Cairo. Examples of tables, adapted in design from ancient Egyptian types, can be seen.

PART II: THE NEAR EAST

Chapter 1: Sumer: Furniture in the early period

1 For a discussion of these two early civilizations and their relationship to each other see Henri Frankfort, *The Birth of Civilization in the Near East*, London, 1954. A comprehensive picture of the Sumerian period is given in S. N. Kramer's *The Sumerians; their History, Culture, and Character*, Chicago, 1963.

2 Leonard Woolley, *The Royal Cemetery* (Ur excavations, II), London, 1934; *Excavations at Ur*, London, 1955.

3 Edith Porada, *Corpus of Ancient Near Eastern Seals in North American Collections*, I, New York, 1948. (The Collection of the Pierpont Morgan Library.)

4 Henri Frankfort, *Cylinder Seals, a Documentary Essay on the Art and Religion of the Ancient Near East*, London, 1939, gives one of the most valuable detailed surveys of Near Eastern seals and their significance.

5 Porada, *op. cit.*, p. 5. Although this and the other 'pig-tailed' seals illustrated are assigned to the Jamdat-Nasr period by Miss Porada, recent excavations at Nippur indicate that they belong to the Uruk period and may antedate the time of the First Dynasty in Egypt.

6 *Ibid.*, p. 17.

7 The so-called 'temptation seal' dates probably from the early post-Akkadian period. The name results from the portrayal of a woman, a god, a serpent and fruit hanging from a tree, but there is no known historical connection between this scene and the story of the temptation in the Garden of Eden.

8 Excavations by the French began at Mari under André Parrot in 1933, and have been continuous except during the Second World War. A summary of the excavations and dramatic illustrations of the major objects found are given by Parrot in his recent book *Sumer* (The Arts of Mankind), London, 1960.

Chapter 2: From the Akkadian period to the end of the Kassite period

1 The individual periods of this era will not be discussed separately, since the political and social aspects are outside the scope of this work and

there is not sufficient material to warrant a separate discussion of the furniture of each period.

2 For a discussion of the Neo-Sumerian or Ur III period see S. N. Kramer, *The Sumerians*.

3 The Gudea statues are beautifully illustrated in A. Parrot, *Sumer*. See note 8, chapter 1.

4 Hammurapi conquered Mari (mentioned in the previous chapter) about 1760 B.C. Henri Frankfort, *The Art and Architecture of the Ancient Orient*, London, 1958, p. 140. See note 4, map 3.

5 *Documents présargoniques*, Paris, 1909, Fsc. 1, 2e partie, 75, i, 3.

6 M. I. Hussey, *Sumerian Tablets*, Harvard Semitic Series, Cambridge, Mass., 1915, 2, 5, iv, 3*f*. Ur III period.

7 Harvard Semitic Series (XV), Cambridge, Mass., 1955, 130 : 25.

8 Armas Salonen, *Die Möbel des alten Mesopotamien*, Helsinki, 1963.

9 *Ibid.*, pp. 227*ff*.

Chapter 3: The Assyrian and Neo-Babylonian Periods

1 Frankfort, *The Art and Architecture of the Ancient Orient*, p. 65, assigns the beginning of an individual art in Assyria to this date.

2 L. W. King, *Annals of the Kings of Assyria*, London, 1902, 246 : 19.

3 *Ibid.*, 365: iii, 62.

4 F. Thureau-Dangin, *Une Relation de la Huitième Campagne de Sargon*, 388, Paris, 1912. Musée du Louvre, Textes cunéiformes III.

5 R. D. Barnett, *The Nimrud Ivories in the British Museum*, London, 1957, pp. 114*f*.

6 Porada, *Corpus of Ancient Near Eastern Seals in North American Collections*, I, nos. 665, 666, 670.

7 *Ibid.*, nos. 672, 673, 675.

8 Nineveh, near Mosul in northern Iraq, was first excavated by Austen H. Layard in 1845, and excavations continued intermittently by the British Museum until 1932. Nimrud also, south of Mosul, has been the object of British excavations at various times from 1845 until the present. Khorsabad, first excavated by Emile Botta and the French from 1843 to 1855, has later been the object of intensive study by the Oriental Institute of Chicago (1929-35).

9 The bas-reliefs from the palace of Tiglath-Pileser III (744-727 B.C.) have been published in full recently, for the first time, by R. D. Barnett and M. Falkner, *The Sculptures of Tiglath-Pileser III*, London, 1962.

10 The bas-reliefs from Sargon's palace at Khorsabad are well illustrated in the publication which followed the excavations at the site by the Oriental Institute of Chicago. Gordon Loud, *Khorsabad*, Chicago, 1936.

11 This and other of Sargon II's building inscriptions can be conveniently found in D. D. Luckenbill, *Ancient Records of Assyria and Babylonia*, II, Chicago, 1927, p. 67, no. 127a.

12 Recently, the Khorsabad sculptures have been moved to the new building of the Iraq Museum where they are effectively displayed with daylight lighting from above. The photographs taken in colour, as well as those in black and white, are owing to the courtesy of the Director of Antiquities in Iraq, Dr Faisal El Wailly.

13 Georges Contenau, *Everyday Life in Babylon and Assyria*, London, 1954, p. 127.

14 André Godard, *Le Trésor de Ziwiyē*, Iran, 1950.

15 Gordon Loud, *Khorsabad*, Part II (The Citadel and the Town), O I P, XL, University of Chicago Press, 1938, p. 104.

16 A. H. Layard, *The Monuments of Nineveh*, London, 1849. Also a *Second Series of the Monuments of Nineveh and Babylon*, 1853.

17 Layard, *Discoveries among the Ruins of Nineveh and Babylon*, New York, 1853, pp. 198-200.

18 J. B. Pritchard, *Ancient Near Eastern Texts*, 1950, p. 288.

19 Herodotus, in describing the defeat of the Persian

fleet by the Greeks, speaks of Xerxes "sitting on his golden throne" as he watched the battle.

[20] For the text see M. Streck, *Assurbanipal*, II, pp. 294*ff.*, lines 16–34; Th. Bauer, *Das Inschiftenwerk Assurbanipals*, II, p. 50, footnote 1. The translation given here, which is only tentative because of the many obscure technical terms, is based mainly on the *Chicago Assyrian Dictionary*.

[21] Teumman was King of Elam in what is now western Iran. For an oracular dream foretelling his defeat see J. B. Pritchard, *Ancient Near Eastern Texts*, Princeton, 1950, p. 451.

[22] Emile Botta, who first excavated Khorsabad in 1853, made a record of his finds in drawings, as Layard did in Nineveh.

[23] A large part of the ivories found by Layard is in the British Museum, and these, together with those found shortly after by Loftus, are discussed in detail by R. D. Barnett, Keeper of the Department of Western Asiatic Antiquities in the British Museum (Barnett, *The Nimrud Ivories in the British Museum*, London, 1957). In this important work, Barnett concludes that the primary purpose of the ivory carvings was for furniture ornamentation. See pp. 129*ff.*

[24] A partial account of these important recent discoveries, with some illustrations, appeared in the *Illustrated London News*, 25 June 1960, and a complete record has since been published in *Nimrud and its remains*, 2 vols. by M. E. L. Mallowan. Those which are illustrated here are by special permission of Prof. M. E. L. Mallowan.

[25] G. Perrot and C. Chipiez, *History of Art in Chaldea and Assyria*, II, London, 1883, p. 314.

[26] R. D. Barnett, *Excavations of the British Museum at Toprak Kale* (near Lake Van), Iraq, XII, pp. 1*ff.*

[27] L. W. King, *Bronze Reliefs from the Gates of Shalmaneser*, London, 1915.

[28] The Cypriot bronzes have recently been discussed by H. W. Catling in *Cypriot Bronzework in the Mycenaean World*, Oxford, 1964.

[29] Layard, *Second Series of the Monuments of Nineveh and Babylon*, London, 1853, denotes this as "spoils from a captured city". The contemporary accounts indicate that the scene is located in North Syria, which, as has been noted in connection with the Alalakh Tablets, was apparently a furniture-making area.

[30] James B. Pritchard, *Ancient Near East in Pictures*, Princeton, 1954, states that the scene probably is from Assurbanipal's Elamite campaigns.

Chapter 4: The Peripheral Regions

[1] Frankfort, *The Art and Architecture of the Ancient Orient*. The term 'The Peripheral Regions' used in this chapter is that employed by Henri Frankfort to describe the neighbouring countries of Mesopotamia, more particularly Asia Minor, Persia, Syria and its extension into Palestine.

[2] Barnett, *Nimrud Ivories in the British Museum*, p. 114. See also notes, chapter 3, Assyrian and Neo-Babylonian periods.

[3] Wiseman, *The Alalakh Tablets*, 1953.

[4] Breasted, *Ancient Records*, II, p. 436.

[5] Excerpts from translation of inscription on a clay hexagonal 'prism' in the Oriental Institute, Chicago. Recorded in J. B. Pritchard, *Ancient Near East Texts*, Princeton, 1950, p. 288. The Hebrew account of the Jerusalem campaign, as found in II Kings, 18 : 13–16, confirms Sennacherib's claim that a huge tribute was exacted from Hezekiah, although it mentions only the gold and silver.

[6] Jack Finegan, *Light from the Ancient Past*, Princeton, 1959, pp. 120–1.

[7] Biblical quotations are taken from the Revised Standard Version.

[8] Kathleen M. Kenyon, *Excavations at Jericho*, London, 1960, vol. I.

[9] Olga Tufnell, *Anatolian Studies, Journal of the British Institute at Ankara*, VI, London, 1956, p. 67. On the basis of the type of dress Miss Tufnell assigns these scarabs to the Hyksos period.

[10] Y. Yadin, *Hazor II*, Jerusalem, 1960.

[11] The taboo against "graven images" was, apparently, never absolute. The instructions for the building of the Ark of the Covenant, given to Moses at the same time as he received the Ten Command-

ments, contain specific direction for the making of "cherubims of gold" (Ex. 25 : 18–20). Also, Solomon's throne was ornamented at the sides with figures of lions. The prophets, however, continued to inveigh against any images that suggested or encouraged the idol worship prevalent in the neighbouring areas, and any representation of the human figure quite likely came under the ban.

12 Sir William Flinders Petrie, *Beth-Pelet I*, London, 1930, pl. LV.

13 For a general discussion of the Megiddo ivories, see Gordon Loud, *The Megiddo Ivories*, Chicago, 1939. See Part I, chapter 3, p. 65, for discussion of the Egyptian god Bes.

14 Kenyon, *Excavations at Jericho*, I, p. 265.

15 These tombs also contained large quantities of pottery and other objects. Wooden bowls and dishes were found in considerable quantities and evidently were commonly used as household utensils. One wall of the tombs frequently had a niche in which there had been placed a lamp with four pinched spouts. It should be noted, however, that although there is a resemblance to the Egyptian tombs in the matter of furnishings, the burial customs were very different. Multiple burials were customary, one body being placed on top of the other, together with its furnishings, and there were no preparations for the continuing care of the spirit in the afterlife as in Egypt.

16 For a list of woods mentioned in the Biblical records see J. D. Douglas (ed.), *New Bible Dictionary*, Grand Rapids, 1962, pp. 1293*ff.*, which lists bay-tree, box-tree, cedar, chestnut, cypress, fir, mulberry-tree, oak, palm-tree, poplar, sycamore-fig, tamarisk and willow as well as less known varieties.

17 Kenyon, *Jericho*, I, p. 265.

18 The word 'turned' is used in a general sense as referring to round legs which appear as though turned in a wood lathe; see Techniques section for further discussion of this subject.

19 Kenyon, *Jericho*, I, p. 531.

20 *Ibid.*, p. 530.

21 These reproductions of the Jericho furniture were made in the summer of 1956 for the Canadian National Exhibition, Toronto, following the original detailed drawings of the excavation's draughtsman, Michael Ricketts. The drawings were supplied to the Royal Ontario Museum by Miss Kenyon, who headed the expedition. Used first in a temporary exhibit at the Canadian National Exhibition, the pieces were later presented to the Museum.

22 Pritchard, *The Ancient Near East in Pictures*, p. 140. Sir Flinders Petrie, *Beth-Pelet I*, pls. XLIV–XLVI. The tomb in which these objects were found was dated to 850 B.C. by the excavator, but it has later been dated to 450–350 B.C. (J. H. Iliffe, *Quarterly of the Dept. of Antiquities in Palestine*, V, 1945, pp. 182*ff.*).

23 Frankfort, *Art and Architecture*, p. 202.

24 See A. Upham Pope, *A Survey of Persian Art*, vol. IV, London, 1938; also E. F. Schmidt, *Persepolis I, Oriental Institute Publications*, vol. LXVIII, Chicago, 1953.

25 See discussion of wood-turning lathe in Techniques, p. 303. From this period on, turnings were very generally used in the Near East, Egypt and Greece.

26 Rodney Young, *American Journal of Archaeology*, LXI, 1957, pp. 319–31, pls. 87–96; LXII, 1958, pp. 139–54, pls. 20–7. The fragments found in the child's tomb (P) and the large tomb (MN) are now in the Ankara Museum.

27 *Ibid.*, LXII, 1958, p. 150.

28 Detail drawings of the finds in the large tomb were made by Dorothy Cox of the Philadelphia University Museum staff at the time of the excavations.

29 One of the most famous paintings from the Tombs of the Nobles at Thebes represents two young princesses seated on brightly coloured hassocks much like those used today in the Near East. An excellent reproduction of the painting by Nina Davies is given in Davies and Gardiner, *Ancient Egyptian Paintings*, Chicago, 1963, pl. LXXIV.

30 Tahsin Özgüç, *Excavations at Altintepe* (Belleten, XXV, no. 98), Ankara, 1961, pp. 269–70. This report, read at the XXVth International Congress of Orientalists in Moscow, gives a detailed account of the discovery of this tomb and its contents.

31 *Ibid.*, p. 271. The word 'reinforced' as used in the report is not clear. It seems probable that the bronze rings were decorations.

PART III: THE AEGEAN

Chapter 1: Introduction

1 Gisela M. A. Richter, *Ancient Furniture: A History of Greek, Etruscan, and Roman Furniture*, Oxford, 1926. A revised and enlarged edition has just been published by Phaidon Press, London. Since the new edition was not available at the time of writing, references are to the first edition. In her original work Cycladic, Minoan and Mycenaean furniture is not discussed.

2 Many discussions of this trade appear in publications by archaeologists and art historians. A recent popular volume which summarizes these studies conveniently is R. W. Hutchinson, *Prehistoric Crete*, London, 1962, pp. 102–12.

Chapter 2: The earliest furniture

1 The small terracotta figure from Sesklo in Thessaly (National Museum, no. 5937), our figure 375, is dated roughly to the Neolithic period. The seated woman, whose head is missing, holds a child in her arms and sits on a stool of which three legs were broken, but are now restored. Both the figure and the stool have painted decoration. Another terracotta figure of the same period from Rafina in Attica appears to represent a low rectangular table on four plain legs, with three holes in the top to receive vases or pots (National Museum, no. 8896), our figure 376.

2 These are illustrated by Christian Zervos in *L'Art des Cyclades*, Paris, 1956, pl. 316. Our illustration (fig. 376), is his pl. 317. This volume discusses the origins and characteristics of Cycladic art and has a fine series of plates illustrating the pottery and figures of this period.

Chapter 3: The Minoan ascendancy

1 Sir Arthur Evans, *The Palace of Minos*, London, vol. I, 1921; vol. II, 1928; vol. III, 1930; vol. IV, 1935.

2 A brief account of the excavations that have taken place in the region of Kato Zakro and the spectacular discoveries appears in an article in *To Vima*,

Athens, by Helen Karapangoti, dated 4 October 1964. A partial translation in English is given in *The Athens News* of 11 October 1964. See also *Archaeology*, XVI, p. 269 and *The Illustrated London News*, 29 February and 7 March 1964.

3 R. W. Hutchinson, *Prehistoric Crete*, London, 1962, pp. 93–100, discusses these early sea-going ships as well as the trade with Egypt, Phoenicia, and the Cyclades, pp. 102, 112.

4 Besides the accounts of Evans and Hutchinson mentioned above, *The Archaeology of Crete*, London, 1939, by J. D. S. Pendlebury, is one of the best general accounts. Among the illustrated books on Minoan art *L'Art de la Crète*, Paris, 1956, by Christian Zervos is outstanding. The many other books on the subject will be found listed in any of the standard bibliographies.

5 Although the throne is popularly called the throne of King Minos, there is no proven association with this mythical character. It has been suggested that this was the throne of a priestess and that the guardian griffins in the background were associated with the religious ritual of the time. Paul MacKendrick, *The Greek Stones Speak*, New York, 1962, p. 95.

6 Evans, *Palace of Minos*, IV, figs. 890, 891. Based on these drawings, several reproductions of the throne were made in wood at the time when interest in this discovery was at its height.

7 Evans, *ibid.*, III, pp. 333–8.

8 Christian Zervos, *L'Art de la Crète*, pl. 462. Photographs of this table and of the carrying chair (fig. 389) and the second tripod table (fig. 391) are owing to the courtesy of Mr Zervos.

9 Evans, *Palace of Minos*, I, pp. 302–14. In describing these faience plaques found by him at Knossos, Evans comments that the mosaic clearly represents town houses, standing in rows, and surmises that where windows are missing on the lower floors this may indicate that a wall stood in front.

Chapter 4: The Mycenaean period in Greece

1 The story of Heinrich Schliemann's excavations and discoveries appears in many historical works on the Mycenaean period. His own reports were

published in *Mycenae*, London, 1878, *Orchomenos*, Leipzig, 1881, and *Tiryns*, Leipzig, 1886.

2 Recent excavations at Thebes by Nikolaos Platon have yielded sensational new information regarding this important Mycenaean site and its relationship to the cultures of the East. Although hindered by the modern buildings of the town, excavations are continuing, and further important discoveries can be expected. Among the finds pertaining to furniture are fine examples of carved ivory ornaments, including two substantial turned ivory posts about nineteen inches high, which were probably supports for a piece of furniture or parts of a canopy. A partial report of these excavations appeared in *The Illustrated London News*, 5 December 1964.

3 C. W. Blegen, *A Guide to the Palace of Nestor*, University of Cincinnati, 1962, gives a full description of the palace and its interior arrangement.

4 Homer, *The Odyssey*, III, 396–9, quoted by Lord William Taylour, *The Mycenaeans*, London, 1964, pp. 92–4.

5 Michael G. F. Ventris and John Chadwick, *Documents in Mycenaean Greek*, Cambridge, 1956, pp. 234–47.

6 L. R. Palmer, *The Interpretation of Mycenaean Greek Texts*, Oxford, 1963, pp. 354–5, 360–1.

7 The principal word differences in the original translations of Ventris, relating to furniture, are *pomegranate* in place of *rosette*, *strutting* instead of *supports*, *grooves* instead of *flame-pattern*, and *encircled* instead of *splay-legged*.

8 Palmer, *op. cit.*, pp. 345–53. Quoted by permission of the publishers, The Clarendon Press. The italics are those which appear in this publication.

9 Reynold Higgins, *Bulletin of the Institute of Classical Studies*, III, London, 1956, pp. 39*ff*.

10 A. J. B. Wace, *Mycenae, 1939–1953*, *Annual of the British School at Athens*, XLIX C, 1954, pp. 238–41.

11 Wace, *ibid.*, plates 38c, 39a, b, c, 40c, e. Photographs of these ivories are owing to the courtesy of Mrs Wace. Special note should be taken also of the carved ivories found recently at Thebes (see note 2 above).

12 Henry Robinson, Director of the American School for Classical Studies, has called my attention to the discovery of several miniature models in the excavations near Corinth. A photograph of this recent find has been given me by Professor Robinson.

13 Homer, *The Odyssey*, XIX, pp. 55–8. English translation by A. T. Murray, London, 1919, pp. 96–7. Also quoted by Richter, *Ancient Furniture*, p. 156, in a different translation.

14 Homer, *The Odyssey*, XXIII, pp. 195–218; translation by Murray, p. 389. Also quoted by Richter, p. 153.

15 The discussion still continues as to precisely who were these invaders, and what were the circumstances of the sudden and almost complete destruction of the Mycenaean palaces. Among the more recent books on Mycenaean history are Frederick Matz, *Crete and Early Greece*, London, 1962; L. R. Palmer, *Mycenaeans and Minoans*, London, 1961; and A. J. B. Wace and F. H. Stubbings, *A Companion to Homer*, London, 1962.

Chapter 5: The Early Greek Period

1 The generally accepted date for the ending of the Archaic period is approximately 475 B.C. following the final defeat of the Persians in 479 B.C. The beginning of the period is usually dated by art historians to about 700 B.C., when the Geometric period in art is considered to have ended.

2 Paul MacKendrick in his popular work *The Greek Stones Speak*, New York, 1962, uses the phrase 'Lyric Age' instead of 'Archaic'.

3 The Harpy Tomb was a limestone structure measuring about seventeen feet high and seven feet square. The marble reliefs were attached to its sides. Its name is derived from the bird-like creatures that are depicted with female heads, arms and breasts (not visible in our illustrations).

4 Narrow saws with small teeth were found in excavations on Crete, and no doubt were part of the usual equipment of the Greek craftsmen. Several bronze saw blades from Gournia on Crete are illustrated in H. B. Hawes, *Gournia*, Philadelphia, 1908, pl. 4, 1–6. Three of these are very narrow.

5 Chronologically the furniture of the Etruscans

belongs with that of Greece. Although local variations occur, in general the furniture styles resemble those of Greece. The relationship that existed is indicated by the many fine painted vases of Greek origin that have been found in Etruscan tombs. For a detailed study of Etruscan furniture reference should be made to Richter, *Ancient Furniture*.

6 Richter, *Ancient Furniture*, p. 86.

7 C. Aldred, in *A History of Technology*, Oxford, 1956, vol. II, chapter 7.

8 Among the woods mentioned by the ancient Greek writers are maple, beech, oak, willow, cedar, cypress, yew, juniper, poplar, fir, lime, olive, elm and pine. Translations of these references are given by Richter, *Ancient Furniture*, pp. 149–51.

9 Although no complete examples of wooden furniture have survived from Greece proper, some Hellenistic pieces have been discovered in other parts of the Mediterranean area (see fig. 450). Perhaps the most valuable materials relating to the earlier woodworking craft are the fragments dating from the eighth century B.C. which have been discovered on the island of Samos, illustrated and described in detail in *Mitteilungen des Deutschen Archäologischen Instituts, Athenische Abteilung*, Berlin, 1953, Band 68, pp. 77–127. Some of the fragments are nicely carved, and in one the remains of a mortise and tenon joint are apparent. There was also found the side-panel of a stool with relief carving in the form of a horse.

Chapter 6: The Continuing Influence

1 The main part of the collection of the Baker Museum for Furniture Research, founded in 1941, is now in Holland, Michigan. A supplementary collection, with a section devoted to craft exhibits, is located in Grand Rapids, Michigan. Fourteen hundred pieces of furniture, mostly antique, are included in the collection, which dates from the Eighteenth Dynasty in Egypt to the present day.

2 The *klismos* and other forms of Classical Greek furniture are now being made in Athens by the Saridis Furniture Factory, after designs by T. H. Robsjohn-Gibbings based on portrayals in painting and sculpture.

Appendix: Techniques

1 J. G. Wilkinson, *Manners and Customs of the Ancient Egyptians*, London, 1837. The best of the later editions is that edited and revised by S. Birch and published in London and New York in 1878.

2 W. M. F. Petrie, *Arts and Crafts of Ancient Egypt*, Edinburgh and London, 1909, chapter XIII.

3 A. Lucas, *Ancient Egyptian Materials and Industries*, 4th edition, revised and enlarged by J. R. Harris, London, 1962. Chapter XVIII deals with woodworking. References to this work are made by permission of Dr Harris.

4 Cyril Aldred, 'Fine Woodwork', *A History of Technology*, vol. I, Oxford, 1954, chapter XXV. The chart illustrated is reproduced from fig. 491, p. 691, by permission of Mr Aldred and the publishers.

5 The origin of each example examined is given by Lucas, who also tells by whom it was identified. Specific references are also given to instances in the ancient texts where woods and their use are mentioned, as well as to more recent studies by archaeologists and historians.

6 Acacia was recommended and used for the steam-bent ribs of a sailing-craft built for the author by a shipyard at Lavagna, near Chiavari, Italy, in 1960.

7 In a section of the 'Palermo Stone', a monument of the Fifth Dynasty, there is reference to the bringing of cedar wood by sea for the building of ships at the time of the Third Dynasty, *c.* 2686–2613 B.C.; it was probably cedar from Syria. J. H. Breasted, *Ancient Records of Egypt*, Chicago, 1906, vol. I, § 146.

8 Richter, *Ancient Furniture*, p. 151. Miss Richter quotes Pliny, *Natural History*, XVI, p. 222, who states that wood was "allowed to dry covered with manure". See also Aldred, *A History of Technology*, II, p. 233, for a discussion of methods used in Greece for seasoning wood.

9 This suggestion was made to the author by Sir Gordon Russell, formerly Chairman of the Council of Industrial Design, London, who is an expert on the subject of woodworking.

10 T. G. H. James in chapter I, p. 7, of the *Introductory Guide to the Egyptian Collections in the*

British Museum, London, 1964, discusses climatic conditions in Egypt.

[11] A full description of this extraordinary example of woodworking is given by Lucas, *Ancient Egyptian Materials and Industries*, 4th edition, pp. 451, 452.

[12] This chart, from C. Aldred's chapter in *A History of Technology*, is reproduced by his permission.

[13] The British Museum has examples also of earlier tools marked with royal names, one having the name of Userkaf of the Fifth Dynasty (about 2490 B.C.). Bronze and copper tools in the British Museum are discussed by A. F. Shore in the chapter on arts and crafts in the *Introductory Guide to the Egyptian Collections*, pp. 208, 212, 213, figs. 77, 79.

[14] This relief appears in the tomb of Ti. The drawing is a detail after G. Steindorff, *Das Grab des Ti*, Leipzig, 1913, pl. CXXXIII.

[15] N. de G. Davies, *The Tomb of Rekh-mi-rē at Thebes*, New York, 1943, vol. II. Our figs. 5 and 6 are details from pl. LIII.

[16] H. E. Winlock, *Models of Daily Life in Egypt from the Tomb of Meket-Re at Thebes*, Cambridge (Mass.), 1955.

[17] For a discussion of glue and its use in ancient Egypt see Lucas, *Ancient Egyptian Materials and Industries*, pp. 4, 5.

[18] Aldred, *A History of Technology*, I, pp. 686, 692, 693. Lucas, *Ancient Egyptian Materials and Industries*, pp. 435, 454.

[19] Lucas, *ibid.*, pp. 449, 450.

[20] Petrie, *Social Life in Ancient Egypt*, London, 1923, p. 153.

[21] Richter, *Ancient Furniture*, p. 152, quotes from this passage from Pliny, *Natural History*, VII, p. 198. See also Aldred in *A History of Technology*, II, pp. 222, 223, on the subject of the lathe.

[22] Aldred, *ibid.*, p. 234, concludes that wood was artificially bent in Greece, probably by steaming.

[23] The author is greatly indebted to Mme Christiane Desroches-Noblecourt, Conservateur-en-Chef of the Egyptian department of the Louvre, for the opportunity of meeting M. Garnier and being given access to these drawings.

[24] Lucas, *Ancient Egyptian Materials and Industries*, p. 354, discusses the various compositions which are called gesso.

[25] Lucas, *ibid.*, pp. 356, 357.

[26] Lucas, *ibid.*, p. 358.

[27] Lucas, *ibid.*, p. 231, states that the specimens of gold-leaf which he has measured personally vary from 0·01 mm. to 0·09 mm. Petrie, in *Arts and Crafts*, p. 96, states that it was often about one-five-thousandth of an inch thick.

[28] Lucas, *ibid.*, p. 352.

[29] Wilkinson, *Manners and Customs of the Ancient Egyptians*, edited and revised by S. Birch, London and New York, 1878, p. 417.

LIST OF COLOUR ILLUSTRATIONS

(*Frontispiece*)
Chest on legs. Wood, partly gilded, with painted texts. H. 2 ft. 3½ in. (69·85 cm.), W. 1 ft. 5¼ in. (43·8 cm.), D. 1 ft. 3¾ in. (40 cm.). XVIIIth Dynasty, *c.* 1350 B.C. From Thebes (tomb of Tutankhamun). Cairo Museum (T.T.403). *Photo: F. L. Kenett*

II Stela of Wepemnefert. Painted limestone. H. 1 ft. 6 in. (45·7 cm.), W. 2 ft. 2 in. (66·04 cm.). IVth Dynasty, *c.* 2590 B.C. From Giza. Robert H. Lowie Museum of Anthropology, University of California, Berkeley. *Photo: W. Stevenson Smith*

III Scene from the tomb of Mereruka. Painted limestone low relief. VIth Dynasty, *c.* 2325 B.C. At Saqqara. *Photo: Oriental Institute, University of Chicago*

IVA Chair of Hetepheres. Wood overlaid with gold. H. 2 ft. 7 in. (78·74 cm.), W. 2 ft. 4 in. (71·12 cm.), D. 1 ft. 2 in. (35·56 cm.). IVth Dynasty, *c.* 2600 B.C. From Giza. Cairo Museum. Replica in Museum of Fine Arts, Boston (see fig. 28). *Photo: Museum of Fine Arts, Boston*

B Chair of Sitamun. Red wood with gilded plaster decoration. H. 2 ft. 6 in. (76·2 cm.), W. 1 ft. 8 in. (50·8 cm.), D. 1 ft. 9 in. (53·34 cm.). XVIIIth Dynasty, *c.* 1400 B.C. From Thebes (tomb of Yuia and Thuiu). Cairo Museum (51113). Photo: replica in Baker Museum for Furniture Research (see fig. 68).

V Chair with side panel of cut-out designs. Red wood painted black, in part gilded and silvered. H. 1 ft. 11 in. (58·42 cm.), W. 1 ft. 3½ in. (39·37 cm.), D. 1 ft. 2 in. (35·56 cm.). XVIIIth Dynasty, *c.* 1400 B.C. From Thebes (tomb of Yuia and Thuiu). Cairo Museum (51111). Watercolour by Howard M. Carter reproduced from T. M. Davis, *The Tomb of Iouiya and Touiyou*, pl. XXXV.

VI Golden throne. Wood overlaid with gold and inlaid with faience, glass and calcite. H. 3 ft. 5 in. (104·14 cm.), W. 1 ft. 9 in. (53·34 cm.), D. 2 ft. 1½ in. (64·77 cm.). XVIIIth Dynasty, *c.* 1350 B.C. From Thebes (tomb of Tutankhamun). Cairo Museum (T.T.91). *Photo: F. L. Kenett*

VII Scene on back of golden throne; see colour plate VI. *Photo: Lehnert and Landrock, Cairo*

VIII Stool. Wood painted white with gilded grille-work. H. 1 ft. 5¾ in. (45·08 cm.), W. 1 ft. 5¾ in. (45·08 cm.), D. 1 ft. 5 in. (43·18 cm.). XVIIIth Dynasty, *c.* 1350 B.C. From Thebes (tomb of Tutankhamun). Cairo Museum (T.T.467). *Photo: F. L. Kenett*

IX Painted chest from the tomb of Kha, also shown in fig. 174. *Photo: Edizioni d'Arte Fratelli Pozzo*

XA Scene showing procession to the tomb. Painted limestone. XVIIIth Dynasty, *c.* 1350 B.C. At Thebes (tomb of Ramose, no. 55). Reproduced from Nina M. Davies, *Ancient Egyptian Paintings*, pl. LXXIII. *Photo: Oriental Institute, University of Chicago.*

B Tomb scene of a banquet. Paint on plaster. H. 2 ft. 5½ in. (74·93 cm.), W. 4 ft. 2 in. (127 cm.). XVIIIth Dynasty *c.* 1450 B.C. From Thebes (probably tomb of Nebamun no. 146). British Museum (37986). *Photo: British Museum*

XI Tomb scene. Painted limestone. XVIIIth Dynasty, *c.* 1400 B.C. At Thebes (tomb of Nebamun and Ipuky, no. 181) *Photo: Metropolitan Museum of Art, New York*

XIIA Standard of Ur. Mosaic of shell, lapis lazuli and coloured limestone. H. 9 in. (22·86 cm.), W. 1 ft. 10 in. (55·88 cm.). Early Dynastic III, *c.* 2600 B.C. From Ur. British Museum *Photo: British Museum*

B Detail of XIIA.

XIIIA Bas-relief. Stone. Neo-Assyrian period, Sargon II (721–705 B.C.). From Khorsabad. Iraq Museum, Baghdad (18629). *Photo: Iraq Museum, Baghdad*

B Detail of XIIIA.

XIV Painted limestone sarcophagus. L. 4 ft. 8⅛ in. (137·5 cm.). *c.* 1400 B.C. From Hagia Triada. Heraklion Museum. *Photo: Hirmer Fotoarchiv*

XV Vase painting: Zeus seated on chair. 550–525 B.C. British Museum (B149). *Photo: British Museum*

XVI Vase painting: chair and small table. 475–450 B.C. Torno Collection, Milan. *Photo: Costa Servici Fotografici, Milan*

LIST OF ILLUSTRATIONS

The list of illustrations gives the Museum numbers and, as accurately as possible, the dimensions where available of each piece of furniture and of the works of art representing furniture, in order both to facilitate reference and to provide a basis for comparison. The plates are not to scale.

335

43a Figure of Sneferu on the curtain box of Hetepheres. Inlaid faience. From Giza. IVth Dynasty, c.2600 B.C. Cairo Museum. Reproduced from G. A. Reisner, *A History of the Giza Necropolis*, II; *The Tomb of Hetepheres the Mother of Cheops*, pl. 11.

43b Figure of Cheops. Engraved on rock. At Hatnub. IVth Dynasty, c.2575 B.C. Reproduced from R. Anthes, *Die Felseninschriften von Hatnub*, pl. 4.

44 Scene from the tomb of Meresankh II. Painted limestone low relief. From Giza. IVth Dynasty, c.2550 B.C. Museum of Fine Arts, Boston. Reproduced from W. Stevenson Smith, *A History of Egyptian Sculpture and Painting in the Old Kingdom*, p. 168, fig. 63.

45 Side of the throne of the statue of Chephren. Diorite. From Giza. IVth Dynasty, c.2550 B.C. Cairo Museum (14). Reproduced in drawing from W. Stevenson Smith, *A History of Egyptian Sculpture and Painting in the Old Kingdom*, p. 36, fig. 11.

46 Part of a scene from the tomb of Meresankh III. Painted limestone low relief. At Giza. IVth Dynasty, c.2500 B.C. Reproduced from W. Stevenson Smith, *A History of Egyptian Sculpture and Painting in the Old Kingdom*, p. 38, fig. 13.

47 Part of a scene from the tomb of Meresankh III (see fig. 32).

48 Part of the sarcophagus of Kauit. Limestone, sunk relief. From Deir el-Bahari. XIth Dynasty, c.2050 B.C. Cairo Museum.
Photo: Lehnert and Landrock, Cairo

49 Scene from the tomb of Ipy. Painted limestone low relief. From Saqqara. VIth Dynasty, c.2300 B.C. Cairo Museum (1536).
Photo: Metropolitan Museum of Art, New York

50 Stela of Rahotep. Limestone. H. 2 ft. 7 in. (78·74 cm.), W. 3 ft. 10 in. (116·84 cm.). From Maidum. IVth Dynasty, c.2575 B.C. British Museum (1242).
Photo: British Museum

51 Stela of Intef. Limestone. H. 11¾ in. (29·84 cm.), L. 1 ft. 2 in. (35·56 cm.). From Thebes(?). XIth Dynasty, c.2050 B.C. Brooklyn Museum, New York (54.66).
Photo: Brooklyn Museum

52 Scene from the tomb of Mereruka. Painted limestone low relief. At Saqqara. VIth Dynasty, c.2325 B.C.
Photo: Oriental Institute, University of Chicago

53 Scene from the tomb of Mereruka. Painted limestone low relief. At Saqqara. VIth Dynasty, c.2325 B.C. (See colour plate III)
Photo: Oriental Institute, University of Chicago

54 Scene of craftsmen from the tomb of Mereruka. Painted limestone low relief. At Saqqara. VIth Dynasty, c.2325 B.C.
Photo: Oriental Institute, University of Chicago

55 Drawing of tables from the tomb of Mereruka (see fig. 53).

56 Drawing of tables from the tomb of Mereruka. Painted limestone low relief. At Saqqara. VIth Dynasty, c.2325 B.C.
Photo: Oriental Institute, University of Chicago

57 Drawing of servants carrying chests from the tomb of Mereruka. Painted limestone low relief. At Saqqara. VIth Dynasty, c.2325 B.C.
Photo: Oriental Institute, University of Chicago

58 Scene of 'draught'-playing from the tomb of Mereruka. Painted limestone low relief. At Saqqara. VIth Dynasty, c.2325 B.C.
Photo: Oriental Institute, University of Chicago

59 Offering-stand of Idy. Copper. L. 1 ft. 3¼ in. (38·73 cm.).

From Abydos. VIth Dynasty, c.2250 B.C. British Museum (5315).
Photo: British Museum

60 Drawing of a sculptor from the tomb of Ti. Painted limestone low relief. At Saqqara. Vth Dynasty, c.2375 B.C. Reproduced from W. Stevenson Smith, *A History of Egyptian Sculpture and Painting in the Old Kingdom*, p. 315, fig. 179.

61 Scene of 'draught'-playing from the tomb of Nykauhor and Sekhem-hathor. Painted limestone low relief. From Saqqara. Vth Dynasty, c.2375 B.C. Reproduced from J. E. Quibell, *Excavations at Saqqara (1907–08)*, pl. LXIV.

62 Drawing of part of a scene with a boat from the tomb of Mereruka. Painted limestone low relief. At Saqqara. VIth Dynasty, c.2325 B.C.
Photo: Oriental Institute, University of Chicago

63 Drawing of part of a scene with a boat from the tomb of Mereruka. Painted limestone low relief. At Saqqara. VIth Dynasty, c.2325 B.C.
Photo: Oriental Institute, University of Chicago

64 Leg of a bed. Hardwood, overlaid with gold and silver foil. H. 1 ft. 6½ in. (46·99 cm.). From Deir el-Bahari. XVIIIth Dynasty, c.1475 B.C. British Museum (21574).
Photo: British Museum

65 Foot-board of a bed. Hardwood, overlaid with gold and silver, and inlaid with silver rings (the board between the uprights is modern). H. 2 ft. 5 in. (73·66 cm.), W. 2 ft. 8 in. (81·28 cm.). From Deir el-Bahari. XVIIIth Dynasty, c.1475 B.C. British Museum (21574).
Photo: British Museum

66 Drawing of relief from the funerary temple of Hatshepsut. At Deir el-Bahari. XVIIIth Dynasty, c.1490 B.C. Reproduced from E. Naville, *The Temple of Deir el Bahari*, IV, p. XCI.

67 Drawing of a relief in the tomb of Surer. At Thebes. XVIIIth Dynasty, c.1400 B.C. Reproduced from T. Säve-Söderbergh, *Four Eighteenth Dynasty Tombs*, pl. XXX.

68 Chair of Sitamun. Red wood with gilded plaster decoration. H. 2 ft. 6 in. (76·20 cm.), W. 1 ft. 8 in. (50·8 cm.), D. 1 ft. 9 in. (53·34 cm.). From Thebes (tomb of Yuia and Thuiu). XVIIIth Dynasty, c.1400 B.C. Cairo Museum (51110). Reproduced from J. E. Quibell, *The Tomb of Yuaa and Thuiu* (Cairo Catalogue), pl. XXXVIII (see colour plate IVB).

69 Drawing of scene on back of chair in fig. 68. By Howard Carter. Reproduced from T. M. Davis, *The Tomb of Iouiya and Touiya*, p. 38, fig. 1.

70 Back view of chair in fig. 68. Reproduced from J. E. Quibell, *The Tomb of Yuaa and Thuiu* (Cairo Catalogue), pl. XXXIX.

71 Side panel of chair in fig. 68. Reproduced from J. E. Quibell, *The Tomb of Yuaa and Thuiu* (Cairo Catalogue), pl. XLII.

72 Side panel of chair in fig. 68. Reproduced from J. E. Quibell, *The Tomb of Yuaa and Thuiu* (Cairo Catalogue), pl. XLI.

73 The small chair of Sitamun. Wood covered with gesso, gilded and silvered. H. 2 ft. (60·96 cm.), W. 1 ft. 3 in. (38·1 cm.), D. 1 ft. 4 in. (40·64 cm.). From Thebes (tomb of Yuia and Thuiu). XVIIIth Dynasty, c.1400 B.C. Cairo Museum (51112). Reproduced from J. E. Quibell, *The Tomb of Yuaa and Thuiu* (Cairo Catalogue), pl. XXXV.

74 Drawing of the scene on the back of chair in fig. 73. By Howard Carter. Reproduced from T. M. Davis, *The Tomb of Iouiya and Touiyou*, p. 43, fig. 4.

75 Chair with cut-out designs on side panel. Red wood painted black, in part gilded and silvered. H. 1 ft. 11 in. (58·42 cm.),

W. 1 ft. 3½ in. (39·37 cm.), D. 1 ft. 2 in. (35·56 cm.). From Thebes (tomb of Yuia and Thuiu). XVIIIth Dynasty, c.1400 B.C. Cairo Museum (51111). Reproduced from J. E. Quibell, *The Tomb of Yuaa and Thuiu* (Cairo Catalogue), pl. XXXIII (see colour plate V).

76 Back of chair in fig. 75. Reproduced from J. E. Quibell, *The Tomb of Yuaa and Thuiu* (Cairo Catalogue), pl. XXXIV.

77 Cabinet. Wood, carved, partly gilded, inlaid with faience. H. 1 ft. 4 in. (40·64 cm.), L. 1 ft. 3 in. (38·10 cm.), W. 10 in. (25·40 cm.). From Thebes (tomb of Yuia and Thuiu). XVIIIth Dynasty, c.1400 B.C. Cairo Museum. Reproduced from J. E. Quibell, *The Tomb of Yuaa and Thuiu* (Cairo Catalogue), pl. XLVI.

78 Cabinet. Wood, gilded and inlaid with faience. H. 1 ft. 8 in. (50·80 cm.), L. 1 ft. 9 in. (53·34 cm.), W. 1 ft. 4½ in. (41·91 cm.). From Thebes (tomb of Yuia and Thuiu). XVIIIth Dynasty, c.1400 B.C. Cairo Museum (51117). Reproduced from J. E. Quibell, *The Tomb of Yuaa and Thuiu* (Cairo Catalogue), pl. XLV.

79 Wig box. Papyrus frame and reed covering. H. 1 ft. 7½ in. (49·53 cm.), L. 3 ft. 6 in. (106·68 cm.), W. 1 ft. 8 in. (50·80 cm.). From Thebes (tomb of Yuia and Thuiu). XVIIIth Dynasty, c.1400 B.C. Cairo Museum (51119). Reproduced from T. M. Davis, *The Tomb of Iouiya and Touiyou*, pl. XLII.

80 Two storage chests. Wood painted to simulate gilding and inlay of ivory and faience. 1. (left) H. 1 ft. 1 in. (33·02 cm.), L. 1 ft. 6 in. (45·70 cm.), W. 1 ft. 1 in. (33·02 cm.); 1. (right) H. 1 ft. 1 in. (33·02 cm.), L. 1 ft. 7 in. (48·26 cm.), W. 1 ft. 1 in. (33·02 cm.). From Thebes (tomb of Yuia and Thuiu). XVIIIth Dynasty, c.1400 B.C. Cairo Museum (51115, 51116). Reproduced from T. M. Davis, *The Tomb of Iouiya and Touiyou*, pl. XLI.

81 Storage chest. Wood, partly gilded and partly painted. H. 6 in. (15·24 cm.), L. 1 ft. 3 in. (38·10 cm.), W. 1 ft. (30·48 cm.). From Thebes (tomb of Yuia and Thuiu). XVIIIth Dynasty, c.1400 B.C. Cairo Museum (51114). Reproduced from T. M. Davis, *The Tomb of Iouiya and Touiyou*, pl. XL.

82a Inside of foot-board of bed in fig. 83.
 b Back of foot-board of bed in fig. 83. Reproduced from J. E. Quibell, *The Tomb of Yuaa and Thuiu* (Cairo Catalogue), pl. XXXI.

83 Bed of Yuia(?). Veneered wood, partly gilded and silvered, with gilded plaster relief-work. H. 2 ft. 6 in. (76·20 cm.), L. 5 ft. 9½ in. (176·53 cm.). W. 2 ft. 6 in. (76·20 cm.). From Thebes (tomb of Yuia and Thuiu). XVIIIth Dynasty, c.1400 B.C. Cairo Museum (51110). Reproduced from the painting by Howard Carter in T. M. Davis, *The Tomb of Iouiya and Touiyou*, pl. XXXVII.

84 Bed. Wood, partly veneered, with silvered ornament. H. 1 ft. 11 in. (58·42 cm.), L. 5 ft. 8½ in. (173·99 cm.), W. 1 ft. 3½ in. (39·37 cm.). From Thebes (tomb of Yuia and Thuiu). XVIIIth Dynasty, c.1400 B.C. Cairo Museum (51109).
Photo: Cairo Museum

85 Bed. Wood painted black, and with white-painted lines representing inlay. H. 1 ft. 10 in. (55·88 cm.), L. 5 ft. 7½ in. (171·45 cm.), W. 1 ft. 3 in. (38·10 cm.). From Thebes (tomb of Yuia and Thuiu). XVIIIth Dynasty, c.1400 B.C. Cairo Museum (51108).
Photo: Cairo Museum

86 Relief. Limestone. H. 11½ in. (29·21 cm.), W. 1 ft. 1¼ in. (33·66 cm.) (approx.). From Amarna. XVIIIth Dynasty. c.1370 B.C. Berlin Museum (14145). Reproduced from G. Steindorff and K. Seele, *When Egypt ruled the East*, fig. 83.
Photo: Dr K. Seele, Oriental Institute, University of Chicago.

87 View inside the tomb of Tutankhamun. At Thebes. XVIIIth Dynasty, *c.* 1350 B.C.
Photo: Griffith Institute, Oxford

88 View inside the tomb of Tutankhamun. At Thebes. XVIIIth Dynasty, *c.* 1350 B.C.
Photo: Griffith Institute, Oxford

89 Side view of golden throne; see description of colour plate VI.
Photo: Metropolitan Museum of Art, New York (Harry Burton)

90 Back view of golden throne; see description of colour plate VI.
Photo: Griffith Institute, Oxford

91 Ceremonial chair and foot-stool. The chair is of ebony and ivory, partly overlaid with sheet gold and inlaid with natural stones, glaze and polychrome glass. H. 3 ft. 4 in. (10·2 cm.), D. 1 ft. 5 in. (44 cm.), W. 2 ft. 3 in. (70 cm.). Cairo Museum (T.T.351).* Foot-stool; see fig. 94.
Photo: Griffith Institute, Oxford
* T.T. no. refers to the object number in the catalogue of the tomb of Tutankhamun. See Helen Murray and Mary Nuttall, *A Handlist to Howard Carter's Catalogue of Objects in Tutankhamun's Tomb*, Oxford, 1963.

92 Back view of ceremonial chair.
Photo: Metropolitan Museum of Art, New York (Harry Burton)

93 Foot-stool. Wood covered with painted gesso. From Thebes (tomb of Tutankhamun). XVIIIth Dynasty, *c.* 1350 B.C. Cairo Museum (T.T.30).
Photo: Metropolitan Museum of Art, New York (Harry Burton)

94 Foot-stool of ceremonial chair. Wood veneered with ivory, faience, glass, ebony and coloured stone figures; partly gilded. H. 3 in. (7·62 cm.), L. 1 ft. 11 in. (58·42 cm.), W. 1 ft. 0½ in. (31·75 cm.). From Thebes (tomb of Tutankhamun). XVIIIth Dynasty, *c.* 1350 B.C. Cairo Museum (T.T.378).
Photo: Metropolitan Museum of Art, New York (Harry Burton)

95 Chair. Reddish wood, partly overlaid with gold, feet sheathed with gold and bronze. H. 3 ft. 2 in. (96·52 cm.), W. 1 ft. 6¾ in. (47·60 cm.), D. 1 ft. 8 in. (50·80 cm.). From Thebes (tomb of Tutankhamun). XVIIIth Dynasty, *c.* 1350 B.C. Cairo Museum (T.T.87).
Photo: Griffith Institute, Oxford

96 Back panel of chair in fig. 95.
Photo: Griffith Institute, Oxford

97 Chair. Wood covered with white-painted gesso. H. 2 ft. 4¾ in. (73·02 cm.), W. 1 ft. 7½ in. (49·53 cm.), D. 1 ft. 3½ in. (39·37 cm.). From Thebes (tomb of Tutankhamun). XVIIIth Dynasty, *c.* 1350 B.C. Cairo Museum (T.T.349).
Photo: Metropolitan Museum of Art, New York (Harry Burton)

98 Side view of chair in fig. 97.
Photo: Metropolitan Museum of Art, New York (Harry Burton)

99 Child's chair. Ebony with gold side-panels and inlay of ivory. H. 2 ft. 4 in. (71·12 cm.), W. 1 ft. 2½ in. (36·83 cm.), D. 1 ft. 3½ in. (39·37 cm.). From Thebes (tomb of Tutankhamun). XVIIIth Dynasty, *c.* 1350 B.C. Cairo Museum (T.T.39).
Photo: Griffith Institute, Oxford

100 Stool. Wood painted white on gesso. H. 11½ in. (29·21 cm.), W. 1 ft. (30·48 cm.). From Thebes (tomb of Tutankhamun). XVIIIth Dynasty, *c.* 1350 B.C. Cairo Museum (T.T.84).
Photo: Griffith Institute, Oxford

101 Stool. Dark red wood with veneers of ivory and ebony, H. 1 ft. 1½ in. W. 11 in. (27·94 cm.) From Thebes (tomb of Tutankhamun). XVIIIth Dynasty, *c.* 1350 B.C. Cairo Museum (T.T.81).
Photo: Metropolitan Museum of Art, New York

102 Stool. Wood inlaid with ivory. H. 1 ft. 1½ in. (34·29 cm.), L. 1 ft. 6½ in. (46·99 cm.), W. 1 ft. 0½ in. (31·75 cm.). From Thebes (tomb of Tutankhamun). XVIIIth Dynasty, *c.* 1350 B.C. Cairo Museum (T.T.83).
Photo: Griffith Institute, Oxford

103 Stools. Wood, partly gilded, inlaid with ivory, originally with leather seats. L. 1 ft. 4½ in. (41·91 cm.) (both). From Thebes (tomb of Tutankhamun). XVIIIth Dynasty, *c.* 1350 B.C. Cairo Museum (T.T.140, 139).
Photo: Griffith Institute, Oxford

104 Side of shrine-shaped chest. Wood overlaid with gold. H. 1 ft. 8 in. (50·80 cm.), W. 10½ in. (29·21 cm.), D. 1 ft. 0½ in. (31·75 cm.) (measurements of shrine). From Thebes (tomb of Tutankhamun). XVIIIth Dynasty, *c.* 1350 B.C. Cairo Museum (T.T.108).
Photo: Griffith Institute, Oxford

105a Stool or table. Wood painted white. H. 11½ in. (29·21 cm.), W. 1 ft. 5 in. (43·18 cm.); (b) top; (c) underside. From Thebes (tomb of Tutankhamun). XVIIIth Dynasty, *c.* 1350 B.C. Cairo Museum (T.T.412).
Photo: Griffith Institute, Oxford

106 Chest on legs (open); see description of frontispiece.
Photo: Metropolitan Museum of Art, New York (Harry Burton)

107 Chest on legs. Wood, partly gilded. H. 2 ft. 2¾ in. (67·94 cm.), W. 1 ft. 5¼ in. (43·80 cm.), D. 1 ft. 3¾ in. (40 cm.). From Thebes (tomb of Tutankhamun). XVIIIth Dynasty, *c.* 1350 B.C. Cairo Museum (T.T.403).
Photo: Metropolitan Museum of Art, New York (Harry Burton)

108 Chest on legs. Wood and ivory. H. 1 ft. 5¾ in. (45·08 cm.), W. 10⅝ in. (26·98 cm.), D. 8⅝ in. (21·90 cm.). From Thebes (tomb of Tutankhamun). XVIIIth Dynasty, *c.* 1350 B.C. Cairo Museum (T.T.56).
Photo: Metropolitan Museum of Art, New York (Harry Burton)

109 Chest. Wood, partly gilded, partly veneered with ivory; shod with silver. H. 1 ft. 4½ in. (41·91 cm.), L. 1 ft. 7 in. (48·26 cm.), W. 1 ft. 5½ in. (44·45 cm.). From Thebes (tomb of Tutankhamun). XVIIIth Dynasty, *c.* 1350 B.C. Cairo Museum (T.T.271).

110 Hieroglyphs commonly used to decorate furniture.

111 Lid of chest in fig. 109.
Photo: Metropolitan Museum of Art, New York (Harry Burton)

112 Painted box. Wood covered with painted gesso. H. 1 ft. 5½ in. (44·45 cm.), L. 2 ft. (60·96 cm.), W. 1 ft. 4½ in. (41·91 cm.). From Thebes (tomb of Tutankhamun). XVIIIth Dynasty, *c.* 1350 B.C. Cairo Museum (T.T.21).
Photo: Griffith Institute, Oxford

113 Side-panel of box in fig. 112.
Photo: Metropolitan Museum of Art, New York (Harry Burton)

114 Chest. Painted wood. H. 1 ft. 7 in. (48·26 cm.), L. 4 ft. 3¾ in. (131·44 cm.), W. 1 ft. 2 in. (35·56 cm.). From Thebes (tomb of Tutankhamun). XVIIIth Dynasty, *c.* 1350 B.C. Cairo Museum (T.T.50).
Photo: Griffith Institute, Oxford

115 Chest with carrying poles. Wood veneered and inlaid with ivory and ebony. H. 2 ft. 0½ in. (62·23 cm.), W. 1 ft. 11½ in. (59·69 cm.). From Thebes (tomb of Tutankhamun). XVIIIth Dynasty, *c.* 1350 B.C. Cairo Museum (T.T.32).
Photo: Metropolitan Museum of Art, New York (Harry Burton)

116 Chest. Wood veneered and inlaid with ivory and ebony. H. 8½ in. (21·59 cm.), L. 10¼ in. (25·73 cm.), W. 9 in. (22·86 cm.). From Thebes (tomb of Tutankhamun). XVIIIth Dynasty, *c.* 1350 B.C. Cairo Museum (T.T.268).
Photo: Metropolitan Museum of Art, New York (Harry Burton)

117 Casket. Wood overlaid with ivory, and with ivory, faience and calcite inlays. H. 2 ft. 1 in. (63·50 cm.), L. 2 ft. 5 in.

(73·66 cm.), W. 1 ft. 4 in. (40·64 cm.) (all approx.). From Thebes (tomb of Tutankhamun). XVIIIth Dynasty, *c.* 1350 B.C. Cairo Museum (T.T.551 – box, 540 – lid).
Photo: Metropolitan Museum of Art, New York (Harry Burton)

118 Pair of storage chests. Wood inlaid with ivory, and with bronze staples. H. 6½ in. (16·51 cm.), L. 11 in. (27·94 cm.), W. 8½ in. (21·59 cm.). From Thebes (tomb of Tutankhamun). XVIIIth Dynasty, *c.* 1350 B.C. Cairo Museum (T.T.493, 494).
Photo: Metropolitan Museum of Art, New York (Harry Burton)

119 Lid of casket in fig. 117. Carved ivory over a wood base (T.T.540).
Photo: Metropolitan Museum of Art, New York (Harry Burton)

120 Chest with sloping top. Wood covered with gold-leaf over a gesso base. From Thebes (tomb of Tutankhamun). XVIIIth Dynasty, *c.* 1350 B.C. Cairo Museum (T.T.44).
Photo: Griffith Institute, Oxford

121 Chest. Wood, veneered with ivory, and with panels of ivory and ebony inlay. H. 11 in. (27·94 cm.), L. 1 ft. 5½ in. (44·45 cm.), W. 11¾ in. (29·84 cm.). From Thebes (tomb of Tutankhamun). XVIIIth Dynasty, *c.* 1350 B.C. Cairo Museum (T.T.267).
Photo: Metropolitan Museum of Art, New York (Harry Burton)

122 Cartouche-shaped chest. Wood, partly gilded, and inlaid with ivory and ebony. H. 1 ft. 0½ in. (31·75 cm.), L. 2 ft. 1 in. (63·50 cm.), W. 11¾ in. (29·84 cm.). From Thebes (tomb of Tutankhamun). XVIIIth Dynasty, *c.* 1350 B.C. Cairo Museum (T.T.269).
Photo: Metropolitan Museum of Art, New York (Harry Burton)

123 Lid of chest in fig. 122.
Photo: Griffith Institute, Oxford

124 Chest with short legs. Wood with ivory inlay. H. 10½ in. (26·67 cm.), L. 2 ft. 1½ in. (64·77 cm.), W. 1 ft. 1 in. (33·02 cm.). From Thebes (tomb of Tutankhamun). XVIIIth Dynasty, *c.* 1350 B.C. Cairo Museum (T.T.585).
Photo: Metropolitan Museum of Art, New York (Harry Burton)

125 Chest. Wood, painted white. H. 1 ft. 7½ in. (49·53 cm.), L. 1 ft. 11½ in. (59·69 cm.), W. 1 ft. 4 in. (40·64 cm.). From Thebes (tomb of Tutankhamun). XVIIIth Dynasty, *c.* 1350 B.C. Cairo Museum (T.T.316).
Photo: Metropolitan Museum of Art, New York (Harry Burton)

126 Game-board and stand. Wood inlaid with ivory, and overlaid in part with gold. H. 3 in. (7·62 cm.), L. 1 ft. 5 in. (43·18 cm.), W. 6 in. (15·24 cm.) (box); H. 7¾ in. (19·68 cm.), L. 1 ft. 8½ in. (52·07 cm.), W. 7 in. (17·78 cm.) (stand). From Thebes (tomb of Tutankhamun). XVIIIth Dynasty, *c.* 1350 B.C. Cairo Museum (T.T.345 – box, 580 – stand).
Photo: Metropolitan Museum of Art, New York (Harry Burton)

127 Box. Papyrus pith, lined with linen, and painted. H. 5½ in. (13·97 cm.), L. 1 ft. 1½ in. (34·29 cm.), W. 1 ft. 1½ in. (34·29 cm.). From Thebes (tomb of Tutankhamun). XVIIIth Dynasty, *c.* 1350 B.C. Cairo Museum (T.T.271a).
Photo: Metropolitan Museum of Art, New York (Harry Burton)

128 Jewel box. Solid ivory with gold fittings. H. 5½ in. (13·97 cm.), L. 6½ in. (16·51 cm.), W. 5 in. (12·70 cm.). From Thebes (tomb of Tutankhamun). XVIIIth Dynasty, *c.* 1350 B.C. Cairo Museum (T.T.54ddd).
Photo: Metropolitan Museum of Art, New York (Harry Burton)

129 Box. Alabaster, with incised painted decoration; knobs of obsidian. W. 7 in. (17·78 cm.), thickness of alabaster, *c.* ½ in. (1·27 cm.). From Thebes (tomb of Tutankhamun). XVIIIth Dynasty, *c.* 1350 B.C. Cairo Museum (T.T.40).
Photo: Griffith Institute, Oxford

130 Canopic shrine. Wood overlaid with gilded gesso; *uraei* inlaid with lapis lazuli and coloured glass. The shrine beneath the canopy is fixed to the sledge by mortise and tenon joints. H. 6 ft. 7 in. (190·66 cm.), W. 4 ft. 1 in. (124;46 cm.),

D. (base) 4 ft. 11½ in. (151·13 cm.). From Thebes (tomb of Tutankhamun). XVIIIth Dynasty, *c.* 1350 B.C. (Cairo Museum (T.T.266).
Photo: Griffith Institute, Oxford

131 Protective goddesses from shrine in fig. 130. Gilded wood. H. 2 ft. 11½ in. (90·17 cm.).
Photo: Metropolitan Museum of Art, New York (Harry Burton)

132 Bed. Wood overlaid with sheet gold; string-mesh mattress. H. 2 ft. 3 in. (68·58 cm.), L. 5 ft. 3 in. (160·02 cm.) (approx.). From Thebes (tomb of Tutankhamun). XVIIIth Dynasty, *c.* 1350 B.C. Cairo Museum (T.T.466).
Photo: Griffith Institute, Oxford

133 Foot-board of bed in fig. 132.
Photo: Griffith Institute, Oxford

134 Bed. Ebony with gilded decoration and string-mesh mattress. H. 2 ft. 5½ in. (74·93 cm.), L. 6 ft. 1 in. (185·42 cm.), W. 2 ft. 11½ in. (90·17 cm.). From Thebes (tomb of Tutankhamun). XVIIIth Dynasty, *c.* 1350 B.C. Cairo Museum (T.T.47).
Photo: Griffith Institute, Oxford

135 Foot-board of bed in fig. 134.
Photo: Griffith Institute, Oxford

136 Folding bed. Wood, painted white; bronze hinges and bronze-shod feet. H. 1 ft. 7½ in. (49·53 cm.), L. 5 ft. 10½ in. (179·0 cm.), W. 2 ft. 3 in. (168·58 cm.). From Thebes (tomb of Tutankhamun). XVIIIth Dynasty, *c.* 1350 B.C. Cairo Museum (T.T.586).
Photo: Griffith Institute, Oxford

137 Folding bed; see fig. 136.
Photo: Griffith Institute, Oxford

138 Bed. Wood overlaid with gilded gesso. H. 2 ft. 4 in. (71·12 cm.), L. 5 ft. 11 in. (180·34 cm.), W. 2 ft. 7½ in. (80·01 cm.). From Thebes (tomb of Tutankhamun). XVIIIth Dynasty, *c.* 1350 B.C. Cairo Museum (T.T.377).
Photo: Griffith Institute, Oxford

139 Bed. Wood, painted white. From Thebes (tomb of Tutankhamun). XVIIIth Dynasty, *c.* 1350 B.C. Cairo Museum (T.T.80).
Photo: Griffith Institute, Oxford

140 Head-rest. Ivory with gilded pins. H. 7 in. (17·78 cm.), W. 11½ in. (29·21 cm.), D. 3½ in. (8·89 cm.). From Thebes (tomb of Tutankhamun). XVIIIth Dynasty, *c.* 1350 B.C. Cairo Museum (T.T.403*d*).
Photo: Metropolitan Museum of Art, New York (Harry Burton)

141 Head-rest. Ivory, partly tinted; gold swivel pins. H. 7¾ in. (19·68 cm.), W. 7½ in. (19·05 cm.), D. 4 in. (10·16 cm.). From Thebes (tomb of Tutankhamun). XVIIIth Dynasty, *c.* 1350 B.C. Cairo Museum (T.T.403*d*).
Photo: Metropolitan Museum of Art, New York (Harry Burton)

142 Head-rest. Glass with gold collar. H. 7 in. (17·78 cm.), W. 11 in. (27·94 cm.), D. 3¼ in. (8·25 cm.). From Thebes (tomb of Tutankhamun). XVIIIth Dynasty, *c.* 1350 B.C. Cairo Museum (T.T.403*a*).
Photo: Griffith Institute, Oxford

143 Lioness couch. Wood overlaid with gilded gesso. H. 4 ft. 5 in. (134·62 cm.) (at head), L. 7 ft. 3¼ in. (231·61 cm.), W. 3 ft. (91·44 cm.). From Thebes (tomb of Tutankhamun). XVIIIth Dynasty, *c.* 1350 B.C. Cairo Museum (T.T.35).
Photo: Cairo Museum

144 Lion couch in a scene of the union of Isis and Osiris. Sandstone low relief. In the Osiris Chapel on the roof of the Temple of Dendera. Roman period, 1st century A.D. Reproduced from *Description de l'Egypte, Antiquités*, vol. IV, pl. 27, 9.

145 Hathor couch. Wood overlaid with gilded gesso, and inlaid with glass. H. 5 ft. 10½ in. (179·07 cm.) at head, L. 7 ft. 9 in. (246·22 cm.). From Thebes (tomb of Tutankhamun). XVIIIth Dynasty, *c.* 1350 B.C. Cairo Museum (T.T.73).
Photo: Cairo Museum

146 Thoeris couch. Wood overlaid with gilded gesso. H. 4 ft. 4¾ in. (134 cm.) at head, L. 7 ft. 8 in. (243·68 cm.). From Thebes (tomb of Tutankhamun). XVIIIth Dynasty, *c.* 1350 B.C. Cairo Museum (T.T.137)
Photo: Metropolitan Museum of Art, New York (Harry Burton)

147 Thoeris head from couch in fig. 146.
Photo: Metropolitan Museum of Art, New York (Harry Burton)

148 Model of a house. Constructed from archaeological evidence found at El-Amarna. XVIIIth Dynasty, *c.* 1370 B.C. Cairo Museum.
Photo: Cairo Museum

149 Model house. Pottery. W. 1 ft. 4 in. (40·64 cm.), H. 6½ in. (16·51 cm.). Middle Kingdom, *c.* 1900 B.C. British Museum.
Photo: British Museum

150 Meket-Re's house. Model of painted wood. H. 10½ in. (26·67 cm.), L. 2 ft. 9½ in. (85·09 cm.), W. 1 ft. 4½ in. (41·91 cm.). From Thebes (tomb of Meket-Re). XIth Dynasty, *c.* 2000 B.C. Metropolitan Museum of Art, New York (20.3.13; from M.M.A. excavation 1919–20, Rogers Fund, with a contribution by Edward S. Harkness).
Photo: Metropolitan Museum of Art, New York

151 Plan and section of a villa at El-Amarna. XVIIIth Dynasty, *c.* 1370 B.C. Reproduced from *Journal of Egyptian Archaeology*, vol. 19 (1933), p. 4.

152 Scene of the house of Djehut-nufer. Painted plaster. At Thebes (tomb of Djehut-nufer, 104). XVIIIth Dynasty, *c.* 1430 B.C. Reproduced from N. de G. Davies, 'The Town House in Ancient Egypt' (*Metropolitan Museum Studies*, 1, pt. 2), fig. 1A.

153 Scene of a house. Limestone low relief. At Thebes (tomb of Surer, 48). XVIIIth Dynasty, *c.* 1400 B.C. Reproduced from T. Säve-Söderbergh, *Four Eighteenth Dynasty Tombs*, pl. XXXVII.

154 Four stools. Painted wood, three with rush seats. a and b: H. 1 ft. 0½ in. (31·75 cm.), L. 1 ft. 4½ in. (41·91 cm.), W. 1 ft. 1 in. (33·02 cm.); c: H. 1 ft. 3 in. (38·1 cm.), L. 1 ft. 3½ in. (39·37 cm.), W. 1 ft. 1 in. (33·02 cm.); d: H. 1 ft. 2½ in. (36·83 cm.), L. 1 ft. 3 in. (38·1 cm.), W. 1 ft. 1½ in. (34·29 cm.). From Thebes (tomb of Kha). XVIIIth Dynasty, *c.* 1400 B.C. Turin Museum (8511, 8512, 8510, 8468).
Photo: Turin Museum

155 Stool. Painted wood. H. 1 ft. 0½ in. (31·75 cm.), L. 1 ft. 10½ in. (57·15 cm.), W. 1 ft. 4 in. (40·64 cm.). From Thebes (tomb of Kha). XVIIIth Dynasty, *c.* 1400 B.C. Turin Museum.
Photo: Turin Museum

156 Stool. Hardwood inlaid with ivory and ebony; bronze swivels, leather seat. H. 1 ft. 9 in. (53·34 cm.), L. 1 ft. 11½ in. (59·69 cm.). From Thebes (tomb of Kha). XVIIIth Dynasty, *c.* 1400 B.C. Turin Museum (8509).
Photo: Turin Museum

157 Stool. Hardwood and leather. H. 1 ft. 6 in. (45·70 cm.), L. 1 ft. 7½ in. (49·53 cm.), W. 1 ft. 7½ in. (49·53 cm.). From Thebes (tomb of Kha). XVIIIth Dynasty, *c.* 1400 B.C. Turin Museum (8507).
Photo: Turin Museum

158 Stool. Painted soft wood, rush seat. H. 1 ft. 1 in. (33·02 cm.), L. 1 ft. 2½ in. (36·83 cm.), W. 1 ft. 2½ in. (36·83 cm.). From Thebes (tomb of Kha). XVIIIth Dynasty, *c.* 1400 B.C. Turin Museum (8614).
Photo: Turin Museum

159 Three-legged stools. Painted wood. a: H. 1 ft. 2 in. (35·56 cm.), L. 1 ft. 3½ in. (39·37 cm.), W. 11¾ in. (29·85 cm.); b: H. 1 ft. 0½ in. (31·75 cm.), L. 1 ft. 6½ in. (46·99 cm.), W. 1 ft. 3½ in. (39·37 cm.). From Thebes (tomb of Kha). XVIIIth Dynasty, *c.* 1400 B.C. Turin Museum (8505, 8506).
Photo: Turin Museum

160 Chair. Painted wood. H. 2 ft. 11¾ in. (90·80 cm.), W. 1 ft. 3½ in. (39·37 cm.), D. 1 ft. 9¾ in. (55·24 cm.). From Thebes (tomb of Kha). XVIIIth Dynasty, *c.* 1400 B.C. Turin Museum (8333).
Photo: Turin Museum

161 Table. Painted wood. H. 1 ft. 6½ in. (46·99 cm.), L. 2 ft. 3½ in. (69·85 cm.), W. 1 ft. 3 in. (38·10 cm.). From Thebes (tomb of Kha). XVIIIth Dynasty, *c.* 1400 B.C. Turin Museum (8257).
Photo: Turin Museum

162 Tables. Reed. a: H. 1 ft. 3 in. (38·10 cm.), L. 2 ft. 3½ in. (69·85 cm.), W. 1 ft. 7½ in. (49·53 cm.); b: H. 11¾ in. (29·85 cm.), L. 2 ft. 7 in. (78·74 cm.), W. 1 ft. 9¼ in. (53·97 cm.). From Thebes (tomb of Kha). XVIIIth Dynasty, *c.* 1400 B.C. Turin Museum (8342, 8343).
Photo: Turin Museum

163 Table on stand. Reed. No measurements available. From Thebes (tomb of Kha). XVIIIth Dynasty, *c.* 1400 B.C. Turin Museum (8229 – lost during the war of 1939–45).
Photo: Turin Museum

164 Scene from a tomb. Limestone sunk relief. At El-Amarna (tomb of Meryre II). XVIIIth Dynasty, *c.* 1360 B.C. Reproduced from N. de G. Davies, *Rock Tombs of El Amarna*, II, pl. XXXVI.

165 Table. Wood. H. 1 ft. 0½ in. (31·75 cm.), L. 1 ft. 6½ in. (46·99 cm.), W. 10 in. (55·88 cm.). From Thebes (tomb of Kha). XVIIIth Dynasty, *c.* 1400 B.C. Turin Museum (8432).
Photo: Turin Museum

166 Chest. Painted wood. H. 1 ft. 1½ in. (34·29 cm.), L. 1 ft. 6½ in. (46·99 cm.), W. 1 ft. (30·48 cm.). From Thebes (tomb of Kha). XVIIIth Dynasty, *c.* 1400 B.C. Turin Museum (8514).
Photo: Turin Museum

167 Chest. Painted wood. H. 1 ft. 3 in. (38·10 cm.), L. 1 ft. 7 in. (48·26 cm.), W. 1 ft. 2 in. (35·56 cm.). From Thebes (tomb of Kha). XVIIIth Dynasty, *c.* 1400 B.C. Turin Museum (8617).
Photo: Turin Museum

168 Chest. Painted wood. H. 1 ft. 2 in. (35·56 cm.), L. 1 ft. 7 in. (48·26 cm.), W. 1 ft. 3 in. (38·10 cm.) (all approx.). From Thebes (tomb of Kha). XVIIIth Dynasty, *c.* 1400 B.C. Turin Museum (8213).
Photo: Turin Museum

169 Wig chest. Wood, partly painted. H. 3 ft. 9½ in. (115·57 cm.), L. 1 ft. 7 in. (48·26 cm.), W. 1 ft. 7 in. (48·26 cm.). From Thebes (tomb of Kha). XVIIIth Dynasty, *c.* 1400 B.C. Turin Museum (8493).
Photo: Turin Museum

170 Bed. Painted wood, string-mesh mattress. H. 2 ft. 3½ in. (69·85 cm.), L. 6 ft. 0½ in. (193·15 cm.), W. 2 ft. 9½ in. (85·09 cm.). From Thebes (tomb of Kha). XVIIIth Dynasty, *c.* 1400 B.C. Turin Museum (8327).
Photo: Turin Museum

171 Bed. Painted wood, string-mesh mattress. H. 2 ft. 2 in. (66·04 cm.), L. 5 ft. 9 in. (174·26 cm.), W. 2 ft. 6 in. (76·20 cm.). From Thebes (tomb of Kha). XVIIIth Dynasty, *c.* 1400 B.C. Turin Museum (8629).
Photo: Turin Museum

172 Stela. Painted limestone low relief, and incised. H. 1 ft. 10¼ in. (56·51 cm.). From Kau el Kebir. XVIIIth Dynasty, *c.* 1470 B.C. Metropolitan Museum of Art, New York (12.182.3), Rogers Fund, 1912.
Photo: Metropolitan Museum of Art

173 Chair. Hardwood with bone inlay. Provenance unknown. XVIIIth Dynasty, *c.* 1400 B.C. Brooklyn Museum (37.40E).
Photo: Brooklyn Museum

174 Back view of chair in fig. 173.
Photo: Brooklyn Museum

175 Chair. Hardwood, similar to fig. 173. H. 2 ft. 6½ in. (77·47 cm.), W. 1 ft. 6 in. (45·70 cm.), D. 1 ft. 7¾ in. (50·16 cm.). Provenance unknown. XVIIIth Dynasty, *c.* 1400 B.C. Rijksmuseum, Leiden (549).
Photo: Rijksmuseum, Leiden

176 Chair. Wood with ivory inlay. H. 2 ft. 10½ in. (87·63 cm.), W. 1 ft. 11 in. (58·42 cm.). Provenance unknown. XVIIIth Dynasty, *c.* 1400 B.C. Louvre, Paris (2950).
Photo: Louvre

177 Drawings of details of the chair in fig. 176. Prepared by the Collège Technique Boulle, Paris.

178 Detail of a tomb scene. Painted limestone. At Thebes (tomb of Rekhmire, 100). XVIIIth Dynasty, *c.* 1475 B.C. Reproduced from N. de G. Davies, *The Tomb of Rekh-mi-re*, pl. LII.

179 Chair. Painted wood. From Thebes (tomb of Sennedjem, 1). XIXth Dynasty, *c.* 1250 B.C. Cairo Museum (27256).
Photo: Fondation Egyptologique Reine Elisabeth, Brussels

180 Statue. Painted limestone. H. 1 ft. 9¼ in. (22·49 cm.). From Deir Durunka in Middle Egypt. XIXth Dynasty, *c.* 1250 B.C. Metropolitan Museum of Art, New York (15.2.1; Rogers Fund, 1915).
Photo: Metropolitan Museum of Art

181 Situla. Engraved bronze. H. (to rim) 1 ft. 4 in. (40·64 cm.). Provenance unknown. XXXth Dynasty, *c.* 370 B.C. British Museum (38212).
Photo: British Museum

182 Chair. Boxwood and ebony with cord-mesh seat. H. 1 ft. 9 in. (53·34 cm.). From Thebes (Burial of Ramose and Hatnufer, near tomb 71). XVIIIth Dynasty, *c.* 1500 B.C. Metropolitan Museum of Art, New York (36.3.152; Rogers Fund, 1936).
Photo: Metropolitan Museum of Art

183 Chair. Hardwood. H. 1 ft. 11 in. (58·42 cm.), W. 1 ft. 5 in. (43·18 cm.), D. 1 ft. 6 in. (45·70 cm.). From Thebes. XVIIIth Dynasty, *c.* 1500 B.C. Metropolitan Museum of Art, New York (12.182.28; Rogers Fund, 1912).
Photo: Metropolitan Museum of Art

184 Chair. Hardwood with ebony and ivory inlay. H. 2 ft. 0½ in. (62·23 cm.), W. 1 ft. 7 in. (48·26 cm.), D. 1 ft. 5 in. (43·18 cm.). From Thebes. XVIIIth Dynasty, *c.* 1450 B.C. British Museum (2480).
Photo: British Museum

185 Chair. Painted wood. H. 2 ft. 5½ in. (74·93 cm.). From Thebes. XVIIIth Dynasty, *c.* 1450 B.C. Staatliche Museen, Berlin (10748).
Photo: Staatliche Museen

186 Drawing of a Bauhaus chair. Reproduced from Bauformen, Stuttgart, *c.* 1937.

187 Chair. Wood. H. 2 ft. 5 in. (74 cm.), W. 1 ft. 4½ in. (41 cm.), D. 1 ft. 7½ in. (50 cm.). From Thebes. XVIIIth Dynasty, *c.* 1450 B.C. British Museum (2479).
Photo: British Museum

188 Chair. Wood. H. 2 ft. 2 in. (65·5 cm.), W. 1 ft. 7 in. (48·6 cm.). Discovered by Mariette. Provenance unknown. XVIIIth Dynasty, *c.* 1450 B.C. Archaeological Museum, Florence (2580).
Photo: F. Barsotti, Florence

189 Side view of chair in fig. 188.
Photo: F. Barsotti, Florence

190 Box seat with solid sides. Limestone low relief. In the Temple of Sethos I at Abydos. XIXth Dynasty, *c.* 1310 B.C. Reproduced from A. M. Calverley, *The Temple of Sethos I at Abydos*, vol. IV, pl. 9.

191 Tomb scene. Painted plaster. H. 2 ft. 1½ in. (64·77 cm.), W. 2 ft. 7½ in. (80·01 cm.). From Thebes (tomb of Sebekhotep, 63). XVIIIth Dynasty, *c.* 1420 B.C. British Museum (920).
Photo: British Museum

192 Stool. Painted wood. H. 1 ft. 2¾ in. (37·46 cm.), L. 1 ft. 2½ in. (36·83 cm.), W. 1 ft. 0¾ in. (32·38 cm.). From Thebes. XVIIIth Dynasty, *c.* 1450 B.C. British Museum (2476).
Photo: British Museum

193 Stool. Wood with ivory elements, ivory inlay and leather seat. H. 1 ft. 3 in. (38·10 cm.), L. 1 ft. 5¼ in. (43·81 cm.), W. 1 ft. 5¼ in. (43·81 cm.). Provenance unknown. XVIIIth Dynasty, *c.* 1400 B.C. British Museum (2472).
Photo: British Museum

194 Stool. White-painted wood, rush seat. H. 4½ in. (11·43 cm.), L. 1 ft. 5 in. (43·18 cm.), W. 1 ft. 2¼ in. (36·19 cm.). Provenance unknown. XVIIIth Dynasty, *c.* 1400 B.C. British Museum (46705).
Photo: British Museum

195 Folding stool. Wood with ivory inlay. H. 1 ft. 7 in. (48·26 cm.), W. 1 ft. 10 in. (55·88 cm.). From Thebes. XVIIIth Dynasty, *c.* 1400 B.C. British Museum (2477).
Photo: British Museum

196 Folding stool. Wood with traces of leather seat. H. 9⅞ in. (25·08 cm.). Provenance unknown. XVIIIth Dynasty, *c.* 1400 B.C. Staatliche Museen, Berlin (12551).
Photo: Staatliche Museen

197 Folding stool. Wood with ivory inlay. H. 1 ft. 3 in. (38·10 cm.), W. 1 ft. 3½ in. (39·37 cm.). From Thebes (tomb of Ani). XVIIIth–XIXth Dynasty, *c.* 1300 B.C. British Museum (29284).
Photo: British Museum

198 Detail of stool in fig. 197.
Photo: British Museum

199 Folding stool. Wood with leather seat. H. 1 ft. 2 in. (35·56 cm.), W. 1 ft. 0½ in. (31·75 cm.), D. 1 ft. 3 in. (38·10 cm.). From Meir. XIIth Dynasty, *c.* 1800 B.C. Metropolitan Museum of Art, New York (12.182.58; Rogers Fund, 1912).
Photo: Metropolitan Museum of Art

200 Folding stool. Wood. H. 1 ft. 1 in. (33·02 cm.), W. 1 ft. 2 in. (35·56 cm.). From Jutland, Denmark. *c.* 1200 B.C. National Museum, Copenhagen.
Photo: National Museum

201 Stool. Wood with carved lion's feet. Seat restored by the British Museum. Provenance unknown. H. 9½ in. (24·13 cm.), W. 15¼ in. (38·73 cm.), D. 16⅞ in. (42·86 cm.). New Kingdom, *c.* 1300 B.C. Baker Museum for Furniture Research, Grand Rapids, Michigan.
Photo: Baker

202 Stool. Wood. H. 1 ft. 0½ in. (31·75 cm.), L. 1 ft. 7½ in. (49·53 cm.), W. 1 ft. 3½ in. (39·37 cm.). From Thebes. New Kingdom, *c.* 1300 B.C. Oriental Institute, University of Chicago (13694).
Photo: Oriental Institute, University of Chicago

203 Stool. Wood. H. 5⅛ in. (13·01 cm.), L. 1 ft. 2½ in. (36·83 cm.), W. 1 ft. 2½ in. (36·83 cm.). Provenance unknown. Middle Kingdom, *c.* 1800 B.C. Egyptian Museum, Stockholm (MM10122).
Photo: Egyptian Museum

204 Stool. Painted wood. H. 10 in. (25 cm.), L. 1 ft. 0⅝ in. (32 cm.). Provenance unknown. Late period, after 850 B.C. Private Collection, Holland.
Photo: J. Möger, Soestdijk, Holland

205 Stool leg. Wood. H. 1 ft. 2⅛ in. (35·87 cm.). Provenance unknown. Late period. Brooklyn Museum, New York (37.42E).
Photo: Brooklyn Museum

206 Stool. Wood. H. 11 in. (27·94 cm.), L. 1 ft. 6⅞ in. (47·94 cm.), W. 1 ft. 5⅜ in. (44·13 cm.). Provenance unknown. Saite period, *c.* 600 B.C. Louvre, Paris (E10780).
Photo: Giraudon, Paris

207 Stool. Wood. H. 1 ft. 3½ in. (39·37 cm.), W. 1 ft. 3 in. (38·10 cm.), D. 1 ft. 3 in. (38·10 cm.). From Thebes. XVIIth–XVIIIth Dynasty, *c.* 1550 B.C. Metropolitan Museum of Art, New York (14.10.4; gift of the Earl of Carnarvon, 1914).
Photo: Metropolitan Museum of Art

208 Stool. Wood. H. 8¼ in. (20·95 cm.), W. 1 ft. 2¾ in. (37·46 cm.). Provenance unknown. XVIIIth Dynasty, *c.* 1450 B.C. Staatliche Museen, Berlin (12553).
Photo: Staatliche Museen

209 Stool. Wood. H. 1 ft. 11 in. (58·42 cm.). Provenance unknown. Ptolemaic period, *c.* 200 B.C. Staatliche Museen, Berlin (13888).
Photo: Staatliche Museen

210 Legs of stools. Wood. a: L. 1 ft. 10 in. (55·88 cm.); b: L. 1 ft. 11 in. (58·42 cm.); c: L. 1 ft. 8 in. (50·80 cm.); d: L. 1 ft. 7½ in. (49·53 cm.); e: L. 1 ft. 8 in. (50·80 cm.). From the Faiyum. Roman period, *c.* A.D. 100. Kelsey Museum of Archaeology, the University of Michigan (10236, 24812b, 24833, 24834, 24823).
Photo: Kelsey Museum of Archaeology

211 Legs of stools. Wood. No measurements available. Provenance unknown. XVIIIth Dynasty – late period, *c.* 1450–750 B.C. Louvre, Paris.
Photo: Giraudon, Paris

212 Stool. Wood. H. 9⅞ in. (25·08 cm.), L. 1 ft. 3⅝ in. (39·68 cm.). Provenance unknown. New Kingdom, *c.* 1300 B.C. Staatliche Museen, Berlin (790).
Photo: Staatliche Museen

213 Stool. Wood. H. 3½ in. (8·89 cm.), L. 10½ in. (26·67 cm.), W. 10½ in. (26·67 cm.). Provenance unknown. Late period, after 850 B.C. Staatliche Museen, Berlin (19359).
Photo: Staatliche Museen

214 Stools and a chair. Wood and rushes. From Thebes (Deir el-Medina). New Kingdom, *c.* 1300 B.C. Reproduced from B. Bruyère, *Rapport sur les Fouilles de Deir el Medineh* (1934–5), p. 48, fig. 21.

215 Stool. Wood and rushes. H. 6¼ in. (15·87 cm.), L. 1 ft. 1½ in. (34·29 cm.), W. 1 ft. 2⅝ in. (37·14 cm.). From Thebes. XIXth Dynasty, *c.* 1250 B.C. Staatliche Museen, Berlin (791).
Photo: Staatliche Museen

216 Stool. Wood and rushes. H. 5¼ in. (13·33 cm.), L. 1 ft. 0¼ in. (31·11 cm.), W. 11¾ in. (29·74 cm.). From Thebes. XVIIth–XVIIIth Dynasties, *c.* 1550 B.C. Metropolitan Museum of Art, New York (14.10.3; gift of the Earl of Carnarvon, 1914).
Photo: Metropolitan Museum of Art

217 Tomb scene. Limestone low relief. At Thebes (tomb of Khaemhat, 57). XVIIIth Dynasty, *c.* 1400 B.C.
Photo: Luxor

218 Tomb scene. Painted plaster. At Thebes (tomb of Menna, 69). XVIIIth Dynasty, *c.* 1420 B.C.
Photo: Luxor

219 Bed. Wood. H. 11 in. (27·94 cm.), L. 5 ft. 3¼ in. (160·65 cm.), W. 2 ft. 3⅜ in. (69·48 cm.). Provenance unknown. XIth Dynasty, *c.* 2050 B.C. Metropolitan Museum of Art, New York (86.1.39; the head-rest 86.1.4).
Photo: Metropolitan Museum of Art

220 Bed. Wood with ivory inlay. W. 2 ft. 2 in. (66·04 cm.) of

the foot-board. From Kerma in the Sudan. XIIth Dynasty, *c.*2800 B.C. Museum of Fine Arts, Boston.
Photo: Museum of Fine Arts

221 Inlays. Ivory and bone. H. of largest, 3 in. (7·62 cm.). From Kerma in the Sudan. XIIth Dynasty, *c.*1800 B.C. Museum of Fine Arts, Boston.
Photo: Museum of Fine Arts

222 Chest. Painted wood. H. 1 ft. 5¼ in. (43·80 cm.), L. 2 ft. 3½ in. (69·85 cm.), W. 1 ft. 2¼ in. (36·19 cm.). From Thebes (burial of Ramose and Hatnufer, near tomb 71). XVIIIth Dynasty, *c.*1500 B.C. Metropolitan Museum of Art, New York (36.3.56.a.b).
Photo: Metropolitan Museum of Art

223 Chest. Wood. H. 1 ft. 2 in. (35·56 cm.), L. 1 ft. 2 in. (35·56 cm.), W. 1 ft. 1¾ in. (34·93 cm.). From Thebes (tomb of Ani). XVIIIth–XIXth Dynasty, *c.*1300 B.C. British Museum (24708).
Photo: British Museum

224 Chest. Painted wood. H. 1 ft. 7 in. (48·26 cm.), L. 2 ft. 6 in. (76·20 cm.). From Thebes (burial of Ramose and Hatnufer, near tomb 71). XVIIIth Dynasty, *c.*1500 B.C. Metropolitan Museum of Art, New York (36.5.A,B).
Photo: Metropolitan Museum of Art

225 Box. Wood covered with painted gesso. H. 5 in. (12·70 cm.), L. 1 ft. in. (33·02 cm.), W. 1 ft. 1 in. (33·02 cm.). From Thebes (tomb of Sennedjem, 1). XIXth Dynasty, *c.*1250 B.C. Metropolitan Museum of Art, New York (86.1.8; various donors).
Photo: Metropolitan Museum of Art

226 Female figure. Wood. H. 6 in. (15·24 cm.). Provenance unknown. XVIIIth Dynasty, *c.*1400 B.C. British Museum (32767).
Photo: British Museum

227 Casket. Wood with ebony and ivory veneers, and silver fittings. H. 8 in. (20·32 cm.), L. 11¼ in. (28·57 cm.), W. 7 in. (17·17 cm.). From Thebes (tomb of Rensonb). XIIth Dynasty, *c.*1790 B.C. Metropolitan Museum of Art, New York (26.7.1438; the vessels outside the box are from Girga).
Photo: Metropolitan Museum of Art

228 Chest. Wood. H. 1 ft. 10 in. (55·88 cm.). Provenance unknown. Late New Kingdom, *c.*850 B.C.(?). Louvre, Paris (2945).
Photo: M. Chuzeville, Paris

229 Casket. Wood and silver and gold fittings, with veneers of ivory, ebony and faience; carnelian inlays. H. 1 ft. 2¾ in. (37·46 cm.), L. 1 ft. 6¼ in. (46·33 cm.), W. 1 ft. 1 in. (33·02 cm.). From El Lahun (tomb of Sit-Hat-Hor-Yunet). XIIth Dynasty, *c.*1800 B.C. Metropolitan Museum of Art, New York (16.1.1).
Photo: Metropolitan Museum of Art

230 Canopic chest. Wood covered with painted gesso. H. 1 ft. 9 in. (53·34 cm.), L. (with sledge) 2 ft. 5 in. (73·66 cm.), W. 1 ft. 8 in. (81·28 cm.). From Thebes (burial of Ramose and Hatnufer, near tomb 71). XVIIIth Dynasty, *c.*1500 B.C. Metropolitan Museum of Art, New York (36.3.53.A,B).
Photo: Metropolitan Museum of Art

231 Toilet chest. Rush and reed, with ebony and ivory knobs. H. 1 ft. 2 in. (35·56 cm.). From Thebes (burial of Queen Menuthotep). XVIIth Dynasty, *c.*1600 B.C. Staatliche Museen, Berlin (1177).
Photo: Fondation Egyptologique Reine Elisabeth, Brussels

232 Tomb scene. Painted limestone. At Thebes (tomb of Nebamun, 17). XVIIIth Dynasty, *c.*1430 B.C. Reproduced from T. Säve-Söderbergh, *Four Eighteenth Dynasty Tombs*, pl. XXII.

233 Tables. Wood painted. a: H. 1 ft. 6¾ in. (47·60 cm.), L. 2 ft. 3½ in. (69·85 cm.), W. 1 ft. 3 in. (38·10 cm.); b: H. 1 ft. 6¾ in. (47·60 cm.), L. 2 ft. 5½ in. (74·93 cm.), W. 1 ft. 3 in. (38·10 cm.). From Thebes (tomb of Kha, 8). XVIIIth Dynasty, *c.*1400 B.C. Turin Museum (8257, 8258).
Photo: Turin Museum

234 Detail of a scene on a coffin. Painted wood. From El Bersheh (tomb of Djehut-nekht). XIIth Dynasty, *c.*1900 B.C. Museum of Fine Arts, Boston (20.1822).
Photo: Museum of Fine Arts

235 Table. Wood. H. 1 ft. 5¾ in. (45·08 cm.), L. 2 ft. 1 in. (63·50 cm.), W. 1 ft. 0¼ in. (31·11 cm.). From Thebes. XVIIth–XVIIIth Dynasty, *c.*1550 B.C. Metropolitan Museum of Art, New York (14.10.5; gift of the Earl of Carnarvon, 1914).
Photo: Metropolitan Museum of Art

236 Table. Wood. H. 11¾ in. (29·85 cm.), L. 1 ft. 8½ in. (52·07 cm.), W. 10¼ in. (26·03 cm.). Provenance unknown. XVIIIth Dynasty, *c.*1450 B.C. Brooklyn Museum, New York (37.41E).
Photo: Brooklyn Museum

237 Table. Painted wood. H. 1 ft. 8 in. (50·80 cm.), L. 2 ft. 2¾ in. (67·94 cm.), W. 1 ft. 6½ in. (46·99 cm.) (of top). From Thebes. XVIIIth Dynasty, *c.*1450 B.C. British Museum (2469).
Photo: British Museum

238 Drawings of tables. From limestone sunk relief scenes in tombs at El-Amarna. XVIIth Dynasty, *c.*1350 B.C. Reproduced from N. de G. Davies, *The Rock Tombs of El Amarna.*

239 Top of table in fig. 238.
Photo: British Museum

240 Pot stand. Wood with painted gesso. H. 2 ft. 3½ in. (69·85 cm.), W. 1 ft. 6½ in. (46·99 cm.), D. 1 ft. 6½ in. (46·99 cm.). From Thebes. XVIIIth Dynasty, *c.*1450 B.C. British Museum (2470; the pot is 42088).
Photo: British Museum

241 Stand. Painted wood. H. 1 ft. 3 in. (38·10 cm.), W. 10 in. (25·40 cm.) (at base). Provenance unknown. XVIIIth Dynasty, *c.*1450 B.C. British Museum (2471).
Photo: British Museum

242 Tomb fragment. Painted limestone low relief. H. 1 ft. 8¼ in. (51·43 cm.), W. 1 ft. 3¾ in. (40 cm.). From Thebes (tomb of Mentuemhat, 34). XXVIth Dynasty, *c.*650 B.C. Nelson Gallery and Atkins Museum, Kansas City (48–28/2; Nelson Fund).
Photo: Nelson Gallery and Atkins Museum

243 Tomb scene. Limestone low relief. At Thebes (tomb of Kheruef, 192). XVIIIth Dynasty, *c.*1380 B.C.
Photo: Oriental Institute, University of Chicago

244 Scene in the lobby of the Nile Hilton Hotel, Cairo, showing furniture based on ancient designs.
Photo: Nile Hilton Hotel

245 Table of metal in the Nile Hilton Hotel, Cairo.
Photo: Nile Hilton Hotel

246 Drawing of a scene on the 'Standard of Ur'. Mosaic of shell, lapis lazuli and coloured limestone. From Ur. Early Dynastic III, *c.*2600 B.C. British Museum (121201).

247 Plaque from the sounding box of a lyre. Shell and bitumen on a wooden backing. H. 8⅜ in. (21·23 cm.). From Ur (royal tomb 789). Early Dynastic III, *c.*2600 B.C. University Museum, University of Pennsylvania, Philadelphia (CBS 17694).
Photo: University Museum, University of Pennsylvania

248 Harp. Wood inlaid with gold, mother of pearl, coloured stones, lapis lazuli, shell and limestone, and gilded. H. 3 ft. 11¼ in. (120 cm.), W. 4 ft. 7 in. (140 cm.). From Ur. Early Dynastic III, *c.*2600 B.C. Iraq Museum, Baghdad (IM8964).
Photo: Iraq Museum

249 Impression of a cylinder seal. Provenance unknown. Jamdat-Nasr period, *c.*2900 B.C. Pierpont Morgan Library, New York (12).
Photo: Pierpont Morgan Library

250 Impression of a cylinder seal. Provenance unknown. Jamdat-Nasr period, *c.*2900 B.C. Pierpont Morgan Library, New York (7e).
Photo: Pierpont Morgan Library

251 Impression of a cylinder seal. Provenance unknown. Jamdat-Nasr period, *c.*2900 B.C. Pierpont Morgan Library, New York (8).
Photo: Pierpont Morgan Library

252 Impression of a cylinder seal. Provenance unknown. Early Dynastic III, *c.*2600 B.C. Pierpont Morgan Library, New York (105e).
Photo: Pierpont Morgan Library

253 Impression of a lapis lazuli cylinder seal. H. 1½ in. (3·81 cm.), Dia. ¾ in. (1·90 cm.) (royal tomb 800). Early Dynastic III, *c.*2600 B.C. University Museum, University of Pennsylvania, Philadelphia (CBS16728).
Photo: University Museum, University of Pennsylvania

254 Impression of a cylinder seal. Provenance unknown. Early Dynastic III, *c.*2600 B.C. Pierpont Morgan Library, New York (113e).
Photo: Pierpont Morgan Library

255 Impression of a cylinder seal. Provenance unknown. Post-Akkadian, *c.*2000 B.C. British Museum (89326).
Photo: British Museum

256 Statue of a seated woman. Stone. From Mari. Early Dynastic III, *c.*2600 B.C.
Photo: Caisse Nationale des Monuments Historiques et des Sites

257 Statue of Ebih-il. Alabaster. From Mari. Early Dynastic III, *c.*2600 B.C. Louvre, Paris.
Photo: Caisse Nationale des Monuments Historiques et des Sites

258 Inscribed plaque in low relief. Stone. H. 9⅝ in. (24·4 cm.), W. 11¼ in. (28·57 cm.). From the Inanna Temple in Nippur. Early Dynastic III, *c.*2600 B.C. Iraq Museum, Baghdad.
Photo: The Oriental Institute, University of Chicago

259 Statue of the goddess Inanna. Stone. From Susa. Second half of 3rd millennium B.C. Louvre, Paris.
Photo: Caisse Nationale des Monuments Historiques et des Sites

260 Fragment of a plaque in low relief. Stone. H. 4 in. (10·16 cm.), W. 4⅛ in. (10·47 cm.). From level VII of the Nintu Temple in Khafajah. Early Dynastic III, *c.*2600 B.C. Iraq Museum, Baghdad.
Photo: The Oriental Institute, University of Chicago

261 Impression of a cylinder seal. Provenance unknown. Old Akkadian period, *c.*2370–2230 B.C. Pierpont Morgan Library, New York (245).
Photo: Pierpont Morgan Library

262 Impression of a cylinder seal. Provenance unknown. Old Akkadian period, *c.*2370–2230 B.C. Pierpont Morgan Library, New York (202e).
Photo: Pierpont Morgan Library

263 Impression of a cylinder seal. Provenance unknown. Old Akkadian period, *c.*2370–2230 B.C. British Museum (103317)
Photo: British Museum

264 Impression of a cylinder seal. Provenance unknown. Ur III period, *c.*2113–2006 B.C. Pierpont Morgan Library, New York (279).
Photo: Pierpont Morgan Library

265 Impression of a cylinder seal. Provenance unknown. Old Akkadian period, *c.*2370–2230 B.C. University Museum, University of Pennsylvania, Philadelphia (Pritchard 525).
Photo: University Museum, University of Pennsylvania (Courtesy of E. Borowski)

266 Impression of a cylinder seal. Provenance unknown. Old Akkadian period, *c.*2370–2230 B.C. Pierpont Morgan Library, New York (231).
Photo: Pierpont Morgan Library

267 Impression of a cylinder seal. Provenance unknown. Old Akkadian period, *c.* 2370–2230 B.C. Pierpont Morgan Library, New York (216).
Photo: Pierpont Morgan Library

268 Impression of a cylinder seal. Provenance unknown. Old Akkadian period, *c.* 2370–2230 B.C. Pierpont Morgan Library, New York (250).
Photo: Pierpont Morgan Library

269 Impression of a cylinder seal. Provenance unknown. Old Babylonian period, *c.* 2017–1595 B.C. Pierpont Morgan Library, New York (315).
Photo: Pierpont Morgan Library

270 Impression of a cylinder seal. Provenance unknown. Old Akkadian period, *c.* 2370–2230 B.C. Staatliche Museen, Berlin (Pritchard 697).
Photo: Staatliche Museen

271 Impression of the cylinder seal of Ur-Nammu, King of Ur (*c.* 2113–2096 B.C.), Ur III period, *c.* 2113–2006 B.C. British Museum (89126).
Photo: British Museum

272 Relief. Stone. From Susa. Old Babylonian period, *c.* 2017–1595. Louvre, Paris.
Photo: Caisse Nationale des Monuments Historiques et des Sites

273 Statue of Gudea, Ensi of Lagash. Diorite. H. 3 ft. $0\frac{5}{8}$ in. (93·63 cm.). From Lagash. Gutian period, *c.* 2140 B.C. Louvre, Paris.
Photo: Caisse Nationale des Monuments Historiques et des Sites

274 Fragment of the stela of Ur-Nammu, King of Ur (*c.* 2113–2096 B.C.). Limestone. H. 1 ft. 4 in. (40·64 cm.), W. 2 ft. 4 in. (71·12 cm.). Ur III period, *c.* 2113–2006 B.C. University Museum, University of Pennsylvania, Philadelphia (CBS 16676).
Photo: University Museum, University of Pennsylvania

275 Relief. Stone. Ur III period, *c.* 2113–2006 B.C. Louvre, Paris.
Photo: Caisse Nationale des Monuments Historiques et des Sites

276 Fragment of plaque. Terracotta. H. 4 in. (10·16 cm.), W. $2\frac{1}{2}$ in. (6·35 cm.). Provenance unknown. Ur III period, *c.* 2113–2006 B.C. British Museum (117940).
Photo: British Museum

277 Stela of Hammurapi, King of Babylon (*c.* 1792–1750 B.C.), inscribed with the Hammurapi Law Code. Diorite. From Susa. Old Babylonian period, *c.* 2017–1595 B.C. Louvre, Paris (SG8).
Photo: Caisse Nationale des Monuments Historiques et des Sites

278 Part of a tablet from a foundation deposit. Stone. H. $11\frac{3}{8}$ in. (28·89 cm.), W. 7 in. (17·78 cm.). From Sippar, *c.* 870 B.C. British Museum (91000).
Photo: British Museum

279 Plaque. Terracotta. H. 5 in. (12·70 cm.), W. $2\frac{1}{2}$ in. (6·35 cm.). From Ischali. Old Babylonian period, *c.* 2017–1595 B.C. The Oriental Institute, University of Chicago (A9345).
Photo: The Oriental Institute, University of Chicago

280 Plaque. Old Babylonian period, *c.* 2017–1595. Louvre, Paris.
Photo: Caisse Nationale des Monuments Historiques et des Sites

281 Fragment of a plaque. Terracotta. Old Babylonian period, *c.* 2017–1595 B.C. Louvre, Paris.
Photo: Caisse Nationale des Monuments Historiques et des Sites

282 Model of a bed. Clay. H. $1\frac{3}{8}$ in. (3·49 cm.), L. $3\frac{15}{16}$ in. (10 cm.). W. $2\frac{3}{8}$ in. (6·03 cm.). From Ischali. Old Babylonian period, *c.* 2017–1595 B.C. Royal Ontario Museum, Toronto.
Photo: Royal Ontario Museum

283 Model of a bed. Terracotta. H. $1\frac{1}{4}$ in. (3·17 cm.), L. $4\frac{1}{2}$ in. (11·43 cm.), W. $2\frac{3}{4}$ in. (6·98 cm.). From Ur. Isin–Larsa period, *c.* 2017–1763 B.C. British Museum (1928–10–10,809).
Photo: British Museum

284 Model of a chair. Terracotta. H. $3\frac{1}{2}$ in. (8·89 cm.). From Ur. Isin–Larsa period, *c.* 2017–1763 B.C. British Museum (12497). *Photo: British Museum*

285 Drawings showing the chronological development of the stone and chair in Mesopotamia, from the Sumerian to the Assyrian period.

286 Impression of a cylinder seal. Provenance unknown. Neo-Assyrian period, *c.* 1000–612 B.C. British Museum (89438).
Photo: British Museum

287 Impression of a cylinder seal. Provenance unknown. Neo-Babylonian period, *c.* 1012–539 B.C. British Museum (89470).
Photo: British Museum

288 Impression of a cylinder seal. Provenance unknown. Neo-Assyrian period, *c.* 1000–612 B.C. British Museum (89655).
Photo: British Museum

289 Impression of a cylinder seal. Provenance unknown. Neo-Assyrian period, *c.* 1000–612 B.C. British Museum (89590).
Photo: British Museum

290 Impression of a cylinder seal. Provenance unknown. Neo-Assyrian period, *c.* 1000–612 B.C. Pierpont Morgan Library, New York (776).
Photo: Pierpont Morgan Library

291 Bas-relief. Stone. H. 7 ft. 9 in. (236·2 cm.). From Nimrud. Neo-Assyrian period, Assurnasirpal II (883–859 B.C.). British Museum (124565).
Photo: British Museum

292 Detail from bas-relief. Stone. H 3 ft. $1\frac{3}{8}$ in. (95 cm.). From Nimrud. Neo-Assyrian period, Assurnasirpal II (883–859 B.C.). British Museum (124565).
Photo: British Museum

293 Bas-relief. Stone. H. 3 ft. $0\frac{3}{4}$ in. (93·8 cm.). From Nimrud. Neo-Assyrian period, Tiglath-Pileser III (745–727 B.C.). Rijksmuseum, Leiden (A1934/6.1).
Photo: Rijksmuseum

294 Bas-reliefs. Stone. H. 9 ft. 6 in. (289·0 cm.) (approx.). From Khorsabad. Neo-Assyrian period, Sargon II (721–705 B.C.). Iraq Museum, Baghdad.
Photo: Iraq Museum

295 Bas-relief. Stone. H. 9 ft. 6 in. (289·0 cm.) (approx.). From Khorsabad. Neo-Assyrian period, Sargon II (721–705 B.C.). Iraq Museum, Baghdad (18630).
Photo: Iraq Museum

296 Bas-relief. Stone. H. 9 ft. 6 in. (289·0 cm.) (approx.). From Khorsabad. Neo-Assyrian period, Sargon II (721–705 B.C.). Iraq Museum, Baghdad (11961).
Photo: Iraq Museum

297 Bas-relief. Stone. H. 9 ft. 6 in. (289·0 cm.) (approx.). From Khorsabad. Neo-Assyrian period, Sargon II (721–705 B.C.). Iraq Museum, Baghdad (D.S.1195).
Photo: Iraq Museum

298 Altar with round top and lion-footed legs. Stone. From Khorsabad. Neo-Assyrian period, Sargon II (721–705 B.C.). Iraq Museum, Baghdad.
Photo: Oriental Institute, University of Chicago

299 Bas-relief. Stone. H. *c.* 4 ft. (122 cm.). From Nineveh. Neo-Assyrian period, Sennacherib (704–681 B.C.). British Museum (12911).
Photo: British Museum

300 Drawing from a bas-relief. Stone. H. *c.* 2 ft. 7 in. (78 cm.). From Nineveh. Neo-Assyrian period, Sennacherib (704–681 B.C.). British Museum (124911). Reproduced from Layard, *Monuments*, II, pl. 23.

301 Drawing from a bas-relief. Stone. From Nineveh. Neo-Assyrian period, Sennacherib (704–681 B.C.). Reproduced from Layard, *Monuments*, I, p. 77.

302 Drawing from a bas-relief. Stone. From Nineveh. Neo-Assyrian period, Sennacherib (704–681 B.C.). Reproduced from Layard, *Monuments*, II, pl. 36.

303 Bas-relief. Stone. H. 6 ft. 6 in. (208·12 cm.). From Nineveh. Neo-Assyrian period, Sennacherib (705–681 B.C.). British Museum (124956).
Photo: British Museum

304 Detail from a bas-relief (fig. 305). Stone. H. 1 ft. 11 in. (58 cm.). From Nineveh. Neo-Assyrian period, Assurbanipal (669–626 B.C.). British Museum (124920).
Photo: British Museum

305 Bas-relief. Stone. H. 1 ft. 11 in. (58 cm.). From Nineveh. Neo-Assyrian period, Assurbanipal (669–626 B.C.). British Museum (124920).
Photo: British Museum

306 Carved panel. Ivory. H. $2\frac{3}{8}$ in. (6·1 cm.), W. 3 in. (7 cm.). From Ziwiye. Neo-Assyrian period, *c.* 8th century B.C. Teheran Museum, Iran (12465).
Photo: Teheran Museum

307 Drawing from a bas-relief by Botta. Stone. From Khorsabad. Neo-Assyrian period, Sargon II (721–705 B.C.). Iraq Museum, Baghdad. Reproduced from Botta and Flandrin, *Monuments de Nineve*, 1, pl. 64.

308 Bas-relief. Stone. H. *c.* 1 ft. 11 in. (*c.* 58 cm.). From Nineveh. Neo-Assyrian period, Assurbanipal (669–626 B.C.). British Museum (124887).
Photo: British Museum

309a Carved panel. Ivory. H. $2\frac{3}{8}$ in. (6·03 cm.), W. $4\frac{1}{4}$ in. (10·80 cm.). From Arslan Tash. 9th century B.C. Metropolitan Museum of Art, New York (Fletcher Fund, 1957) (57.80.5).
Photo: Metropolitan Museum of Art

309b Reverse of carved panel in fig. 309. Ivory. H. $2\frac{3}{8}$ in. (6·63 cm.), W. $4\frac{1}{4}$ in. (10·80 cm.). From Arslan Tash. 9th century B.C. Metropolitan Museum of Art, New York (Fletcher Fund, 1957) (57.80.5).
Photo: Metropolitan Museum of Art

310 Carved panel. Ivory. H. $4\frac{1}{2}$ in. (11·43 cm.), W. $4\frac{5}{8}$ in. (11·74 cm.). From Nimrud. 8th century B.C. Metropolitan Museum of Art, New York (Rogers Fund, 1958) (58.31.3).
Photo: Metropolitan Museum of Art

311 Carved panel. Ivory. H. $6\frac{1}{4}$ in. (15·87 cm.), W. 3 in. (7·62 cm.). From Nimrud. 8th century B.C. Metropolitan Museum of Art, New York (Rogers Fund, 1961) (61.197.6).
Photo: Metropolitan Museum of Art

312 Carved panel. Ivory. H. $4\frac{5}{16}$ in. (11·43 cm.), W. $2\frac{1}{4}$ in. (5·72 cm.). From Nimrud. 8th century B.C. Metropolitan Museum of Art, New York (Fletcher Fund, 1957) (59.107.11).
Photo: Metropolitan Museum of Art

313 Carved panel. Ivory. H. $3\frac{3}{16}$ in. (7·5 cm.), W. $7\frac{3}{4}$ in. (19·68 cm.). From Nimrud. 8th century B.C. Metropolitan Museum of Art, New York (Rogers Fund, 1961) (61.197.8).
Photo: Metropolitan Museum of Art

314 Carved panel. Ivory. H. $4\frac{5}{8}$ in. (11·74 cm.). From Nimrud. 9th–8th century B.C. Iraq Museum, Baghdad.
Photo: Iraq Museum

315 Carved panel. Ivory. H. $3\frac{1}{4}$ in. (8·25 cm.). From Nimrud. 9th–8th century B.C. British Museum (118147).
Photo: British Museum

316 Carved chair back. Ivory. H. 1 ft $1\frac{13}{16}$ in. (35·09 cm.), W. 1 ft. $7\frac{3}{4}$ in. (50·16 cm.). From Nimrud. 8th century B.C.

Metropolitan Museum of Art, New York (Rogers Fund, 1959) (59.107.1).
Photo: Metropolitan Museum of Art

317 Drawing of a carved panel. Ivory. H. 2½ in. (6·35 cm.). From Nimrud. 8th century B.C. British Museum (118179). Reproduced from the Catalogue of the Nimrud Ivories by R. D. Barnett.

318 Carved panel. Ivory H. 3 in. (7·62 cm.). From Nimrud. 9th–8th century B.C. British Museum (118120).
Photo: British Museum

319 Carved bed panel. Ivory. H. 1 ft. 10 in. (55·88 cm.), W. 2 ft. 7½ in. (80·01 cm.). From Nimrud. 9th–8th century B.C. British Museum (132691).
Photo: British Museum

320 Panel, possibly the head-board of a bed. Ivory. H. 2 ft. 1 in. (66 cm.), W. 2 ft. 9 in. (84 cm.). From Nimrud. 9th–8th century B.C. Iraq Museum, Baghdad (62721).
Photo: Iraq Museum

321 Panel, similar to fig. 320. Ivory. H. 2 ft. 1 in. (66 cm.), W. 2 ft. 9 in. (84 cm.). From Nimrud. 9th–8th century B.C. Iraq Museum, Baghdad (62722).
Photo: Iraq Museum

322 Panel, similar to fig. 320. Ivory. H. 2 ft. 1 in. (66 cm.), W. 2 ft. 9 in. (84 cm.). From Nimrud. 9th–8th century B.C. Iraq Museum, Baghdad (62723).
Photo: Iraq Museum

323 Carved sphinx. Ivory. H. 5 in. (12·70 cm.). Provenance unknown. Metropolitan Museum of Art, New York (Gift of Mrs George D. Pratt, 1936, in memory of George D. Pratt) (36.70.8).
Photo: Metropolitan Museum of Art

324 Carved lion's leg. Ivory. H. 4½ in. (11·5 cm.). From Nimrud. 9th–8th century B.C. British Museum (118269).
Photo: British Museum

325 Carved foot. Ivory. H. 1 ft. (32 cm.). From Nimrud. 9th–8th century B.C. British Museum (118190).
Photo: British Museum

326 Drawing of a carved angle piece and leg. Bronze. From Toprak Kale. 8th–7th century B.C. Collection M. de Vogüé, Paris. Reproduced from A. Salonen, Tafel LXII, *Die Möbel des Alten Mesopotamien*.

327 Angle piece. Bronze. H. 3¼ in. (8·5 cm.), W. 5⅞ in. (15 cm.). From Toprak Kale. 8th–7th century B.C. British Museum (91251).
Photo: British Museum

328 Female centaur. Bronze. H. 9¼ in. (23·7 cm.). From Toprak Kale. 8th–7th century B.C. British Museum (91247).
Photo: British Museum

329 Lion's paw. Bronze. H. 7½ in. (19 cm.). From Toprak Kale. 8th–7th century B.C. British Museum (91164).
Photo: British Museum

330 a: End section of a table. Bronze. H. 2 ft. 5½ in. (75 cm.). From Nimrud. 8th–7th century B.C. b: End section of a stand. Bronze. H. 11¾ in. (30 cm.). From Nimrud. 8th–7th century B.C. British Museum (22491, 119458).
Photos: British Museum

331 Stand. Bronze. H. 5 in. (12·5 cm.). From Curium, Cyprus. 8th century B.C. British Museum (1920–12–20, 1).
Photo: British Museum

332 Drawings from a bas-relief. Stone. From Nineveh. Neo-Assyrian period, Sennacherib (704–681 B.C.). Reproduced from Layard, *Monuments*, II, pl. 40.

333 Drawing from a bas-relief. Stone. From Nimrud. Neo-Assyrian period, from the palace of Assurnasirpal II (883–859 B.C.). British Museum (124548). Reproduced from Layard, *Monuments*, I, pl. 30; Budge, *Assyrian Sculptures; Reign of Ashur-nasir-pal*, pl. XVI.I.

334 Drawing from a bas-relief. Stone. From Nineveh. Neo-Assyrian period, from the palace of Sennacherib (704–81 B.C.). From Nimrud. Reproduced from Layard, *Monuments*, I, pl. 77.

335 Bas-relief. Stone. From Nineveh. Neo-Assyrian period, c.650 B.C. Staatliche Museen, Berlin (VA965).
Photo: Staatliche Museen

336 Stela. Stone. From Ras Shamra. c.13th century B.C. Aleppo Museum.
Photo: Dr Pritchard, University Museum, University of Pennsylvania, Philadelphia

337 Detail from a carved sarcophagus. Stone. From Byblos. c.13th century B.C. Beirut Museum.
Photo: Dr Pritchard, University Museum, University of Pennsylvania, Philadelphia

338 Detail from a carved stela. Stone. From Zinjirli. 8th century B.C. Staatliche Museen, Berlin.
Photo: Dr Pritchard, University Museum, University of Pennsylvania, Philadelphia

339 Relief. Stone. From Zinjirli. 8th century B.C. Staatliche Museen, Berlin.
Photo: Staatliche Museen

340 Stela. Stone. From Ras Shamra. 8th century B.C. Louvre, Paris (AO3027).
Photo: Caisse Nationale des Monuments Historiques et des Sites

341 Stela. Stone. From Ras Shamra. 14th century B.C. Aleppo Museum.
Photo: Dr Pritchard, University Museum, University of Pennsylvania, Philadelphia

342 Impression of a cylinder seal. L. 1⅜ in. (3·5 cm.), Dia. ½ in. (1·2 cm.). From Tell es Sa'idiyeh. c.8th century B.C. University Museum, University of Pennsylvania, Philadelphia.
Photo: University Museum, University of Pennsylvania

343 Impression of a cylinder seal. L. 1⅜ in. (3·5 cm.), Dia. ½ in. (1·3 cm.). From Tell es Sa'idiyeh. c.8th century B.C.
Photo: University Museum, University of Pennsylvania

344 Drawing of two scarabs. From Lachish and Gezer. Late 2nd millennium B.C. Reproduced from *Anatolian Studies*, VI, 1956.

345 Statue of a seated man. Stone. From Hazor. Middle of the 2nd millennium B.C. Palestine Archaeological Museum, Jerusalem.
Photo: Palestine Archaeological Museum

346 Statue of a seated man. Stone. From Hazor. Middle of the 2nd millennium B.C. Palestine Archaeological Museum.
Photo: Palestine Archaeological Museum

347 Engraved lid of a box. Ivory. From Tell el Farah. 14th century B.C.

348 Drawing of the side panel of a box. Ivory. From Megiddo. 13th–12th century B.C. The Oriental Institute, University of Chicago (01M, A22270). Reproduced from Gordon Loud, *Megiddo Ivories*, pl. 32, 160c.

349 Drawing of a plaque. Ivory. From Megiddo. 13–12th century B.C. Palestine Archaeological Museum, Jerusalem.

350 Carved openwork plaque of a Bes figure. Ivory. H. 4 in. (10 cm.). From Megiddo. 13th–12th century B.C. Palestine Archaeological Museum, Jerusalem (PAM 38.781).
Photo: The Oriental Institute, University of Chicago

351 Carved openwork plaque of a sphinx. Ivory. H. 4 in. (10 cm.). From Megiddo. 13th–12th century B.C. (01M, A22213).
Photo: The Oriental Institute, University of Chicago

352 Small box with Assyrian winged lions. Ivory. H. 2⅜ in. (6 cm.). From Megiddo. 13th–12th century B.C. Palestine Archaeological Museum, Jerusalem (PAM 38.816).
Photo: The Oriental Institute, University of Chicago

353 Drawing of fragments of a bench. Wood. From Jericho. c.1600 B.C. Reproduced from Kathleen M. Kenyon, *Jericho*.

354 Drawing of fragments of a stool. Wood. From Jericho. c.1600 B.C. Reproduced from Kathleen M. Kenyon, *Jericho*.

355 Drawing of fragments of a table. Wood. From Jericho. c.1600 B.C. Reproduced from Kathleen M. Kenyon, *Jericho*.

356 a–d Drawing of construction details of furniture from Jericho. c.1600 B.C. Reproduced from Kathleen M. Kenyon, *Jericho*.

357 Panel of an inlaid toilet box. Wood with bone inlay. L. 7½ in. (19·05 cm.), W. 5½ in. (13·97 cm.). From Jericho. c.1600 B.C.
Photo: Royal Ontario Museum, Toronto

358 Reconstructed bench with woven top. Wood. H. 1 ft. 4 in. (40·64 cm.), L. 3 ft. 4 in. (101·60 cm.), W. 1 ft. 4 in. (40·64 cm.). From Jericho. c.1600 B.C. Royal Ontario Museum, Toronto (956.193.3).
Photo: Royal Ontario Museum

359 Reconstructed table. Wood. H. 1 ft. 2 in. (35·56 cm.), L. 4 ft. 11½ in. (151·13 cm.), W. 1 ft. 7½ in. (49·53 cm.). From Jericho. c.1600 B.C. Royal Ontario Museum, Toronto (956.193.1).
Photo: Royal Ontario Museum

360 Reconstructed stool with woven top. Wood. H. 1 ft. 8½ in. (52·07 cm.), L. 1 ft. 4½ in. (41·91 cm.), W. 1 ft. 4½ in. (41·91 cm.). From Jericho. c.1600 B.C. Royal Ontario Museum, Toronto (956.193.2).
Photo: Royal Ontario Museum

361 Stool. Bronze. From Tell el Farah. 6th century B.C. Palestine Archaeological Museum, Jerusalem (1142).
Photo: Palestine Archaeological Museum

362 Bed. Bronze. From Tell el Farah. 6th–4th century B.C. Palestine Archaeological Museum, Jerusalem (1143).
Photo: Palestine Archaeological Museum

363 Fragment of a bas-relief. Stone. From Susa. c.9th century B.C. Louvre, Paris.
Photo: Dr Pritchard, University Museum, University of Pennsylvania, Philadelphia

364 Stela of Meli-Shipak. Stone. From Susa. 12th century B.C. Louvre, Paris (64 Y 33).
Photo: Caisse Nationale des Monuments Historiques et des Sites

365 Relief from the Treasury. Stone. From Persepolis. c.524 B.C. Persepolis, Iran.
Photo: The Oriental Institute, University of Chicago

366 Carved openwork furniture panel. Wood. From Gordion. 8th century B.C. Ankara Museum.
Photo: University Museum, University of Pennsylvania, Philadelphia

367 Fragments of furniture. Wood. From Gordion. 8th century B.C. Ankara Museum.
Photo: University Museum, University of Pennsylvania, Philadelphia

368 Drawing showing the contents of the 'Royal Tomb' at Gordion. c.725 B.C. Reproduced from *American Journal of Archaeology*, 1958.
Photo: University Museum, University of Pennsylvania, Philadelphia

369 Drawing of reconstructed standing screen by Dorothy Cox. From Gordion. *c.* 725 B.C. Ankara Museum.
Photo: University Museum, University of Pennsylvania, Philadelphia

370 Inlaid screen. Wood, with boxwood and yew inlay and bronze studs. H. 3 ft. 1⅜ in. (95 cm.), W. 2 ft. 7½ in. (80 cm.). From Gordion. *c.* 725 B.C. Ankara Museum.
Photo: University Museum, University of Pennsylvania, Philadelphia

371 Drawing of the face of the standing screen by Dorothy Cox. From Gordion. *c.* 725 B.C. Ankara Museum.
Photo: University Museum, University of Pennsylvania, Philadelphia

372 Drawing of one of eight similar tables from the 'Royal Tomb' at Gordion by Dorothy Cox. H. 8¼ in. (51·5 cm.). *c.* 725 B.C. Ankara Museum.
Photo: University Museum, University of Pennsylvania, Philadelphia

373 The 'pagoda table' in situ. Wood. H. 2 ft. 1⅝ in. (65·08 cm.), top 2 ft. 5½ in. (74·93 cm.) × 1 ft. 0⅜ in. (31·43 cm.). From Gordion. *c.* 725 B.C. Ankara Museum (5212 W 80).
Photo: University Museum, University of Pennsylvania, Philadelphia

374 Drawing of reconstructed 'pagoda table' at Gordion by Dorothy Cox. *c.* 725 B.C. Ankara Museum.
Photo: University Museum, University of Pennsylvania, Philadelphia

375 Terracotta statuette: mother and child. H. 6¼ in. (16 cm.). From Sesklo, Thessaly. *c.* 3000 B.C. National Museum, Athens (5934).
Photo: C. Constantopoulos, Athens

376 Terracotta model table. From Rafina, Attica. *c.* 3000 B.C. National Museum, Athens (8896).
Photo: C. Constantopoulos, Athens

377 Marble statuette. H. 6⅞ in. (17·3 cm.). From Thera. *c.* 2500 B.C. Badisches Landesmuseum, Karlsruhe (B864).
Photo: Badisches Landesmuseum

378 Stone statuette, fragmentary. From Naxos. *c.* 2500 B.C. National Museum, Athens (8833).
Photo: C. Constantopoulos, Athens

379 Marble statuette. H. 11⅜ in. (29 cm.). From the Cyclades. *c.* 2500 B.C. Metropolitan Museum of Art, New York (Rogers Fund, 1947) (47.100.1).
Photo: Metropolitan Museum of Art

380 Back view of fig. 379.
Photo: Metropolitan Museum of Art, New York

381 Marble statuette. H. 8⅞ in. (22·5 cm.). From Keros, near Amorgos. *c.* 2500 B.C. National Museum, Athens (3908).
Photo: National Museum, Athens

382 Back view of fig. 381.
Photo: National Museum, Athens

383 Marble statuette. H. 6½ in. (16·5 cm.). From the Cyclades. Virginia Museum of Fine Arts, Richmond.
Photo: Lee Boltin

384 Cast of throne from Knossos. H. 5 ft. (152·4 cm.). Ashmolean Museum, Oxford.
Photo: Ashmolean Museum

385 Measured drawing of throne (fig. 384). From Evans, *Palace of Minos*, 4, figs. 890, 891. See Chapter 2, note 1.

386 Painted terracotta sarcophagus. From Knossos. *c.* 1400 B.C. Ashmolean Museum, Oxford.
Photo: Ashmolean Museum

387 Painted terracotta sarcophagus. From Knossos. *c.* 1400 B.C. Ashmolean Museum, Oxford.
Photo: Ashmolean Museum

388 a: Minoan steatite seal: altar-table with four legs and projecting poles. b: Minoan agate seal: altar-table with four legs to a side and intervening supports. c: Clay seal impression: woman seated on stool with straight legs and stretchers. From Knossos. d: Clay seal impression: woman seated on stool. From Little Palace, Knossos. e: Clay seal impression: 'The Young Minotaur' on folding stool. From Knossos. Reproduced from Evans, *Palace of Minos*, 4, figs. 26, 452b, 376b, 322, 321.

389 Terracotta model of carrying chair. H. 4 in. (10·5 cm.). From the Palace, Knossos. *c.* 1750 B.C. Heraklion Museum (HM2583).
Photo: G. Xylouris

390 Stone table with three supports in the form of half-rosettes. H. 5¾ in. (14·5 cm.). From the Palace, Knossos. *c.* 1500 B.C. Heraklion Museum (HM65).
Photo: G. Xylouris

391 Terracotta model of three-legged table. H. 3⅞ in. (10 cm.). From the Palace, Knossos. *c.* 1500 B.C. Heraklion Museum (HM8923).
Photo: G. Xylouris

392 Faience mosaics depicting house-fronts. From the Palace, Knossos. *c.* 1750 B.C. Heraklion Museum (HM1–2).
Photo: G. Xylouris

393 a: Linear B tablet (TA715) from Palace of Nestor, Pylos. *c.* 1200 B.C. National Museum, Athens. b: Drawing of inscriptions on Linear B tablet above which describe tables of ebony, ivory and yew wood. Drawing courtesy of C. W. Blegen.
Photo: University of Cincinnati

394 Ivory ornaments from furniture. From the House of Shields and House of Sphinxes, Mycenae. 1250–1200 B.C. National Museum, Athens.
Photo: Mrs A. J. B. Wace

395 Terracotta models of chairs. From Mycenaean tombs. 1400–1200 B.C. National Museum, Athens.
Photo: National Museum

396 Terracotta model bed. H. 1⅛ in. (3 cm.). From a tomb near Corinth. *c.* 1350 B.C. Corinth Museum.
Photo: American School of Classical Studies, Athens

397 Terracotta model chair. H. 5¼ in. (13·5 cm.). From a tomb near Argos. *c.* 1350 B.C. National Museum, Athens.
Photo: C. Constantopoulos, Athens

398 Impression from gold signet ring from Tiryns. *c.* 1400 B.C. National Museum, Athens. Reproduced from Evans, *Palace of Minos*, 4, fig. 385.

398a Detail from fig. 398, showing chair with cross-legs and high back. Reproduced from Evans, *op. cit.*, fig. 329.

399 Hexagonal wooden box, covered with gold. H. 3¼ in. (8·26 cm.). From Mycenae. *c.* 1550 B.C. National Museum, Athens (808–11).
Photo: C. Constantopoulos, Athens

400 Vase painting: Odysseus slaying the suitors. *c.* 450 B.C. Staatliche Museen, Berlin.
Photo: Hirmer Fotoarchiv, Munich

401 Terracotta seated figure. From Boeotia. Late 7th or early 6th century B.C. National Museum, Athens (13257).
Photo: C. Constantopoulos, Athens

402 Back view of fig. 401.
Photo: C. Constantopoulos, Athens

403 Terracotta seated figure. H. 4⅞ in. (12·3 cm.). Late 8th century B.C. Metropolitan Museum of Art, New York (Fletcher Fund, 1931) (31.11.8).
Photo: Metropolitan Museum of Art

404 Terracotta seated figure. H. 8¼ in. (21 cm.). Made in Boeotia *c.* 580 B.C. British Museum (769).
Photo: British Museum

405 Terracotta model table. From Cyprus. *c.* 8th century B.C. Metropolitan Museum of Art, New York (74.51.1790).
Photo: Metropolitan Museum of Art

406 Marble seated figure (headless). Inscribed ARGEMO. H. of seat 1 ft. 4½ in. (41·91 cm.), D. 1 ft. 5 in. (43·18 cm.). From Arcadia. *c.* 650–640 B.C. National Museum, Athens (6).
Photo: C. Constantopoulos, Athens

407 Detail of leg from fig. 406.
Photo: C. Constantopoulos, Athens

408 Limestone 'hero relief'. From Laconia. *c.* 550 B.C. Staatliche Museen, Berlin.
Photo: Staatliche Museen

409 Marble relief. From Paros. *c.* 550 B.C. Staatliche Museen, Berlin.
Photo: Staatliche Museen

410 Marble relief from the Harpy tomb at Xanthus in Lycia. *c.* 500 B.C. British Museum (B287).
Photo: British Museum

411 Marble relief from the Harpy tomb at Xanthus in Lycia. *c.* 500 B.C. British Museum (B287).
Photo: British Museum

412 Marble relief from the Harpy tomb at Xanthus in Lycia. *c.* 500 B.C. British Museum (B287).
Photo: British Museum

413 Marble relief from the Harpy tomb at Xanthus in Lycia. *c.* 500 B.C. British Museum (B287).
Photo: British Museum

414 Limestone statue. From near Tripolis, in Arcadia. *c.* 630 B.C. National Museum, Athens (57).
Photo: C. Constantopoulos, Athens

415 Marble relief, 'cat and dog fight'. From Athens, Themistoclean wall. *c.* 500 B.C. National Museum, Athens (3476).
Photo: National Museum

416 Terracotta relief (restored): Pluto and Persephone seated. From Locri. 470–460 B.C. National Museum, Reggio di Calabria.
Photo: Soprintendenza alle Antichità della Calabria

417 Terracotta relief (restored): woman placing garment in chest. From Locri. 470–460 B.C. National Museum, Taranto (832).
Photo: Soprintendenza alle Antichità della Puglia

418 Vase painting: couches and tables, from Corinth. 625–600 B.C. Louvre, Paris.
Photo: Hirmer Fotoarchiv, Munich

419 Vase painting: couches and tables. 520–510 B.C. Musées Royaux d'Art et d'Histoire, Brussels.
Photo: Hirmer Fotoarchiv, Munich

420 Vase painting: couch and table. 530–500 B.C. Antikensammlungen, Munich.
Photo: Kohlroser, Munich

421 Vase painting: Zeus seated on throne. *c.* 460 B.C. British Museum (E410).
Photo: British Museum

422 Drawing of vase painting: Poseidon seated on throne. *c.* 470 B.C. Cabinet des Médailles, Paris. Reproduced from Efter, *Monumenti Inediti*, I, 1829–33, pl. 52 (see Richter, fig. 34).

423 Drawing of vase painting: Zeus seated on chair. c.460 B.C. National Museum, Palermo. Reproduced from *Archäologische Zeitung*, XXVIII, 1870, pl. 33 (see Richter, fig. 37).

424 Vase painting: Zeus seated on chair decorated with forepart of horse. c.540 B.C. British Museum (B147). *Photo: British Museum*

425 Bronze model of three-legged table (support for statuette of girl). H. 2 in. (5 cm.). From Vulci. Etruscan. 525–500 B.C. British Museum (599). *Photo: British Museum*

426 Terracotta sarcophagus: couple on couch. From Cervetri. c.525 B.C. Louvre, Paris (5194). *Photo: Archives Photographiques, Paris*

427 Vase painting: slave carrying a table. c.470 B.C. National Museum, Athens. *Photo: C. Constantopoulos, Athens*

428 a and b Side and front view of bronze table leg. 1st century B.C. (?). National Museum, Palermo. *Photo: Lo Cascio, Palermo*

429 Vase painting: boy carrying couch and table. 500–475 B.C. Ashmolean Museum, Oxford (1890–29). *Photo: Ashmolean Museum*

430 Vase painting: couch with carved goat's legs. 500–475 B.C. Villa Giulia Museum, Rome. *Photo: Gabinetto Fotografico Nazionale*

431 Vase painting: drawing showing a couch being transported by a donkey. From a vase in Fürtwangler and Reichhold, *Griechische Vasenmalerei*, II, pl. 120 (see Richter, fig. 193).

432 Vase painting: stool. 515–510 B.C. National Museum, Tarquinia. *Photo: Hirmer Fotoarchiv, Munich*

433 Vase painting: Zeus seated on a cross-legged stool. 550–525 B.C. Vatican Museum, Rome. *Photo: Anderson, Rome*

434 Vase painting: cross-legged stool with running-scroll ornament. 500–475 B.C. British Museum (E61). *Photo: British Museum*

435 Painted terracotta plaque: cross-legged stool and chair. c.550 B.C. Staatliche Museen, Berlin (1811.26). *Photo: Staatliche Museen*

436 Drawing of a vase painting: cross-legged stool with carved goat's legs. c.450 B.C. Museum für antike Kleinkunst, Munich. Reproduced from Fürtwangler and Reichhold, *Griechische Vasenmalerei*, I, pl. 4 (see Richter, fig. 112).

437 Vase painting: Zeus seated on chair. c.550 B.C. British Museum (W38). *Photo: British Museum*

438 Vase painting: Midas seated on chair. c.425 B.C. Vatican Museum, Rome. *Photo: Alinari, Florence*

439 Vase painting: Hestia seated on chair. 515–510 B.C. National Museum, Tarquinia. *Photo: Hirmer Fotoarchiv, Munich*

440 Vase painting: the classic chair. 500–475 B.C. Staatliche Museen, Berlin. *Photo: Staatliche Museen*

441 Vase painting: the classic chair. c.450 B.C. British Museum (E189). *Photo: British Museum*

442 Vase painting: the classic chair. c.450 B.C. Ashmolean Museum, Oxford. *Photo: Ashmolean Museum*

443 Vase painting: satyr carrying chair. c.450 B.C. British Museum (E465). *Photo: British Museum*

444 Lead model of chair. Uncertain date. British Museum (Life Room 636). *Photo: British Museum*

445 Vase painting: variation of classic chair with small table. 475–450 B.C. Torno collection, Milan. *Photo: Costa Servici Fotografici, Milan*

446 Vase painting: carpenter at work. c.500 B.C. British Museum (E23). *Photo: British Museum*

447 Part of the east frieze of the Parthenon. c.445 B.C. Acropolis Museum, Athens. *Photo: Greek Archaeological Service, Athens*

448 Stele of Demetria and Pamphile. c.325 B.C. Kerameikos Museum, Athens. *Photo: Greek Archaeological Service, Athens*

449 Stele of Hegeso. c.400 B.C. National Museum, Athens (3624). *Photo: Megaloconomou Bros, Athens*

450 Wooden table with three legs. H. 2 ft. 4½ in. (72·5 cm.). 2nd or 3rd century B.C. From Egypt; of Hellenistic design. Musées Royaux d'Art et d'Histoire, Brussels. *Photo: Musées Royaux d'Art et d'Histoire*

451 Drawing of classic chair by Thomas Hope. Reproduced from T. A. Strange, *English Furniture, Woodwork, Decoration etc. during the Eighteenth Century*, p. 367, fig. 1.

452 Classic chair of Empire style. Schlossmuseum, Berlin. Reproduced from Hermann Schmitz, *Deutsche Möbel des Klassizismus*, III, Stuttgart, p. 134.

453 Napoleonic classic chair with gold-embroidered bees. French, c.A.D. 1810. Baker Museum for Furniture Research. *Photo: Holland Illustrative Photography*

454 Chair of Empire style. Mahogany. French, c.A.D. 1810. Baker Museum for Furniture Research. *Photo: Holland Illustrative Photography*

455 Chair of Directoire style. Black and gold. English, c.A.D. 1820. Baker Museum for Furniture Research. *Photo: Holland Illustrative Photography*

456 Bas-relief. Gypseus alabaster. H. 9 ft. 7 in. (292 cm.). From Khorsabad. 8th century B.C. Louvre, Paris.

457 Examples of joints. From Old Kingdom coffins, c.2500–2250 B.C. Reproduced from the drawing by Cyril Aldred in Singer, Holmyard and Hall, *History of Technology*, I, p. 691, fig. 491.

458 Carpenter's tools. Wood and bronze blades and lashings of leather and linen. L. of axe-haft 2 ft. 5½ in. (74·93 cm.). Mostly from Thebes. XVIIIth Dynasty, c.1450 B.C. British Museum (22834, etc.). *Photo: British Museum*

459 Joiners at work. Painted limestone relief. At Saqqara (tomb of Ti). Vth Dynasty, c.2400 B.C. Reproduced from G. Steindorff, *Das Grab des Ti*, pl. CXXXIII.

460 Cabinet making. Painted limestone. At Thebes (tomb of Rekhmire, no. 100). XVIIIth Dynasty, c.1475 B.C. Reproduced from N. de G. Davies, *The Tomb of Rekh-mi-Ré*, pl. LII.

461 Furniture makers. Painted limestone. At Thebes (tomb of Rekhmire, no. 100). XVIIIth Dynasty, c.1475 B.C. Reproduced from N. de G. Davies, *The Tomb of Rekh-mi-Ré*, pl. LIII.

462 Model of a carpenter's shop. Painted wood. L. 2 ft. 2 in. (66 cm.), W. 1 ft. 8½ in. (52·07 cm.). From the tomb of Meketre in Thebes. XIth Dynasty, c.2000 B.C. Cairo Museum (J. d'E. no. 46722). *Photo: Metropolitan Museum of Art*

463 Miniature furniture. Painted wood. From the tomb of Meketre in Thebes. XIth Dynasty, c.2000 B.C. a: Chair. H. 6 in. (15·24 cm.). Metropolitan Museum of Art, New York (part of no. 20.3.1. Gift of Edward S. Harkness and Rogers Fund). b: Two figures seated on stools. H. 7 in. (17·78 cm.). Metropolitan Museum of Art, New York (part of no. 20.3.2. Gift of Edward S. Harkness and Rogers Fund). c: Bed, chair and chests. L. of bed 8 in. (20·32 cm.). Cairo Museum (part of J. d'E. no. 46720). d: Chair, as in c. H. 6¼ in. (15·88 cm.). *Photos: Metropolitan Museum of Art*

464 Furniture making. Painted limestone. At Thebes (tomb of Rekhmire, no. 100). XVIIIth Dynasty, c.1475 B.C. Reproduced from N. de G. Davies, *The Tomb of Rekh-mi-Ré*, pl. LV.

465 Detail drawings of furniture joinery from XVIIIth Dynasty Egyptian furniture. Collège Technique Boulle, Paris.

466 Detail drawings of furniture joinery. Collège Technique Boulle, Paris.

Measured drawings by Miss M. S. Macdonald-Taylor

467 Chair. From Thebes. XVIIIth Dynasty. British Museum (2480). See fig. 184.

468 Chair. XVIIIth Dynasty. Brooklyn Museum (37. 40E). See fig. 173.

469 Chair. XVIIIth Dynasty. Archaeological Museum, Florence (2580). See fig. 188.

470a Painted and decorated stand for holding a vase. XVIIIth Dynasty. British Museum (2470). See fig. 240.

470b Stool. White painted wood, rush seat. XVIIIth Dynasty. British Museum (46705). See fig. 194.

471 Cross-legged stool with inlaid duck's heads. XVIIIth Dynasty. British Museum (2477). See fig. 195.

472 Lattice-type stool, originally painted white over gesso. XVIIth Dynasty. British Museum (2476). See fig. 192.

473 Low rectangular table, painted over gesso. XVIIIth Dynasty. Turin Museum (825F). See fig. 233.

474 Toilet box with compartments. XVIIIth Dynasty. British Museum (24708). See fig. 223.

INDEX

Figures in *italics* indicate pages on which illustrations will be found.